Early Childhood Education in the Home

To my husband, Martin, and to Marty, Charles, John, Mary Ann, Michael, and Judy Clare. who brought us much happiness during their childhood and continue to do so as young adults.

Early Childhood Education in the Home

Elinor Tripato Massoglia

DELMAR PUBLISHERS
COPYRIGHT ©1977
BY LITTON EDUCATIONAL PUBLISHING, INC.

All rights reserved. No part of this work covered by the copyright hereon may be reproduced or used in any form or by any means — graphic, electronic, or mechanical, including photocopying, recording, taping, or information storage and retrieval systems — without written permission of the publisher.

LIBRARY OF CONGRESS CATALOG CARD NUMBER: 76-14091

Printed in the United States of America
Published Simultaneously in Canada by
Delmar Publishers, A Division of
Van Nostrand Reinhold, Ltd.

Jeanne Machado, Consulting Editor

Elinor Gunnerson, Early Childhood Education Series Editor

DELMAR PUBLISHERS • ALBANY, NEW YORK 12205
A DIVISION OF LITTON EDUCATIONAL PUBLISHING, INC.

Preface

Early Childhood Education in the Home embraces the author's basic philosophy — that a person who works with young children should be a practitioner of both early childhood and adult education. This person needs

- Knowledge of child growth and development and the ability to create learning activities that respond to the needs of the growing child.
- Skill in working with adults to make possible open communication and close working relationships with staff, parents, and community agencies.
- Ability to apply the principles of adult learning to help parents become more effective teachers of their own children.

The author, Elinor Tripato Massoglia, proposes a framework around which a new role can be developed — early childhood/adult educator. To accomplish this goal, the author draws on her experience as a teacher of young children and youth, as an educator involved in preservice and in-service teacher training, as a person with much experience in working with parents, and as the mother of six children of her own.

Many of the concepts and procedures described were developed by Dr. Massoglia, field-tested with her own children, shared with other parents, and pursued during a teaching career that spans thirty years. As early as 1942, her master's thesis (*Authors at Six*) described the individualized program in which she taught first graders to read by helping them to write their own storybooks. Parents were encouraged to visit, observe, and carry on similar activities in the home. This innovative practice took place at a time when many other educators viewed parent involvement as being synonymous with parent interference.

Early Childhood Education in the Home is divided into eight sections. Each is self-contained and enables students to begin wherever their own interests or needs lie. The book is addressed to all persons who deal in some way with parents and early childhood education — parents themselves may find it helpful.

Section 1 considers the parent as a teacher and sets the stage for exploring the potential of home-based early childhood education. The components of a program are identified and described. The unit on social action provides a basis for understanding how a community can become involved in starting programs for young children.

Section 2 explores the role of the home visitor and concentrates on her tasks, training, and those with whom she works. The need for a good communication system is emphasized. Some systems for delivering services are presented, and home visitor tasks are discussed as ways to help parents become skillful teachers of their own children. Some approaches are drawn from actual experiences; others are creative ideas to challenge innovators — those who seek new and unusual ways to do ordinary things.

Section 3 concentrates on the need to view parents as any other adult learner who seeks information or skills. The principles of adult learning are applied to parents, and some appropriate learning situations are identified. A workshop, drawn from several different real-life situations, is presented as a one-day program for parents.

Section 4 considers child growth and development and the importance of parental skills in creating a home-learning environment that promotes the child's maximal growth. Suggested activities for home learning are described as parent enablers — ways by which the child can learn and grow.

Section 5 presents material which the author draws from her experiences as a parent, teacher, preservice and in-service teacher-trainer, and parent educator.

Section 6 stresses the importance of models worthy of imitation. One unit describes ways to work effectively with parents in early childhood centers and suggests ways by which the training can be transferred to the home situation.

Section 7 emphasizes the importance of keeping accurate records and suggests ways to evaluate a child's growth and progress. Stressed is the need to make evaluations based on specific objectives.

The author gained much valuable experience in developing a home-based educational program for her own children when the family moved frequently during her husband's career as an army officer. Concerned with the need for continuity and sequence in the education of children of military personnel, she developed a *Growth and Progress File* for her own children. This was subsequently published by *U.S. Lady Magazine*. The file enabled parents to keep a record of the progress their children were making. As a teacher, she held frequent meetings for parents, and helped them provide learning experiences for their children at home and in the community.

Dr. Massoglia has taught at all levels on the continuum from kindergarten to college, both here and abroad. Her numerous writings cover a wide range of topics published over the years. Her early training took place at the Mills Training School for Kindergarten-Primary Teachers (later Mills College of Education) in New York City. She holds a B.S. and an M.A. from the School of Education, New York University, covering early childhood, elementary education, and teacher-training. In 1972, she earned a doctorate in adult and community college education from North Carolina State University at Raleigh.

At present, Dr. Massoglia teaches at North Carolina Central University. She is also actively involved in the Adult Education Association of United States, the Association for Childhood Education, and the American Home Economics Association.

The Delmar Early Childhood Education Series includes

    Creative Activities for Young Children — Mayesky, Neuman, and Wlodkowski
    Teaching Young Children — Beatrice Martin
    Early Childhood Experiences in Language Arts — Jeanne Machado
    Administration of Schools for Young Children — Phyllis Click
    Early Childhood: Development and Education — Jeanne Mack
    Home and Community Influences on Young Children — Karen VanderVen
    Experiences in Music for Young Children — M.C. Weller Pugmire

Contents

SECTION 1 GOALS AND OBJECTIVES

Unit 1	Establishing Home-based Objectives.	1
Unit 2	Identifying and describing Program Components.	9
Unit 3	Creating Home-based Programs	22

SECTION 2 ORIENTATION TO HOME VISITING

Unit 4	The Home Visitor	31
Unit 5	Developing Workplans.	41
Unit 6	Administrative Planning and Operating	56
Unit 7	Delivering Services	67

SECTION 3 PARENTS ARE ADULT LEARNERS

Unit 8	Knowing the Adult Learner.	80
Unit 9	Creating Adult Learning Situations	90
Unit 10	Planning Workshops.	104

SECTION 4 CHILD DEVELOPMENT AND PARENT ENABLERS

Unit 11	Viewing Human Development.	115
Unit 12	What Infants Learn and Parent Enablers	126
Unit 13	What Toddlers Learn and Parent Enablers	140
Unit 14	What Preschoolers Learn and Parent Enablers.	152

SECTION 5 MATERIALS FOR HOME-BASED LEARNING

Unit 15	Firsthand Experiences.	163
Unit 16	Objectives and Activities.	179
Unit 17	Creating Media for Learning.	193

SECTION 6 MODELING SKILLS

Unit 18	Identifying the Modeling Approach.	209
Unit 19	Working with Parents in Centers	220

SECTION 7 FAMILY DEVELOPMENT

Unit 20	The Family Unit.	233
Unit 21	The Play Way to Family Development.	243

SECTION 8 RECORD-KEEPING AND EVALUATION

Unit 22	Developing a Record System.	255
Unit 23	Evaluation	264

Appendix A 277
Appendix B 279
Appendix C 285
Appendix D 288
Appendix E 289
Answers to Review Questions 290
Acknowledgments 300
Index 303

Section 1 Goals and Objectives

unit 1 establishing home-based objectives

OBJECTIVES

After studying this unit, the student should be able to
- Support the view that parents need skills that will help them to be effective teachers of their own children.
- Identify five concerns of early childhood education.
- Discuss five principles of learning and tell how parents can demonstrate them in home-based early childhood programs.
- List and describe at least five things that parents do when "teaching" is taking place.

A *child's home* is wherever he lives under the guidance of one or more persons who assume responsibility for his well-being. He may live with his *natural* (biological) parents or *surrogate* (substitute) parents.

Home may be a dismal, drab flat in the smog-filled ghetto, or it may be a countryside mansion fit for a king. Although differing widely in appearance, the two homes share a common purpose. Each provides the environment in which the child's early development takes place.

The outward appearance of the home is not as important as the quality of life within it. A rich home does not insure success; a poor one does not deny it. To foster maximal growth and development, every home must be responsive to the needs of each child who lives there.

PARENTS AND THEIR NEEDS

A *need* is described as any gap that exists between what a person does and what he should do or wants to do. It implies that an imbalance exists that can be changed by desirable new input.

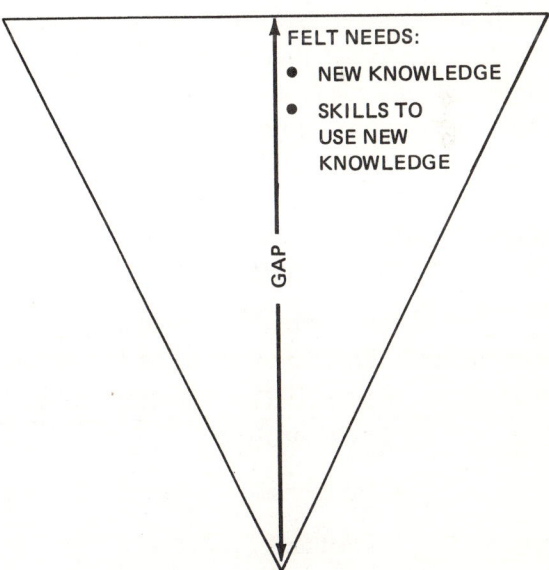

Fig. 1-1 Parents participate in programs to the extent that they recognize their felt needs and are able to meet them. As new skills are gained, the competence of the parent is broadened.

Section 1 Goals and Objectives

Parents who seek or accept help with their children demonstrate that they have "felt needs" for new knowledge and skills. The evidence indicates that parents and parents-to-be have needs in the field of parent-child development. Research shows that a strong relationship exists between parents who have skills and children who can cope with their world.

The phenomenal sales of such books as Haim Ginott's *Between Parent and Child* and Dr. Benjamin Spock's *Baby and Child* indicate that millions of people are seeking a greater understanding of child development concepts, principles, and skills. Participation in Head Start programs also demonstrates that parents are willing and capable of becoming actively involved in the education of their children. More than two million parents annually consult family service agencies to seek information, understanding, and skills necessary to guide children. Promising results from the home-based child development programs are significant. Parents provided many of the activities and services that their children would receive if enrolled in established centers. These factors form a basis for further action in the field of parent-child development.

HOME START AS A CATALYST FOR ACTION

The United States Office of Child Development (OCD) began a Home Start demonstration in March 1972. Sixteen centers throughout the country explored the ways in which parents with low incomes can provide in the home setting the same comprehensive services as Head Start. The demonstration effort ended on July 1, 1975.

The evidence indicates great success in training parents to be *enablers* — effective and efficient teachers of their own children. The crucial role that parents play in the development of their children was highlighted. The great demand for Home Start training guidelines, home-based curriculum materials, and other pertinent information reflects a readiness for further action on a nationwide scale.

Home Start programs take into account local cultural, ethnic, and language characteristics. Existing community resources and services are identified and used as needed. These include parent involvement and educational, social, and health (including medical, dental, nutritional, and mental) services for children and their families.

The goal of Home Start is to broaden and expand parent skills; parents emerge as "child development specialists," with the

TYPES OF GROWTH
• Intellectual
• Emotional
• Social
• Physical
• Language

Fig. 1-2 Parent skills can enrich the total development of children.

Fig. 1-3 Intellectual growth takes place when parents provide opportunities that help the child explore and experiment with things in his environment.

Unit 1 Establishing Home-based Objectives

knowledge and skills needed to enrich the total development of their children. Home Start programs rely a great deal on home visitors for working with parents. Training is focused on helping the child accomplish developmental tasks in all types of growth.

- Intellectual: developing thinking processes that help him acquire, store, arrange, and rearrange information concerning his world.

- Emotional: being sensitized to his feelings and knowing how to handle them; learning to feel "good" about himself.

- Social: getting along with others — showing consideration, accepting responsibility, sharing, practicing self-control, and listening as well as talking.

- Physical: developing a healthy body through good eating habits, rest, physical exercise, safety precautions, and personal hygiene.

- Language: using communication skills as a two-way process — receiving and transmitting ideas, feelings, and information.

The idea of home-based learning recalls the words of philosopher John Dewey: "What the best and wisest parent wants for his own child, that must be the community want for all of its children." This suggests that assistance should be available to all parents who want to help their children.

The present discussion assumes that all parents want to be Dewey's "best and wisest parent." The "how to" is presented here as choice alternatives that serve different parents and families. A creative approach suggests ways to guide them in making selections appropriate to child and family needs.

CONTEMPORARY CONCERNS OF EARLY CHILDHOOD EDUCATION

Early childhood means that period of life in which a child's intellectual, emotional, social, and physical qualities are in the formative stages. Early childhood education focuses on programs that are deliberately intended to affect the learning and development of children. The word *program* is a flexible term including any plan or procedure, service or activity that helps the child or his parents.

Contemporary thinking about early childhood education is concerned with

Fig. 1-4 With a contented kitten asleep in her arms, a young child is sensitized to her feelings. She learns the meaning of taking care of a loved one.

Fig. 1-5 Children need to know that adults care about them and what they think.

Section 1 Goals and Objectives

(1) the child's total development from birth to the beginning of his formal education; (2) the early detection of health and educational handicaps; (3) the home environment of the child and opportunities for personal growth and development in his home; (4) the competence of parents as effective teachers of their own children; and (5) the influence of families in the total process of child development.

There is support for the view that there may be value in giving more attention to the parent than to the child. The parent not only is the first teacher the child has, but also continues to influence him for an indefinite future time. A competent parent is a competent teacher, available at all stages of a child's development.

Whether a child is physically strong, intellectually capable, and emotionally balanced is affected greatly by the quality of parental skills. A child's parents are like his basic textbook. It is in the home setting that the child meets his first problems. He learns to solve his problems and he faces the consequences of his actions. The child also evaluates his experience in terms of avoiding or repeating his action.

Ideally, the concept of providing services for early child development begins before the child is born. What the fetus experiences *in utero* may profoundly affect what he is like when he enters the world. Providing services for this early child development has led many public and private efforts to stress concern for the health of expectant mothers — prenatal and postnatal care. Provision for an adequate diet for newborn and very young children is part of these services, along with education for prospective and new parents.

PARENTS AS TEACHERS

A *teacher* can be described as anyone who consciously guides the experiences and behavior of an individual so that learning takes place. *Learning* is a change in behavior. It occurs as the individual interacts with his environment, fills a need, and is thereby able to cope with his environment. *Teaching* is the dynamic human transaction that takes place as teacher and learner interact.

Parents are teaching when they

- Help the child to see more clearly what his family holds as true and what they reject as false.
- Listen to the child and assist him in clarifying his own values, attitudes, feelings, ideas, and problems.
- Answer questions that enable the child to understand his world and gain meaning from it.
- Let the child experiment and practice with new ways of thinking and doing.
- Create a climate that promotes learning. Arrange a stimulating home environment. Let children propose, plan, collect, organize, assimilate, reproduce, create, and carry on activities that are natural and valuable for them.
- Give the child love and affection, understanding, and security — opportunities for building a healthy self-concept and self-esteem.

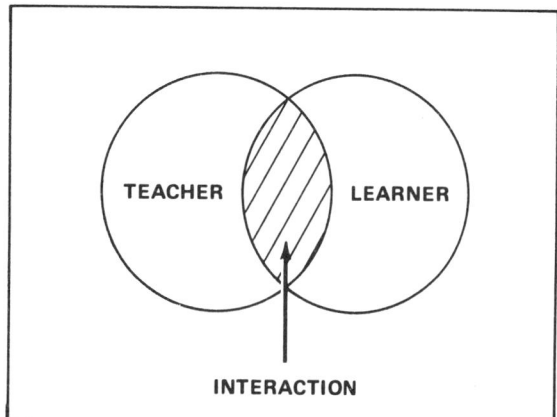

Fig. 1-6 **Teaching and learning take place when the teacher and learner interact.**

Unit 1 Establishing Home-based Objectives

Fig. 1-7 A warm embrace makes a child feel wanted and secure.

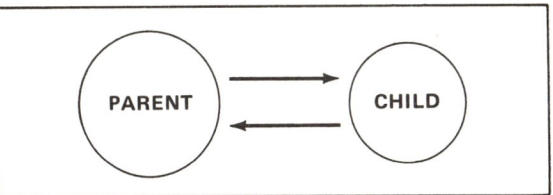

Fig. 1-8 The one-to-one relationship in home-based learning gives the child a unique program that is unequaled in any later learning that takes place in school-based programs.

ADVANTAGES OF HOME-BASED LEARNING

Parents who are effective teachers of their children can capitalize on every experience the child has — to insure positive growth. The child is not limited to preconceived *behavioral objectives* that tell exactly what the child is to do, the conditions under which he is to do it, and the extent to which his performance is accepted.

Parents function as program builders capable of identifying, planning, and carrying out worthwhile learning activities appropriate for the child. The child's horizons are expanded toward anything that he wants to know or needs to know at any point in time. What parents teach is compatible with family goals and values; the child is not confused by differing viewpoints.

There is some evidence that very young children learn better in home-based programs than they do in traditional approaches to early education. Perhaps this is related to the remarkable teacher-child ratio that parents establish. The one-to-one situation is unequaled in any later learning that takes place in school-based programs.

The parent-teacher creates a genuine climate for developing the idea of lifelong learning.

- Locate problems and help the child gain the ability to solve them: Where are you stuck? What do you think is getting in the way? What do you think can be done about it? How can I help you?
- Show the child how to do certain things through demonstration-type teaching designed to develop his motor-perceptual skills: Call his attention to what he is to do, and how he is to do it. Help him tie a shoelace, fasten a zipper, button his coat.
- Examine the family's cultural heritage to help the child gain insight to his questions: Who am I? What am I? Why am I? What can I be?
- Examine with the child other cultures in the community to discover answers to his questions: Who are you? What are you? Why are you? How can we work together "to be"?
- Expect the child to perform; accept what he does; respect his action, idea, or product.

- The child learns early in life to value learning experiences.
- Parents set a positive example for learning by sharing experiences with the child and guiding his efforts to a satisfying goal.

5

Section 1 Goals and Objectives

- Praise and commendation that parents give immediately reinforce behaviors, making them more likely to recur. Parents liberate the child's mind through continuous development of independent habits of study and problem solving.
- Home is the place in which the child learns how to live.
- Living is learning one's way through life by experiencing, doing, undergoing, reacting, and coping with each day.

ESSENTIAL PRINCIPLES OF LEARNING IN HOME-BASED PROGRAMS

Learning should be problem centered. The parent's task is to provide situations in which the child sees a broad range of problems from which to select. When the child sees a real problem, he is motivated to seek some kind of solution.

Learning should be experience centered. The parent has knowledge of the child's backlog of experiences and understandings that can be used to facilitate new learning. Genuine participation by the parent increases the child's motivation, adaptability, and speed of learning.

Experiences should be meaningful to the learner. Effective parents guide learning when problems are real and are initiated by a need that the child sees as his own. Interest, readiness, and capacity to understand are present. The child himself sets his goals. The parent starts him on the process of developing necessary skills that help him to learn and to grow.

Experiences must be geared to the learner's mental, physical, and social maturity. Home-based learning provides a variety of activities and instructional materials. Each child is enabled to learn in his own way and at his own pace. Materials of learning, seen as the child's actual experiences in the home, are always readily available tools. They cost nothing, and they neither ignore the child's interests nor run counter to them.

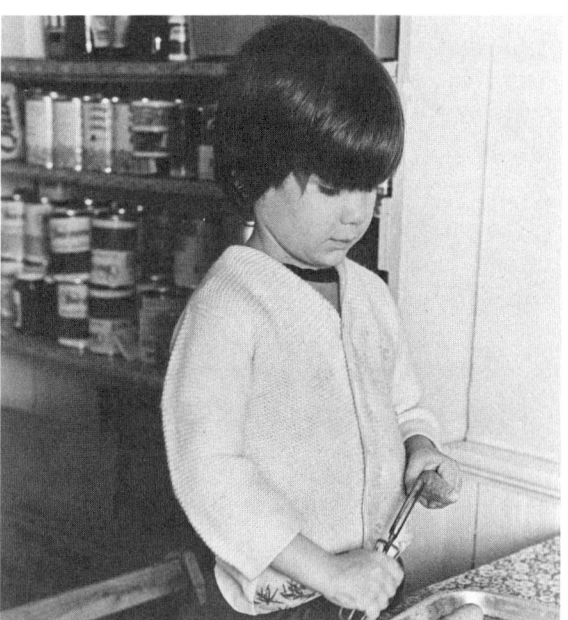

Fig. 1-9 Materials of learning, seen as the child's actual experiences in the home, are tools that are always available.

The learner must have feedback (knowledge of results) about progress he is making toward his goals. Behaviors during the learning process are modified by their consequences. *Positive reinforcement* (praise or reward) assists the child in finding and fixing correct responses. Parents give feedback immediately after the desired behavior occurs, thereby strengthening and reinforcing it.

The security of the learner must be protected. Parent-teachers "prize" the learner: his feelings, opinions, and potential. Parents help the child to develop a healthy self-concept. They give the child protection when it is needed and courage to progress. The fear of failure, guilt, and embarrassment is reduced.

SUMMARY

The child's home provides him with his first and most influential teachers — his parents or surrogate parents. Home-based child development programs are created by parents who are trained. Specific knowledge, understandings, and skills help parents become effective teachers of their own children.

Contemporary thinking in early childhood education focuses on (1) the total development of the child, (2) the competence of parents, (3) the influence of family and home environment, and (4) the early detection of possible developmental handicaps.

Parents have needs in rearing their children. Data show that people want more information about rearing children. People participate in programs to the extent that their felt needs are met.

Home-based teaching puts into practice some essential principles of learning: (1) learning should be problem centered; (2) learning should be experience centered; (3) experiences should be meaningful to the learner; (4) experiences must be geared to the learner's mental, physical, emotional, and social maturity; (5) the learner must have feedback (knowledge of results) about the progress he is making toward his goals; (6) the security of the learner must be protected.

A child's parents are the basic textbooks that provide the foundation for future learning. They enable a healthy mind in a healthy body.

SUGGESTED ACTIVITIES

- Visit an early childhood center. Observe.

    a. Find learning activities that parents can guide in the home setting.

    b. Ask for permission to examine the center's daily activity schedule. Think of ways to adjust the schedule to fit a home-based program.

    c. Identify and record any learning resources that parents can tap for home use.

    d. Share your findings with your peer group. Prepare a composite list of ideas discussed by the group. Put the list in your resource file.

- Go to a library or resource center. Locate an article describing Home Start, the demonstration program sponsored by the Office of Child Development. Ask for help if you need it.

    a. Write the name of the article in correct reference form. Examples are listed.

    > Westinghouse Learning Corporation. *The Impact of Head Start.* Athens: Ohio University, 1969.

    > Yarbrough, Willard V. "Preschool Goes to the Mountains." *American Education.* Vol. 9, July 1973, pp. 27-31.

    b. Summarize main ideas.

    c. Give your own reaction to the ideas. Confirm or contradict what you read, but give evidence to support your stand.

    d. Discuss the article in class. File your notes. If you can duplicate them, give copies to your peer group.

Section 1 *Goals and Objectives*

REVIEW

A. Define and describe each of the following terms.

   1. Need
   2. Intellectual growth
   3. Emotional growth
   4. Social growth
   5. Physical growth
   6. Language growth
   7. Learning

B. Give five facts that suggest parents need skills.

C. State briefly contemporary concerns of early childhood education.

D. Discuss ways in which parents are teaching during the course of every-day living with the child.

E. State at least five essential principles of learning that operate in home-based programs.

unit 2 identifying and describing program components

OBJECTIVES

After studying this unit, the student should be able to

- Discuss comprehensive services available to children and their families who are participating in home-based programs.
- List ten resources available to most communities.
- Create a card file of local services offered.

What makes up a program is determined in part by the situation in which the program exists. The term *situation* is defined to include the location in which the program is placed and the circumstances, conditions, or state of affairs the location gives to the program.

The location is important because it holds the people and things that are a part of the program, including available resources. How people regard the program and how they respond to it create conditions that affect it.

If people see a thing as pleasurable, they may support it. If they see it as painful, they may reject it. People also see things as being "good" or "bad." The ideas that people have about something affect the manner in which they respond to it.

In a situation where citizens care about others and their needs, there are groups that can become part of any effort to help families. Many organizations, agencies, and associations, directly or indirectly, provide services to the community. These are the *components:* the people, places, and things that make possible home-based programs.

LOCATING RESOURCES

Some communities have listings of civic and social organizations that give the names and addresses of persons to contact and their telephone numbers. This information is often provided in published or printed form. The local Chamber of Commerce or Community Planning Services may locate lists.

It is wise to adapt printed listings to meet individual needs. Card files are established. Components of home-based programs include education, health services, welfare and social services, and parent involvement. A partial breakdown of the education component is presented in figure 2-3. Other subheadings are found in HEW's Home Start Program.

When a service group is identified, the name, address, contact person, and telephone number are recorded on a file card. Personal contact is made and the outcome is noted on the card. Figure 2-5 provides a basic framework that is helpful.

The manner in which community resources are listed is not so important as the way in which they are used. There must be a system that helps to link resources in the community with families, who may then make a selection from a variety of options. A continuity of services should be made available to parents, which enables them to develop independence and competency in child rearing. This system should individualize and tailor home-based programs to children and families by involving parents in the identification and selection of services, gaps

Section 1 Goals and Objectives

PROTECTIVE SERVICES

I. To report, or seek action in behalf of:

    a. abused child   b. neglected child

Make reports to:

    Anne Daughtridge, Supervisor
    Protective Services Division
    Durham County Department of Social Services
    P.O. Box 810
    Durham, North Carolina
    Telephone: 688-6351, Extension 354

Services offered:

    casework   psychological testing
    day care   family planning
    foster care   adoption
    homemaker

II. Child Advocacy Commission

Service offered to all children in need (retarded, emotionally or physically deprived, neglected, etc.)

Purpose:

1. to plan and coordinate work of existing agencies in related areas
2. to speak for the child's needs (advocate)
3. to act as a referral body
4. to follow up to insure proper and prompt care

Requests for service should be made to:

    Mr. Larry Stegall
    Child Advocacy Commission
    P.O. Box 1151
    107 N. Market Street
    Durham, North Carolina 27702
    Telephone: 919-682-1129

Fig. 2-1 A booklet containing comprehensive services available to families provides workers with a valuable source of information.

Abstracted from: Day Care Task Force, *Programs and Community Resources for Day Care,* (Durham, N.C.: Community Planning Services, August 1973), pp. 39-40.

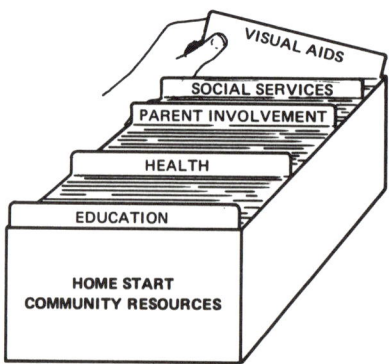

Fig. 2-2 A shoe box makes a handy container for a resource file.

Unit 2 Identifying and Describing Program Components

Education Component
- Universities, colleges, and community colleges
- Libraries, museums, art institutes and galleries, zoos, planetariums
- Local, state, and national departments of education
- Local, state, and national education associations, including all levels: early childhood, elementary, secondary, and adult education
- The Cooperative Extension Service
- Public and private schools
- Service clubs and fraternal organizations: Elks, Rotary, Kiwanis, Lions, Cosmopolitans, Knights of Columbus, etc.
- YMCA and YWCA organizations
- Church-affiliated groups offering educational services
- National associations organized to help children and their families: Child Study Association of America, Child Welfare League of America, etc.
- Community Coordinated Child Care Council

Fig. 2-3 A partial breakdown of the education component is shown. These are the categories under which cards listing specific groups are filed. Cards listing topics are helpful, too. Examples are music, recreation activities, and similar items.

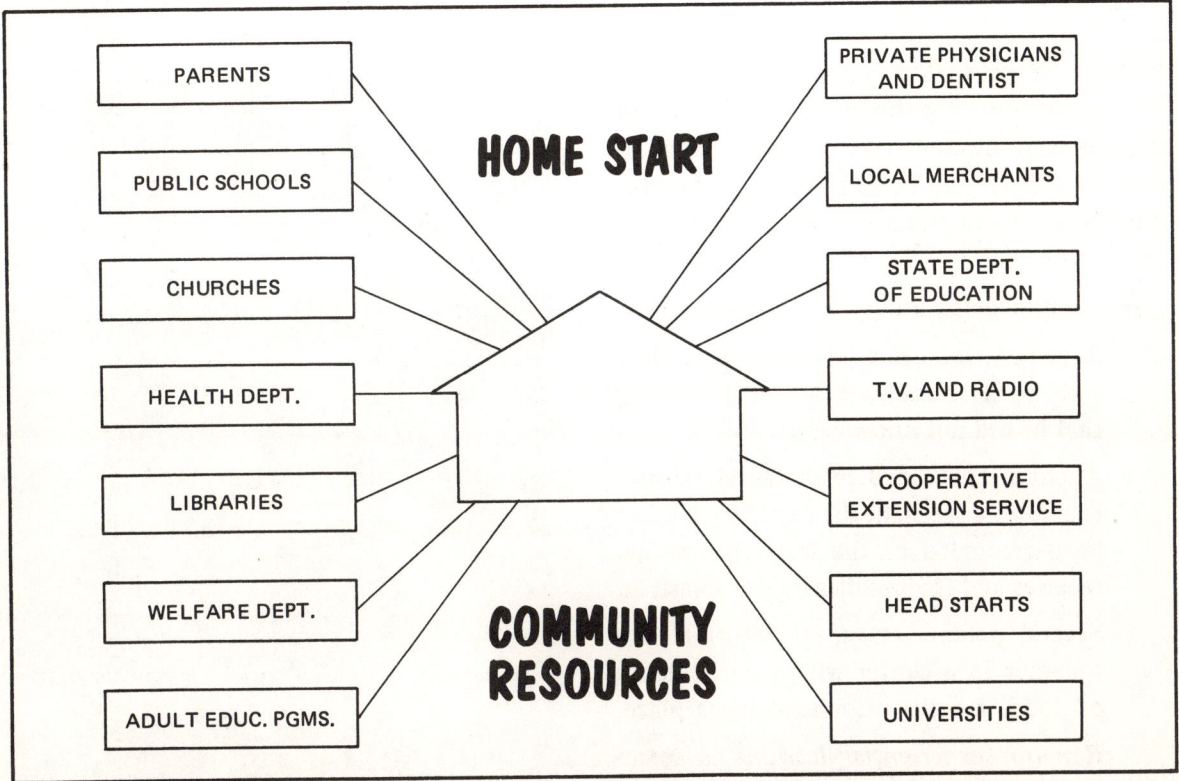

Fig. 2-4 Shown is HEW's Home Start Program linked with many community resources.

SOURCE: Office of Child Development, *A Guide for Planning and Operating Home-Based Child Development Programs*, DHEW Pub. No. (OHD) 75-1080 (Washington, D.C.: U.S. Department of Health, Education and Welfare, June 1974).

Section 1 Goals and Objectives

```
COMPONENT        Education                          CATEGORY    Drama
TYPE OF SERVICE  Puppet Show Presentation
CONTACT PERSON   Secretary at Hill House            TELEPHONE   682-0339
LOCATION OF SERVICE  N.C. Museum of Life & Science Auditorium
                     433 Murray Ave., Durham, N.C. 27707
COST   Free      AGES SERVED   3-6
WHEN AVAILABLE   For one week in October, December, February, and March. Four performances
                 each morning. Auditorium seats approximately 100.
ARRANGEMENTS     Advance notice requested (1-3 weeks)
COMMENTS   3/8/75 Excellent show. Repeat next year. Performance was presented by Junior
           League Puppeteers
```

Fig. 2-5 Items recorded on a file card provide important information for planning purposes. When services are changed, a new card replaces the outdated one.

that may appear as the needs of families change and grow should be avoided.

DEFINING EDUCATION

Education is defined as the process of lifelong learning that begins at birth and ends with death. It can be informal: unplanned, unstructured, or without any recognizable or stated goals.

- A child helps a peer to tie his shoelace.
- A person watches a television quiz show and learns something about a country that he did not know exists.
- A child, frightened by a thunderstorm, is able to cope with the experience when he is reminded of the water his garden receives and the puddles he can splash in.
- Several parents attend an informal get-together in a center where a discussion of toddler toilet problems takes place.

Random experiential learning is something that just happens during the everyday course of a person's life. A child may stop a play activity to watch someone change a tire.

No one is guiding his learning, but he "looks" and then he "sees." One "thing" comes off, and another "thing" goes on. Something

Fig. 2-6 Skill in learning to tie a shoelace comes with practice. The learning situation is both unplanned and unstructured.

must be wrong with the "off thing," he reasons. The experience is incidental, but the child does learn from such random experiences. An adult, unfamiliar with the tire-changing process, also may learn.

Formal education is learning that is (1) planned and directed toward identified goals and objectives, (2) guided by someone qualified to do the job, (3) sponsored by those who offer the opportunity on a credit or noncredit basis, (4) organized as a voluntary or compulsory experience, and (5) usually given recognition by diplomas, badges, certificates, ribbons, tokens, stars, or some other symbol of achievement, upon completion of the course or program.

People who work with parents need to recognize the many different situations in which learning takes place. Parents who are aware of the importance of everyday experiences make the child's world a powerful laboratory for learning.

EDUCATION COMPONENT

The aim of the education component is to help the child by helping his parents. Increased knowledge and understanding of general early childhood development enables parents to be better educators of their children. It is like creating a temporary Siamese twin connection between a child and his parents. What affects one flows naturally to the other. Parent skills are like a heartbeat. Competence is the source of "life" — successful parenting.

Competencies that make up the goals of the education component include the parents' ability to

- Make the most of educational opportunities that arise in the course of everyday living.
- Utilize the resources and services in the community to help the child reach maximal growth: intellectually, socially, physically, and emotionally.
- Select, plan, and carry out worthwhile learning activities for the child and the family.
- Gain useful information and skills through workshops, sewing and woodwork craft centers, toy-lending libraries, and other learning situations.
- Work independently to find appropriate solutions to child-rearing problems as they arise.

Establishing linkage with resources is easier when a resource file is available. This indispensable tool is a valuable time saver. The following suggestions explore ways to broaden and expand the possibilities of some resources listed in the file.

Universities, colleges, and community colleges have a wealth of human resources (people) and facilities that can be tapped for home-based early childhood programs. A question must be answered: How can people be motivated to participate? People are motivated when they see a real opportunity to fill an important need. Institutions of higher learning are always on the lookout for ideas that improve their services and raise their ratings. What is needed are ideas that hit at the heart of some of their "how-to" problems. How-to

- Become more responsive to student needs.
- Develop new and dynamic programs.
- Create innovative approaches to learning.
- Restore vitality to departments that are losing students (example: foreign languages).

Department chairpersons have a vested interest in constantly improving offerings. Listed are some departments and suggested ways to involve them in home-based programs. (Listings are suggestions, not formulas. Any effort to try them is done through program sponsors who can make necessary arrangements.)

Section 1 Goals and Objectives

Home Economics and Education Departments

Students in both home economics and education departments work with children and parents to integrate theory and practice. A *theory* is an explanation, or educated guess, that can be tested. The ideas are what is tested. *Practice* is what is done when ideas are being tried.

There are many theories or ideas that can be tried — the possibilities are endless.

- Parent education experiences for pre-service teachers are in the real world. Child care is caring for children.
- College professors have a unique opportunity to work with children and parents to demonstrate what they say in their classes.
- Classroom lectures are replaced by self-study texts. Regular class time is replaced by visits to homes and tasks related to course work: food service, nutrition, child care, consumer education, and sewing.
- A telephone service is established and monitored by students who provide information that parents seek.
- A storage bank of lessons is created by students who are "on call" to parents who seek help in teaching something specific to their children.
- The potential of cottage-based classes is explored. "Classes in the Kitchen" (the instructor goes to the student) are common as parents learn how to use home tools for early childhood learning. College students tape their lessons and submit them with an evaluation. Students, parents, and children profit from the experience.
- College students develop many workshops in lieu of term papers. A final examination is an opportunity to demonstrate teaching ability instead of writing about it.
- Weekend college (Saturday and Sunday) classes are held to enable working parents to attend. Entire families participate.

Psychology Department

The science dealing with the study of living things and their behavior is called *psychology*. The psychologist who studies human beings is concerned with the person as a social being, an individual self, and as a biological system (what he is made of).

Students studying about people and their behavior find home-based child development programs a real-world laboratory for learning. Instructors guide them in their search for knowledge. The possibilities are endless.

- College students help parents assess the needs of children through appropriate testing procedures studied under the department.
- Parents learn ways to provide children with feedback that motivates more learning.
- Learning about child discipline is a team effort between a psychology student and parents. Both learn and the child profits.
- The child's home is a unique situation for observing children and learning about their behavior. The college student learns and shares his knowledge with parents — who also learn.

Sociology Department

The relationships among people and how they behave in their group are the concern of *sociology*. What happens before people interact and what results from their interaction are topics of special study. Students gain experience and contribute services in some of the ways listed.

- They assist, as assigned, in the gathering of necessary information from families. They perform crisis intervention, such as drug counseling, when assigned.
- They learn how to establish working relationships with a wide variety of agencies and institutions and how to coordinate activities of parents and resources.
- They gain a broad knowledge of community services that contribute to the care, growth, and development of children and their families.
- They work with immigrants from another culture to help them learn to live in a "new" world.
- They learn about cultures from immigrants with whom they work.
- The range of job opportunities for a sociology student is explored: social workers, counselors for community services, agricultural extension services, home-based program workers.

Business and Economics Departments

Departments of business and economics are concerned with the management of income, expenses, and meeting the material needs of people. Students studying in these areas have much to share with all socioeconomic levels.

- They give information helpful in buying and selling goods, setting up home records for taxes, ordering from catalogs, and balancing checkbooks.
- They assist, as assigned, in the task of bringing together families who need funds with sources of funds.
- They help in examining the want ads with parents, assist them in preparing for job interviews and in finding ways to improve job skills.
- They guide parents in identifying their own needs and seeking services on their own.

Other Departments

Other university and college departments that have much to contribute include

- Biology and other science departments.
- Music and art.
- English, drama, radio and television.
- Recreation and physical education.
- Foreign languages (assist with parents who do not speak English well, or cannot speak English at all).

Libraries

Libraries make valuable contributions to the education component. Local and state resources may include a *materials curriculum*

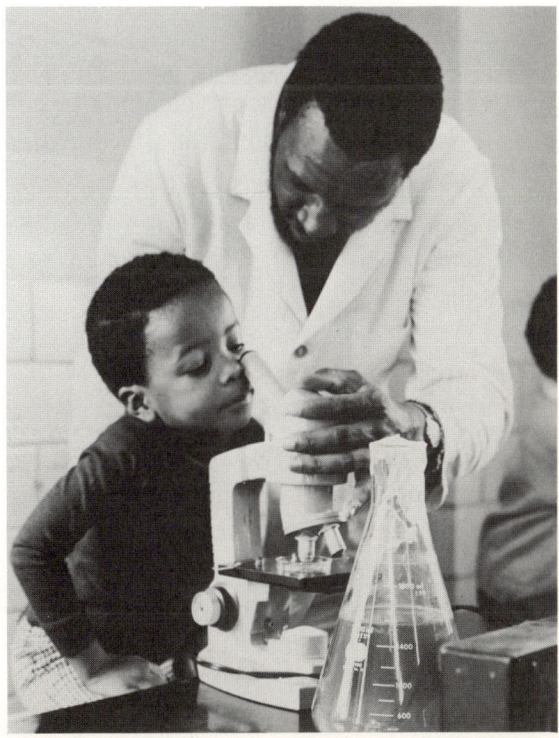

Fig. 2-7 A college professor shares his biology laboratory with a group of preschoolers. Shown is a child held spellbound by what he "sees."

center, a place where learning materials and audiovisual aids are kept. Libraries offer program workers, parents, and/or children opportunities to

- Obtain library cards and borrow books, records, filmstrips or slides, paintings, and prints for home or center use.
- Listen to stories, puppet shows, and lectures. See and hear talking books, slide presentations, and movies.
- Participate in discussion groups, workshops, and seminars on topics related to parenting or personal interests.

Department of Education

State and local departments of education provide

- Sources of funds and services not covered by other agencies.
- Counseling and testing for parent employment.
- State-supported training and education offered in high schools, community colleges, or other public adult education institutions.
- Parent education courses and programs given under public research-based projects.

Cooperative Extension Service

The Cooperative Extension Service, often referred to as "Agricultural Extension," has a long history of helping people. It is composed of three parts: federal, state, and county extension services. The Service operates through a cooperative arrangement between the state land-grant college or university in each state and the United States Department of Agriculture.

Extension agents serve both rural and urban areas. They are concerned with social, economic, and cultural needs of the people. A

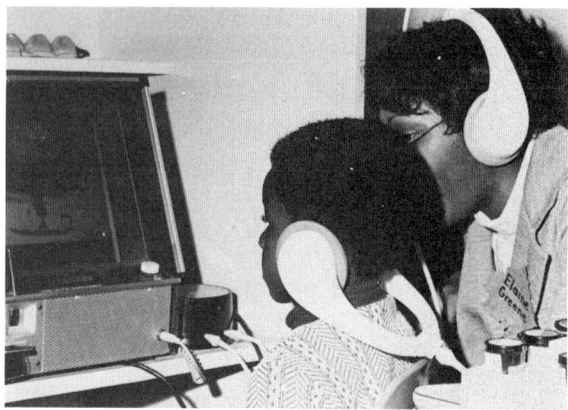

Fig. 2-8 A toy-lending library provides the child with many opportunities to listen, look, and learn.

close relationship is maintained with social service and educational groups designed to meet special needs. Agents provide learning experiences through personal contact, group activities, and mass media methods.

Services provided by agents, free of charge, include a wide range.

- Home and family living assistance.
- Marketing and consumer education.
- 4-H Clubs for youth activities.
- Published bulletins and pamphlets to help urban and rural people; radio and television programs.
- Demonstrations of new methods and changes in farming and homemaking practices.

HEALTH COMPONENT

The aim of the health component is a healthy mind in a healthy body for the child and his family. A full range of services covers nutrition, dental health, physical and mental health, and safety education. Emphasis is placed on the prevention of problems and correction when necessary and possible.

Some health goals are listed:

- Evaluate the child health status at the time he enters the program. A complete physical examination includes screening

COMMUNITY SOURCES OF FUNDS AND SERVICES FOR HEALTH CARE:

1. Private practitioners of medicine, dentistry, optometry, psychology — individual or group.	1. May provide all types of health services (consultation and planning, administrative, examinations and screening tests, treatment, immunizations, health education and continuing health supervision) on a volunteer contract, or fee for service basis.
2. Health departments — city, county, regional and state.	2. May provide all types of health services. Some may be free for all children or for certain children as part of existing programs, some may be purchasable. Health departments may provide funds to purchase services from other sources.
3. School health programs.	3. Same possibilities as health departments.
4. Clinics — run by hospitals, medical schools or other agencies.	4. May provide all types of health services, usually on contract or fee for service, but some services may be free for all or some children.
5. Prepaid medical groups.	5. May provide complete range of services to children of members of group. May accept families or children as new members of group.
6. Armed Forces medical services.	6. May provide medical preventive, diagnostic and treatment services to children of Armed Forces personnel. Dental services usually available only at remote posts. Facilities may be greatly overburdened so that only acute medical care is actually available.
7. Neighborhood health centers.	7. May provide comprehensive health services without fee for children living in geographically defined neighborhoods served by centers.
8. Comprehensive child health centers.	8. May provide comprehensive health services without fee to children who are in the defined population served by the center.
9. Dental service corporations.	9. May provide planning and administration of dental services for day care children for a contracted fee.
10. Special voluntary agencies and public agencies (see Table II).	10. May provide funds or services for screening or treatment and rehabilitation of certain health problems. Each agency is usually concerned with a single category of illness.
11. State crippled children's programs.	11. May provide funds or services for screening or treatment and rehabilitation of certain health problems. Limited to certain categories of illness which vary from state to state and within states.
12. Medical assistance under Title XIX "Medicaid."	12. Provides funds to purchase diagnostic and treatment services for a wide range of health problems for poor children. Exact services paid for and rules for eligibility vary from state to state.
13. Insurance and prepayment plans.	13. Provide payment for certain kinds of health services for children of families covered by policies.
14. Community mental health centers.	14. Diagnostic and treatment services for individual children, program consultation and in-service training.

Fig. 2-9 A list of community sources of funds and services for health care is an important reference for persons working with families.
SOURCE: A. Frederick North, Jr., MD, *6 Health Services: A Guide for Project Director and Health Personnel,* DHEW Pub. No. (OCD) 73-12 (Washington, D.C.: Office of Child Development, U.S. Department of Health, Education and Welfare), p. 11.

Section 1 Goals and Objectives

SOME SPECIAL HEALTH AGENCIES WHICH MAY HELP WITH DAY CARE HEALTH SERVICES:

1. Catholic, Protestant, Jewish Welfare Associations.
2. Family service associations.
3. Lions Club.
4. Other fraternal organizations: Civic clubs, women's clubs, and Parent Teacher Associations.
5. Associations for the blind or for prevention of blindness.
6. Associations for retarded children, cerebral palsy, crippled children and for children with special diseases.
7. Tuberculosis associations.
8. Mental health associations.
9. Visiting Nurse Association.

1. Money for services, social services.
2. Psychological, psychiatric and social services.
3. Eyeglasses for needy children.
4. Money or volunteer help for special projects.
5. Vision screening, special services for vision impaired children.
6. Special services for retarded and handicapped children.
7. Tuberculin testing and follow-up.
8. Psychological and social services, mental health consultations.
9. Home nursing and home visiting.

Fig. 2-10 Agencies that work with Day Care Centers give help to all persons who need assistance. These agencies are an asset to a home-based child development program, too.
SOURCE: A. Frederick North, Jr., MD, *6 Health Services: A Guide for Project Directors and Health Personnel,* DHEW Pub. No. (OCD) 73-12 (Washington, D.C.: Office of Child Development, U.S. Department of Health, Education and Welfare), p. 11.

tests, checking past records, parent interviews, and observations of the child.

- Provide remedial services to correct existing problems as much as possible.
- Provide necessary immunizations, fluoride treatment (to prevent tooth decay), and other preventive measures to insure future health.
- Help all family members to improve their present health and to take steps to keep in good health.
- Make sure that parents know what services are available for health care and what sources of funds are available for these services (if needed).

Resources for health services are comprehensive. Many are listed in figures 2-9 and 2-10.

SOCIAL SERVICES

The aim of the social services component is to help all parents resolve the problems that they face at home, at work, and in their community. It is more than welfare and related benefits. It is an effort to match parents and their problems with agencies and services that can help them.

Although social services utilize other community resources, some specific goals are identified.

- Guide parents to existing social and psychological services that provide assistance with problems: psychological services, drug counseling, job training, employment counseling, housing, financial aid, and recreational programs.
- Coordinate the efforts of other service organizations that help people: civic

groups such as American Legion, Rotary Club, Lions Club, Elks, Odd Fellows, and Veterans, for example.

- Assist protective organizations (child advocacy, guidance centers) in seeking action in behalf of children and their families. Services are specific.

PARENT INVOLVEMENT COMPONENT

Involving parents in the education of their children is what this text is all about. Some desirable goals have been identified already. Other valuable outcomes are presented.

When existing parent skills are broadened and expanded and new ones developed, both the child and his parents profit.

- Parents have a unique opportunity to reconstruct their own past. Creative activities and skills development, not experienced before by parents, can be gained as their children learn. A parent who has never molded clay, painted a picture, participated in dramatic presentations, or enjoyed other creative activities may grow and develop with the child.

- People who care about each other can strengthen and reinforce the bond between them by sharing experiences. Children learn to value parents who care and share with them.

- Parents who develop new skills may develop a new self-image — one of increased worth and ability.

- Parents who learn to work effectively with their children can fill in any gaps that may occur during the children's school years.

- Parents who learn how to work effectively and efficiently with young learners may wish to expand their work, as volunteers or paid employees. Many opportunities for career development exist in early education.

- Parents with education know-how can serve on advisory councils, school boards, and other school-related community groups. By contributing their services toward the improvement of education in the community, they improve conditions that affect their own children.

- Reaching children through their parents may be an economical way of providing early childhood programs. Center-based activities require building facilities, equipment, and money to staff and operate the formal program. A home visitor, working directly in the home, can reach many more people at a fraction of the cost.

- Working with parents in the home enables the home visitor to help change any conditions that may stand in the way of learning.

CAUTIONS

Community resources are like a giant umbrella that is available to all members of a community. The umbrella is ready, willing, and able to give "cover" to people who seek options in resolving their problems.

Nevertheless, it is important that those planning to use these resources in home-based programs examine all ideas carefully. Sponsors and workers must plan in terms of their own situation. What may be acceptable in one situation may be rejected in another. Problems are avoided when new ideas or things that appear to be different are discussed and approved before the idea is used.

SUMMARY

The situation in which a program is located affects the number of resources available. There are many organizations and

Section 1 Goals and Objectives

agencies that contribute to the four components of home-based programs: education, health, social services, and parent involvement. A listing of community resources is necessary.

Education is a lifelong process that takes place as people live and learn their way through life. Learning is a change in behavior. Teaching takes place when teacher and learner interact.

People are motivated to participate in programs when their needs are met. Organizations have needs, too.

SUGGESTED ACTIVITIES

- Start a community resource file. A suggested procedure is given.

    a. Get a shoe box and file cards to fit.

    b. Make a divider for each of the four components of home-based child development programs: education, health, social services, and parent involvement.

    c. Turn to the yellow pages of your local telephone directory. Find organizations and agencies to list under the components identified. Make a card for each group. Include name, address, and telephone number.

    d. Contact five groups by telephone. Ask them about their work. See if any are involved in Head Start or Home Start programs. List their services. Check figure 2-5 for information to include.

    e. CAUTION: If you are in a class with other students, divide the cards so that each organization is telephoned only once. Share your finding with your class.

- See if your community has a printed resource listing. If so, compare it with your list. See how many groups you located on your own. Add any that you did not find.

- If your community does not have a printed resource list, see if you can help some group make one. Perhaps this can be done as a class project. Discuss the matter with your instructor or the group with whom you make the list.

- Visit some of the resources. See how many new ideas and how much information you gain.

REVIEW

A. Define and describe each of the following terms.

   1. Situation
   2. Program components
   3. Education
   4. Random experiential learning
   5. Formal education

B. Identify each of the following as being either informal or formal learning.
   1. A child is watching fire fighters at practice.
   2. A professor is giving a lecture.
   3. A student is looking up some information in the library.
   4. A student is taking a course presented on television.
   5. A teacher is giving a final examination.
   6. A family is visiting the zoo.
   7. A student is using a self-study textbook for a course he is taking.
   8. A toddler is watching her mother bake a cake.
   9. A student enrolls in a correspondence course.
   10. A lifeguard is taking water-safety training.

C. Briefly answer each of the following.
   1. What is the aim of the education component?
   2. How would you go about setting up a community resource file?
   3. State four health goals in the home-based program.
   4. What is the aim of the social services component?

unit 3 creating home-based programs

OBJECTIVES

After studying this unit, the student should be able to
- Give at least four reasons why the concept of social action is an important tool for citizens.
- Describe the concept of social action as a tool for planning home-based programs.
- Examine the process described as it relates to a local situation.
- Select ideas that apply to the local situation.

There is evidence that parents need skills and information to make them effective parents and teachers of their own children. There are community resources that can help them. The question is "How can parents and resources come together?"

SOCIAL ACTION

A good way to begin is to work through social action, group plans that are made deliberately to change the way something is done. New ways are developed and necessary alterations are made in the old way.

Social action begins when two or more persons recognize a problem, talk about it, and decide to do something about it. They draw other interested persons into the group by "planting the seed," by stimulating others and arousing their interest in the problem.

The activities of these interested persons involve group decisions concerning what is to be done and a general agreement to act on the decisions. Important information is gathered to use in the decision-making process. People with authority or power to get the job done are members of the group.

It is useful to understand the concept of social action as a tool for all citizens. People who see a problem need are able to locate other people interested in searching for alternative ways to resolve the problem. When a community is confronted with problems, its citizens have a keen insight into ways to approach the problem. The citizens who understand social action processes are better prepared to become a part of it. When new programs are being explored, prospective workers are able to "plug in" at whatever level seems best for them.

Does the concept of social action apply to creating home-based child development programs? The fact that the question is raised implies that some thought has already been given to the idea of home-based learning activities. Once a problem is identified, the next step is the search for possible solutions. That is what social action is all about.

The answer to the question is, "Yes, social action can be used in creating home-based child development programs." The process is not a simple one that can be described

---

Social action begins when one or more persons recognize a problem, talk about it, and decide to do something about it. They draw other persons into the group.

Fig. 3-1 "Planting the seed."

briefly. Nor is it something that can be given in the precise terms of a cake recipe. It is possible, however, to present a thumbnail description of what happens when social action takes place.

SOCIAL ACTION IN PROGRAM PLANNING

When social action is involved in program planning, ten tasks are presented. The breakdown is an arbitrary one. Each task identifies an objective and pertinent questions to consider. Programs that evolve are choice alternatives designed to meet the needs and life-styles of different people in a particular community.

Task One: Identifying the Community

All action takes place in situations. People act in situations that are related to their physical and social worlds. Problems that people have exist in those worlds.

The community is the "real world" in which home-based programs are to operate. A description of the community is needed.

- Territory: setting, size and geographic location.
- Human resources: residents, racial makeup, religions, professions and occupations, socioeconomic levels, population, and cultural and ethnic influences.
- Natural resources: water, vegetation, and weather.
- Man-made resources: roads, buildings, and communication systems (including all ways people share information).

Pertinent questions are raised to obtain relevant information.

- Where is the community located? How large an area does it cover? What is the population?
- Who are the people in the community? What are their habits, beliefs, racial and ethnic identities?
- What do the people do for a living? What professions and occupations are identified?
- What are the natural resources in the community? How does the climate affect the lives of the people?
- How much does the community invest in roads and in public and private buildings?
- What investment does the community make in education? What is the educational level of the people who live there? What is the attitude toward education?
- What is the attitude of the community toward people who share a value system different from the majority?
- What forms of communication respond to the needs of the community: television, radio, newspapers?
- What transportation facilities are available?

Task Two: Determining That a Problem Exists

Someone may think that there is a need for home-based programs, but more information is needed to verify it. Thoughts are *subjective* — something that comes from the feelings of the person thinking. What is needed is *objective* evidence — something that exists as an object or fact. Objective evidence is real and can be verified. When a check is made the same information comes out.

There are a number of different ways to determine the existence of a problem. Some ways are listed on page 24.

COMMUNITY ELEMENTS
• Territory
• Human resources
• Natural resources
• Man-made resources

Fig. 3-2 A description of the community is needed.

Section 1 Goals and Objectives

- Contact organizations in the community to survey interest in home-based child development programs.
- Locate other community resources serving children and families each day (for example, family day-care centers, family day-care homes, public home visitor programs, and center-related programs for parents).
- Volunteers and staff of concerned organizations conduct a survey through various means (door-to-door contacts, telephone calls, mail, and community meetings).

Sources of information can be found in the community resource list prepared earlier. A few are highlighted.

- Community action agencies
- Religious organizations
- Agricultural extension services
- Public health departments
- Area planning councils
- Public and private schools
- Industrial organizations
- Human resources committees

There are some specifics that must be included in the information gathered. Questions are grouped under three headings: children, parents, and staff.

- Children
  1. How many are in the age range eligible for services?
  2. How many are currently being served by existing resources?
  3. How many are not being served by existing resources?
  4. How many families desire services? What is the number of children and their ages per family?

- Parents
  1. What is the number of parents who work full time, part time, and are unemployed?
  2. What services are desired by parents through home-based programs?
  3. What is the willingness of parents to participate in parent group sessions? What is the attitude toward intervention?
  4. What are the geographic locations of families, and what transportation facilities are needed to reach them?

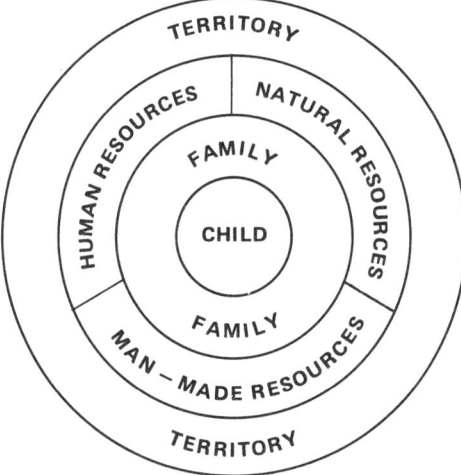

Fig. 3-3 The child is shown in the center of his world. His family make up the human beings in his immediate environment. Other factors that have an impact on his growth and development surround the child.

Fig. 3-4 People in a community express their love for children in different ways. Shown is a unique way of saying, "We care."

- Staff
    1. What is the number of present workers who are well-informed about home-based programs — what are they, how do they function?
    2. What is the number of persons who can utilize the findings of research to develop effective programs?
    3. What is the number of persons (volunteer or paid) who wish to broaden and expand services to reach all who seek help?
    4. What is the number of workers capable and willing to assume leadership roles?
    5. What is the number of existing centers ready to assume new responsibilities in working with parents?

The number of people making the survey varies with the community and the people in it. Concerned organizations and agencies often send representatives to participate in planning and reporting results to respective organizations. A small group may be very effective in laying the groundwork for future action. A large group can be equally effective. A working group is the requirement — a group of people who recognize what needs to be done and do it.

It is wise to work through existing community action groups. "Piggybacking" on an education-oriented group such as the PTA or social welfare may bring much support. Information gained through the survey is pooled and examined.

Task Three: Examining the Data and Formulating Objectives

The survey establishes a clear community interest in home-based services. The need is wide and varied. Based on the survey, answers to the following questions are found.

- What community organizations and agencies lend their support?
- Do existing programs take care of present needs? How can present services be expanded to serve more people? Are administrators open to suggestions for expansion?
- What are the advantages of totally home-based programs for early childhood education? Disadvantages?
- What sources of funds are presently available? How can additional funds be obtained?
- Are there "seasonal fluctuations" in the need for services? Do seasons or assignments cause families to move: migrant workers, military personnel, sales representatives, public health workers, diplomatic corps, foreign service workers?

The **"What do we have?"** question is answered. Facts and figures are on hand. The **"What do we need?"** responses support the social action group: home-based programs are needed and wanted by parents. The question is raised, **"What shall we do about it?"**

A "brainstorming" session is an excellent way to get new ideas from a group. All participants in the discussion submit ideas. Creative thinking is encouraged. No ideas are discussed until all members have spoken. It is important to remember that the first consideration is what can be done, not how it can be done.

After all suggestions are listed, they are discussed. Each idea stands or falls on its own merit. Unworkable ideas are discarded in favor of workable ones. Program objectives are formulated by the group.

Task Four: Selecting the Plan to Follow

The plan selected is approved by the group. A set of sound reasons for making the selection is given.

Section 1 Goals and Objectives

- The plan meets the needs of the greatest number of people. It enables the greatest amount of individualization in meeting the needs of children and families.

- Persons who have the necessary skills to work with parents are identified and available for the plan selected. Provisions exist for training additional staff needed and for in-service training on a continuing basis.

- The plan is compatible with the values, beliefs, attitudes, and culture of those who are served and of those who provide the services.

- The plan focuses on total families. Included are the working parent(s) and other family members who are away from home during the day. Group activities allow a full and continual involvement of parents and children.

- Transportation problems are resolved. Staff working with parents have transportation facilities. Parents have a way to get to training sessions away from home, if necessary.

- The comparative cost is about the same as other plans considered. The present plan gains financial support from several organizations that want to use parent programs in their own work.

Task Five: Obtaining Approval to Go Ahead with the Plan

In any program involving the community, it is necessary for *authority* figures (those who can give the "license to act") to give their approval. Sometimes the key figures in the community serve in that capacity. It is at this point that citizens become involved in the sense that they can help "push" the program forward.

Task Six: Communicating the Idea to the General Public

Public support often is gained through information released in newspapers and on radio and television. People who understand issues are more apt to be open-minded about giving support to related programs.

At this stage there is a need for people who have time to make contacts necessary in spreading information. It is important to reach the people who need the services, too.

Task Seven: Moving the Public to Vote for or Against the Plan

When new programs are initiated, funds are crucial. A public that understands the importance of the program is more apt to lend support. Funds may be legislated at the local or state level. Federal funding often is available, when certain conditions are met. People who want new programs to be funded give support to federal legislation that deals with the problem.

Task Eight: Organizing Resources to Carry Out the Program

At this stage, a plan of work is developed. In keeping with stated program objectives, an organizational plan is made. What is to be done, who is to do it, and the conditions under which it is to be done are all part of this plan.

Persons to be responsible for carrying the program forward are identified. Training plans are made. Resources are mobilized: physical facilities (as needed), financial support, communications, and human resources.

Task Nine: Moving Toward the Activities and Carrying Out Program Objectives

The primary concern is the coordination of activities. It involves carrying out the plan of work effectively and efficiently. It means ironing out any problems that arise.

ESSENTIALS OF SOCIAL ACTION

- Identify the community
- Determine the problem
- Examine data
- Formulate objectives
- Select a plan
- Gain approval
- Communicate the idea
- Vote for or against the plan
- Organize resources
- Move toward change
- Accomplish the objectives
- Measure the results
- Evaluate the effects of the program

Fig. 3-5 Social action is an important skill for all citizens in a community. Knowing about social action helps people give support to projects that can improve the quality of life in the community.

Task Ten: Measuring the Extent Objectives are Realized and Evaluating the Effects of the Program

Measurement means *how much;* evaluation means *how good.* Tests, interviews, questionnaires, discussions, and other means are used to measure objectives. Through these techniques, information is obtained that is helpful in determining the extent to which objectives are met.

Evaluation is the process of determining how good the program is in meeting the stated objectives. Evaluation is an ongoing part of all good programs. Periodic assessments provide an opportunity to make adjustments in the program, when existing conditions do not meet needs.

FUTURE DIRECTIONS

Communities planning to expand services to young children may gain support from their regional HEW office (see Appendix for addresses).

Home Start Training Centers

At the end of Home Start as a demonstration, Home Start Training Centers (HSTC) were funded through the Office of Child Development regional offices. Each *regional cluster,* two or more U.S. Department of Health, Education and Welfare (HEW) regions working together, established common goals and objectives for centers.

- To serve as sites for providing information and assistance helpful in copying ideas from existing programs for children and their families.
- To provide training and know-how in tasks necessary to carry out home-based programs.
- To highlight the role of parents as teachers and developers of their own children.

National Network of Resources

The goal of the HEW Home Start concept is to develop a nationwide resource and training network to assist local Head Start home-based programs. As time and resources permit, services and assistance may be expanded to reach other child development programs and public schools.

- To help them improve their own efforts in home-based early education.
- To offer assistance and guidelines in training workers to perform their tasks as well as workers in the training centers.
- To work through the regional cluster to conduct training sessions within the geographic area covered by the cluster.
- To compile, publish, and distribute HSTC materials developed by the national network.

Utilizing Existing HSTC Resources

The manner in which a community can tap the resources in a regional HSTC is an

Section 1 Goals and Objectives

MATERIALS FOR PROGRAM DEVELOPMENT

- A training guide designed to meet the needs of local home visitors.
- A resource file listing community institutions, agencies, and organizations which can provide services, materials, or advice.
- A home visitor's kit of basic games, toys, and other learning materials.
- Cultural and ethnic materials to meet individual interests and needs in the community.
- Other education media for program sharing (libraries, public school systems, state departments of education) as made available.
- Mini-courses for home visitor training made available by community colleges, continuing education divisions of local universities, or other institutions of higher learning.

Fig. 3-6 Librarians can assist in locating much-needed information and ideas for program development.

individual matter. Suggestions to communities can be made only in terms of the local situation and the HEW region in which each community exists. However, there are some hints that may apply in general.

- Locate the regional HSTC. Have community representatives make arrangements to visit the center and observe.
- Identify and obtain, if possible, any published materials provided by the center. Obtain all available HEW information and guidelines related to home-based programs.
- Have local planners become thoroughly familiar with the most recent literature on home-based early education programs. People with research know-how can interpret for planners the findings of special projects.

- Ask the local library to assist in gathering material. Education Research Information Center (ERIC) has a great deal of up-to-date information that can be tapped.
- Discuss the literature as it may apply to local situations. Make a list of "good" ideas. Reject those that do not apply to the local situation.
- Persuade a local college or university to submit a proposal for HEW funds, if the community comes up with new ideas that can be tried and tested.

SUMMARY

The social action process involves seeing a problem and initiating action that leads to solutions. Social action can be helpful in starting home-based child development programs in a community. It is a useful tool for all citizens.

A thumbnail sketch of social action, as presented in the foregoing discussion, lists ten tasks: (1) identifying the community, (2) determining that a problem exists, (3) examining the data and formulating objectives, (4) selecting the plan to follow, (5) obtaining approval to go ahead with the plan, (6) communicating the idea to the general public, (7) moving the public to vote for or against the plan, (8) organizing resources to carry out the program, (9) moving toward the changes necessary in carrying out program activities, and (10) measuring the extent to which objectives are realized and evaluating the effects of the program.

SUGGESTED ACTIVITIES

- Find a social action group in your community. Ask if you can attend a meeting. See if you can determine what tasks are in progress.

- Attend a meeting of the local board of education. See if you can find some elements of social action at work during the course of the meeting.

- Locate some problem in your community that you think can be resolved through social action. Using the steps presented in this unit, work out a plan that you would follow. Tell what might result from the plan.

- Check your daily newspaper. Find articles that deal with ways that people initiated action and carried it out through group action. Look for items about young children.

- Share your findings with your peer group. Ask your instructor to give you some feedback on your activities, especially in designing your plan.

REVIEW

A. Indicate the best choice for each of the following.

1. According to the author, social action is

    a. a change that takes place during the course of everyday living.
    b. a plan deliberately made to change the way something is done.
    c. a special program of community entertainment.

2. Which of the following does not apply to social action?

    a. It is a simple process that can be described briefly.
    b. It is a complicated process that requires an adequate explanation for full understanding.
    c. It cannot be described.

3. Which of the following statements is *subjective?*

    a. The survey showed that there are fifty families who want to participate in home-based programs.
    b. The principal said, "I think that you should be able to find about fifty preschoolers among the families in our school district."
    c. "Let's include this game in the program," said the teacher. "They ought to like it. Last year's class voted it to be their favorite game."

4. When a group gets together for a "brainstorming" session,

    a. they should ask for ideas and discuss each one as they go along.
    b. they should ask that each person go home and write down his ideas and bring them to the next group meeting.
    c. they should ask for ideas and discuss them after everyone has had an opportunity to contribute.

5. The term, "license to act," as discussed in this unit means

    a. the right to act in a dramatic performance.
    b. the freedom to do whatever the person wants to do.
    c. the authority figure's (figures') official approval.

B. Respond to the following questions in your words. Be as creative as possible.

1. Without any concern for expense, how would you advertise (communicate to the public) the idea of home-based early child development programs?

2. Name and discuss the social action process as presented in this unit.

3. Discuss some ways in which you might be able to tap the resources of an existing HEW Home Start Training Center.

Section 2 Orientation to Home Visiting

unit 4 the home visitor

OBJECTIVES

After studying this unit, the student should be able to

- Explain the meaning of the term *qualified home visitor.*
- Tell what a home visitor does.
- State four ways in which the home visitor may unintentionally stray from program goals.

A *home visitor* is just what the term implies: a person who visits homes. The purpose of the visit is to help parents build a home-based, early education program for the target child. The *target child* is the first concern of the home visitor and the parents with whom she works.

When necessary and appropriate, the home visitor extends her services to other children in the family. She may do something that contributes to the well-being of any other person who is part of the family.

In the present context, the visitor may visit any parent in any home. The goal is to reach all parents who want to provide an excellent learning environment for their children.

WHO CAN VISIT

A home visitor can be any qualified person capable of giving assistance, guidance, and

Fig. 4-1 Planning is an important task before a visit takes place.

Fig. 4-2 The home visitor arrives.

Section 2 Orientation to Home Visiting

resource information to parents in need of help. She must be able to model (show) the way she wants the parents to act. She models by doing whatever needs to be done. The parents imitate the action.

In general, *qualified* means those home visitors who possess the knowledge and skills required. These qualifications include successful experiences as a parent, or with parents. Home visitors must also have a knowledge of the cultural background and language of those to be served. They must possess the ability to relate to the problems of others and have the requisite information and skills to do the job.

Academic credentials may vary according to the individual situation for which assistance is sought. Requirements may be minimal where a neighbor-to-neighbor attitude is needed to affect parental change. The important quality is exceptional aptitude in working creatively with children and their parents.

Career development for home visitors can provide a self-improvement program. Easy access to a staff member who can give appropriate in-service training provides the home visitor with guidance that she needs to work effectively.

Home visitor credentials may be quite different in other situations. Expectations are apt to be more demanding if parents of gifted children seek assistance, if the parents are themselves well educated, or if the social, emotional, or physical needs of children and/or their parents require someone with professional credentials.

WHAT A HOME VISITOR DOES

The *job description* of the home visitor tells the general duties that are to be performed. Tasks may fall into three categories: sponsoring agency, home visit, and community related.

Sponsoring Agency Tasks

Sponsoring agency tasks may vary with individual groups, but a home visitor may expect to

Fig. 4-3 A hearty greeting is exchanged.

Fig. 4-4 The home visitor turns to her file box. It is her professional tool kit.

- Engage in training sessions as outlined by sponsors.
- Participate in other training as required.
- Seek assistance from appropriate agency personnel, as needed, to improve services to children and their families.
- Submit required records as necessary for meeting program objectives.
- Confer at specified times with those responsible for planning and coordinating the program.

Home Visit Tasks

The tasks of the home visitor have a built-in flexibility to meet the special needs, characteristics, and expectations of local situations. A home visitor may expect to

- Develop a plan tailored to the individual needs of each family for whom she is responsible.
- Spend a specified time with each family (usually once or twice a week, for an hour-and-a-half to two hours).
- Carry out the day-to-day activities of the work program, as outlined in each family plan.
- Keep necessary records: child and family information, records of referrals, follow-up of referrals. *Referrals* are those cases that are directed toward someone else for services or information.
- Be available on call by families, at night and on weekends.

Fig. 4-6 The child carries on his task by himself.

Fig. 4-5 One child is given a task.

Fig. 4-7 The home visitor calls attention to a learning objective.

Section 2 Orientation to Home Visiting

Community-Related Tasks

Duties that link the program with the local community fall into this cateogry. The home visitor should

- Know what existing resources and services (set fee, reduced fee, no fee) are available in the community.
- Understand how to coordinate, integrate, and utilize resources on an as-needed basis to provide social, health, nutritional and psychological services for program children and their families.
- Prepare and deliver family referrals to support agencies in the community and include a follow-up on all referrals.
- Make parents aware of agencies in the community that provide adult education experiences that can meet people's needs.
- Maintain community support for the program.

Job Performance

What the home visitor actually does in carrying out specified objectives is called *job performance*. There is no one approach followed in home visits, for each situation is considered on an individual basis.

The visitor is concerned primarily with adult-oriented behaviors that help parents (or surrogate parents) to become more effective teachers of their preschool children. Building on existing family strengths and involving parents are seen as the major means of improving the quality of children's lives.

Sometimes the work concentrates on the child to make easier any task concerned with physical, social, emotional, and intellectual development.

- Helping the parent plan, prepare, and serve the child nutritious meals.

Fig. 4-9 The child works with guided practice.

Fig. 4-8 A demonstration is given to show what is to be done.

Fig. 4-10 Independent practice helps to set the skill.

Unit 4 The Home Visitor

- Demonstrating physical activities that are body building and fun for the preschooler.
- Guiding parents in accepting the feelings, emotions, interests, limitations, and capacities of the child.
- Showing how assisting with a household chore can become a constructive learning experience for the child.
- Using as teaching tools, elements of the child's environment at home and away: household articles, magazines, television, newspapers, neighborhood stores, and natural phenomena, for example.
- Introducing homemade games for learning: involving counting, classifying, and identifying objects.
- Helping the child and his family build success bases that enable them to cope with any failures.

Home visitors may also take parents to the community library to help locate books of particular interest to them or their children. Arrangements may be made for parents to utilize other library services that may be available.

- Viewing films being shown at the library.
- Borrowing a film, or filmstrip, and a projector for home use.
- Listening to records in the library or borrowing them for home use.
- Checking out, from the toy-lending division, toys appropriate for the target child or other children in the family.
- Obtaining information concerning forthcoming events: storytelling, puppet

Fig. 4-12 The home visitor calls mother's attention to an important point.

Fig. 4-11 The child receives praise for a job well done.

Fig. 4-13 Mother reads a story.

Section 2 Orientation to Home Visiting

shows, special film festivals, lectures, workshops or seminars designed for parent education.

DEPENDENCE AND INDEPENDENCE

In the DARCEE (Demonstration and Research Center for Early Education) program for low-income mothers, home visitors are trained to place the mother in a dependent role. The reason given is that a person must first be "dependent on the individual who is going to help her learn how to be independent."[1] Gaining independence is seen as a process of learning.

As a mother in the DARCEE program becomes skillful, she is given more responsibility. The process continues until the mother takes over all of the teaching herself.

DARCEE mothers come from low-income families. The educational level of parents may create the need for much help when they start their home-based work. These parents may be quite comfortable in a "dependence" role.

In other socioeconomic groups, parents may not feel the same. They may see the dependence role as an effort to "take over." Perhaps the dependence-independence role of different groups may be judged best by seeing how much parents can already do by themselves.

What the home visitor needs to do is to see herself in the role of change agent. The home visitor who is trained to be a change agent has skills that help her to make decisions concerning dependence and independence in working with parents.

A *change agent* is a person who is trained to

- Identify a need for change.

[1] Rosemary Giesy, ed., *A Guide for Home Visitors*, (Nashville, Tennessee: Demonstration and Research Center for Early Education, George Peabody College, 1970), p. 35.

- Plan for the change in terms of the interests, needs, abilities, and culture of the people to be changed.
- Create a working relationship with those who need the change, and build their trust and confidence.
- Unset old ideas that might stand in the way of making the new ideas work.
- Work with the people in practicing the new ideas until the new way becomes a habit with them.
- Stop working with the people when they are able to continue without help.
- Make sure that the people with the new ways know where to go in case they need help in the future.

PROBLEMS OF THE HOME VISITOR

Deeply imbedded in the objectives of the home visitor is the aim to be a listener, helper, advisor, and friend to the entire family being served. In an effort to gain the confidence, cooperation and friendship of parents, the home visitor may unintentionally sabotage her own program. She may be guilty of

- Setting up too many formal activities instead of allowing for much informal give-and-take.
- Concentrating her work efforts on the child instead of the parents.
- Allowing parents to become too dependent on her, instead of encouraging them to become self-sufficient through increased responsibility.

ROLE OF CHANGE AGENT
- Identify a need for change
- Plan for the change
- Create a working relationship
- Unset old ways
- Help people practice new ways
- Break away when new ways are set
- Keep in touch

Fig. 4-14 A change agent helps people to change by working from a position of dependence on the agent to independence in continuing what is learned.

- Gearing her program toward middle-class values, attitudes, and appreciations instead of creating a program based on the uniqueness and strengths of each family.

In keeping with the principles of adult learning which are discussed later in unit 8, sponsoring agencies should involve home visitors in identifying and carrying out their own training needs. Too often trainers find it easier to fit people to preconceived or packaged subject matter than it is to take time to discover what is needed, why it is needed, and how the adult learner can relate to what is needed.

Failure to involve the home visitors in their own training becomes a problem of frustration and failure.

HOW A HOME VISITOR IS TRAINED

In identifying, selecting, and training home visitors, some crucial questions must be answered.

- What tasks are to be performed by the visitor?
- What enabling skills are needed to perform each task?
- What educational requirements are necessary to develop the enabling skills?
- What experience is necessary to develop competence?

The responsive trainer treats the preservice home visitor as a person. She is seen as the main reason for the training program. Her experiences and ability are discovered and used in planning and carrying out the kind of learning program that fits her adult nature. The home visitor is regarded as a learner, and her needs are satisfied. In general, the program is practical and broadly based.

Preservice training may be as short a period as three to four weeks, with emphasis on continuing, in-service training. Or, the entire training period may be as long as the time that it takes to obtain a degree from a community college or other institution of higher learning. The latter may be true in the case of a trainee who needs highly specialized skills.

WHAT THE HOME VISITOR SHOULD KNOW

The home visitor should be able to

- Show skills in her job performance.
- Identify the needs of people in terms of their background, interests, and culture.
- Locate the services and agencies that provide the help that children and their families may need.
- Work effectively in showing people new ways of doing things and helping them to adopt the ideas.
- Work independently in homes without the need for constant supervision by her trainers.
- Continue her own training by knowing how to recognize what she does not know and how to get the necessary skills and information.

PERSONAL CHARACTERISTICS OF THE HOME VISITOR

The personal characteristics of the trainee are crucial. The success or failure of the home-based program rests heavily upon the visitor's unique personality and past experiences. Some desirable qualities are listed.

1. A healthy, well-integrated self-concept and a personality that responds to people and to which people respond.
2. Knowledge and skills proved in helping children and their families in real-life situations.

3. Ability to create a climate of mutual trust and understanding through
- Maturity gained with experience.
- Sensitivity to the rights and feelings of others.
- Flexibility gained by the ability to change her own behavior and plans to accommodate other persons.
- Empathy developed by sympathetically listening to others and learning how to see things from the standpoint of other people.
- Motivating forces that come from within: a desire to learn, ability to change, and a commitment to learning and developing new skills for herself.

HOME VISITOR AS A CATALYST FOR CHANGE

The concept of the home visitor can become a positive force in a democracy that seeks maximal growth and development for all of its citizens. If more than lip service is to be given to the words "provide for individual differences," then a way must be found to provide home-based education for all children whose parents need help.

Fig. 4-15 Time out to let the children talk about something that interests them.

- Physically handicapped
- Emotionally disturbed
- Mentally limited
- Economically deprived
- Socially constrained
- Academically gifted

What is learned from the development of programs serving young children can be studied to broaden and extend the services of home visitors to learners from infancy to old age. Education for lifelong growth and development can become a reality.

The field is wide open to those who are concerned with the needs of people. Educators and others have a standing invitation to accept the challenge.

SUMMARY

Home visitors help parents create home-based learning situations for preschoolers.

Fig. 4-16 The lessons are over. Everyone plays a game: "We are birds."

Fig. 4-17 The day's lessons are discussed. Plans are made for the next visit.

Unit 4 The Home Visitor

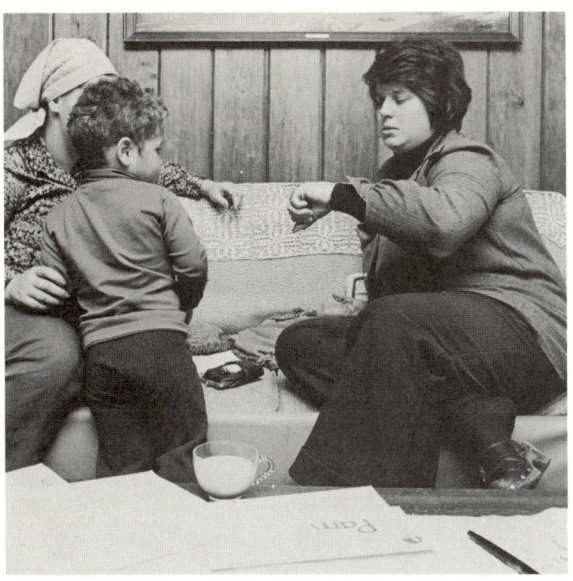

Fig. 4-18 It's time to leave.

Fig. 4-19 The home visitor leaves. She will be back another day.

Parents are trained to be the major means of guiding the healthy growth and development of their own children.

A special program is planned for each child and his family. The program is centered around materials and people in the child's home and resources and services in the community.

The home visitor possesses the knowledge and skills needed to plan and carry out the program. She has access to people who can help her.

SUGGESTED ACTIVITIES

- Interview a home visitor in your community. Find out

    a. How her agency identifies, selects, trains, and assigns home visitors.

    b. What she does on the job.

    c. What kind of community resources and services are accessible to her.

- Check your file box of resources and services available in your community.

    a. Compare your list with that given to you during your interview with the home visitor.

    b. Visit some of the resources and services agencies on your list. Take an inventory of specific services offered by each group that you contact.

    c. Rearrange your own list in a descending order, starting with the greatest number of services at the top. Continue downward with the next highest, and the next — until you place the smallest number at the bottom. Discuss your findings with a member of your peer group, an instructor, staff member, or other interested person.

39

Section 2 Orientation to Home Visiting

REVIEW

A. Define the following terms as they were used in this unit.

   1. Home visitor
   2. Job description
   3. Job performance
   4. Change agent
   5. Home visit tasks

B. Name the three categories into which home visitor tasks may fall.

C. Describe the tasks that fall into the categories named in question B.

D. List four things that must be known in the identification, selection, and training of home visitors.

E. Indicate the best choice for each of the following.

   1. A home visitor means someone who
      a. Has a college education.
      b. Can do something special.
      c. Has permission to visit orphans.
      d. Visits friends at home.

   2. Preservice training of home visitors may
      a. Take three to four weeks.
      b. Take two years.
      c. Vary.
      d. Take four years.

   3. The home visitor is concerned primarily with
      a. What the child does at home.
      b. How the child relates to siblings in the home.
      c. Adult-oriented activities.
      d. Ways to teach the young child.

   4. The home visitor should see herself as
      a. Setting up a formal program for the child.
      b. Sizing up each situation for an informal give-and-take.
      c. Finding the weaknesses in the family situation.
      d. Making toys and games to give the parents.

   5. The success or failure of a home-based program rests heavily upon the
      a. Kinds of problems that the visitors face.
      b. Nature of the child and his family.
      c. Resources and services available.
      d. Personality and past experiences of the home visitor.

unit 5 developing workplans

OBJECTIVES

After studying this unit, the student should be able to

- Discuss the following important considerations in making workplans: change, planning, intervention, culture, family value system, cultural baggage.
- List and describe four basic questions that are the concern of every worker and apply them to home visit situations.
- Develop a workplan file that contains carefully planned material that can serve as a model for other workplans.
- Prepare a workplan and present it in a simulated or real-life situation.

The task of planning is one of preparation for *change,* a variation or alteration in form, quality, or state of being. The home visitor is a change agent who attempts to change or alter the way parents are doing something. She does her job by demonstrating the advantages of a new way. She may provide ideas for action where none exist.

Planning is the process of working out a broad outline of the things that need to be done and the methods for doing them. A carefully made plan of work provides the home visitor with a basis for making important decisions.

- Deciding the direction of the work with the child, his parents, and the family.
- Determining the goals of the program being developed.
- Selecting the strategies (courses of action) necessary for making the right decisions at the right time.

INTERVENTION AND CULTURE

Home visitors must always be aware of the fact that home-based programs are a type of *intervention,* an interference in the affairs of another. When parents seek help, or accept it, they are in effect inviting into their homes new values, ideas, and attitudes. Intervention changes the lives of people. Persons providing help must understand the impact that their efforts have on the value system of those they serve.

A *family value system* means family standards. It includes moral, social, and emotional beliefs and attitudes. Family values are building blocks that parents provide, helping to make the child what he is.

The child is *socialized* when he acquires the value system of the group into which he is born. Through the process of *socialization,* the child not only learns about his group, but becomes a functioning member of it. His family helps him to develop a "sense of belonging" and a strong "we" feeling with shared family experiences.

Parents have both the right and the responsibility to train their children as they choose. Consequently, the home visitor's plans must recognize, respect, and utilize the resources of the target child's cultural background.

Culture is the social heritage of people — a way of life. It includes everything that an individual learns and shares as a member of society.

- The rules which govern the behavior of the people.
- The manner of thinking, acting, and feeling about certain things.
- The material products which the people produce and use.
- The knowledge and beliefs of the group.
- The language and methods of interacting with each other.

Wherever they go, people carry with them *cultural baggage.* It is a product of a person's experience in his own society. It provides a framework through which he sees and judges the world and other people's behavior. It is also a source of misinformation about another culture. What a person says, does, or feels in his own culture may not be acceptable in another.

No amount of training can erase a person's cultural baggage. It is deeply rooted in each person's personality. But, well-planned training helps home visitors to

- Identify and examine their own culture.
- Identify and examine the culture of families with whom they work.
- Identify and examine cultural differences that may create conflict between home visitor and parents.
- Refrain from labeling cultural differences as "good" or "bad" for children and their families.

The aim of the home visitor is not to change families into a new image but to work with parents for needed change.

BASIC QUESTIONS FOR WORKERS

There are four basic questions that home visitors must ask themselves.

- What is the major **purpose** of my work?
- What **process(es)** shall I employ in doing by job?
- Who are the **persons** with whom I am involved in providing services: sponsors, cooperating organizations and agencies, and the child, his parents, and family?
- In what **place(s)** are my services given?

Purpose

The home visitors' purposes are the products of their own view of the task and that of their sponsors. The organization or agency that sponsors the program has objectives, too. The philosophy and objectives of the visitors must be compatible with that of the sponsors.

The primary purpose of the program is to help the child by improving the parenting skills of both father and mother. Plans are made for reaching the parents, the target child, and other children in the family. Senior citizens in the home may also be drawn into the program.

Processes

There are different ways to reach the same goals. It is important for workers to know what options are open. A wide range of choices increases the worker's capacity for meeting the needs of different people.

Fig. 5-1 Older children in a family give the baby a "sense of belonging" by sharing their love, attention, and activities.

The home visitor uses whatever materials and methods can help her accomplish desired goals. She must be selective in finding the right activity for the right person.

Persons

The ability to work effectively with people is related to how well the persons involved know each other. Not only must the home visitor know about the child and his family, but they in return must know something about her.

The home visitor must reveal herself as a person who takes a positive approach to all situations. She shows equal respect for the low-income mother of limited background and for the well-educated mother. She does not judge the first one for living in the poorly cared for home that is often part of poverty. Nor does she condemn the second mother for not being able to make use of her education in dealing with the problems of her own child.

Confidential information learned in a home visit is respected by the worker. She keeps to herself things that she sees and hears that are not related to her business. She inspires trust in parents.

A pleasant smile, kind words, an appreciation of the family's culture, and the ability to make people comfortable can tell much about a home visitor. Communication lines with sponsors, supervisors and other need-to-know people must be kept open. The home visitor must see herself as the member of a team that helps people.

Places

Activities between parents, the target child, and the home visitor usually take place in the child's home. The visitor is concerned with living conditions that affect learning in the home.

Resources for learning, adequate space in which to learn, and people with time to spend with children are vital needs. The well-trained home visitor is able to assist parents in broadening and expanding the use of existing resources and in providing missing resources for learning in the home environment.

When necessary, the home visitor's services are given in places outside the home. She may take parents and the child to the library, a social agency, or to any other place where family needs are met.

The worker must be familiar with all opportunities for learning that exist in the home and in the community. Her resource file gives her a broad view of options. It can serve her well if she keeps the file current.

LONG-VIEW PLANS

Long-view plans are a structure from which later plans are made. Unlike a classroom teacher, whose long-view plans represent the yearlong program, the home visitor's long-view plans may or may not be used.

A classroom teacher can predict what is needed because her class is made up of children who are more alike than they are different. The teacher plans for like needs and provides for individual differences. The home

Fig. 5-2 Many opportunities for learning exist in the community. Organizations offering special exhibits each year can be listed in the home visitor's resource file.

Section 2 Orientation to Home Visiting

visitor faces the task of dealing with many different people having unpredictable needs.

To enable her to deal with her problem realistically, the home visitor's long-view plans are presented as a resource file of workplans. A *workplan file* is made up of tangible materials that are ready for use. The file serves as a professional "tool kit" that expands the visitor's capability for tailoring activities to fit different families.

Developing a workplan file before making visits is a mechanism for involving the home visitor in her own training. She is able to broaden and expand her knowledge of children and parent skills, while she is preparing materials to help both. The workplan file relates to the set of goals and objectives for the entire program.

The way a workplan file is organized depends upon the person who is to use it. What goes into the file depends upon the usefulness of the material. Each home visitor must decide for herself. The only requirement is that the plans are flexible, accessible, and useful.

SUGGESTIONS FOR MAKING A WORKPLAN FILE

The following filing system is a great help to many preservice and in-service teachers. It is offered to generate ideas that help home visitors to devise a plan of their own.

Creating Storage Space

When needed materials accumulate, everyone is faced with the problem of finding some out-of-the-way place for storing them. Filing cabinets are expensive and take up valuable space.

A file, created from a cardboard box, costs little or nothing. It has the added advantage of being portable. File boxes can be stored on book shelves — a convenient location for easy access.

Making a Storage File

- Get a cardboard box large enough to hold manila folders.
- Make an attractive collage, or "stained glass" type covering, using scraps of colored paper taken from mail order catalogs or magazines. Small triangles are cut and pasted on the box, so that each triangle slightly overlaps another. Apply several coats of shellac or clear varnish to protect the collage, and give a finished look. If available, scraps of contact paper are an excellent substitute for the catalog cutouts. Contact paper has the advantage of requiring no paste.
- Find a larger box that fits over the top of the decorated box. Cut the larger box to a size appropriate for a cover.

Fig. 5-3 Making a workplan file is an important part of a training program. The task includes selecting activities, preparing and presenting them to the training group in simulated (make-believe) teaching situations, and then working with one or two children in the "real world."

Some people like to use narrow boxes, so that several fit on a book shelf. A good idea is using one for each component, or major topic of home-based child programs. Sharing with another person multiplies the resources.

Home visitors may wish to help individual families to start a file containing items of interest and need to family members: medical records, games, learning materials, for example. Parents can start a file of learning materials for their first child

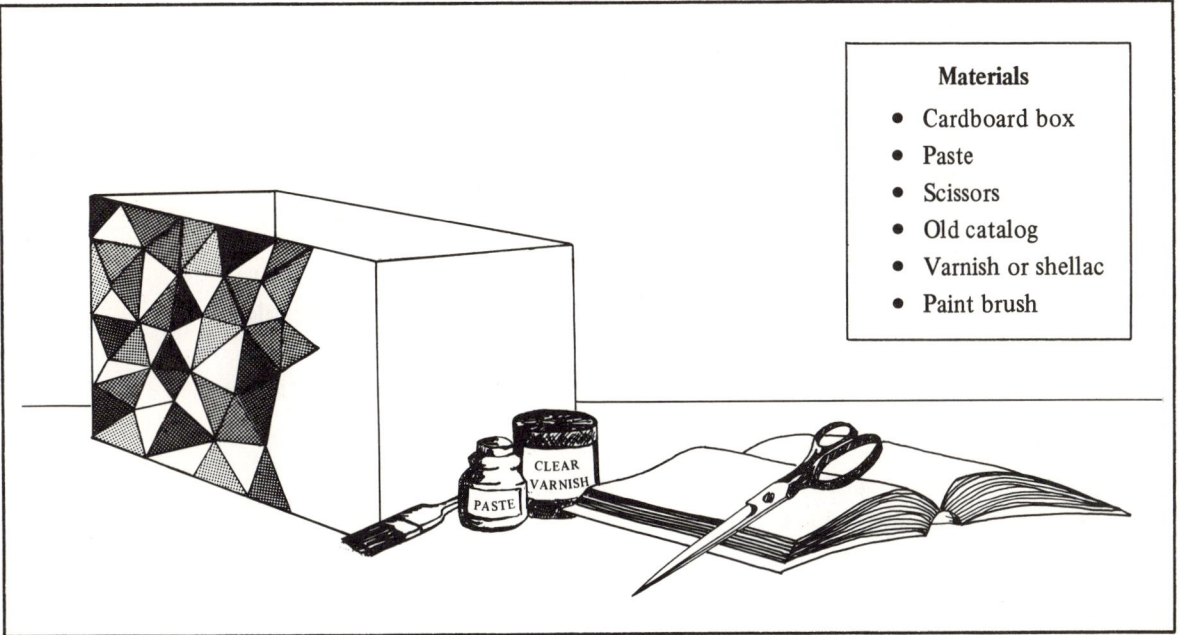

Fig. 5-4 A workplan file is easy to make and costs almost nothing.

Materials
- Cardboard box
- Paste
- Scissors
- Old catalog
- Varnish or shellac
- Paint brush

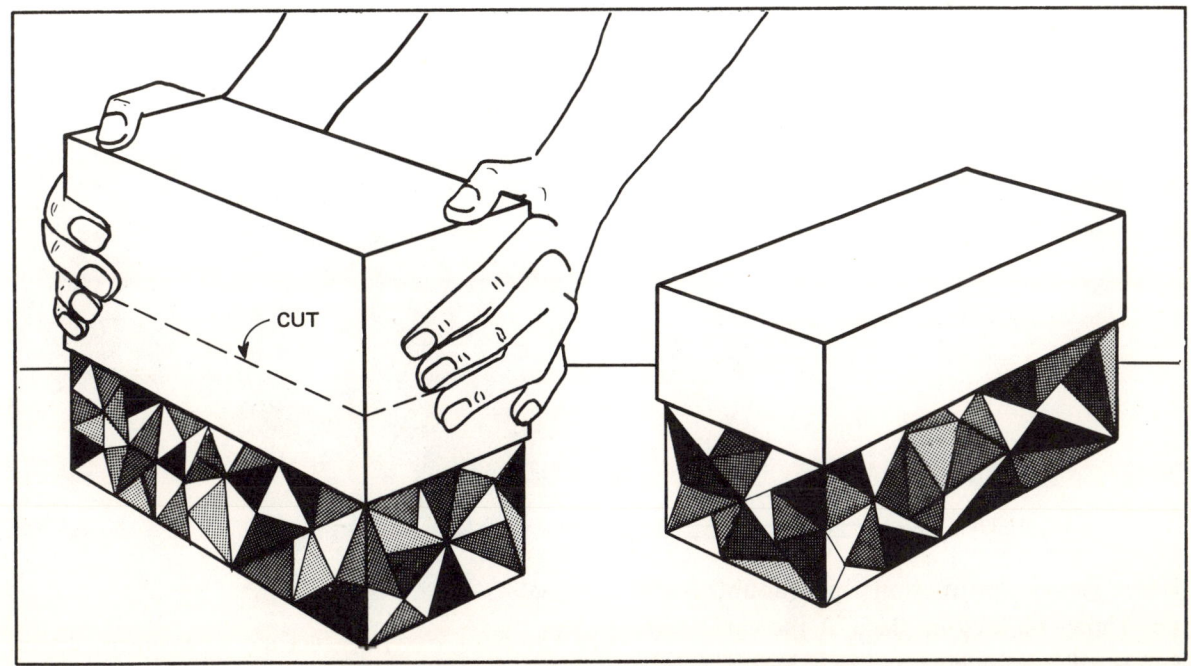

Fig. 5-5 A larger box, fitted to the base, is cut to size — making a handy cover for the workplan file.

Section 2 Orientation to Home Visiting

and can develop the file further with subsequent offspring.

Selecting the Folders

The selection of folders depends upon the availability of funds. Three types are listed.

- Manila folders: These are the most expensive, but take the least time and effort to prepare.
- Large envelopes: These may be purchased as new items or obtained from offices that discard used ones.
- Homemade folders: These may be made from cardboard boxes. The sides of a cardboard box are cut to make two 9 x 12 sheets. An edge of each is placed on a twelve-inch strip of wide masking tape, so that there is a space of 3/4 inch or more between each sheet. A second strip of masking tape is placed over the other, binding together both sheets of cardboard. Holes may be punched at the top of each sheet and string inserted to make a portfolio tie. Thus:

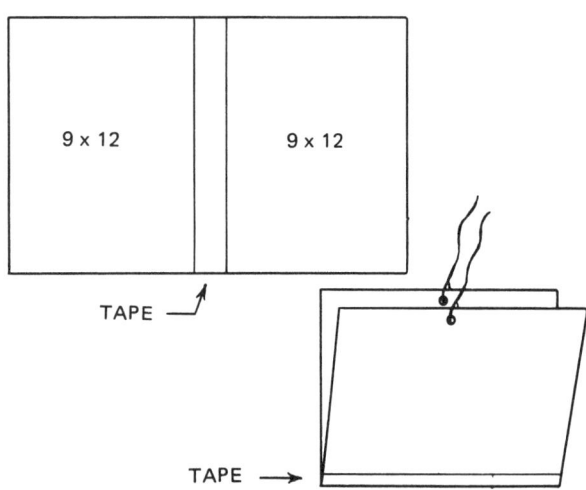

Note: Heavy construction paper (double thickness) may be used in place of the cardboard. Gummed reinforcements can help to keep the string from tearing the paper.

Preparing the Folders

Make a list of topic headings to be included in the file. Topics should include any service that the home visitor performs and information related to her work. Some topics are listed.

- Alcoholism
- Art Ideas
- Child Development
- Crafts
- Discipline
- Drug Education
- Family Assignments
- First Aid Treatment
- Free Films Available
- Health Services
- Language Activities
- Music
- Number Experiences
- Nutrition and Foods
- Parent Effectiveness Training
- Physical Fitness
- Record-keeping Forms
- Reference Books
- Sex Education
- Science Activities
- Tests
- Visual Aids

Fig. 5-6 Workplan files are a time-saving device. Sharing them multiplies ready-resources with a minimum of time and labor for each person involved.

Unit 5 Developing Workplans

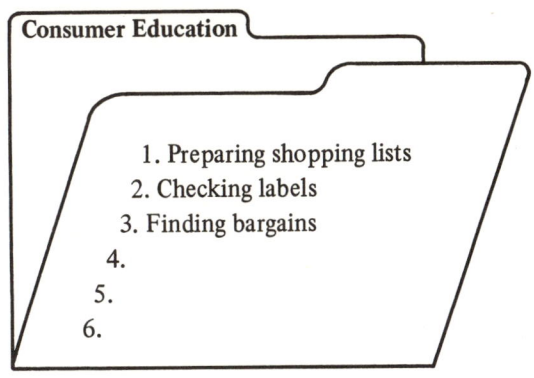

Fig. 5-7 Following its number, the name of each workplan is written on the outside of the folder. On each workplan a corresponding number is written in the upper left-hand corner of the workplan. Each number is written with the paper in horizontal position so that it can be easily located in the folder.

Organizing Material

A file box may contain much useful material, but it is of little value if the material is "lost" in a folder. One solution to the problem is given.

- The first time a workplan is ready for a folder, a number is placed on the item, and a corresponding one is placed on the outside of the folder. The title of the insert follows its number on the folder. A sample is shown in figure 5-7.

- As new workplans are added, more numbers follow. Workplans are filed in sequence.

A similar procedure is followed for all topics. By numbering and listing the contents on the outside of each folder and filing each item consecutively inside, much valuable time is saved.

For increased efficiency, holes are punched in workplans before they are filed. When an item is needed, it is withdrawn and placed in a loose-leaf notebook used for plans and records. Each workplan is returned to the file after being used.

Subtopics

A workplan file, assembled over time, contains many subtopics. A breakdown of three major topics is shown in figures 5-8, 5-9, and 5-10.

The only reason for including something in the file is an affirmative answer to the question, "Can this material be used sometime?"

PREPARING WORKPLANS

Whether a workplan is based on a long form, figure 5-11, or a short form, figure 5-12, depends upon the skills of the person who will use the plan. An inexperienced person, or a home visitor-in-training, may find the long form helpful in analyzing topics to create learning experiences. When guided in developing each plan, the learner can become skillful in

- Identifying worthwhile tasks for young children.

- Presenting learning activities effectively.

- Evaluating the outcome.

The short form is helpful for those persons who can think through a plan without writing the details. This is a skill that comes through practice. The home visitor, using the short form, may prepare workplans that can be used by parents. Additional needed information can be given verbally to parents.

47

Section 2 Orientation to Home Visiting

Language Activities

1. Stories (outlines for recall)
2. Poems
3. Finger Plays
4. Picture File to Motivate Storytelling
5. Themes for Dramatic Play
6. Word Games for Target Child
7. Homemade Language Games for Family
8. Films for Family Viewing
9. Filmstrips Available
10. Lending-library Language Materials
11. Sample Letters for Parents to Use as Models in Their Correspondences (how to return an item, how to order something by mail, thank-you notes, invitations, etc.)
12. How To Order from a Mail-order Catalog (copies of various forms available from companies)

Fig. 5-8 Many activities in the workplan file can be used independently by parents. The possibilities for advanced planning are endless.

HEALTH: First Aid

1. General Directions for Giving First Aid
2. Emergency First Aid
3. Treating Shock
4. Respiratory Emergencies and Artificial Respiration
5. Convulsions
6. Swallowed Objects and Choking
7. Poisoning: Causes, Symptoms, Treatment; Preventive Measures
8. Drugs: Use and Abuse
9. Treatment of Burns; Prevention of Accidents
10. Insect Bites and Emergency Treatment
11. Treating Cuts and Bruises
12. Plans for Home Safety: Checklist

Fig. 5-9 Subtopics under the health component are many and varied. First aid information is an imperative. A course in first aid and personal safety is recommended for home visitor training. Parents should be encouraged to participate in first aid classes offered in their community.

Unit 5 Developing Workplans

HOLIDAY: Crafts

1. Decorations for the Christmas Tree
2. Hanukkah: Festival of Lights
3. How to Make a Pinata
4. Holiday Crafts from Many Lands
5. How to Make a Jumping Jack Santa Claus
6. "Easy-to-make" Easter Baskets
7. Coloring Easter Eggs
8. Making Inexpensive Holiday Cards
9. How to Make a Paper-folded Envelope
10. Christmas Gifts Made from Waste Materials
11. Valentines
12. Holiday Decorations for the Home
13. How to Make a Paper Bag Mask for Halloween
14. Halloween Masks
15. Spring Flower Containers Made from Waste Materials

Fig. 5-10 Holidays lend themselves to increased family activities. Decorations in the home add to the festive feeling.

WORKPLAN OUTLINE: Long Form

- Name of the activity
- Aims, goals, or objectives
- Background information
- Suggested learning activities
- Materials and resources for learning
- Procedures
- Checks or evaluation techniques
- Leads (What next?)
- References: home visitor, parents, child
- Notes (Effectiveness? Changes? Repeat?)

Fig. 5-11 A workplan contains important information to be tapped for the right person at the right time.

WORKPLAN OUTLINE: Short Form

- Objectives
- Materials
- Procedure
- Checks
- Leads (What next?)

Fig. 5-12 A simple outline can be used when the home visitor gains skill in planning. It can be used for parents, too.

Section 2 Orientation to Home Visiting

Components of the workplan are presented. Pertinent questions to be asked are included.

- **Name of the activity:** For what need does the activity provide? How can it be described briefly?
- **Aims, goals, or objectives:** What goal is the activity supposed to accomplish? What is the desired change in behavior; that is, what is the learner supposed to be able to do after being exposed to the learning experience? What need is met?
- **Background information:** What should the home visitor know about the topic? What questions should she be able to anticipate and answer? What information can be given to the learner? How much background information is appropriate for the learner's interest, ability, or needs?
- **Learning activities:** What desirable and worthwhile learning experiences help to meet the objectives? In how many different ways can the objectives be met? What difficulties may be faced? What cautions must be taken, if any?
- **Materials and resources:** What materials of instruction are needed? Where can the materials be obtained? Can they be made from easily-obtained waste materials? What resources are available to enrich the activity?
- **Procedures:** What ways are suggested to meet objectives? How can the learner be motivated to take part in the activity? What sequence of tasks is recommended in presenting the needed information? What special needs of the learner must be considered?
- **Checks or evaluative techniques:** What progress can be expected of the learner? When should the learner be given help in his task? How can a person tell when the learner is having difficulty? How can a system of checks (evaluation) be part of the ongoing activity?
- **Leads:** What next? How can the experience lead toward other worthwhile activities for the learner? How can he build on this experience to create more knowledge? What specific activities are related?
- **References:** What references are available for the home visitor? Are there books that can be used by the child or his parents? (A librarian can assist in selecting reading materials for parents — to accommodate readers from high- to low-level reading ability.)
- **Notes:** What suggestions are made for future use of the workplan? How did others in the learner's training group react to the simulation (practice in group) exercise? How did learners outside the training group react? What changes should be made before the workplan is used again?
- **What other family members can be doing** is a topic the home visitor may wish to add. When the home visitor is working with the child and his parents, it may be necessary to provide activities for other children in the family. Giving the matter some thought during the development of workplans may be the best time to start. Whether plans for other children in the family are a part of the specific workplan or whether a separate section is provided in the workplan file is something the home visitor must decide for herself. Although a workplan appears to be a "ready-to-go lesson," the home visitor must be selective. She must choose the right activity to fit the needs of those with whom she works. Activities are altered to fit the learner — the reverse must never be true.

A SAMPLE WORKPLAN (LONG FORM)

Name of Activity: *The Story of the Little Red Hen*

Objectives:

- Promote listening skills.
- Tell a story that uses repetition as a primary literary device.
- Spark the young child's interest in creating his own stories by using repetition as a structural device.
- Encourage the child to participate in storytelling by having him join in during the presentation.
- Arouse the child's interest in wanting to know from where food comes.

Background information:

The little red hen makes some bread through a sequence of tasks and events.

- She finds some wheat.
- She plants the wheat.
- She harvests the wheat.
- She takes the wheat to the miller.
- She bakes the bread.
- She and her chicks eat all the bread, because no one wanted to help her with the work.

Suggested learning activities:

Selections must be made in terms of the child's maturity level and interests. He may

- Hold cardboard cutouts as an animal "speaks."
- Join in repeating the little hen's question: "Who will help me?" and in repeating the answer: "Not I. . ."
- Draw pictures to illustrate the story.
- Imitate animals as they "speak."
- Take a trip to a wheat field, if possible.
- Examine a sample of wheat.
- Talk about new words, such as harvest.
- Visit a bakery shop to see bread being made.
- Eat some bread — just as the hen and her chicks did.
- Bake some bread.
- Heat some "brown and serve" rolls to enjoy the smell of bread baking; eat the bread.

Materials and resources:

Selections are made as needed.

- Storybook
- Recorded story
- Animal cutouts
- Samples of wheat
- Ingredients to make bread
- Permission to visit bakery
- Crayons and drawing paper
- Brown and serve rolls

Procedures:

Select as appropriate.

- Show the child a sample of wheat. Say, "I have a story about a hen who found some wheat just like this."

> **A Sample Workplan (Long Form) (con't)**
>
> - Show a storybook; arouse interest; tell the story.
> - Line up cutouts in the order of each animal's appearance. Have the child pick up the animal and hold it as the animal "speaks."
> - Use a record storybook kit.
> - Other procedures as appropriate.
>
> Checks:
>
> See how well the child listens to the story. Note facial expressions that display pleasure. See how much participation is spontaneous on the part of the child. Do not urge him to take part, but encourage him if he shows an interest.
>
> Leads:
>
> Make up a repetition story about the child. It might be developed along these lines: Once there was a little boy named Charlie. Every morning he got out of bed with a skip, and a hop, and a jump-jump-jump! He went to breakfast with a skip, and a hop, and a jump-jump-jump! (Ask the child to name other things that he does. Then add: "with a skip, and a hop, and a jump-jump-jump!")
>
> Have the child make up his own story. Tell more stories of repetition such as *Billy Goats Gruff* and *Gingerbread Man*.
>
> References:
>
> A copy of the storybook.
>
> Notes:
>
> Additions or other comments about presentation. List any changes that should be made before the workplan is used again.

Fig. 5-13 A sample workplan

SCENARIO: A WORKPLAN IN ACTION

Presented is an example of what might happen when the storytelling workplan is put into action. The home visitor makes no attempt to use all ideas. She selects only what seems most suitable for the target child. She plans as needed for other family members. The discussion begins with a brief description of the situation, the overall plans made for the visit, and the materials and activities.

The Situation

Miss Davis is a home visitor who was asked by her sponsors to visit Mrs. Clark. A television commercial brought the program to the attention of Mrs. Clark.

Mrs. Clark is a *parent without a partner* (there is no male who assumes the "father" role in the home). She is the twenty-one-year-old mother of three children: Tad, four-years old; Jimmy, two-and-one-half; and Dana, four-months old. Mrs. Clark is eager to provide opportunities for her children that she never had.

In the home is Mrs. Clark's grandmother, a woman in her early sixties. She likes to make things for the children. She appears to be in good health.

Home Visit Plans

The home visitor plans for all members of the household.

- A storytelling demonstration for the mother. Objective: to show how a story can be a learning experience with many desirable outcomes.

- A mobile of paper-folded birds (see unit 12 for directions) for the baby's crib. Objective: to help the baby learn to focus attention on an object.
- A homemade toy of nested boxes for Jimmy. Objective: to help the child discover relationships between objects of different sizes.
- Knitting needles for the grandmother. Objective: to provide materials for creativity; to set the stage for a visit to the senior citizen recreation center.
- A story for the target child with objective drawn from the workplan already described.

Materials Needed

- Animal cutouts
- A written copy of the story to give the mother
- A wheat sample (real or artificial)
- Several soda crackers
- A rolling pin
- Knitting needles and wool
- Two sheets of waxed paper
- Some flour
- Brown and serve rolls
- Jelly and peanut butter
- A knife for spreading
- An electric blender

The Actual Visit

When Miss Davis arrives, the family is waiting for her. The children have been "scrubbed and dressed" for the event. It is evident that Mrs. Clark wants the children to look their best. Miss Davis interprets this as a positive attitude.

After greeting everyone, the visitor starts a welcome song, *If You're Happy*. The children and the adults sing the song and clap their hands at the right time.

With everyone in a happy mood, the visitor gives the senior citizen the needles and wool. The mobile is tied to the baby's crib. Jimmy is placed on the floor and given the boxes with which to play. The boxes are separated, but can be nested.

Storytelling procedure. The visitor then begins the story for the target child.

Home visitor (HV): "I have a story about a little hen who found something that looked like this." (Hold up wheat.) "Have you ever seen anything like it?" (Waits for child and parent to respond.)

HV: "Yes, it might look like. . ." (She gives positive feedback.)

HV: "Listen to the story. Maybe you can help me tell it. See if you can find a place where you can help in telling the story." (She tells the story.) As she says the name of an animal, the home visitor holds up a cutout. She offers the first one to Tad, but he refuses it. She places the object on the table. She continues with her story. When she comes to a repetition — her eyes widen and she makes a motion with her hands for Tad and his mother to join in. They get the point. Jimmy stops his play with the boxes and joins the storytelling group. He chimes in with the others. The home visitor finishes the story.

HV: "What part of the story did you like best?" (She does not ask a question requiring only a *yes* or *no* response. She stimulates the listeners to think. She pauses for Tad to answer.)

HV: "I like that part, too." (She supports him.)

The home visitor shows Tad the flour. He holds some in his hand. They talk about it. Tad tastes it. He spits it out. She tries to develop an understanding of the word *grind* by putting one cracker between the sheets of waxed paper and showing Tad how to "grind" the cracker with the rolling pin. Tad enjoys the "grinding" until the cracker is powdery. The home visitor then puts a cracker into the blender to show that a machine can make the cracker become very fine, somewhat like the flour.

HV: "People who make flour out of wheat use machines. They do different things to change the wheat into flour." (She compares the work of the blender with that of the miller.)

> The HV and the mother put the brown and serve rolls into the oven. A menu for lunch is prepared. Attention is drawn to the scent or smell of the rolls as they are being baked. Peanut butter and jelly sandwiches are included in the lunch menu.

After the storytelling session, the home visitor discusses many desirable learnings that can be gained through stories. She gives Mrs. Clark a typed copy of the story. She also plants the idea that Mrs. Clark could learn more about children by continuing her education at the local community college. The worker mentions the mothers who work as teacher aides in the local day care center. She then prepares a summary of what was done, and makes plans for the next visit.

SUMMARY

Planning is the process of working out a broad outline of the things that need to be done and the methods for doing them. Home visitors must take into consideration the value system of the families with whom they work. Home visitors must examine their own cultural baggage to make sure that cultural differences do not conflict with the culture of families with whom they work.

Every worker is concerned with (1) the purpose of the work, (2) the process(es) through which this work is done, (3) the person(s) with whom she/he interacts, and (4) the place(s) where the services are rendered.

A classroom teacher's long-view plans represent the program to be followed during the school year. A home visitor's long-view plans are presented as a resource file of ideas and guidelines which help in developing personalized programs for families. Plans for other children in the family are included.

Preparing a number of long-form workplans helps the home visitor to develop skill in examining topics through which the child can learn. After she develops skill in planning, a short form can be substituted.

SUGGESTED ACTIVITIES

- Organize a class team to prepare and share workplans for a resource file. A suggested procedure follows.

    a. Cooperatively make a comprehensive list of topics.

    b. Divide topics among team members.

    c. Each member prepares workplans for selected topics.

    d. Group discusses completed workplans. If necessary, revisions are made.

    e. Duplicate revised workplans. Each team member gets a complete set.

- Make a resource file box for workplans. Add something creative to your box. Perhaps you can make a fishnet carrying bag, attach straps for handles, or provide wheels for greater mobility. You may even design a more practical file. Be creative.

- Locate several parents with whom you can share some of your workplans. Get some feedback from them. How helpful was the material? Did the parents think that the child(ren) enjoyed the activities? Do the parents have any suggestions? Would they like to borrow more workplans? Relate your experiences to the class.

Unit 5 Developing Workplans

REVIEW

A. Match each item in Column II with the correct item in Column I.

I	II
1. Change	a. Acquiring the value system of the group into which the person is born.
2. Culture	
3. Intervention	
4. Long view plan	b. Preparation for change
5. Socialization	c. A framework through which people see and judge the world and other people's behavior.
6. Planning	
7. Cultural baggage	
	d. An interference in the affairs of another
	e. A variation or alteration in form, quality, or state of being.
	f. Everything that an individual learns and shares as a member of his society.
	g. A structure from which later plans are made.

B. Briefly answer each of the following.

1. Why is it necessary for a home visitor to do advanced planning?

2. What information should be included in a long form workplan?

3. Name at least three subtopics that can be categorized under each of the four components of home-based programs in early childhood education: education, health, social services, and parent involvement.

4. Prepare a long form workplan on any topic of your own choosing. Have your instructor check your plan. Make any changes that may be suggested. Present your plan to an appropriate learner, tape-recording your work as you progress. Present the tape recording to your instructor for a final performance-based evaluation.

unit 6 administrative planning and operating

OBJECTIVES

After studying this unit, the student should be able to

- Define and describe an organization.
- Discuss the seven activities (POSDCoRB) necessary in administering a program.
- Compare a good reporting system with a communication system.

Every home visitor has a *sponsor,* the organization that employs her and to whom she is responsible. An *organization* is defined as

- A human system that has an arranged way for two or more people in the system to behave — in their thinking, feeling, and acting in the system.
- People who are a unit, because each member shares goals and objectives set by the system.
- People who have objectives of their own that fit in with those of the system.
- People who have some way of being identified with the system.
- People who interact with each other as they carry out their tasks for the group.
- People who expect to carry out tasks that are a part of their job and who expect others in the system to carry out certain other tasks.

Society is organized. People spend all of their lives in some organization. It is through organization that society is held together. People achieve their goals through their organizations, either directly or indirectly.

When speaking of organizations it is important to bear in mind that an organization is not a "thing." It is made up of human beings.

The home visitor's sponsor sees as its role the task of carrying out the *administrative process* of the organization; that is, making decisions that affect the program and the goals of the organization, and taking action to achieve the goals of the program. *Administrators* are those persons in the organization who are responsible for seeing that the goals of the program are fulfilled.

Organizations that may sponsor home-based child development programs are wide and varied. No effort is made to identify specific sponsors in the present discussion. Given instead is a brief description of necessary administrative tasks and a list of people in the organization who may perform those tasks.

P	O	S	D	Co	R	B
l	r	t	i	o	e	u
a	g	a	r	r	p	d
n	a	f	e	d	o	g
n	n	f	c	i	r	e
i	i	i	t	n	t	t
n	z	n	i	a	i	i
g	i	g	n	t	n	n
	n		g	i	g	g
	g			n		
				g		

Fig. 6-1 POSDCoRB makes sense when each letter becomes the start of a word.

POSDCoRB

A man once asked what work is done by the president of the United States.[1] He answered his own question with the word "POSDCoRB." The response makes no sense until each letter becomes the start of a word: PLANNING, ORGANIZING, STAFFING, DIRECTING, COORDINATING, REPORTING, AND BUDGETING.

The words that the letters stand for are activities said to be necessary to run the office of the President. POSDCoRB is helpful also in looking at the work of those who sponsor and administer home-based early education programs.

Planning

Once an organization decides to sponsor home-based services, effective planning is crucial. An administrative staff is needed to work out the broad outline of what needs to be done.

It is important to involve in the planning as many people as possible who are to be affected by the plans. Among those included may be

- Policy makers and/or representatives of the sponsors.
- Parents.
- Available staff members.
- Advisory board members.
- Representatives from the community agencies to be involved.
- Consultants.

Objectives are stated, and the methods for achieving them are discussed. The success of the program may rest heavily on how well plans are made and carried out.

[1] Luther Gulick and L. Urwick, eds., *Papers on the Science of Administration,* (New York: Institute of Public Administration, 1937), p. 13.

Organizing

Through organizing, the setup for the entire program is created. The *line of authority* is established — who is responsible to whom.

Necessary facilities may be included in the organization plan: what services are offered, and in what place. Sites outside the home are identified and described. The best possible arrangement for meeting objectives is adopted.

Staffing

Staffing is seen as a process made up of several parts.

- Creating a climate for work that makes people feel comfortable, socially and emotionally, as they do their jobs.
- Developing job descriptions that are subject to change when the work gets underway. What the worker should be able to do is a part of the description.
- Identifying, recruiting, and selecting qualified staff for the program. Although existing staff members are utilized, it is often desirable to hire some people from the outside. New workers tend to bring in new ideas.
- Providing *preservice training* (before the job begins) and *in-service training* (while the job is being done).
- Evaluating the people concerned, the process involved, and the purposes of the job. It is important to bring together for an exchange of words both the person making an evaluation and the person being evaluated. Self-evaluation is also an important part of the process.
- Maintaining good working conditions for the workers.

A vital part of in-service training is *staff development.* This refers to the opportunities that exist for workers to improve their skills on the job. It may also include opportunities to continue their formal education.

Adult night schools and community colleges in the area may be drawn into the training programs for home-based education workers. Arrangements can be made for a worker to study and continue to improve and develop needed skills, and to qualify for advancement to a new job with more responsibility.

Directing

The *director* of a program is the person who serves as leader. *Directing* refers to the director's responsibility for

- Interpreting the policies and objectives of the program to the persons who need to know.
- Implementing (carrying out) plans by putting them into action.
- Making important decisions and putting them into orders or directions for others to follow.
- Making evaluations that affect the ongoing activities.

The director of a program serves as leader, but other persons often assist in the task of making decisions and putting them into action.

There are many other people in a program who are responsible for some kind of directing. The process they follow is similar to that of the director, but they operate at a lower level of authority.

Coordinating

Administrators coordinate the efforts of those working in the total program. Suggestions for corrections or improvements in services are noted. Appropriate action is taken. A well-coordinated program has a built-in system for preventing and correcting problems that arise.

Reporting

A good reporting system may be compared to a good communication system. It is a two-way street that involves "listening" as well as "telling." It is an exchange of information, ideas, or opinions. This is true whether the interaction has two people in a one-to-one relationship or two hundred people in a large complex organization.

Effective communication is the heart of any organization. Every act of speech is a listening act for someone else. One person writes what another person may read. Sometimes nonverbal (unwritten or nonoral) messages are given and received in the form of gestures: a wave of the hand, a raised eyebrow, a frown, or the like. Nonverbal messages often reveal what a verbal message may conceal.

Every communication, or message, begins with a motive. The motive is a need for some action or information. The sender recognizes this need, as shown in figure 6-2. Several steps can be seen.

- Message: The message is prepared.
- Sending: The message is sent through whatever means seems best.
- Receiving: The message is received.
- Reacting: The receiver reacts to the message.
- Acting: The receiver acts on the message.
- Feedback: A feedback loop shows that the sender gets knowledge of the results of his message.

There are three major processes in a communication system. Figure 6-3 shows how these processes work.

- Incoming impression: A message is perceived ("seen") by someone who listens to what is said or reads the message. One or more of the five senses may help the message to be perceived.

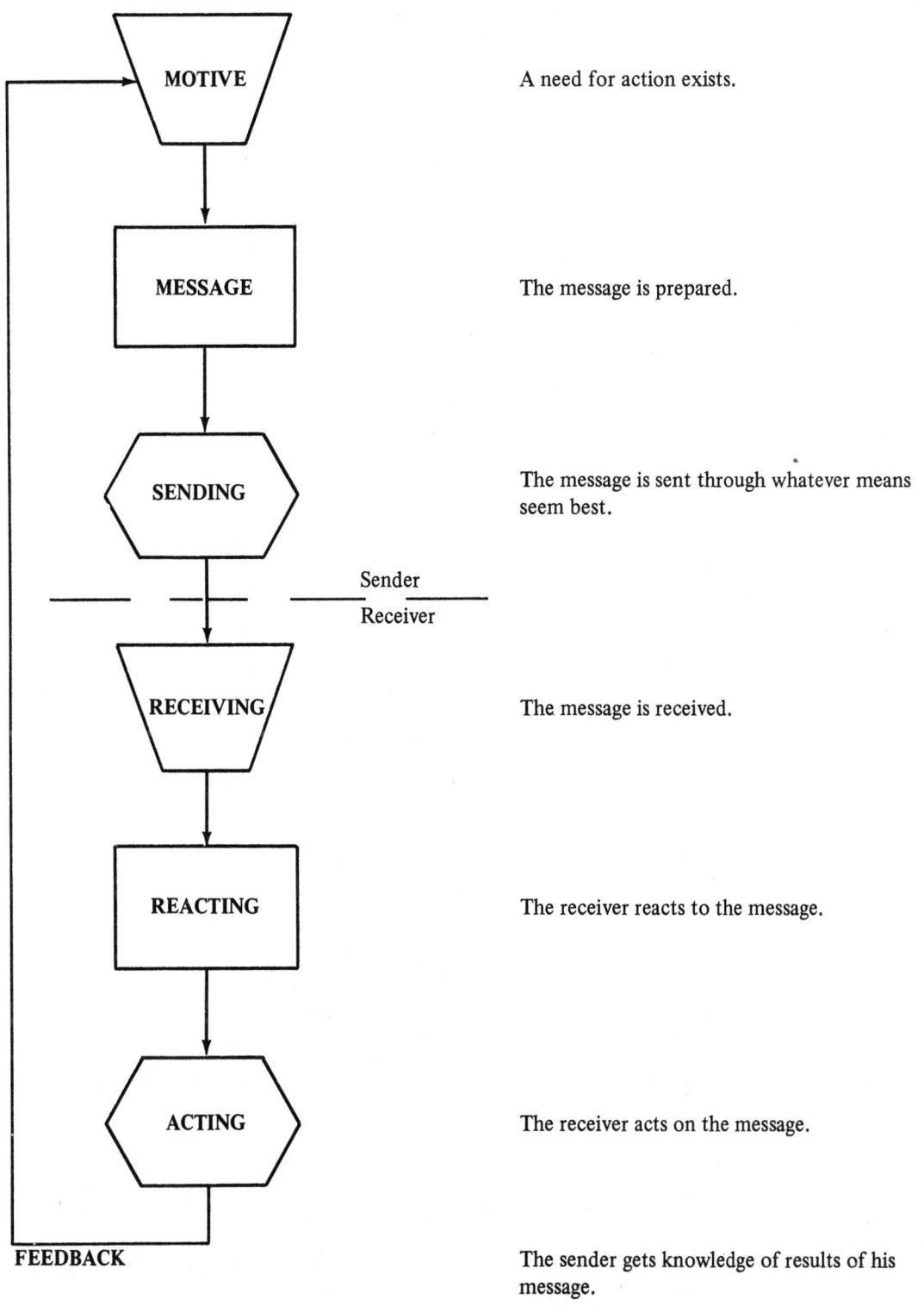

Fig. 6-2 A flowchart shows what happens to a message from start to finish.

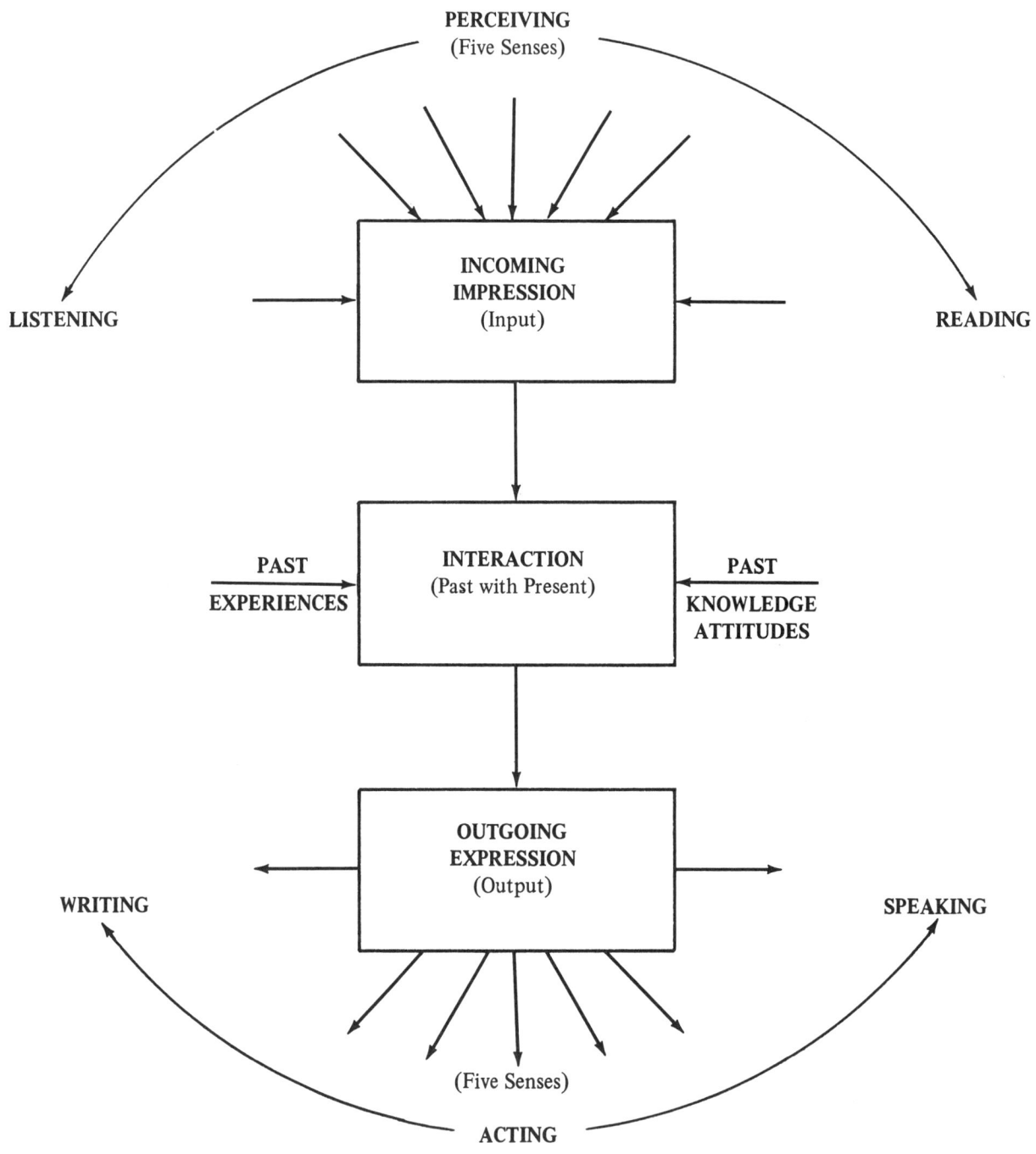

Fig. 6-3 Major processes that take place in a communication system.

- Interaction: The message is received. The receiver "gets the idea." His past experiences, attitudes, and knowledge help him to decide how to react to the message. The receiver may accept or reject what is sent.
- Outgoing expression: The receiver of the message acts out his "response." He may respond in oral or written language. When appropriate, he may also use any one of his five senses (touching, tasting, feeling, seeing, hearing) in his response.

A communication is not complete until the sender receives feedback on his message. Communication is always a two-way street.

A good reporting system also has overlapping staffs to promote teamwork and cooperation among workers. Overlapping staffs

- Provide for certain persons to meet with other workers up and down the line.
- Enable workers to know what is going on both above and below their place in the organization.
- Make workers feel that there are no "secrets" holding information that affects them, or that they ought to know to work well in their organization.
- Help to build good morale among workers by making them feel that they are important in the organization and to it.

There are different ways to provide for overlapping staffs in an organization. Figure 6-4 shows one method. Three groups of workers are shown, starting from the top and moving downward. Arrows show that workers exchange information up and down the line. Messages may be oral or written, preferably both. Written messages that are exchanged and explained lessen the chance of having people misunderstand what is said. Those responsible for the exchange often attend meetings held by workers above and below them. How an organization makes provision for the exchange is an individual matter.

Overlapping staffs help the director of a program do a better job. He is kept well informed. A good reporting system serves as a "troubleshooter." Problems can be prevented or resolved quickly when

- The director knows what is going on in the organization.
- The director gives messages clearly and makes sure that they are understood.
- The director makes provision for effective communication in the organization.
- All workers know what is expected of them and are provided with what they need to carry out their tasks.

Budgeting

All programs need funds. *Budgeting* is the process of planning in detail for all expenses

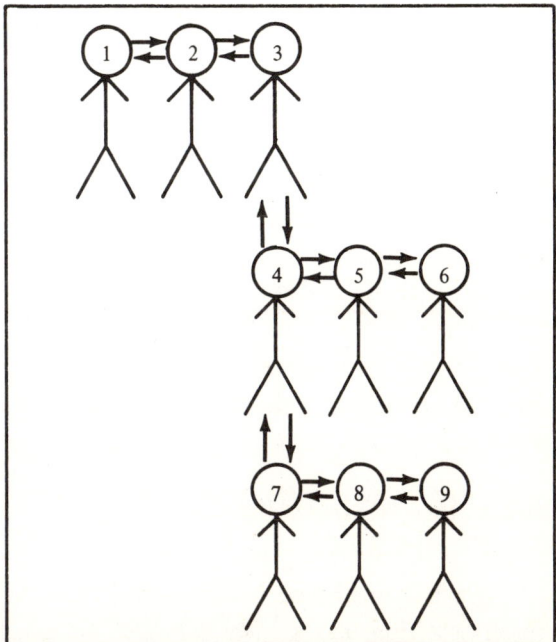

Fig. 6-4 Overlapping staffs pass important information to workers up and down the line.

Section 2 Orientation to Home Visiting

involved in a program. Budgeting is based on staffing needs.

- Money for salaries is set. Salaries should compare favorably with other jobs in the community that call for like tasks and responsibilities.
- Arrangements are made for obtaining funds for required materials and services. Who will account for the funds and who will control use of the money are part of the plans.
- Funds are set aside for any materials and services that are "special" — not included in the basic needs.
- Funds for any required facilities are set.
- Insurance needs are considered. When a home visitor uses her own car, additional insurance may be needed because the car is being used for business purposes. Liability insurance is important to protect the program against any law suits that may arise. Accidents may injure the home visitor or those with whom she is working. Personal liability insurance is needed, too.

The program also needs protection from the actions of a home visitor that may result in a law suit. Giving out certain information about a family may be called "an invasion of privacy." It is necessary for sponsors to spell out in detail what actions and activities are appropriate for the home visitor. The home visitor must be protected against law suits that may arise as she carries out her tasks.

IDENTIFYING DIFFERENT STAFF MEMBERS

Each home-based program may have different staffing needs. No rule can be made that will apply in all situations. Each program selects on an individual basis.

The following types of staff are utilized in meeting the needs of respective programs.
- Director
- Assistant Director/Child Development Specialist
- Family Education Specialist
- Coordinator of Preservice and In-service Training
- Nutrition Specialist/Coordinator
- Health Coordinator or Medical Specialist
- Speech Pathologist
- Supervisor for Home Visitors
- Social Worker/Coordinator
- Supervisor for Home Visitors
- Home Visitors
- Parent Coordinators

Tasks for each job and the qualifications specified are made in the light of each situation. A sample job description for a home visitor is presented in figure 6-6. It provides a basic framework around which staff requirements can be tailored to fit local home visitor needs. The selection of staff members remains an individual matter.

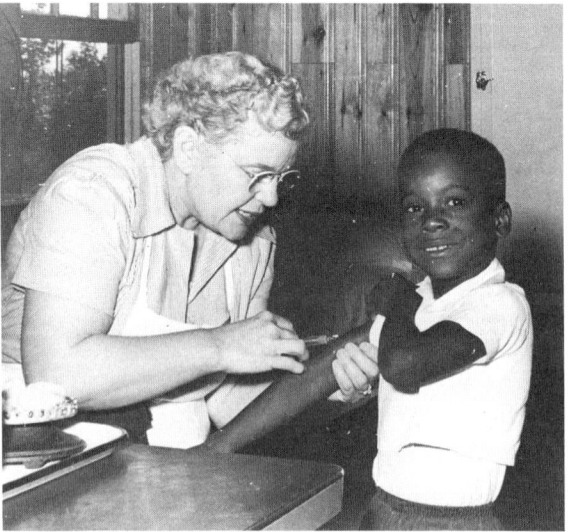

Fig. 6-5 Health services are an important part of a program concerned with the total development of the young child.

JOB DESCRIPTION

JOB TITLE: Home Start Visitor

SALARY RANGE:
CLASSIFICATION:

DUTIES OF JOB

1. Meets one-half day weekly with the Supervisor to plan and coordinate Home Start Program.
2. Is responsible for spending a minimum of two (2) hours per week (except for weeks set aside for training and re-assessment) with each individual family enrolled in Home Start.
3. Is responsible for carrying out day-to-day activities of the work program as outlined by grantee agency.
4. Is constantly concerned and works to maintain community support for Home Start.
5. Participates in all training designed for Home Start staff.
6. Makes family referrals to other agencies and facilitates the referral process.
7. Keeps records of referrals, follow up of referrals and other family records as deemed necessary for meeting program objectives.
8. Must be available on call by families at night and on weekends.
9. Must participate in occasional group activities of or for parents.
10. Develops a developmental plan for each family, taking into consideration the individual needs of the family members.
11. Is responsible for assistance from supervisors and other agency personnel in an effort to better serve individual families.

JOB SPECIFICATIONS

Educational Requirements: Must have participated in Head Start Supplemental Training courses previously offered by ARVAC or other CAP training.

Experience Required: Must have been employed as a Community Service Aide or Head Start Teachers or Aide with ARVAC, Incorporated, for at least two (2) years.

Home Start Visitor Training:
1. Head Start Supplemental Training.
2. Public Service Careers Training.
3. Monthly In-Service Training.
4. Special Workshops for Home Start or Head Start.

Responsibility: Must be a responsible person. Must be able to handle confidential information, without sharing it inappropriately. Must be able to plan and organize her work. Must be able to work without constant supervision.

Personal Traits: Must be a listener. Must be able to delegate responsibilities to other people. Must be mild natured, respected in the community, responsive, and an emotionally stable individual. Must be trustworthy. Must have an interest and concern for low income families. Must have an interest in children and their development. Must be able to adapt to a variety of situations and be able to work with other people on the behalf of clients.

Section 2 Orientation to Home Visiting

Job Description (con't)

Manual Skills: Must be able to drive an automobile. Must be adept to assembling equipment and supplies.

Supervision Available: A supervisor with five (5) years of previous experience at working with children and/or low income families.

Fig. 6-6 A sample job description for a home visitor.
SOURCE: Office of Child Development, *A Guide for Planning and Operating Home-Based Child Development Programs*, DHEW Pub. No. (OHD) 75-1080 (Washington, D.C.: U.S. Department of Health, Education and Welfare, June 1974), pp. A-15, A-16.

FOUR "Cs" TO SUCCESS
- Competence
- Confidence
- Cooperation
- Communication

Fig. 6-7 Vehicles to a successful program are shown.

PLANNING WITH STAFF

Most programs provide home visitors with a supervisor, or professional staff member, who is available to them at all times. Four to six home visitors may share the same supervisor. Or, supervision tasks may be divided among staff members. Additional help may be given by specialists who are responsible for seeing that services are delivered and coordinated properly. Supervisors provide on-the-job help in homes, as well as office-based guidance, to plan and discuss actions and activities.

The number of planning sessions for home visitors varies. The background and experience of workers determines both the kind of supervision and the amount. When the first visits are made, more frequent supervision is desirable. As the worker gains in ability and confidence, more responsibility is given along with more independence in carrying out plans.

Whenever a home visitor wants to try a new idea, or explore an area in which she has not yet worked, it is important that the plans be discussed in detail with her supervisor. An effective and efficient program can be achieved only when workers consider themselves as a team.

Four things are offered as vehicles to a successful program: competence, confidence, cooperation, and communication.

- Competence on the part of all workers.
- Confidence in self and others.
- Cooperation with all persons involved in the program.
- Communication flowing fully and freely.

SUMMARY

Every home visitor has a sponsor, the organization that employs her and to whom she is responsible. An organization is not a "thing." It consists of human resources who carry out their jobs in meeting the objectives of the group to which they belong.

The home visitor's sponsor is responsible for carrying out the administrative tasks of the home-based program. Administrative tasks include planning, organizing, staffing, directing, coordinating, reporting, and budgeting (POSDCoRB).

The problem of staffing is that of creating a climate for the workers; developing the job description; identifying, recruiting, and selecting qualified staff; and providing pre-service and in-service training.

Unit 6 Administrative Planning and Operating

Effective communication is the heart of a good program. A communication system includes incoming impression (message), interaction (receiver "gets the idea"), and outgoing expression (receiver acts out his response).

Overlapping staffs help all workers to give and receive information up and down the lines. A good reporting system can be a "troubleshooter."

Planning with supervisors is an important part of the home visitor's tasks. On-the-job supervision is provided as needed.

SUGGESTED ACTIVITIES

- Make arrangements through your instructor to visit the administrator of a home-based early child development program. If none are available in your community, substitute a center-based program.

    a. Ask the administrator to discuss with you the tasks described in POSDCoRB (write the seven words on a card). Share your findings with your class.

    b. See if you can obtain permission to examine any written job descriptions that tell what is done by workers in the program.

    (1) Discuss the jobs with your instructor and your class. Find out what kind of training is needed for each job.

    (2) Identify and write the tasks that you can already perform. List other skills that you need to qualify for one or more of the jobs. Tell how you would go about getting the needed skills.

    (3) Share your "training needs and plans" with your instructor. Get some feedback from her.

    c. Ask your instructor to show the class a sample plan for one or more of the tasks described in POSDCoRB. Perhaps she will give you a copy of the plan or help you to prepare a sample for your file.

    d. Look at the flowchart in figure 6-2. Use it to follow the flow of some message that you sent or received. Compare your flowchart with that of one of your classmates.

    (1) See how the flowchart discussions are similar. Compare them to find differences.

    (2) Try to find a better way to send the same messages.

    (3) Ask other classmates to share their flowcharts with you. Discuss.

    e. With your class, assemble a check list of factors that enable the group to understand messages that are received by them.

    f. With your class, assemble a check list of factors that the group must remember whenever they send messages.

REVIEW

A. Define each of the following.

1. Sponsor
2. Organization
3. Administrative process
4. Line of authority

Section 2 Orientation to Home Visiting

- B. List the seven administrative tasks that result when each letter in POSDCoRB becomes the start of a word.
- C. Compare the meaning of the terms *preservice training* and *in-service training*.
- D. Tell why staff development is important.
- E. Using the terms *incoming expression, interaction,* and *outgoing expression,* tell how a communication system works.

unit 7 delivering services

OBJECTIVES

After studying this unit, the student should be able to

- Apply the concept of delivery system to home-based early childhood programs.
- Discuss three alternatives for delivering services.
- Identify and describe three skills that parents need and the corresponding home visitor tasks that help parents get these skills in the areas of home-based education, health, social services, and parent involvement.

Whenever goods or services are needed, a system must be provided for delivering them. A *delivery system* is a combination of parts that are interrelated, and

- Contribute to a specific operation in the form required, at the place required, and at the right time.
- Produce information that "feeds back" to other parts of the system.
- Produce continuous interaction between parts, and thus help to maintain the system.

The concept of delivery system is applied to home-based early childhood programs.

- A sponsor sees the need for a program with objectives.
- A home visitor has the task of accomplishing some of the objectives.
- The objectives are fed to the home visitor who, in turn, utilizes all components of the program: education, health, social services, and parent involvement. A program is planned through which the objectives can be met. The program provides inputs to the system.
- The home visitor works in meeting the needs of the child, his parents, and his family. Two processes are seen: developing new knowledge and skills and managing the learning activities.
- Out of the processing of information comes practice — *observable behavior* (that which can be seen) called output.
- An evaluation or checking device shows the results — the extent to which learning objectives are met.
- A feedback loop takes knowledge of results (KOR) back to the point of origin — the objectives — where the home visitor decides what must be done next.

If goals have been reached, then new objectives are made and the process starts all over again. If goals have not been reached, a new set of learning activities may be made to accomplish unmet objectives. Action is based on the needs of the individual situation. No fixed procedure can be established.

DELIVERY OPTIONS

A variety of options are open for delivering early education services. Each sponsoring group selects the most effective arrangement possible for meeting program needs. The system created must be right for each situation.

Section 2 Orientation to Home Visiting

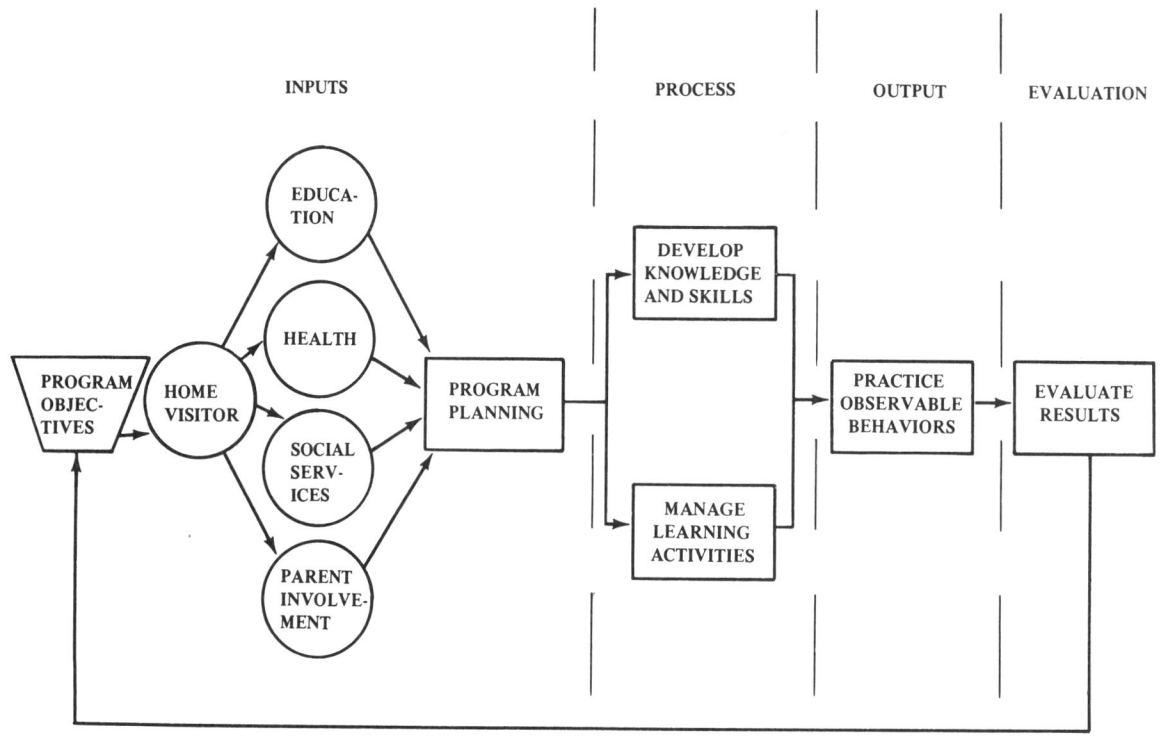

Fig. 7-1 A delivery system for home-based early education programs.

One or more of the following may work in a given program. Although the term *home visitor* is used, there may be other persons who organize and guide activities.

Home Visit

The primary means for delivering services may be through the home visitor who works directly with the child, parents, and family. Visits may be supplemented by occasional center-based experiences with other parents and their children.

Sometimes the home visitor meets with groups of neighborhood parents. Meeting places may rotate, moving from one home to another. For some of the parents, group work may be a stimulating social experience. The home visitor's work is supplemented by television, news bulletins, field trips, and the like.

Mobile Units

A specially designed mobile classroom van, or remodeled bus, travels to different

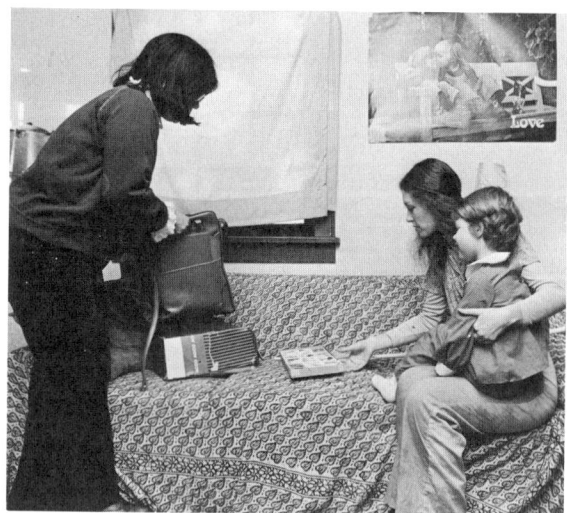

Fig. 7-2 The primary means for delivering services is through the home visitor.

areas for the purpose of holding demonstration classes for children and their parents. The van is well equipped to meet a wide variety of needs like those found in a high quality early childhood center.

Equipment includes air conditioning and heating, movie and slide projectors, television set, tape recorder and listening posts, stove, refrigerator, and chemical toilet. Teaching aids include books from an affiliated circulating library, an easel, flannel boards, records, puzzles, manipulative toys and educational games.

Child-sized tables, chairs, and equipment create a classroom atmosphere where children gain in social growth by sharing, working together, and following directions. Children are offered different experiences depending on their knowledge and previous experience in the group.

Classroom activities in the van are planned to correlate with a television program that explores interesting things for children to see and do. The home visitor shows parents how to carry on activities introduced by the television show.

Among offerings to parents are workshops, craft-making sessions, workplans to follow, and bulletins announcing new television schedules or shows. Home visitors may also provide information concerning needed services for health or welfare.

Research has demonstrated that mobile units are an effective and economical alternative to other programs of early education. Parents accept mobile units combined with TV shows.

Toy-lending Libraries

In a library-centered situation small groups of mothers role-play a series of "learning episodes" in which their children will (1) acquire cognitive skills and (2) learn how to solve problems. A mother in the community serves as group leader. She enables each mother to take home, weekly, a toy which the group has practiced using in a variety of ways. Parents may borrow the toys for home use.

The program usually includes a basic sequence of eight introductory toys with filmstrips and cassette tapes that show parents how to play each game. A booklet for parents and a course-leader manual are provided. All parents who want to improve their parenting skills have access to these materials. A home-based early education program for a young child may be started in the nearest public library.

Parent Cooperatives

Parent cooperatives, nursery schools organized and operated by parents, are in existence in various forms. A newer approach is that of neighborhood women who share their talents in working with their own children and those of neighbors. Through a wide assortment of materials and services that mothers share, young children expand their experiences in learning at home and away. For each, learning is living fully every day.

When workshops are offered in the community, mothers take full advantage of the opportunities. With the help of workshop leaders, participants work with basic tools and materials to learn by doing — and by trial-and-error methods. As parents explore what can be done with materials, they direct their own learning experiences concretely.

The ideas that are gained are brought back to the neighborhood group. The group adapts the ideas to their own children's needs. Learning packages are often prepared with the aid of workshop leaders or trained toy demonstrators.

Parents control the educational process, but use in their efforts all resources that exist in the community. Parent cooperatives are made up of parents who work together as a team in every sense of the word.

Pediatrician-sponsored Groups

A child development program that comes from the efforts of pediatricians provides more than preventive medicine. It is a

Section 2 Orientation to Home Visiting

Chapel Hill Pediatrics, P.A.
Pediatric And Adolescent Medicine

ROBERT J. SENIOR, M.D.
CHARLES I. SHEAFFER, M.D.
WILLIAM G. CONLEY III, M.D.
R. MEADE CHRISTIAN, JR., M.D.

DOCTORS' BUILDING
901 WILLOW DRIVE
CHAPEL HILL, N.C. 27514
TELEPHONE (919) 942-4173

Child Development and Child Behavior Management Sessions

Parent Call-In and Come-In Time

During the past several years parents have been asking for information concerning their child's development and the management of his behavior. To help answer this need, Chapel Hill Pediatrics, P.A., and the Division for Disorders of Development and Learning (DDDL) planned and conducted a pilot series of child development and child behavior management discussion sessions. Staff in Psychology, Nursing and Social Work from the DDDL led the discussion groups. The response to these sessions was quite favorable and they will continue to be offered.

The October-March schedule will be a series of child development and child management sessions for the parents as follows below. Preregistration through the Pediatric receptionist at 942-4173 is required.

Date	Age	Time
October 9, 16, 23	13-18 months	(8-9 p.m.)
November 6, 13, 20	19-30 months	(8-9 p.m.)
December 4, 11, 18	31 mos. - 4 yrs.	(8-9 p.m.)
January 8, 15, 22	5 years	(8-9 p.m.)
February 12, 19, 26	6-7 years	(8-9 p.m.)
March 11, 18, 25	8-9 years	(8-9 p.m.)

In addition, a Parent Call-In time and Parent Come-In time will continue to be offered twice weekly. This time is offered for parents to discuss with a professional person questions about their child's development and/or behavior. The Parent Call-In time will be on Monday and Wednesday afternoons from 3:30-4:14, and the telephone number is 929-1873. If this number is busy, please dial 942-4173 between 4:00 and 4:15, leave your name and telephone number, and one of the staff members will return your call. The Parent Come-In time will be 4:15-5:00 on Monday, Tuesday, and Wednesday afternoons. Appointments can be made through the Pediatric receptionist, 942-4173.

Many of you have had your children's developmental progress checked at 9 months of age by use of the Denver Developmental Screening Test. We are now *expanding this service to include 3 year olds* as well as 9 month olds. You can make an appointment for your child anytime between 30-36 months of age for this service. Appointments may be made through the office receptionist.

A bibliography in child development and child management has been compiled. This is in the form of a card file in the Pediatric receptionist area. Several books will be available for review but will not be on loan. The cost and place that the books can be purchased or borrowed will be noted in the card file.

No charge is made for any of the above services.

Fig. 7-3 Described is a home-based child development program that emerged from the efforts of pediatricians concerned with the (1) total development of children, and (2) parenting skills of parents. Training sessions take place away from home. Parents use information and learning materials in the home.

unique opportunity for parents to check, under professional supervision, the growth and development of their children. Physical, intellectual, emotional, and social well-being are seen as one main objective — helping the whole child.

Community Learning Centers

The need for a base to coordinate services may be met by community learning centers. A child development specialist — hired by the city, social welfare agency, or other group — serves as a source of information.

Her base may be only an office in City Hall or an old school building, but she is qualified to help parents with their problems.

The ideal center is one with well-equipped rooms where people can learn about learning. They can watch others teach and learn. They can learn how to do what they see, when someone is there to assist them.

Child Development Centers

The concept of the child development center was used as a model in Head Start centers for disadvantaged children. The assumption is that what happens to a child in his family is important in his growth and development.

Child development centers draw together all resources in a community which can add to the child's total development. Professional workers in the fields of education, health, welfare and related areas are part of the effort to build a home and school program for each child.

Activities are organized around a classroom and a play area. In addition to the learning needs of young children, workers deal with physical, social, and medical problems of children enrolled. Nonprofessionals have a part in the program. Parents have an important role. They are drawn into developing policies and participating in the program.

Child development centers often have an affiliation with a university. Sponsors of home-based programs, and others who wish to start them, should see what help they can get from their local universities.

In the delivery systems described in this unit, not all use home visitors. However, for each system common goals are planned and met: a healthy self-concept and cognitive development for the young child and increased skills for his parents *as parents*.

MEETING NEEDS

The first visit to a home is a crucial one, for it may mean the family's commitment to the program. Good relationships can be made by learning the names of family members, letting the family talk about their interests, and making family members feel that what they do is important. A tape recording of music the child may like, puppets, a family game, or a story may serve as "icebreakers." Recipes, a notice of a special community affair, or the sharing of some free material that responds to family interests may get the parents to participate.

A follow-up visit may yield information related to

- **Family relationships and roles:** Who are the family members? How do they feel about themselves and each other? Who takes leadership role(s) in the family?

Fig. 7-4 A healthy, happy child is the goal of all home-based early childhood programs.

Section 2 Orientation to Home Visiting

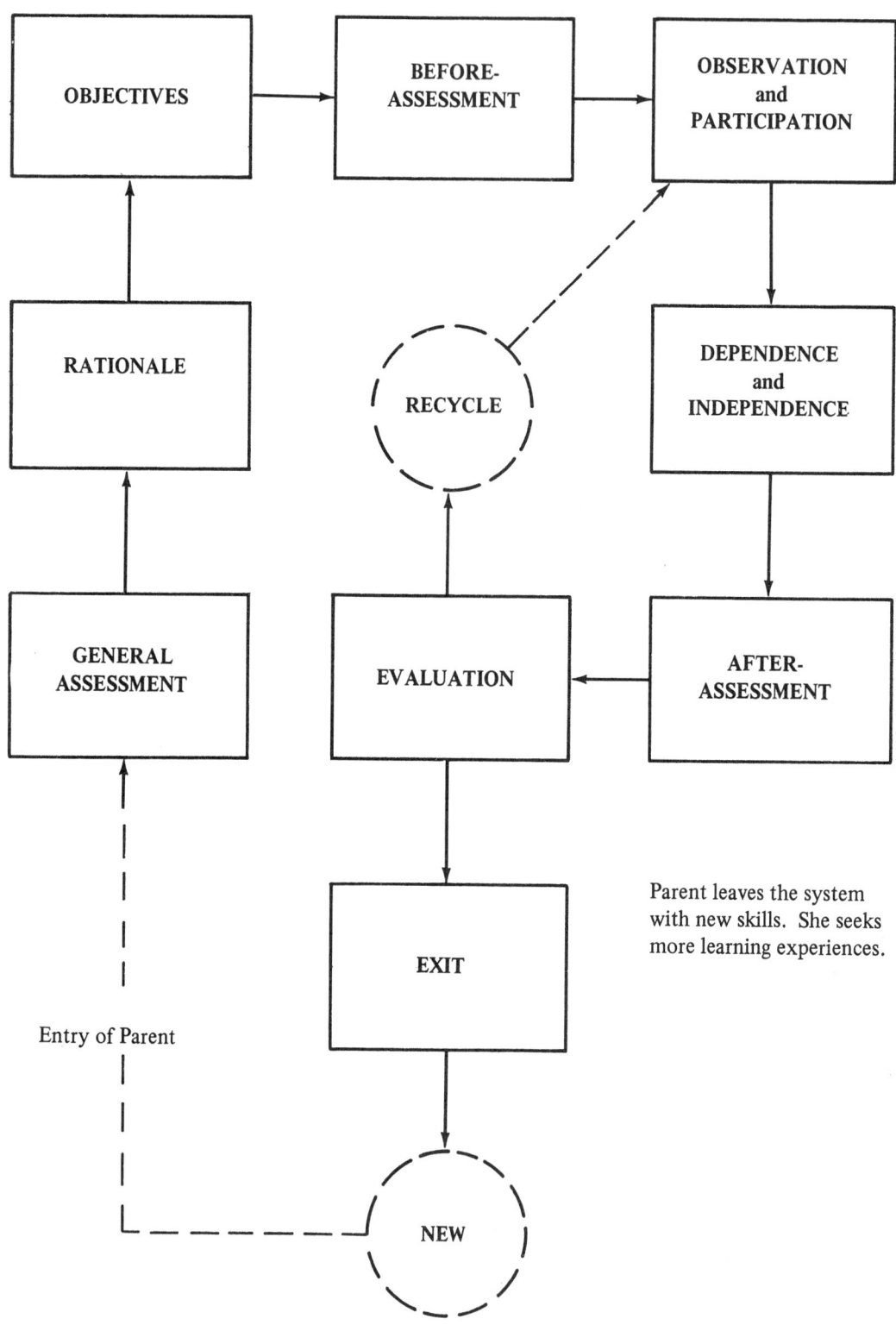

Fig. 7-5 A flowchart shows how learning tasks are met in training programs for parents.

- **Family cultural and ethnic living patterns**: What is the life-style of the family? What are their attitudes about education, health, and nutrition? How do they cope with problems? Is there evidence of social problems, drugs, alcoholism, disease, or child abuse? What do family members do in their leisure time?
- **Family in relation to the community**: How does the family utilize community resources? What do they get? What do they give? How do they feel about the community?
- **Family hopes and aspirations**: How does the family cope with everyday problems of living? What are their plans for the future? How can the program guide them toward greater skill and independence in meeting their goals?

CAUTION: All information obtained must be as objective as possible. Subjective reports can be misinterpreted unintentionally. Recent laws authorizing parents to examine all records at their request makes careful handling of reports an imperative.

When needs are identified and objectives established, the home visitor taps her workplans and community resource file to organize programs. Materials are modified, if needed, or additional materials are made to meet a new situation. Figure 7-5 shows how the learning tasks are met.

- **Entry**: Parent enters the program.
- **General assessment**: A general picture of the home situation is made. Through informal talks a broad view of what parents already know about child development is gained.
- **Rationale**: Parents are guided in seeing ways through which they can help their child by taking part in the program. They are made aware of the importance of parent skills in home-based education. Parents are involved in examining reasons why a certain change or skill may be needed. They learn why old ways of doing things with their child can be changed to new and better ways.
- **Objectives**: Learning objectives are made for developing a certain parent skill. Parents are involved in setting the objectives.
- **Before-assessment**: What parents already know about the skill is found — before the learning activity takes place. Plans are made to help parents fill in any gaps between what they know, and what they would like to know — or need to know.
- **Observation and participation**: The parents watch the home visitor model the new skill with the target child. The parents observe and then discuss what they saw. The parents practice the skill in working with the child.
- **Dependence and independence**: Guided by the home visitor the parent continues to practice. As the parent develops skill, the home visitor starts to give up control of the situation. When the parent is ready, he/she gets full control of the teaching task. The parent works from a position of dependence toward independence.
- **After-assessment**: What can the parent do after the learning experience is

Fig. 7-6 **The parent watches the home visitor work with the child.**

Section 2 Orientation to Home Visiting

determined? The parent and home visitor make the assessment together.

- **Evaluation**: Evaluation means looking at something to see how good it is. The home visitor and the parents look at the new skill. If the parents can do what they are supposed to do, feel confident, they may exit (leave) the system. They then go back to general assessment to see what skill can come next, and why it should be developed. If they do not feel comfortable about the work, or show signs of needing more practice, they are recycled back to dependence-independence to continue practice with guidance.
- **Exit**: The parent leaves with a new skill and goes back to the general assessment to see what comes next in the program.

EDUCATION SERVICES

Education focuses on getting knowledge and on getting skills to use that knowledge. Listed are parent skills needed, and home visitor tasks that enable parent skills.

Parent Skills

Parents need the ability to promote the child's physical, intellectual, emotional, and social growth by

- Establishing in the home a climate that leads to learning.
- Using materials and experiences that encourage the child to explore, question, experience, do, and progress toward greater maturity.
- Providing for sensory activities that enable the child to learn by touching, tasting, seeing, hearing.
- Fostering creative expression through paints, crayons, clay, blocks, stories, dramatic play, utilization of waste materials in creating, and other media.
- Creating many opportunities for the child to make decisions, solve problems, and work on projects of his own choosing.

Fig. 7-7 The young child learns to make choices by having a chance to choose.

Fig. 7-8 The young child sees a problem and seeks some kind of solution.

Unit 7 Delivering Services

Fig. 7-9 Play space is provided for the child to work on her task.

- Taking preventive measures against hazards to physical safety and well-being.
- Guiding the child toward a sense of positive identity as a self, as a member of his family and ethnic group, and as a competent person with his own place in the world.
- Utilizing all community services and resources to help the child and his family to live rich and fulfilling lives by developing in the best way that they can.

Home Visitor Tasks

The purpose of home visitor tasks is to enable parent skills by guiding them in identifying and using home opportunities and community resources by

- Helping parents to organize in the home work-play areas recognizable by the child, for example, art, music, games, dressing up, block building, clay modeling, discovery centers.
- Stressing the importance of giving the child some place for storing his personal things and for being alone to think and grow.
- Demonstrating the use of household materials and activities as tools for learning: setting the table, making a bed, sorting the laundry, using measuring cups and spoons to "discover" equivalent amounts and sets.
- Teaming with parent to make something useful from scrap and waste materials: storage chests, wagons, puzzles, bookshelves, games, and other items. Motivating the parent to make other articles for the family.
- Securing guides to accompany children's television shows which are shown locally to make television viewing a more active, less passive, tool for learning. Preparing a simplified guideline for parents who need less difficult reading matter.
- Going with parent and child to show how the child can learn in his community: what fire fighters do, what the library shares, how things are bought and sold, who keeps people well, and the like.
- Providing ways for parents to interact with other parents in the home, in the center, or in the community.
- Locating courses that parents may wish to take in a local adult or continuing education center. Assisting parents who need help in making necessary arrangements to go on with their studies.

HEALTH SERVICES

Health inputs focus on a group of services that meet the health needs of parents and their families. Suggestions that follow emphasize the prevention and correction of conditions that can affect the well-being of the family group.

Parent Skills

Parent skills include the ability to recognize and practice with the family good habits of safety, sanitation, nutrition, physical and mental well-being, by

- Recognizing the importance of a balanced diet.
- Being aware of danger signals and symptoms that may need special treatment: alcoholism, drugs, venereal disease, child discipline, atypical child behavior, infections.
- Knowing where to go to get health services, and understanding how to make necessary arrangements to use them.
- Knowing elementary first aid and important health practices.
- Keeping a check list to make sure that safety precautions are kept in the home.

Home Visitor Tasks

Home visitor tasks enable parent skills by

- Teaching parents how to plan well-balanced, appetizing meals that use the four basic food groups.
- Providing parents with important consumer information: planning, budgeting, and buying food. Helping eligible persons to get food stamps. Locating sources of surplus commodities that can be obtained through some Agricultural Extension Services.
- Arranging for parents to make use of the wealth of information and demonstrations offered through local Agricultural Extension Services, such as

    Sewing Clothes for Handicapped Persons
    Making Inside Home Improvements
    Building or Remodeling Homes
    Preparing Home Gardens
    Canning and Freezing Food
    Sponsoring Senior Citizen Activities

- Going through the right channels to arrange for the child's physical examination: urinalysis and hemoglobin tests; dental examination; and tests for the presence of lice, worms, impetigo, and other infections (when necessary). Making necessary referrals and providing for follow up to make sure that services continue.
- Discussing with parents the need to take steps to see that handicapped persons receive needed care, or to continue any rehabilitative services that may be in progress.
- Helping parents to prepare a safety check list by examining with them electrical outlets, exposed wires, steps, shelves, storage places for poisonous materials, medicine cabinets, dangerous tools and equipment, and other things that may be a health or safety hazard.

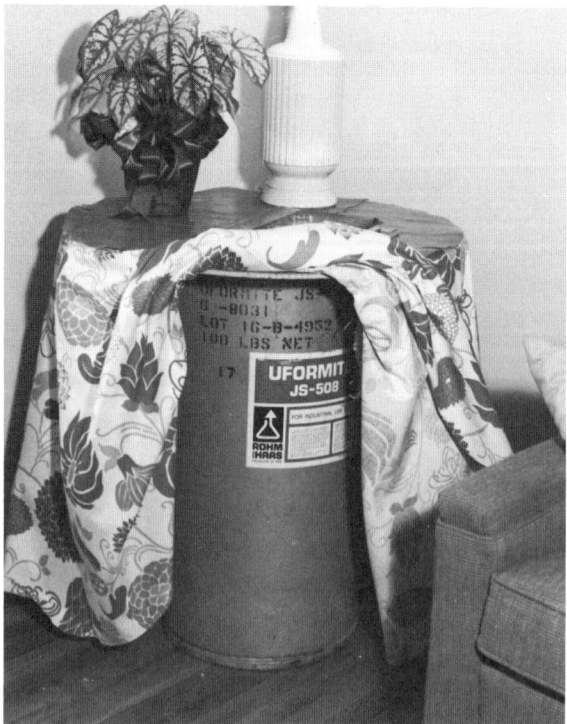

Fig. 7-10 Extension agents offer many services which can be tapped by parents. Shown is a model of a useful table made from an old storage can.

SOCIAL SERVICES

In the broadest sense social services include all the assistance that a community may provide for its citizens: (1) welfare and economic assistance, (2) recreation facilities, (3) libraries, (4) counseling services for vocational or mental health, (5) job training. There may be some overlapping with health services, but a good delivery system provides for cooperation between workers and avoids duplication of services.

Parent Skills

Parent skills include the ability to function effectively in helping family members to avoid or lessen problems in personal relationships, physical and mental health by

- Knowing where to go for help with legal or economic problems and knowing how to obtain services.
- Providing the family with wholesome housing, or knowing where to go for help in finding housing or improving the existing home.
- Contributing to community health and progress by cooperating with local agencies that try to improve all conditions that may be a health threat to citizens.

Home Visitor Tasks

Home visitor tasks enable parent skills by

- Helping parents to assess social problems in the family and leading them to agencies that provide aid.
- Arranging for counseling in such areas as employment, drugs, family planning, education, marriage, and disease.
- Sharing a community resource file and showing parents how to make use of the local telephone book in preparing a directory of resources tailored to the family.

PARENT INVOLVEMENT

Involving parents in the early education of their own children is the goal of home-based child development programs. The idea of parents as teachers of their own children is not new. Throughout the history of early childhood education, many writers called attention to the close bond between parent and young child. It is this bond that causes the parent to be the prime influencer of the young child's learning and development.

The present stress on home-based education is an effort to use the parent's influence in getting the young child off to a healthy and happy start in life. By improving their parenting skills, both father and mother can improve the quality of that life.

Parent Skills

The desired outcome of home-based early childhood programs is parents who have

- Confidence in themselves.
- Competence in teaching their own children.

Fig. 7-11 A very important part of a home visit is the opportunity for the parent and home visitor to discuss their program.

Section 2 Orientation to Home Visiting

- Independence in making decisions that affect the young child and other family members.
- Knowledge necessary to know when and where to go for help when difficult problems arise.

Home Visitor Tasks

Home visitor enables parent skills by
- Governing her efforts by the pace to which parents can absorb and use new experiences.
- Providing each group of parents with its own tailored program and timetable.
- Developing new skills in working with parents and new perceptions of what makes up a viable relationship between parents and those who help them with parenting tasks.

The focus of all these efforts is the child. The goal is the strong foundation every child needs as he grows and gradually becomes able to take care of his own needs. The outcome is a person of maximal growth and development who is able to live in and understand the world about him and to contribute to his world.

SUMMARY

When goods and services are needed, an effective and efficient system must be provided for delivering them. A delivery system for early education programs calls for objectives, inputs, outputs, a checking device for evaluation, and feedback.

There are a variety of ways through which home-based program objectives can be met. The home visitor is the primary means for organizing programs for parents. Other delivery systems may include mobile units, toy-lending libraries, parent cooperatives, pediatrician-sponsored groups, community learning centers, child development centers, and television programs.

The first visit to a home is an important one that may affect the family's attitude toward the program. An icebreaker helps to engage the child's interest. A warm, friendly conversation between parents and visitor can create a good working relationship.

The home visitor uses an instructional system for some activities. The system includes general assessment of the situation, rationale, objectives, before-assessment, observation and participation, dependence and independence, after-assessment, evaluation, and exit.

The objectives of the four components of home-based programs are delivered through ways seen as most appropriate by sponsors, workers, and parents.

SUGGESTED ACTIVITIES
- Visit your local library. Inquire about a toy-lending library.
    a. If the library has one, examine the materials. Make a list of those you would like to share with your class. Reserve a date for borrowing the materials to take to your class.
    b. If your library does not have a toy-lending library, see if you can persuade your librarian to borrow some materials through interlibrary loan.
    c. Role-play with your peer group. Follow up with young children if they can be brought to class.
    d. Make a tape recording of your work with your peer group or with the children. Evaluate your performance by asking yourself these

questions: Were the materials appropriate to the age level and interest level of the children? Did they respond positively? Did the activity keep their interest for five or more minutes? Did they demonstrate the performance expected?

    e. If you are unable to obtain materials through your local library, perhaps you can find a nursery school teacher who can accommodate you.

- Visit the nearest agricultural extension office. Ask to see materials distributed by home and family life agents. See how many services are similar to tasks performed by home visitors. Share your findings with your class.

- See if arrangements can be made for you to go along with an extension agent when she is working with families. Relate your experience to your class.

- If possible, ask the agent to visit your class. Prepare a list of questions that the class may wish to ask. (Be sure to write a "thank you" note following the visit of the extension agent.)

REVIEW

A. Define each of the following.

    1. Delivery system
    2. Inputs
    3. Outputs
    4. Feedback
    5. Evaluation, or checking device
    6. Mobile classroom
    7. Toy-lending library
    8. Observation-participation
    9. Dependence-independence
    10. Before-assessment

B. Briefly answer each of the following.

    1. State at least five ways through which early education services can reach children in their homes.

    2. Identify four kinds of information that is helpful in assessing the needs of children and their families.

    3. List the learning tasks that are met in training programs for parents.

    4. List five skills that parents need. Describe home visitor tasks that can enable those skills for each of the following components: health services, social services, education.

    5. Give your own ideas concerning the parent involvement component and what it means.

Section 3 Parents Are Adult Learners

unit 8 knowing the adult learner

OBJECTIVES

After studying this unit, the student should be able to

- Define briefly the following terms: parenting, adult learner, andragogy, pedagogy, busywork, developmental task, teachable moment, recurrent task, identity crisis, sense of trust.
- Identify and describe at least four principles of adult learning.
- Discuss the tasks of parents from the standpoint of developmental tasks or critical periods.

Parents come in all sizes, shapes, and age groups. Like a band of raw recruits reporting to an induction center, they have backgrounds that vary in both education and experience. From the college professor to the cabinetmaker, however, parents have three things in common: they are parents; they have children; and they have a moral and legal responsibility to provide for the wellbeing of their children — a task met through parenting.

There is no task that is so demanding and for which people have so little training as *parenting,* which may be described as

- All of the child rearing tasks performed by parents themselves and the needed services that they obtain from others.
- All of the tasks performed by other persons in the community who contribute to the child's development.
- All of the tasks performed by organizations and agencies concerned with the child's total development as a citizen and person in his own right.

Parenting is seen as a team effort for which parents assume roles of both responsibility and leadership. They are responsible for seeing that the child's needs are met. When situations arise that require outside help, parents must be able to

- Identify the need.
- Recognize that a problem exists that requires the services of other persons.

Fig. 8-1 Adult learning efforts are usually voluntary and may take place in formal or informal situations.

- Know what assistance is available and know when, where, and how it can be obtained.
- Find the best way to solve their problems.

Parents assume a leadership role when they take the initiative — when they lead the child toward experiences by which he can grow and learn. Parenting is more than loving the child and giving him food, shelter, and clothing. It is helping him to grow and change as his world changes. It requires that parents change, too. Parents can change by becoming adult learners.

PARENT-ADULT LEARNERS

In the present context, an *adult learner* is a mature person who is no longer required by law to go to school. He is under no obligation to take part in public education of any kind. If he studies his efforts are usually voluntary and may take place in formal or informal situations.

A *learner* is a person who is learning — who is undergoing a change in behavior. Learning takes place as the learner interacts with his environment and fills a need. With his need met, the learner is able to cope with his environment.

Parents who seek solutions to problems which they meet during the parenting process are in effect adult learners. When they try different ways to solve a problem, they undergo changes in behavior. When they find a satisfactory solution, a need is filled and they are able to cope with their situation. Thus the parents have "learned" how to solve the problems.

Ability and willingness to change in a changing world is essential. To be able to change is to learn. To be efficient is to be able to change often. To be effective is to go on changing to face new problems and solve them in the best way possible. These are the learning tasks of parents.

Principles of Adult Learning as Applied to Parents

Adults come to the learning situation with years of experience in living. Unlike the child who is seeking first experiences, the adult is the older product of many experiences. Differences between child and adult learners have led some adult educators to come up with a new school of thought for adult learning.

Malcolm Knowles calls it *andragogy*, the "art and science of helping adults learn."[1] He believes that adults are self-directed learners who need methods, techniques, and materials geared to them — not to children. Knowles keeps the term *pedagogy*, the science of teaching children, for child learners. But he goes on to say that andragogy has much to offer those who teach children.

No matter what term is used, the fact remains that each learner needs to be seen as an individual with his own set of attitudes, interests, needs, experiences, and motives for learning. The learner also needs to be guided to reach his highest level of performance in all that he does.

The adult's experiences must be considered when he is in a teaching-learning situation because he is then able to relate new ideas to past experiences, giving new information greater meaning. New information becomes easier for him to remember if it ties in with something in his past. Adults are also likely to be set in their thinking, giving them strong feelings about what is right and what is wrong — and what is for them. Adults may resist new ideas that run counter to what they believe. It may be necessary to unset old ideas, before new learning can take place.

[1] Malcolm Knowles, *The Modern Practice of Adult Education,* (New York: Association Press, 1970), p. 38.

Section 3 Parents are Adult Learners

Example: The mother of nine children believes that she cannot become pregnant if she is nursing her baby. This old wives' tale must be "unset" before the woman is ready to receive information concerning birth control.

Adults tend to be impatient in meeting learning objectives.

- Adults are concerned with here-and-now usefulness of information and skills that they learn.
- Adults seek meaningful experiences that can serve them in meeting their goals.
- Adults resist anything that looks like *busywork,* something that has no purpose beyond the activity itself. They do not like to feel that they are wasting their time when they could be doing something "useful."

Example: A mother has a bad morning trying to find things to keep her children busy. She cannot afford to buy toys and games. When the home visitor comes in the afternoon, she tells the mother that teaching aids can be found in the home. The mother is interested in learning how to use measuring cups, pots and pans, and other items to teach her child and keep him busy. The here-and-now quality is there. She sees something she can use right away. She becomes involved in working with her child.

Adults have strong reasons for learning.

- Parents who work with their children are motivated.
- Involved parents want their children to succeed.
- Adults are willing to work toward goals that they see as their own.
- The adult learner is a voluntary one whose successes in learning generally lead him to seek and find more success.

Example: Parents are involved in making homemade toys and games for their children. The materials used are free or inexpensive. When the toys and games are made, the parents can see their value. The stage is set for making more things.

Adult learners are independent in their actions.

- Adults do not like to have others tell them what to do, as if they were children. Therefore, parents must be involved in their own training.
- Adult learners are often quick to begin something that really arouses their interest. They may stop just as quickly when their interest is not held.

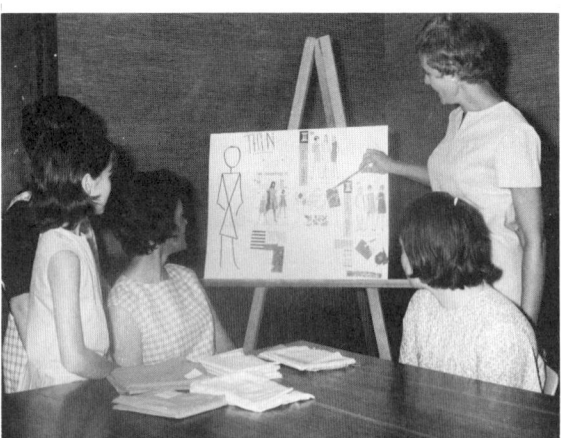
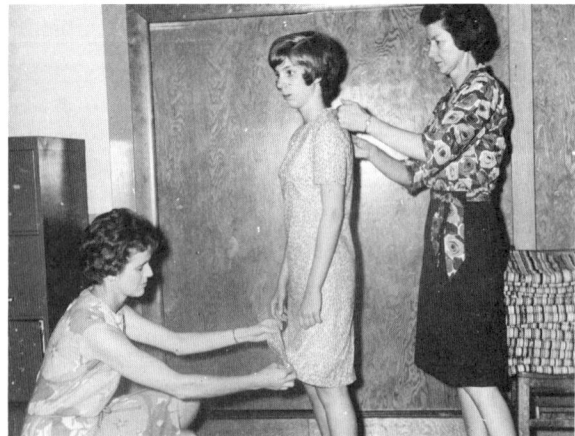

Fig. 8-2 Adults seek meaningful experiences that can serve them in meeting their goals. Providing clothes for a family is an important parenting task.

Unit 8 Knowing the Adult Learner

- Adults tend to be uncomfortable if they are put in a dependent position. When she can, the home visitor uses ideas that the parent has.

Example: A mother is being trained to use the four basic food groups in preparing menus. To find something that she can use, the home visitor asks the mother for favorite family recipes. This puts the mother in the lead, for the task begins with her knowledge. Her ideas count. She has good feelings toward the person who makes her feel that way. In turn, the mother may be willing to listen to the home visitor.

Adults are sensitive to failure in learning activities.

- Although all learners are sensitive to failure, adults are more so; they have a *low tolerance level.*
- Lack of success can cause adult learners to drop out of a program.
- Adult educators can build a success base for learners by starting with tasks that cannot fail.

Example: A mother wants help with a child who is a poor eater. The home visitor prepares a food-tasting session for the child and his parent. She shows the child pictures of food which she has in her plan. The child chooses what he thinks he may like. He helps his mother prepare the new dish. He eats the food that he helped cook. If the home visitor is skillful, the parent sees some success in changing the child's interest in food. Both parent and child are more apt to repeat the activity and try another new dish.

Adults are used to being treated as mature persons.

- Home visitors must never "talk down" to parents.
- Adults resent being treated like children.
- Adults like to have a part in making decisions that affect them.

- Parents with greater knowledge and academic ability may prefer to receive some information in written form, instead of being told.
- When an adult makes a mistake, there should be no comment or reprimand that makes him feel "scolded."
- Home visitors must avoid making parents feel that their job is being taken over by someone else.

Example: An older child in the family presents a discipline problem that gets out of hand. The home visitor helps by making the parents feel that they are not alone. She lets them know that other parents often have like problems. With skill and understanding, the home visitor goes through channels to get help. The parents are never criticized, but are led toward some options to solve the problem.

Adults can learn no matter how old they are.

- Studies show that adults can learn and change their way of doing things.
- Physical activities may slow down, but it is possible for adults to stay mentally alert all through life.

Fig. 8-3 Adults are willing to work toward goals they see as their own. Shown are persons discussing homemaking problems.

Section 3 Parents are Adult Learners

- Senior citizens in good health may be able to make some valuable contributions to home-based programs.

Example: Persons who have reached later maturity may welcome the opportunity to work with children. Many senior citizens are giving their time and skills to help people learn. Figure 8-4 shows a S.T.E.P. (Seniors Tutor for Educational Progress) tutor at work with a child.[2]

Program planners may wish to explore ways by which senior citizens can help in local home-based programs. A person sixty-four years of age does not lose his skills when he turns sixty-five. Senior citizens may

- Serve as consultants to the program. There are many people who like to keep busy and feel needed.

- Serve as supervisors during home visits. Professional persons may welcome the opportunity to continue to use the skills they have. The home visitor may like the informal on-the-job training experiences that result.

- Take the role of surrogate grandparents for the family. Today's world often finds families spread far and wide. Senior citizens may be able to fill a gap for families who have few chances to link their lives with the past.

- Keep the child busy while the home visitor talks with the parent. Stories, worksheets, or just plain "talk" can fill the need.

- Lend a "listening" ear to mothers. There is something about age that seems to inspire confidence in some people. A parent may find it easier to talk to an older person and discuss family problems.

- Prepare materials for home use. Senior citizens may be able to spend an afternoon working at a center. If not, it may be possible to go to them. The social experience is apt to have great appeal for those who take part.

What can be done depends on the local situation and the senior citizens who may be

Fig. 8-4 Many senior citizens are giving their time and skills to help people learn. Shown is a tutor at work with a school child.

Fig. 8-5 Creative thinking on the part of program planners is the key to action. What can successful gardeners bring to a home-based program?

[2]Project S.T.E.P. (Seniors Tutor for Educational Progress), Redding Schools, Redding, Connecticut.

interested. Good health is essential if older persons are to be involved. Creative thinking on the part of program planners is the key to action.

TASKS OF ADULT LEARNERS

When parents are seen as adult learners, what are some of their tasks? How can these problem areas be examined and described? How can an understanding of adult tasks help people who want to help parents do a good job?

There are no easy answers. This discussion takes a brief look at two ways to approach the problem.

Developmental Tasks

The first approach uses the developmental tasks concept. A *developmental task* is one that comes up at a certain point in an individual's life. Each task is something which a person must learn to cope with effectively, if he is to achieve a happy and successful later life. If he fails to master his tasks, he faces unhappiness in his life, disappointment and sometimes "punishment" by society, and difficulty with later tasks which he must face.

Robert Havighurst has identified certain tasks which an individual must face at each of six periods in life. He starts with the tasks of the infant and deals with the entire life cycle from the cradle to the grave.

Developmental tasks are seen as something created by three conditions. When they are present, Havighurst says that the "teachable moment" has come.[3] The three conditions are

- **The individual's own timetable for physical and mental growth**: he must be ready for his task and have the capacity to do it.

[3]Robert J. Havighurst, *Developmental Tasks and Education*, Third Edition, (New York: David McKay, Inc., 1972), p. 2.

- **The individual's own values, motives and goals**: he must be willing to face his task with success as his goal.
- **The cultural forces around the individual**: he is faced with pressure to do what is expected of him by society.

Some tasks are recurrent — they occur over and over again. Getting along with one's age mates is an example. Other tasks are not recurrent. They take place at one time only, such as learning to walk and toilet training.

For adults who fall into the early adulthood group, Havighurst sees the conventional way of life: choosing and learning to live with a marriage mate, raising a family, taking care of a home, and becoming a part of a community. The adult in this group is just getting started in his occupation or life's work.

Developmental Tasks and Different Ways of Life

A close look at the tasks described for early adulthood suggests the need for caution. Not all people in today's society share middle-class values. It is important that home visitors, and other adult educators, recognize unlike views and respect the people who share them.

Mating and marriage. For some persons, mating and marriage may be unrelated. Temporary living arrangements, trial marriages, sexual activity with no attachments, and other like relationships are seen as acceptable.

Another group may form marriage contracts that spell out the rights and duties of partners before they are wed. Included are provisions for ending the marriage if rules are broken.

When children are a part of an arrangement that adults end, adjustments may be difficult. Children may face living with a single parent. Parents-without-partners have problems unique to that condition. A home visitor who understands some of the problems is better able to help parents in coping with them.

Children and families. In some homes, the concept of family may mean to a child, "the people I live with." The father figure may be more than one male. A mother figure may mean several women with whom the child relates in his home.

The person who says to a child, "Draw a picture of your family," may need to restate the direction. "Draw a picture of the people you live with" allows for more options and life-styles. It also helps the child to feel accepted as he is. There is no risk that he sees himself as being set apart from his peer group, because his home life is not like theirs.

Careers and occupations. Many people in today's society are not interested in conventional work. They live a life that is related to their beliefs. A simple, back-to-nature lifestyle may not fall into any conventional definition of a job.

When the developmental tasks concept is applied to parents as adult learners, it needs to be tailored to fit the culture of persons concerned. The knowledge, beliefs, values, and attitudes of people are what make them what they are. What they are, and what they want to be, create the framework around which they are helped best.

Those who work with adults must be open-minded and without bias in their work. What is offered to parents must be done in the light of human qualities that make each person what he is.

Critical Periods

The concept of critical periods, or identity crises, is another way to look at the problems people face in life. An *identity crisis* is defined as that which occurs when something interferes with a person's development. What takes place then may be the opposite of what is desired.

For example, a person may develop mistrust of people instead of trust. Early in life a person learns to trust or mistrust people. A child trusts his mother when she responds to his needs — he knows that she will take care of him. He feels loved and wanted when she holds him and loves him; he learns that he has no fear of falling and trusts her.

A sense of trust is the feeling that everything is all right. It is like saying, "I'm O.K." This desire for trust goes on throughout life. People need this feeling to face new tasks and new problems. They need to know that other people can be trusted, too.

Erikson believes that a person must be able to cope with certain stages in his development if a healthy personality or "self" is to result.[4] Success at one stage makes possible success at the next stage. Each person must be able to

- Learn to trust his world and things in it: a sense of "trust." (birth to 12 months)
- Learn to be independent by exploring his world to know what is in it: a sense of "autonomy." (1-3 years)
- Learn to carry out plans and ideas that are his own: a sense of "initiative." (4-5 years)
- Learn the feel of *accomplishment,* or that he can do things in his world: a sense of "accomplishment." (6-12 years)
- Learn who he is, what he is, and what he can be: a sense of "identity." (13-16 years)
- Learn the meaning of friendship, love of others, and self-love: a sense of "intimacy." (16-18 years)
- Learn how to become a parent and express concern for all children: a "parental" sense. (18-25 years)

[4]Erikson, Erik K. *Childhood and Society,* (New York: W.W. Norton, 1950).

- Learn how to accept the life cycle and what it holds for him from the cradle to old age: a sense of "integrity." (25 years on)

A person who is unable to cope with each stage faces crises which must be resolved if he is to go on to his next stage. He may feel inferior and doubt his self-worth. He may be unable to do things for himself. He may have a sense of guilt. He may be unable to accept himself or to reach out to others. He may be too immature to be a good parent. He may reach old age with a low value on himself, distrustful of the world, and critical of all things in it.

The home visitor may find some parents who are in one of the periods of crisis. She must be able to start where they are and help them to move on in their own development. Letting them learn that they can trust her is a good point of departure.

HOME VISITORS AS ADULT LEARNERS

The home visitor is an adult educator. She must be an adult learner, too. As an adult learner, the home visitor should

- Broaden and expand her ability to gain new information and increased skill in using new knowledge.
- Keep up with current events to improve her own mind and to be able to discuss topics of interest or concern to parents.
- Sharpen her skill in reaching parents and children by developing creative and innovative ideas.
- Increase her knowledge of people and their problems — to gain greater skill in meeting their needs.
- Keep herself well informed on community resources: services, agencies, organizations, and other groups that help people.
- Maintain good health and mental alertness by giving herself only the best of care: proper diet, adequate rest, physical exercise, mental stimulation, and social experiences.
- Expand her knowledge of children: how they learn — and how they learn best.
- Continue to grow in her ability to sell home-based early education programs to people who need help or to those who can provide it to others.

SUMMARY

Parenting includes all the child-rearing tasks performed by parents and the needed services that they can obtain from others. Parents must be able to provide for the child's needs themselves or to provide the services of others who can.

An adult learner is a person who learns because he wants to learn something. Parents are in effect adult learners.

Andragogy is the art and science of helping adults learn. It views adults as self-directed learners. Pedagogy is a term used to describe the science of teaching children.

The principles of adult learning are important and must be considered when programs are planned for parents:

- Adults come to the learning situation with years of experience in living.
- Adults tend to be impatient in meeting learning objectives.
- Adults have strong reasons for learning.
- Adult learners are independent in their actions.
- Adults are sensitive to failure in learning activities.
- Adults are used to being treated as mature persons.
- Adults can learn no matter how old they are.

A developmental task is something which a person must learn to cope with effectively, if he is to achieve a happy and successful later life. If he fails to master his early tasks, he faces unhappiness and failure with later tasks.

Not all people share middle-class values. It is important to recognize unlike views and respect the people who share them. What is offered to parents must be done in the light of the human qualities that make each person what he is.

An identity crisis is that which occurs when something interferes with a person's development. What takes place then may be the opposite of what is desired. If people are to develop a healthy personality, they must develop a sense of trust, autonomy, initiative, accomplishment, identity, intimacy, parental concerns, and integrity.

The home visitor serves as an adult educator when she works with parents. She must be an adult learner, too. This requires more knowledge, more skills, and a constant search for ways to do her job in the best way possible.

SUGGESTED ACTIVITIES

- Make a list of tasks which parents must meet during the parenting process. The list may be seen from three points of view.

    a. Things that they must be able to do themselves.

    b. Things that they must do for their children.

    c. Tasks they face as family members in a community.

- Find examples of the principles of adult learning as described in this unit. You may wish to consider the following:

    a. How experiences help adults to learn certain new tasks.

    b. Examples of adults being in a "hurry" to learn something, or to meet a learning objective.

    c. Adults trying to learn something "on their own."

    d. Adults as independent people.

    e. Adults wanting to be treated like mature persons.

    f. Older persons in the community who are in a learning situation.

- Make arrangements to discuss the following topics with several people in your class. You may wish to divide the topics among members of the group.

    a. How parents can develop a child's sense of "trust" from early childhood.

    b. How parents can help a child test himself and his powers as he seeks "autonomy" (independence).

    c. How parents can model the type of behavior that shows the child how he can develop "initiative" for himself.

    d. How parents can provide opportunities for a child to succeed and develop a sense of "accomplishment."

e. How parents can provide their child with guidance, or a helping hand, as he tries to find his own "identity."

- Interview five parents. Ask each to give you (in order of importance) five problems that they face in parenting.

    a. Write each list on a separate sheet of paper.

    b. Examine the lists carefully. See if there are any common problems.

    c. Arrange the problems in groups (that you decide upon), so that you can tally the results. Topics that may be used include discipline, finicky eaters, lying, nightmares, sleeplessness, bedwetting, frequent illness, temper tantrums, disobedience, and running away.

    d. Share your findings with your class. Start a discussion concerning ways that the problems might be lessened, or solved. Get feedback from your instructor. (Perhaps she may be able to invite some parents to class to join in the discussion.)

REVIEW

A. Define each of the following.

   1. Parenting
   2. Adult learner
   3. Andragogy
   4. Pedagogy
   5. Busywork
   6. Developmental task
   7. Teachable moment
   8. Recurrent task
   9. Identity crisis
   10. Sense of trust

B. Identify and describe four principles of adult learning as described in this unit.

C. Discuss the tasks of parents as "developmental tasks" or as "critical periods" as described in this unit.

unit 9 creating adult learning situations

OBJECTIVES

After studying this unit, the student should be able to

- Describe parent education as a continuous cycle of events.
- Identify and describe at least three methods that may be used in adult learning situations.
- Compare two adult education learning methods, defending the one of personal preference.

Creating adult learning situations for parents is the task of parent education, defined as using educational techniques to help parents

- Develop skill, competence and independence in parenting.
- Build their self-esteem through greater success in parenting.
- Inspire strengths in families.
- Insure the maximal growth and development of the child.
- Provide for the child's personal well-being.
- Help the child to reach his highest potential in all facets of his life.

Parent education is that part of adult education that helps parents in one of their adult roles — parenting. While adult education refers to efforts to help any adult perform any of his roles, parent education is geared toward a specific adult role. In this context parent education is designed for persons who are already parents.

Parent educators are all persons who provide some kind of training, assistance, or information to help parents in performing their tasks. Included among parent educators are home visitors and any other person who is part of the program.

The term *preparental education* is reserved for training that takes place before a person becomes a parent.[1] It is that which is offered to young people in high schools and colleges and to adults anywhere — who expect to be parents at some future time.

The present discussion is concerned with those parents actively engaged in parenting as described in this text. Preparental education is not included, although many concepts discussed can be applied to preparental education, too.

ELEMENTS IN PARENT EDUCATION

Every parent educator must consider the following elements in creating a situation for parent education.

- The **method**: the way parents are organized for the purpose of learning. The approach must be suited to purposes of the learning experience and the persons who are exposed to it.
- The **techniques**: the skillful ways that the activity is managed so that learning takes place. People become bored with monotonous activities. A skillful parent educator uses a wide variety of ways to interest people in what is being done.

[1]Orville G. Brim, Jr., *Education for Child Rearing*, (New York: The Free Press, 1965), p. 25.

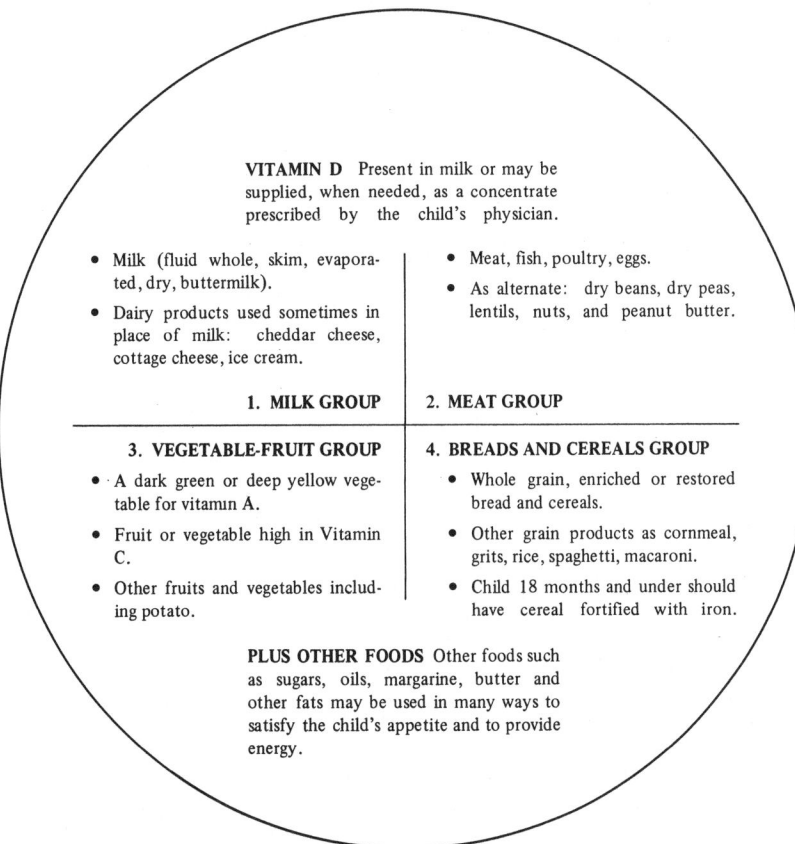

Fig. 9-1 The Basic-4 food plan is shown. Serving sizes may differ — small for young children, extra large (or seconds) for very active teenagers. Knowing the Basic-4 is being able to put them to use.

- The **devices**: all the things, conditions, or "tricks of the trade" that the parent educator uses to increase the probability that learning takes place. Adults progress most rapidly in learning situations that involve dealing with realistic problems. Most adults are impatient with abstractions — they want things that are real to them.

ACTION IN PARENT EDUCATION

Learning is an active process. People learn as the result of what they do, not as the result of what someone else does. The action must always focus on the learner, rather than on the person who is guiding the learner.

Why is this? Education is learning and learning is change — behavioral change in an individual. Behavioral change does not truly become part of a person until the change is reinforced through use.

For example: a mother can memorize a list of the four basic foods that provide the daily needs of her family. But she does not actually "learn" about them until she practices using the information in planning and preparing meals for her family. The mother, in short, must be involved in the process of learning. It is what she does that she learns.

No one knows for sure how people learn anything, but the search goes on for ways to make people learn better and faster. The only way to see if learning has taken place is by observing the behavior of people — by seeing what they say and do.

Section 3 Parents are Adult Learners

PARENT SKILLS AND THE BASIC-4 PLAN

Level One: The parent is able to

- Identify the four basic food groups.
- Tell what foods fall into each group.
- State the amount of each food needed by a child each day.

Level Two: The parent is able to

- Maintain the skill learned at Level One.
- Prepare a sample meal plan for breakfast, lunch or supper and dinner.
- Choose the right foods for each meal.
- Cook and serve the meal.

Level Three: The parent is able to

- Maintain the skills learned at Levels One and Two.
- Plan meals for an indefinite period, using a variety of foods based on the Basic-4 plan.
- Differentiate daily menus which are nutritionally sound from those which are not.
- Explain food needs as related to growth rate and age.
- Evaluate all meals planned before preparing them.

Fig. 9-2 Shown are three levels of understanding in the use of the Basic-4 food plan. They can be helpful in determining the performance level of the person responsible for seeing that the child's needs are met in food and nutrition.

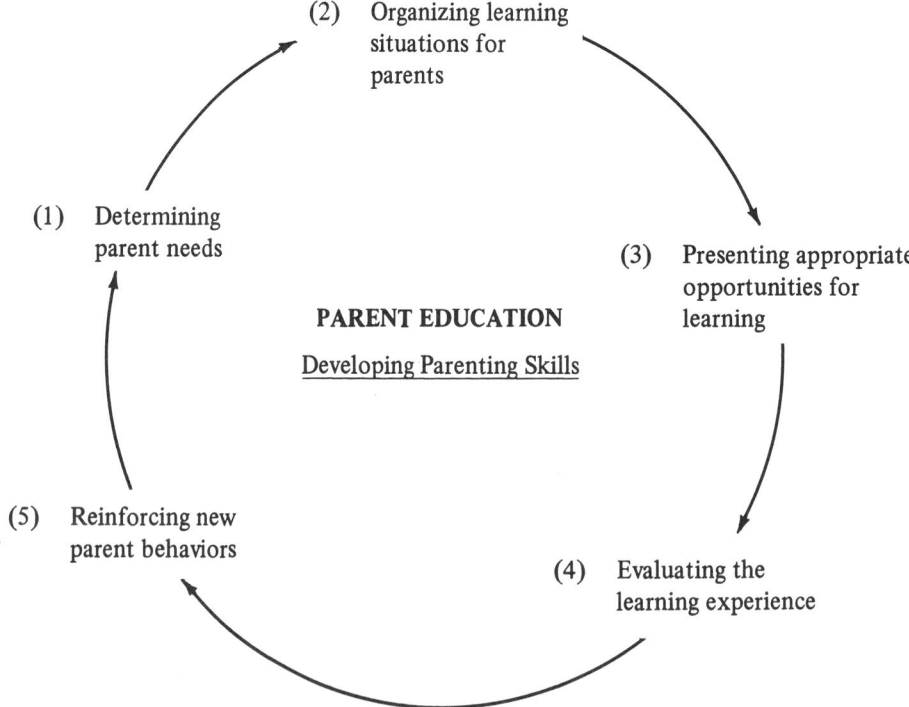

Fig. 9-3 Parent education is shown as a continuous process of training events.

Parent educators must build into the learning situation ways for parents to apply new learnings in their day-to-day lives. Parent education is active learning. It is training parents to do things for their children and with their children. When new ways in the behavior of parents can be seen, learning has taken place.

A Cycle of Events

Parent education is shown as a continuous process in figure 9-3. The cycle of events includes

- Determining parent needs.
- Organizing situations for parent learning activities.
- Presenting appropriate opportunities for learning to the right person, in the right way, and at the right time.
- Evaluating the learning experience.
- Reinforcing new parent behaviors.

As one need for a parenting skill is met, another objective for learning takes its place. The cycle begins all over again.

METHODS OF INSTRUCTION

The methods of adult education are all the ways by which mature persons learn. A wide variety of options is needed to meet the needs of parents as they learn to cope with each stage in a child's development.

No approach can serve all adult learners. The parent educator should ask one important question, "What method can help parents learn best and use what is learned?" The selection must be what is "best" for the parents involved.

Some common training methods are offered. The list is far from complete, but gives an idea of what can be done.

Individual Study

There are many adults who like to study on their own. Individual study provides them with opportunities for self-directed, self-paced learning. The adult works on an individual basis but is helped to achieve identified goals.

- Printed matter is provided in the form of a how-to-do-it book, or study sheets. Library books, correspondence courses, and other printed matter fall into this category. The reading level of the material is matched to meet the educational level of the parent. High and low levels are considered.
- Electronic methods for self-study include films, television programs, telephone courses, and computer work. The learner may or may not be provided with other related material.

What a parent does, during individual study, leads to a skill that is needed in solving a parenting problem. This method has great appeal to self-directed learners and to parents who have a high level of formal education.

To insure a successful self-study program for parents, the parent educator must be able to

- Plan a program for individualized study.
- Find materials that are appropriate for each learner.
- Guide individualized study.
- Help the learner practice what is learned.
- Help the learner evaluate the learning experience in terms of his own goals.

Group Activities

The following are descriptions of typical group study methods. Certain roles are usually common to all group techniques.

- **Moderator or leader:** the person who sees that the activity moves along as planned. He may serve as discussion leader.

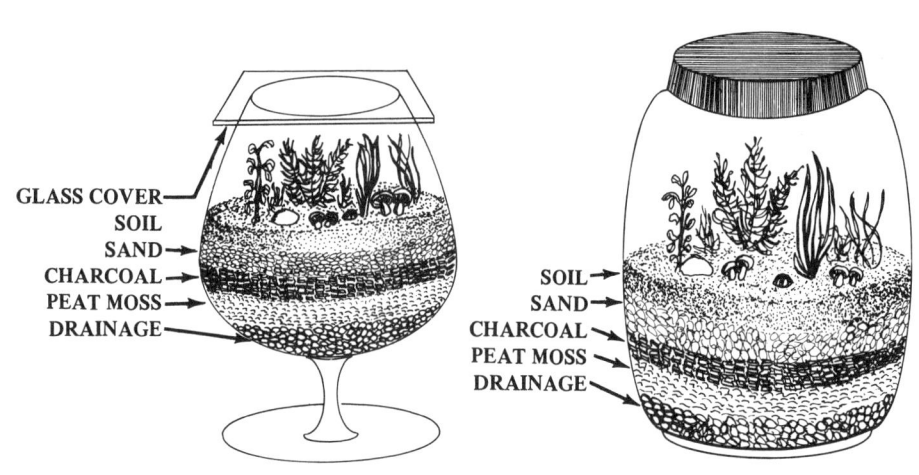

HOW TO BUILD A TERRARIUM

A terrarium is a small greenhouse which can be built in a *glass container*. A good terrarium can be made from a large jar with a tight-fitting cover, or a large brandy snifter with a piece of glass cut to fit over the top of the container.

To make a good terrarium, do the following in the order given:

1. Line the bottom of the jar with a *drainage layer* (1 1/2 to 2 inches): pebbles, coarse sand, gravel, charcoal or a mixture of these.
2. Add a thin *layer of moss* on top to keep the soil out of the drainage material.
3. A layer of crushed or *chipped charcoal* helps to keep the soil sweet and free from a sour smell.
4. Add a thin layer of *gravel,* about the size of peas. Coarse sand may be used instead.
5. Place *soil* in the center. It can be made up of 1/3 peat moss, 1/3 good garden soil and 1/3 coarse sand. Packaged potting soil can be used but it may need to be loosened with a bit of peat moss and sand. The layer of soil should be slightly moist, very light and loose.
6. Wet the roots of *plants* and place them in a depression in the top layer of soil. Add any decorations desired.
7. Plants can be found in the woods, or purchased. Some are
    - Moss: pincushion, fern-leaved, hair-cap.
    - Fungi: small mushrooms, molds, rusts, toadstools.
    - Ferns: royal, sensitive
    - English ivy, ice plant, partridge berry, evergreen seedlings.
8. Plants should be small so that they do not touch the top of the terrarium. Moisten the soil well.
9. Leave the container uncovered for two or three days. Then cover tightly.
10. If kept covered, the terrarium need not be watered. Moisture evaporating from the plants and excess water condenses on the glass inside and precipitates. If it becomes dewy and too difficult to see inside, remove the cover and wipe off the excess moisture. Replace cover.

Fig. 9-4 Printed matter is used in individual study.

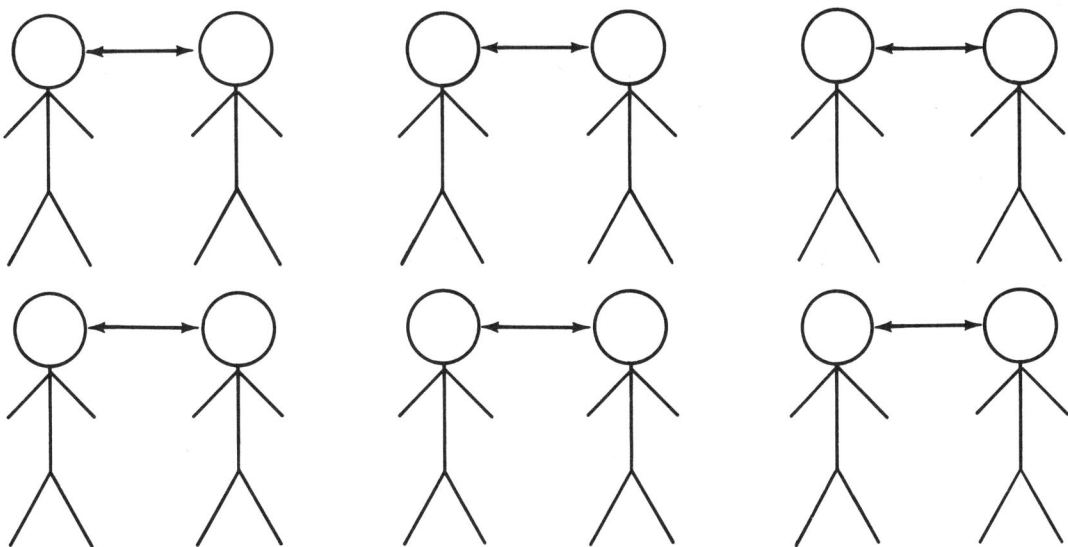

Fig. 9-5 Sometimes a large group is divided into dyads (pairs) who discuss a main idea before the large group comes together again.

Fig. 9-6 Buzz groups give all persons in a training group an opportunity to give their ideas. This large group is divided into triads (three persons) to discuss the main idea, for about five minutes.

- **Recorder:** the person who keeps a record of what takes place. He may take notes or make tape recordings of the session.
- **Observer:** the person whose task is to see how the group works as individuals and as members working together toward a common goal.

Depending on the specific requirements that group study methods are designed to satisfy, these special roles may or may not be included. Consequently, they are not given in the following descriptions or shown in the figures.

Small-group activities for learning can take several different forms.

- An **interview** takes place when one or more resource persons are questioned by one or more participants. It is a method that is used when the topic being covered does not lend itself to a more formal presentation.

- **Buzz groups** give all persons in a training program a chance to discuss their ideas. A topic is selected. The group divides into *dyads* (two persons) or *triads* (three persons). About five minutes are taken

95

Section 3 Parents are Adult Learners

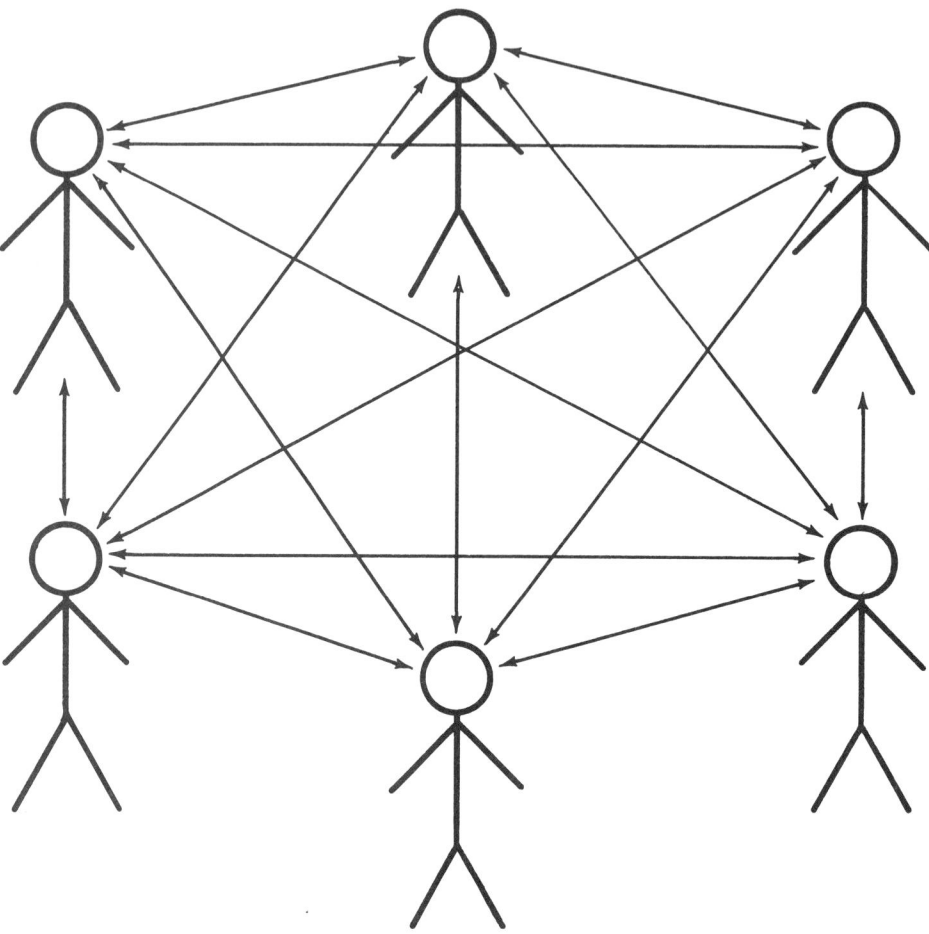

Fig. 9-7 Brainstorming enables all members of a group to give their ideas, before the discussion takes place. Creative thinking is encouraged.

for the groups to discuss the main topic. Each person gives his ideas. When the dyads or triads join to form the large group again, buzz group ideas are shared with all members.

- **Brainstorming** is a process that permits all members of a group to contribute ideas related to a problem or topic of concern to the group. When all ideas have been given, each is discussed. The goal of this technique is creative, rather than practical, thinking. Ideas rise or fall on their own merit.

- **Demonstration** shows a parent how to use something or perform a task that can be seen, heard, or felt. The parent repeats the activity under the supervision of the parent educator. Oral discussion of the activity is an important part of the method.

Demonstration-type activities can be used in all teaching-learning situations that call for some type of performance, no matter what the level.

Figures 9-8, 9-9, and 9-10 show demonstrations taking place at three levels. An extension agent shows preservice teachers how to create successful terrariums. Preservice teachers share their skills with five-year-old children. The children report back to their peer group and show them how to make a terrarium. The goal is the

Unit 9 Creating Adult Learning Situations

Fig. 9-8 Extension agent shows preservice teachers how to make a terrarium.

Fig. 9-9 Preservice teachers help young children make a terrarium.

Fig. 9-10 Several young children show their peer group how to make a terrarium.

same, but each group works in a manner most appropriate for the learners involved.

- **Discussion** works as a teaching technique when two or more people meet informally to talk about a topic or problem of mutual concern. People who take part do so on a common basis; there is something that ties them into a group. They may have similar roles (as parents or home visitors). They may have done some assigned reading that is to be discussed. They may share some other educational experience (as participating in a parent training session).

- **Seminar** sessions include an expert who leads a discussion among people who are receiving some kind of special training. The expert usually begins by presenting background information on the topic, often raising important questions. A discussion, guided by the expert, gives the group an opportunity to explore the topic further.

- **Simulation** is an educational experience described as a make-believe form of a real life situation. It can be compared to a game in which people act out what happens when they interact with people and things in the "real world." The parent educator gives the group opportunities to make decisions or take action before members repeat the tasks in a real life situation. Simulations are planned by those providing the training.

- **Role-playing** is done by a small group of persons who act out a real life situation

97

in front of another group. The participants make up their parts as they go along. After the performance, a discussion takes place to relate the role-playing to the real life problem.

- **Skits** are short, rehearsed dramatic acts involving two or more persons who work from a prepared script. The main ideas of the skit are drawn from events or incidents that may occur when members of the group are working. As a teaching technique, skits call attention to tasks or skills of importance to the group.
- **Workshops** are small-group meetings where people work on topics, problems, or things that are derived from the people present. A group of fifteen to thirty people come together to improve their skills. The group shares information and suggests ways that members can deal with a problem more effectively. The problem is converted to choice alternatives from which each member may find a workable solution to use "back home."

To insure the success of small-group activities in parent education, the parent educator must be able to

- Plan, organize, and carry out a wide variety of learning activities in which adult learners can be active.
- Prepare or locate materials that can be used.
- Demonstrate language ability in both speaking and writing.
- Serve as discussion leader, but not give the idea that being a leader is being an authority.
- Bear in mind that a discussion leader's task is to (1) guide the group to express itself in an orderly way; (2) help the group to focus on one point at a time; (3) keep the discussion or activity moving toward solutions to problems; (4) clarify points when necessary; (5) give a brief summary of points as the discussion moves along; and (6) help the group to summarize what it has achieved.
- Make sure that parents feel comfortable and free as they give and get ideas.
- Apply the principles of adult learning to the parents who are in the process of change.

Large-group activities involve any number of people who come together for a set purpose. It is not the most productive way to develop parenting skills. But it can "break the ice" for later work that takes place in small groups.

Very often a program may begin with a general session, or large-group meeting. There are several techniques that can be used effectively. The selection is usually made when the target group is known.

- **Lectures** are formal speeches that are prepared and presented by a person who is considered an expert on the chosen topic. The group has a chance to ask questions about some point in the speech. Or, they may ask for more information.
- **Panel** techniques bring together a group of four to eight speakers who are experts on their assigned topic. The panel carries on a conversation-type activity in front of the group of parents. A *moderator*, or leader, keeps the panel in order and makes sure that each person has equal time to speak. The panel covers their assigned topic in depth. The listening group is invited to ask questions of any speaker on the panel, during the last part of the session.
- **Forum** techniques consist of a discussion that takes place after a topic has been introduced in some way: speaker, panel,

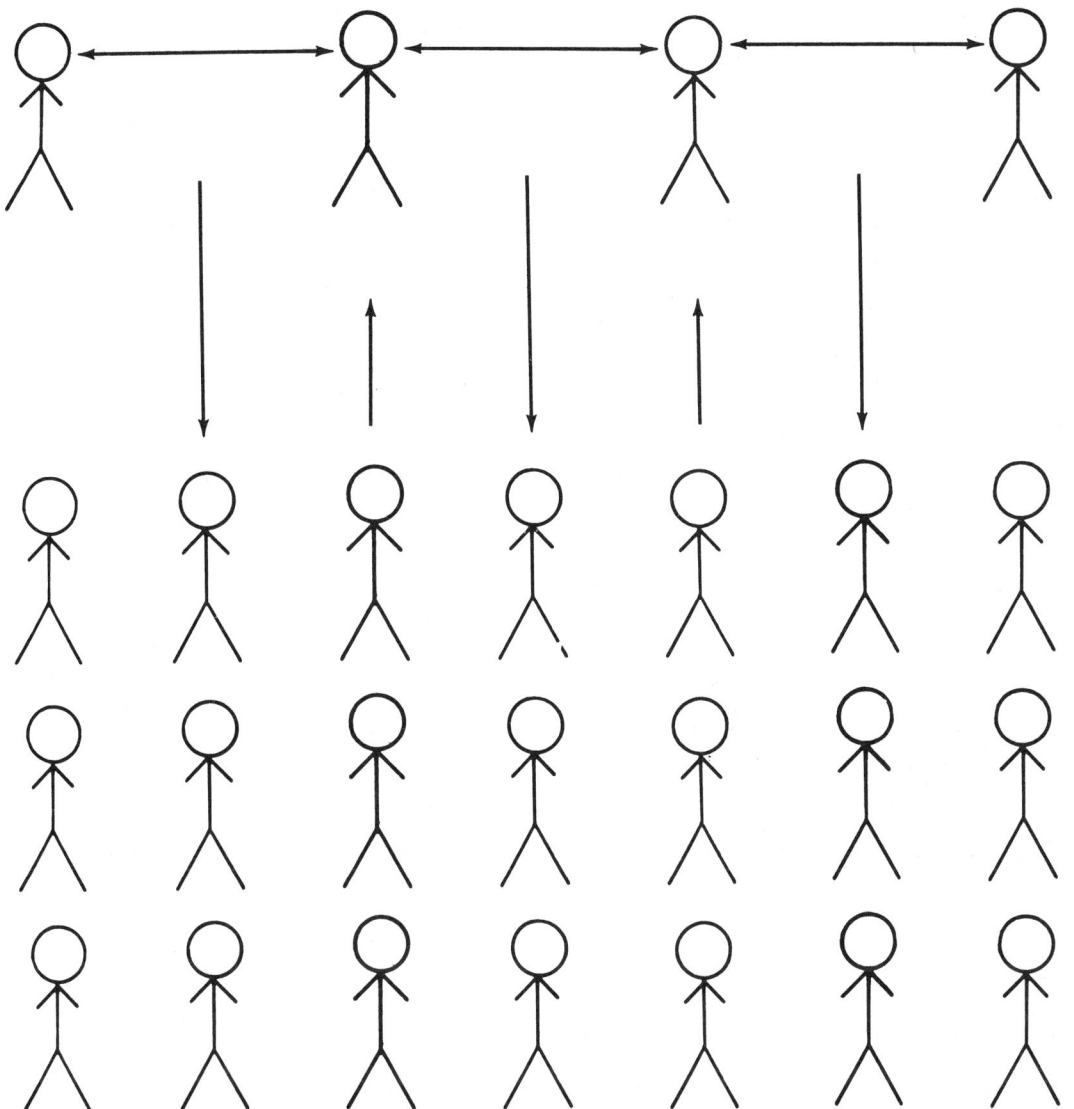

Fig. 9-11 Large-group activities usually begin with a general session where a "telling group" gives information to a "listening group." Toward the end of the session, the listening group is invited to ask questions.

skit, film. A moderator insures that order is kept and that each person gets a chance to voice his views.

- **Symposiums** have more audience listening than active participation. A symposium consists of a series of prepared lectures given by several resource people. Each speaker gives one side of the topic, taking about twenty-five minutes for the presentation. The audience is given time to raise questions from the floor.

To insure the success of large-group activities in parent education, the parent educator must be able to

- Identify topics and techniques that have appeal to parents who are the adult learners.
- Plan and organize a program that gives parents the type of activity most suited to them.
- Obtain the use of adequate space and facilities to accommodate the people who are participating.

- Locate qualified people to take part in the program.
- Advertise the program to reach all groups for whom the event is planned.
- Deal with problems that arise when speakers must cancel out at the last minute and also be able to cope with any other unforeseen problems.
- Work well with people of any race, color, creed, and ethnic identity.

TOPICS TO CONSIDER

There are many topics of concern and interest to parents. Whether learning activities take place in a large or small group is an individual matter. The decision lies in the local situation.

Topics that are too broad can be broken down into subtopics. Listed are areas in which many parents express an interest.

- Alcoholism and Children
- Arts and Crafts for Young Children
- Child Growth and Development
- Child-rearing Practices
- Consumer Education
- Drug Use and Abuse
- Family Finances
- Family Relationships
- Family Fun
- Games for the Whole Family
- Gifted Children and Their Needs
- Health and the Growing Child
- Marriage and Family Relationships
- Mental Retardation and Learning
- Parent-Child Relationships
- Reading Readiness
- Sex Education for Young Children
- Storytelling
- Venereal Disease

WHERE ADULTS CAN LEARN

Every community offers endless opportunities for adult learning. In many cases parents and children can learn together. Other opportunities are geared toward the adult and the problems that he meets in his day-to-day life.

Listed are places where parents can gain information and develop skills to improve the quality of their lives and that of their family.

Established Educational Institutions

- Adult high schools that meet during the day, at night, on weekends, or at all of these times
- Community colleges and technical institutes
- Colleges and universities

Informal Educational Institutions

- Libraries, museums, and art galleries
- Planetariums and zoos
- Concert halls (orchestras) and opera houses (operas)
- Theaters (movies and plays)

Social Organizations

- Church-affiliated learning centers
- Businesses and corporations
- Government agencies
- Unions and other labor groups

Voluntary Organizations

- Local, state, and national organizations
- Churches and other places of worship
- Community clubs
- Councils, committees, and social action groups

Mass Media

- Television shows designed for informal and formal learning experiences
- Radio programs
- Newspapers and magazines
- News bulletins

LEARNING MEDIA

Media for learning refers to anything used to increase the probability that the desired change in behavior takes place. They are the means through which parent educators can put "life" into training programs. Media for learning help parents get, hold, and use what is taught.

The term *learning media* includes more than audiovisual aids, such as films, tapes, and charts. The present focus is on having the adult learn through the use of all his senses: sight, sound, touch, taste, and smell. That is used which is considered best for teaching the needed skill.

Learning media that can spark adult learning are listed. One or more may be used in a given situation.

Seeing

- Books
- Bulletin board displays
- Cartoons and comics
- Catalogs
- Chalkboards
- Charts
- Computer-assisted instruction
- Diagrams
- Dioramas
- Discussion guides
- Displays
- Filmstrips and movies
- Flannelboards
- Globes
- Graphs
- Homemade materials
- Information sheets
- Magazines and periodicals
- Magnetic boards
- Manuals and study guides
- Maps
- Mock-ups
- Models
- Newspapers
- Objects
- Paintings, pictures, posters
- Puppets
- Radio
- Reading lists
- Simulations
- Television
- Slides and specimens
- Worksheets

Hearing

- Computer-assisted-instruction (sound)
- Conference, lecture
- Films (sound)
- Models (with sound)
- Objects (with sound)
- Radio
- Tapes and records
- Television (sound)

Feeling

- Globes
- Models
- Objects
- Samples

Section 3 Parents are Adult Learners

Tasting and Smelling

- Objects
- Samples

Parent education may be compared to selling goods. A sale can be made only when there is something to sell and someone to buy. When people see something that they can use – they will buy. When parents see a program that can help them – they will come. When the program holds their interest – they will stay. Appropriate learning media may help to keep them there.

SUMMARY

Creating adult learning situations for parents is the task of parent education. It is training geared toward a specific adult role, parenting, and is for persons who are already parents. Preparental education refers to training that takes place before a person becomes a parent.

Parent educators include all persons who provide some kind of training for parents. Elements in parent education include methods, techniques, and devices.

Parent education is active learning. It is what parents do that they learn. The training program must provide ways for parents to apply new learnings in their day-to-day lives.

Parent education is seen as a continuous cycle of training events. When one goal is met, another takes its place. The methods of parent-adult education are all the ways by which mature persons learn. The best method is what is best for the learners.

Methods of instruction may include individual study, small-group activities, and large-group activities. Small-groups may include interviews, buzz groups, brainstorming sessions, demonstrations, discussions, seminars, simulations, role-playing, skits, and workshops. Among large-group activities are panels, lectures, forums, and symposiums.

There are many topics that interest parents. Training programs must provide many opportunities for parents to learn what they want to know. Media for learning must be appropriate.

SUGGESTED ACTIVITIES

- Arrange to visit an adult learning situation, such as, evening high school or community college. Observe a class in session.

    a. List the instructor behaviors that you see when teaching-learning takes place.

    b. List the learner behaviors that you see when teaching-learning takes place.

    c. Compare the two lists. Explain why you feel that the learner(s) were or were not actively engaged in the process of learning.

    d. Using the lists of learning media given in this unit, check the media you observe. Tell what learning media you would use if you were the instructor.

- Arrange to observe a training session for teachers, parents, or teacher aides. Identify the learning method used. Tell whether or not you feel the method is appropriate for the group. State reasons for your view.

- Act as an observer in your own class. List any methods, techniques, and media you observe that were mentioned in this unit.

- Select a technique that you would like your class to try. Help your instructor select a topic, plan the activity, and carry out the plan. Discuss the activity and the outcome.

REVIEW

A. Define each of the following.
   1. Parent education
   2. Parent educators
   3. Preparental education
   4. Method
   5. Technique
   6. Device

B. Describe parent education as a continuous cycle of events.

C. List eight small-group activities for adult learning.

D. Compare two adult learning methods, giving reasons why you prefer one of them.

E. List at least fifteen learning media that can be used as visual stimuli to learn.

unit 10 planning workshops

OBJECTIVES

After studying this unit, the student should be able to

- Discuss the general characteristics of a workshop.
- Identify and describe three steps necessary in skill learning during workshop sessions.
- Compare the tasks of the coordinator, staff, and resource person in workshops.
- Describe at least five things that parents can do in workshop situations.

Workshops provide a method for training any group of people interested in a common goal or involved in a common problem. Most are similar in that

- Workshops provide for meeting individual needs. Each learner is able to work out a program of personal study, for which he receives help from the group.
- Workshops offer flexible learning situations. There are times when a participant may wish to drop one activity in favor of another. Effective planning permits people to move at will from one group to another. The staff must be able to meet problems when they arise and still get the job done.
- Successful workshops have the active involvement of all members. Most of the time is spent in small groups where people work on activities that concern them. Buzz groups, role-play, simulations, skits, or special forms of discussion may take place.
- Workshop staffs plan, conduct, and evaluate the activities.

WORKSHOP CHARACTERISTICS

- Provides for meeting individual needs.
- Offers flexible learning situations.
- Requires active involvement of members.
- Promotes self-learning.
- Keeps members involved in "learning by doing."
- Enables members to move about at will.
- Lets people learn from each other and the staff.
- Includes large-group and small-group interaction.
- Permits a wide range of learning activities.
- Makes it possible to have large numbers participate.

Fig. 10-1 A workshop session can meet the needs of a large number of people effectively and efficiently.

Unit 10 Planning Workshops

> **SKILL LEARNING**
> - Build an understanding of the concept.
> - Provide for demonstration, guided practice and positive feedback.
> - Practice at home until the skill is "set."

Fig. 10-2 Shown are three steps in building skills.

- Workshop materials and resources are available to all persons in the group. What is offered is appropriate for the group.
- Workshops promote self-learning by helping members plan what they can do. They carry out their plans at their own direction and at their own rate. They evaluate what they do in terms of goals set as their own.
- Workshops for parents enable them to learn what they are interested in learning instead of what someone else thinks that they should learn. Opportunities for learning are created, but parents must make their own search.
- Workshops may vary in the period of time set for the program. The activity may be concentrated in several hours, or the program may be expanded to several days or weeks.

WORKSHOPS IN TRAINING PROGRAMS

Workshops mean "learning by doing," a concept that has great appeal to adult learners. Parents seeking new and better ways to meet their parenting tasks find workshops a good way to learn from each other and from the workshop staff.

During workshop sessions, parents need to go beyond an imitation of what someone else does. It is important that they learn why a certain task aids the child in his growth and development. When parents recognize the worth of an activity, they are better able to find other tasks of equal value.

Three steps are identified in providing parents with the techniques of skill learning in workshop sessions:

- An understanding of the concept involved is built. Talks, discussions, worksheets, demonstrations, and the like give parents a good view of what is to be done, why it is to be done, and how it is to be done.
- An opportunity is provided for demonstration and guided practice. Parents watch a step-by-step demonstration given by the staff. Individually, or in groups, parents are guided in performing the task successfully. Positive feedback helps to reinforce learning.
- Continued practice brings confidence and competence to parents. When they practice the skill in the home situation, the home visitor gives feedback that helps to "set" the skill.

WORKSHOP PLANNERS

The *coordinator* of a workshop is the person who assumes roles of leadership and guidance in planning and carrying out the program. The listed tasks can be expected of a program coordinator:

- Sees that the right kind of planning group is selected by the program sponsors, or by him.
- Makes sure that members selected for other committees know what their job is and sees that they do it.
- Serves as discussion leader for committees and provides them with information that they need in doing their job.
- Helps to develop objectives for the workshop.
- Knows the elements of a good program and sees that each element is considered.

Section 3 Parents are Adult Learners

COORDINATOR TASKS CONCERNING RESOURCE PERSONS

1. Contact a potential speaker by mail or telephone. Extend the invitation, specifying any funds available to meet his commitment. If he is not to be paid, be sure that this is made known when the invitation is extended.
2. Follow up a telephone call by restating in writing what was said during the telephone conversation.
3. When the speaker confirms his agreement to participate, obtain necessary information:
   - Correct spelling of speaker's name and preferred title: Dr., Mrs., Mr., Miss, Ms.
   - Correct job title, preferred mailing address (home or business), and telephone number for emergency purposes (during workshop).
   - Title of presentation (if self-selected) and requirements for audiovisual aids to be used.
   - Hotel requirements (when speaker comes from a distance).
4. Send out a tentative agenda and time allowed for each presentation (if more than one person is to speak).
5. Obtain a copy of the speaker's vita form, if a news release is to be made.
6. If the speaker travels by air (when funds are available this might apply), someone should meet him at the airport. If it is not possible to meet him, he should know in advance where he is to go, and how he is to get there.

Fig. 10-3 To avoid any misunderstandings, the coordinator must give and get all necessary information.

- Gathers information that is needed concerning the location of the workshop, participants and their training needs, budgets, and the role of sponsors.
- Gives information to resource persons and helps them to know what is expected of them.
- Reviews any evaluation data available from prior workshops that can be helpful in planning the present one.
- Keeps sponsors, or policy-making group, informed as necessary.

The workshop *staff* consists of all persons who are responsible for carrying out the program. They may or may not be the people who did the planning. Staff members may serve in one or more of the following capacities: instructor, resource person, discussion leader.

Resource persons are people who are usually brought in from outside to contribute a special skill, information, or opinion that is related to the workshop goals. Resource persons are most helpful when they have had experience with the kinds of problems that face the group.

There is a wide range of skills that resource people can bring to workshops. They can

- Show the group how to perform a new teaching technique.
- Share experiences that help the group to gain insight into the solution of their own problems.
- Demonstrate skills in role-playing, panel discussions, and use of learning media or contribute other skills that help the group to learn.

PLANNING TASKS

Committees are organized to deal with decisions that must be made in planning the workshop. No hard-and-fast rule can be made in stating which committee is to perform

COMMITTEES HELPFUL IN PLANNING AND CONDUCTING WORKSHOPS

Committee	Tasks
Program	• Develops program plans in detail.
	• Finds people for the program.
	• Selects training staff for the workshop.
Arrangements	• Makes arrangements for rooms, equipment, audiovisual aids, supplies, coffee breaks.
Hospitality	• Greets workshop members.
	• Assumes responsibility for any social activities (receptions, luncheons).
	• Performs courtesy services for members.
Registration	• Provides people and equipment for registration.
Publicity	• Brings public attention to workshop.
	• Sees that potential members hear about it.
	• Arranges television and radio spots.
	• Prepares and gives out news releases, if appropriate.
Exhibits	• Arranges for needed space.
	• Recruits exhibitors when desirable.
Evaluation	• Decides how the success of the workshop can be measured.
	• Prepares and collects information after the workshop.
Reports	• Determines what records must be kept.
	• Decides how to share workshop results.

Fig. 10-4 Shown are some workshop committees. How many are used is based on the local situation.

what tasks. Nor can a rule-of-thumb be given to state how many committees are needed.

The following tasks must be met in planning most workshops. Each group decides how many work groups are needed and which tasks each committee is to perform.

- Program objectives are established. Problems to be dealt with are identified. General information to be presented and behavioral changes to take place are part of the planning decisions.

- Participants are identified. Learning experiences are planned to meet their needs. The number of people that can take part is set.

- A location and calendar date are selected. Meeting rooms are reserved as required. Arrangements are made for coffee breaks or meals that are to be included.

- Promotion and publicity help are organized. What is to be advertised and how the information is to be given are important decisions. If notices are to be mailed, it is necessary to consider duplicating costs, postage, and envelopes in the budget. A member of the group may contact radio, television, and newspaper reporters if the workshop meets the requirements for full coverage (spreading the word far and wide).

- Each session in the workshop is designed to be an effective learning situation. Techniques to be used and appropriate learning media are selected. Sometimes a resource packet is prepared to "brief" the participants. Schedules, rooms, and information about resource people and staff members are often among the briefing materials.

- Provision is made for administrative tasks: supplies (name tags, registration, signs), equipment, stenographic help, and janitor and custodial services.
- The cost of the workshop and financing problems are crucial. Limited funds can lead to only limited activities.

WHAT PARENTS CAN DO IN A WORKSHOP

The number of things that parents can do in a workshop seems endless. Listed are some activities that have been successful in workshops for parents of young children.

- Making toys and educational games for children.
- Experimenting with art materials.
- Exploring the world of science to discover ways that young children can learn through their five senses.
- Learning to use filmstrip and movie projectors, tape recorders, and learning machines available for home use.
- Designing and using puppets in storytelling.
- Participating in dramatic play to develop skills for home use.
- Role-playing situations that take place in their homes, as a means of finding possible solutions to problems.
- Examining children's books in the light of what makes a book appropriate for a young child.
- Being exposed to information and material that help them to learn more about child growth and development.
- Viewing and discussing movies that show how children grow and develop in a way that is natural for them.
- Engaging in body movement and dance activities that they can carry out with their own children.
- Discussing in the group, a home teaching-learning situation with their children that the workshop planners televised for the workshop.
- Watching a television show for children and exploring ways to make the program a learning experience for their children.

HOW WORKSHOPS ARE CONDUCTED

A workshop usually begins with a general session that brings together the entire group. Important information is fed to participants. What is said, and how it is handled, depends upon the purpose for which the workshop is conducted. A one-day workshop may proceed along these lines:

- **Opening session** to present person(s) responsible for the program: sponsors (when appropriate), coordinator, staff members, resource persons.
- **Introductory statements** to describe the procedure to be followed.
- **Information** to provide participants with background information on the topic or central theme to be covered. A large-group format is used: lecture, panel, symposium, or whatever serves best the workshop purpose.
- **Question-answer period** to give members an opportunity to ask the speaker(s) questions concerning what was said. Sometimes questions raised by the "listening group" are discussed in small group sessions that follow.
- **Coffee break** (about 15 minutes) to give the group a chance to stretch and

circulate. Social interaction between members of the group helps to bind them into a teamlike spirit.

- **Members divide into small groups** for discussions, demonstrations, practice under expert guidance, or for whatever is the purpose of the small group.

- **Recess.** A luncheon meeting may include a guest speaker. If not, social interaction between members is the behavioral goal. Sometimes no luncheon arrangements are made, so that the group can make their own contacts. Workshop packets often include a list of eating places, stressing those that are inexpensive, to help members suit their own tastes, food and funds.

- **Afternoon Session.** When the afternoon session opens, one of two options is used in most cases. In one way, small-group sessions continue, summarizing their work for a later large-group session. In another way, the large-group meets again for a particular purpose, or discussion, which is followed by more small-group action.

- **A final session** gives members an opportunity to learn about the small-group activities. Reports may be given. Summary statements are made by persons assigned the task. Members may receive a copy of the summary later.

- **Exhibits** are handled according to who is exhibiting, and what is shown. Members usually have an opportunity to see exhibits before, during, or after the workshop. When book exhibits are included among exhibitors, it may be necessary to pack materials before the close of the workshop. Planners should make sure that there is a time set aside for seeing exhibits.

A WORKSHOP IN ACTION

A college instructor wants to provide preservice teachers with an opportunity to develop their skills as early childhood educators. Included among the skills identified is the ability to work with parents to help them become teachers of their own children.

The instructor arranges

- To place students in a local preschool center where they work one or two hours each week. They are involved in using the educational games and toys that they make in connection with their course work.

- To give a workshop for parents to show them how to make some of the toys and games that their children enjoy.

Workshop Objectives

The workshop is designed as a *culminating* (end of unit) activity for the course. The preservice teachers are to demonstrate that they are able to

- Select learning activities that meet the needs, interest, and abilities of the children.

- Make worthwhile games and toys that can help skill-learning.

- Work with the children to achieve goals that can be met with homemade materials.

Fig. 10-5 Early childhood students are planning a workshop session.

Section 3 Parents are Adult Learners

- Show parents how to make educational games and toys and to carry out other learning activities for their children.
- Prepare and televise a lesson that shows what the preservice teachers do when they work with the children. Show and discuss the tape during the workshop.
- Present, for parent discussion, a film that shows how children grow and learn in a manner that is natural for them.
- Help parents to develop new skills as they teach their own children.
- Work effectively with parents of young children.

Committees and Plans

Committees are set up to accomplish the following tasks. Work groups set their own procedures and get their jobs done.

- Workshop plans are prepared. Decisions are made concerning what is to be done, who is to do it, and in what way it is to be done.
- Waste materials are collected to be used during game and toy-making sessions.
- Arrangements are made to borrow ready-made materials from the local toy-lending library.
- A display of library materials is planned: books, games, toys, records.
- A preregistration form is prepared and sent to parents. An interest inventory is included to find out which of the listed items are of interest to parents. The inventory helps planners to provide what parents want and need.
- Arrangements are made for news release in the local newspaper. Photographs and a follow-up story are to be done during the workshop.
- A list of waste materials needed is posted in several places on campus. Students arrange to pick up whatever is available.
- Handouts are prepared for the workshop sessions.
- Requests are sent to companies that offer free materials that can be used in workshop packets. Other stores give usable items for the packets: pencils with company labels, small calendars, English-to-metric-system conversion charts, calorie charts, shopping-list pads, and other items used for advertising. Donators are acknowledged in the workshop program.
- Arrangements are made with a local food vendor to fill orders given at the time of the workshop registration (for a scheduled lunch hour). (CAUTION: Money is collected before the order is telephoned. A receipt is given, and each person's name is recorded on a checklist. Meals are distributed to those who return their receipts.)

The Action

9:00-9:30 Registration

- Parents arrive and are greeted by the hospitality committee. Name tags are made.

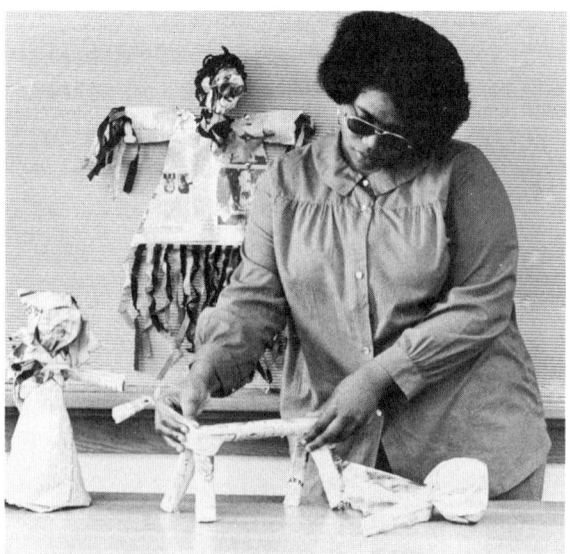

Fig. 10-6 A popular activity is newspaper art.

Unit 10 Planning Workshops

WORKSHOP CHECKLIST

1. Meeting room arrangements (items selected as appropriate):
   - Chairs and tables in number needed.
   - Rostrum and microphones.
   - Audiovisual equipment, screens, and operator.
   - Electric or wooden pointer.
   - Chalkboard with chalk and eraser.
   - Flip chart stand (if required).
   - Recording equipment and operator (when taping sessions).
   - Lighting system.
   - Signs as needed for meeting room (or rooms).
   - Coffee and soft drinks for breaks.
   - Provisions for smokers and nonsmokers (separate sections)
2. Registration area:
   - Signs as required to assist in registration.
   - Personnel to man registration desk.
   - Telephone and typewriters (or access to them).
   - Registration packets — agenda, name tags, announcements and brochures, handouts when needed.
   - Bulletin board to post messages (usually needed when meetings are large, or extend over several days).
   - Supplies: paper, pencils, pens, tape, stapler, message forms, clips, eraser, scissors, magic marker, etc.
3. Press room (usually required only when workshops are part of a large conference or convention).
   - Tables, chairs
   - Typewriters
   - Telephone
   - TV coverage
4. Miscellaneous information:
   - Transportation information.
   - Eating arrangements and receptions (if required).
   - Instructions/information for speakers.
   - Duplicating facilities (if required).
   - Attendance certificates (often given during large conferences, conventions, and workshops).

Fig. 10-7 A comprehensive workshop checklist. Items are selected to accommodate the size and requirements of the workshop.

- Parents circulate in the room with exhibits. They see a display of things that preservice teachers have used in working with the preschool children.

- Several college classrooms are used for the workshop. Parents visit each room to see bulletin boards and materials on display.

Section 3 *Parents are Adult Learners*

9:30-10:30 Meeting of the Total Workshop

- The group is greeted. College students do this.
- Members are asked to introduce themselves and shake hands with the person sitting next to them. This breaks the ice and the workshop is underway.
- Staff members are introduced. Workshop procedures are explained in a very brief talk.
- The professor is identified as the resource person. The topic: *Creative Activities for Children.* An interesting presentation includes slides, a skit, and audience participation in songs and fingerplays for children. Concepts covered by the resource person include music, art activities, mathematics games, play, and craft work.

10:30-10:40 Question-Answer Period

- Questions are raised and answered.
- A recorder makes notes of the questions asked by parents.

10:40-10:50 Coffee Break

- Members relax and move about the area.
- Soft drinks are available (with charge) for those persons who do not drink coffee.

10:50-11:50 Small-group Sessions

- Each of four rooms is set up as a learning center for the topics covered by the resource person: music, art activities and craft work, mathematics, games, play. (College students are in charge.)
- Parents move at will from one learning station to another. College students guide parents in the selection of tasks. Tape-recorded explanations of games are available at some tables.
- In the craft class, parents receive shopping bags for storing the things they get and the things they make.
- The resource person moves from one learning station to another to make sure that all goes well.

11:50-1:00 Lunch Break

- Members exchange their receipts for the lunch. Soft drinks are available (for a charge).
- Salt, pepper, napkins, and water in paper cups are available. A trash can is ready for the cleanup.
- No speaker is available, but in one corner of the room, slides are shown. An explanatory tape recording is played during the lunch period. Interested persons may sit there.
- Several tables are reserved for persons who do not smoke.

1:00-2:00 Small-group Sessions Continue

- Members may visit other groups or continue what they were doing during the morning session.
- A film is shown in the large-group meeting room. There is time to repeat the movie, so that everyone can see it. This is an extra offering to accommodate those parents who do not wish to continue the activity-type learning.

2:00-2:15 Break

- Drinks are available.
- Members return to the large-group room.

2:15-3:00 Large-group Activity

- Activities during this time vary. Parents share with others what they have made. A discussion follows involving parents in describing ways that the materials can be used at home.

- The resource person guides the parents in the direction of role-play. Cards are distributed describing what is to be done. Some members received blank cards on which they are to make up their own role-play activity. College students and parents team up for the role-play. Photographs may be taken for the local newspaper.

3:00-3:15 Summary and Evaluation

- Program activities are summarized.
- Evaluation forms are completed by participants.
- The group departs.

After-Action Report

The workshop staff prepares a complete report of all action. Facts about committees, program, resource materials, and participants are recorded. Newspaper releases and other publicity are included. Photographs of learning stations are valuable data for persons planning workshops at some future time. The evaluation results are a part of the report.

The implications are that college students and their instructor can be used in home-based early education programs. With the barest minimum in funds, the instructor can invite parents to participate in making course work an interesting learning experience for all persons involved:

- The preservice teachers who have a real laboratory for learning.
- The children who profit by what the college students do with them and with their parents.
- The instructor who finds new and better ways to help people learn.

SUMMARY

A workshop is a method for training any group of people who are interested in a common goal or involved in a common problem. Workshops provide for meeting individual needs. They are flexible. They require the active involvement of all members of the group. Workshop means "learning by doing."

Three steps in skill learning are (1) understanding the concept involved, (2) demonstrations and guided practice, and (3) continued practice until the skill is set.

Workshop planners include a coordinator who assumes leadership roles, and a staff that gets the job done. Resource people provide special skills, information, or opinions that are related to workshop goals.

Committees are responsible for seeing that their respective tasks are carried out in planning and conducting the workshop. The number of committees needed is based on the local situation.

Parents can be actively involved in making toys and games for their children, experimenting with materials, role-playing, and taking part in many other activities.

Workshops usually begin with a general session that brings together the entire group. Provision is made for small-group activities. People work on things that interest them.

A summary usually ends the workshop. An after-action report is a record of

- What the workshop was about.
- Who planned and carried out the activities.
- Who took part in the workshop.
- What happened during the workshop sessions.
- What people learned as shown in their evaluation of their experiences in the workshop.

Section 3 Parents are Adult Learners

SUGGESTED ACTIVITIES

- Plan a workshop for parents that you can do with your peer-group. "How to" suggestions follow:

  a. Make a list of topics with the aid of the class.

  b. When all topics have been given, discuss them with the class.

  c. Select the topic that interests the majority of the group.

  d. Have the group plan with committees.

  e. Present the workshop for the group.

  f. Evaluate the experience with your classmates.

  g. Get the feedback from your instructor.

- Following procedures suggested by your instructor, make arrangements to attend a workshop in a school nearby. Ask if you may observe; an invitation to participate may be extended. Make a report to your class.

- See if you can present a workshop for parents in a nearby preschool center. Perhaps your instructor will offer to serve as resource person for the group.

- Find books that tell about workshops. List good ideas.

REVIEW

A. Define each of the following.

   1. Workshop
   2. Coordinator
   3. Workshop staff
   4. Resource person
   5. Skill-learning

B. List and briefly describe five characteristics of a workshop.

C. Briefly answer each of the following.

   1. What is meant by the statement, "Workshops mean 'learning by doing' "?

   2. Why do workshops usually begin with a general session?

   3. Using the skill learning procedure described in this unit as your guide, tell about a learning experience that you had in which the selected procedure was or was not used. Tell what effect the procedure that was used had on your ability to truly learn the skill.

   4. Using the skill learning procedure, tell how you would teach a young child how to do something: tie a shoelace, put his toys away, clean a paint brush, fasten a zipper, or perform another task that he needs to know.

Section 4 Child Development and Parent Enablers

unit 11 viewing human development

OBJECTIVES

After studying this unit, the student should be able to

- Define and describe the following terms: child development, growth, maturation, development, learning, givens.
- Identify at least five ways that children grow and develop along lines that are similar.
- Describe three different views of development.
- Discuss the four areas of child growth and development: identify the area, describe it, and give examples.

Parents who want to help their children may find information in books, newspapers, magazines and on television or radio shows. They may gain ideas from these sources that are sometimes difficult for them to understand because the viewpoints given are often inconsistent. A suggestion that parents find in one source may be rejected in another. The result is that they are often confused and do not know what to believe.

DEFINING GROWTH AND DEVELOPMENT

All persons who work with children need knowledge which helps them as individuals decide what advice to accept and what to reject. Needed is an understanding of the factors that enter into growth and development. Knowing the young child and his needs enables parents to create an environment that helps the process.

Important Definitions and Descriptions

When people talk about the same thing, each may give his words a different meaning. This can cause confusion about what is said. The following terms are defined and described to give a common frame of reference to the present discussion.

Child Development. *Child development* refers to the process, or series of steps, that take place in a child through time as he changes from a helpless newborn to a person of some independence. Four terms are commonly used to describe the process: growth, maturation, development, and learning.

Growth. *Growth* deals with some increase in size such as height, head size, or some other physical dimension. It may be seen as an increase in quantity. For example, a child's body is much larger at three months that it was at birth.

Maturation. *Maturation* refers to the process by which a child grows from within. It applies to his inner, organic forces that help him to grow as an individual. Maturation can be viewed as an increase in quality. An example is the fact that a child sits before he stands.

He draws a circle before he draws a square. A certain degree of physical maturation is basic to the use of his physical powers.

In the first stages of his life, the child's physical powers have a great effect on all other powers. His goal is the immediate satisfaction of his physical drives. When he is hungry he cries for food and demands it at once. When he is tired, he may squirm, fidget, or cry.

Development. *Development* refers to a stage that the child achieves at any particular time in his growth and maturation process and that can be described. When the outside forces in the child's environment come in contact with his inside forces of maturation, development takes place. For example, the child eats nourishing food and runs and plays in the sunshine. Development is the product of his inner forces that use the food, exercise, and sunshine to help him grow and mature.

Learning. *Learning* is defined as a change in behavior that takes place when an individual interacts with his environment, fills a need, and is thereby able to deal with that environment. Learning is active. A person learns by what he does, not by the action of someone else. An example is a child watching a person working with finger paints. Although his observation may lead him to know what to do, the child does not really learn finger painting until he does it himself. His "need" is the desire to know and do.

Learning is a many-sided concept. There are many *theories* (educated guesses, explanations, or bets) about the way learning occurs. A brief look at some of the theories follows.

- *Developmental theory:* Learning occurs because growth simply takes place. The child goes through stages of development that all humans follow. A simple task must be learned before a more complex one can follow. The learner is seen as one who wants to become all that he is capable of becoming, over time.

- *Reinforcement theory:* Learning takes place because people of all ages respond to rewards and punishments. If a behavior is rewarded, it is likely to be repeated — and learned. If a behavior is punished, it is stopped — to avoid or end that punishment.

- *Association theory:* Learning takes place because people, and animals, respond automatically to certain kinds of stimuli. A nurse dressed in a white uniform may give a baby an immunization shot. The child experiences pain. An association is made between the white uniform and the pain that the wearer of the uniform makes the child experience. The baby subsequently fears any person dressed in white. From his experience

Fig. 11-1 Children may watch their parents dance, but they do not really "know" about dancing until they try it for themselves.

he has learned that white and pain are related. He learns to fear everything "white."

- *Cognitive theory:* Learning takes place because the child uses his present mental ability to learn as much as he can. New concepts and ideas gained are used to help him learn in new and more difficult situations. In effect the child is seen as the organizer of his own experiences.

What parents need to know is that there is no one way that is "best" for learning. What works for one child may not be successful with another. What produces appropriate behavior for a child at one age may bring the very opposite behavior when he is older. For example, a young child may lose interest in something that he is told he may not have. An older child's interest may increase if told the same thing.

Parents can be guided in trying different approaches, depending on the particular situation and the particular child's needs. They may find encouragement in the fact that there are options.

A good rule to follow is — if it works, use it. Parents need to know that acquiring the skills necessary for learning is more important than acquiring different kinds of information. For example, being able to count the right number of forks needed at the dinner table is more important than saying numbers without understanding.

Rote learning, repeating facts without understanding, may keep the child from being actively involved in the learning process. Parents need to know that placing too much emphasis on rote learning may prevent the child from the kind of experiences that lead to learning. By setting up an environment that involves the child with objects, ideas, and actions, parents encourage all kinds of learning.

FACTORS IN HUMAN DEVELOPMENT

Each child grows and develops along lines that form a very similar pattern. In most essential ways, children are more alike than they are different. Parents and others who guide them require an understanding of principles which affect the child's growth and development.

Fig. 11-2 A corner for themselves provides children with an opportunity to plan and direct their own learning experiences. Each child becomes an "organizer."

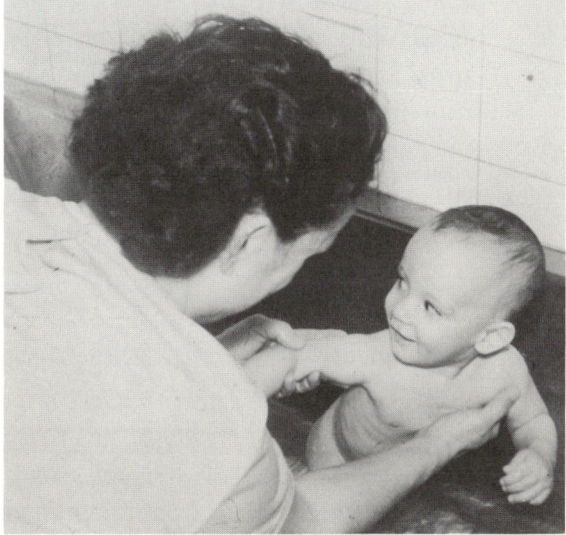

Fig. 11-3 Physical, intellectual, social and emotional growth are interrelated and tend to proceed together. A baby's bath promotes his physical well-being and helps him to learn through all of his senses.

If his environment does not deprive him of normal growth, each child follows a sequence that is much the same:

- Growth is a continuous process but is not always steady.

- Physical, intellectual, social, and emotional growth are interrelated and tend to proceed together.

- Functioning in one area of development cannot really be understood without taking a look at each of the other areas.

- Behavior is influenced by the needs of the child.

- The child and his peers react in basically the same ways to people and things in their environment: fear, interest, cooperation, aggression, and withdrawal.

- The child goes from a state of dependence to increasing independence.

- All children require feelings of personal satisfaction, satisfaction in relation to others, and satisfaction in relation to things.

- Social skills grow out of feelings of security and confidence that the child gains from interactions with the people, objects, and events in his world.

- All children are interested in learning about the world in which they live.

Factors Which Affect Growth and Development

A discussion of factors which affect growth and development really begins before birth, during the period of prenatal growth. *Prenatal growth* takes place from the moment of conception until the time of birth which is normally nine months later. To insure the healthy development of her unborn child, the mother must

- Receive medical care to prevent conditions that can harm her physically (infections, excessive weight gain, anemia, high blood pressure).

- Eat properly, exercise according to the doctor's orders, and get rest to avoid fatigue.

- Avoid smoking, unnecessary medicines, and exposure to x-rays that can have serious effects on the growing fetus.

- Seek tests, when needed, that can detect any one of many problems that could be present in the unborn child. Knowing if problems exist can help

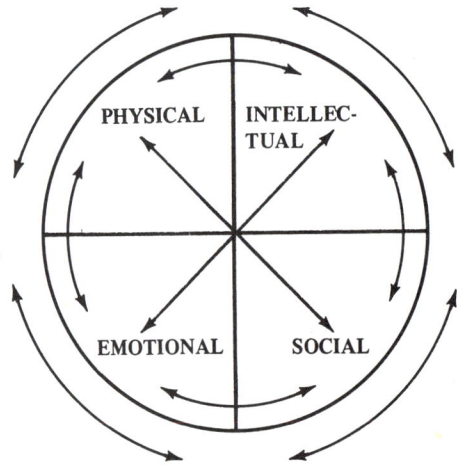

Fig. 11-4 All areas of child growth and development are interrelated. Something that affects one area influences the other areas.

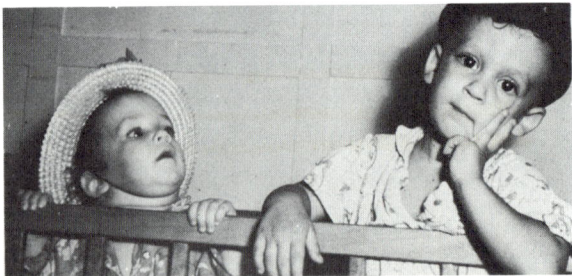

Fig. 11-5 Behavior is influenced by the needs of the child. Shown is a four-year-old who finds that his baby sister is not the responsive playmate that he seeks.

doctors take any available measures to lower the child's chance of birth defects.

The concern for health includes that of the father as well as of the mother of the unborn child. The presence of disease, such as syphilis, may infect the mother. In turn, her infection does harm to the unborn child. A doctor must take appropriate steps to protect the unborn child.

When a child comes into the world and grows, he is more like other children than he is different. He is like others; he is also a unique individual unlike all others. It is necessary that parents understand and respect these differences in order to meet the child's individual needs.

Every child comes into the world with his own set of *givens* — the characteristics, traits, and features that make him unique. Givens in a real sense are what nature gives him at the moment of conception.

There is little that can be done to change the impact that his givens may have on the child's development. They set the limit on what he can achieve in life even with the best opportunities. For example, a child may have little interest or ability in playing the piano. No amount of training can force the child to become a concert pianist, if his givens fail to lead him in that direction. He may learn to play, but the quality of his performance can not place him at the concert level.

It is important that parents understand that a child has limits. Knowing about limits helps the parents to find his assets and promote their development.

- The child is shaped by the interaction of his inborn heredity, the world around him, and his individual differences. His personality trends result from his givens, early experiences, and conditions that continually recur.
- Each child is a changing person who is affected by the society and culture in which he lives. Each comes from a different background of experience and has developed different understandings. Each moves through growth sequences toward maturity at his own rate.

Different Views of Development

Attempts to describe development — and what it is that takes place in the child — result in many different viewpoints. It is not important to go into a discussion of theory. But it is helpful for parents to know that what takes place can be seen from at least three major viewpoints.

One view is that development can be described as changes that take place in the child as he grows and matures as his nature intends. Parents can understand this view better when the child is compared to plants with potential for growth.

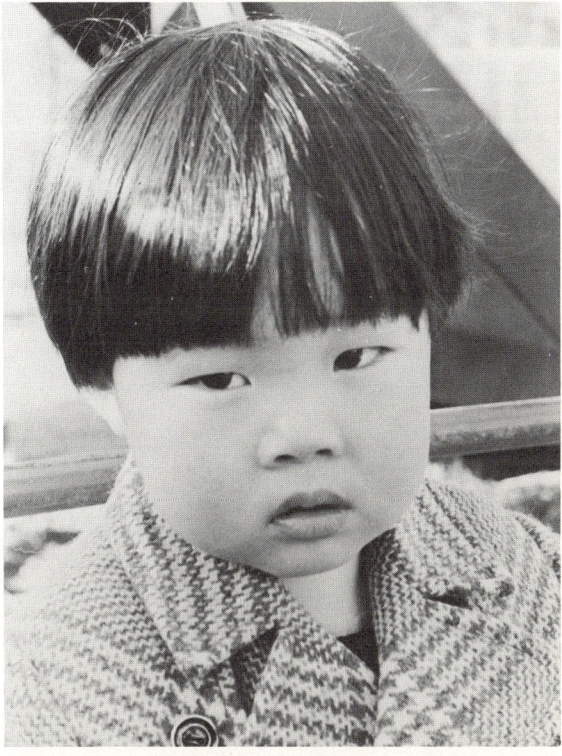

Fig. 11-6 All children are interested in learning about the world in which they live. The ability to "see" is an important part of a child's development.

For example, when plants are cultivated and receive nutrition from sun, soil, and water — something that they get from outside — they grow. The young child also has potential for growth. He grows and develops in a warm, comfortable setting that lets him meet his needs and explore his natural interests. But, only when there is potential inside can full growth take place.

Another view is that development can be described as changes that take place in the child as he responds to stimuli in his environment. It is through *nurture* (environmental influences) that he learns.

The child imitates what he sees others doing. Rewards that he gets increase the likelihood that he repeats the response. Punishment may cause him to avoid or stop the response completely. When a child sees his parents doing something, he imitates what he sees as something worthy of imitation. What he sees and does is what he learns.

According to this view it is important for the child to see people model the kind of behavior that is expected of him. He needs the presence of adults who themselves act in accepted ways. He needs their rewards for his behavior when they feel it is good and worthwhile.

Fig. 11-8 While providing toys that develop the "mothering" concept, parents must not lose sight of the fact that young girls, too, need things that they can get into, ride, explore, and build.

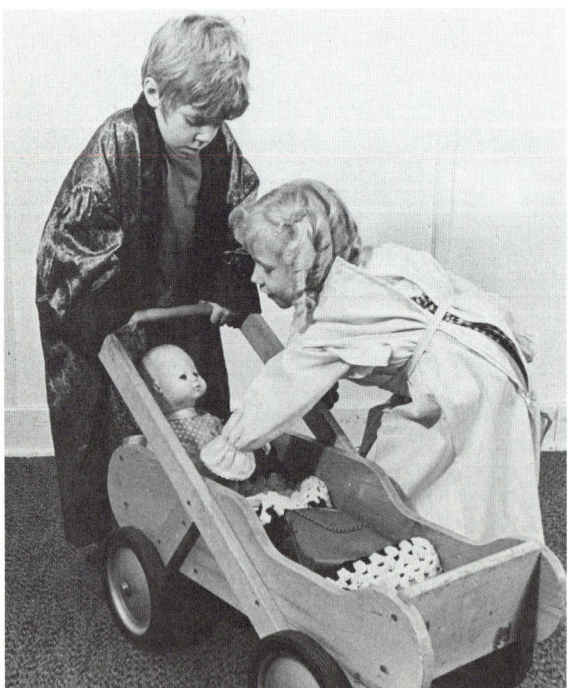

Fig. 11-7 All children need opportunities by which they can role-play family life activities.

Fig. 11-9 Children imitate what they see others doing. It is important that parents let their children see them reading to develop the idea that reading is a worthwhile activity.

A third view describes development as a middle ground between the approaches of nature and nurture. Both are seen as being equally active in shaping the child's development.

The explanation of this view is not yet complete. Even so, the middle ground is divided into two parts. One places emphasis on the emotions and personality development of the individual. The other emphasizes the need for each person to construct a cognitive map for himself.

A *cognitive map* is made up of all the concepts (interrelated ideas and experiences) which a person develops and uses to guide his behavior. The map evolves from experiences that begin in infancy. It can be compared to a storage bank of information from which a person draws from his past to understand something in his present life.

The middle ground has five sets of influences that affect the way that human growth and development takes place from birth to adulthood:

- Maturation and genetic factors.
- Experience gained in the environment.
- Givens that enable developmental tasks.
- Encounters with other people who share their world of objects, places, ideas, and events.

AREAS OF CHILD GROWTH AND DEVELOPMENT

There are four important areas of child growth and development that must be considered in any attempt to know the child and his needs. These are the physical, the intellectual, the emotional, and the social.

No real division exists because each area is somewhat dependent on and is influenced by the others. They are divided only in an attempt to understand the child better. The division makes it easier to explain the areas to the parents.

Physical Growth

A child's physique and rate of growth are individual matters which may be the product of factors that influence him. Included are givens, nutrition, illnesses, disease immunity, and the balance of glands that control growth.

The child's body responds in its own way to the world around it. The nature of the child's environment can promote or prevent his well-being. An environment that meets his basic needs helps the child to be a happy, healthy person. He is able to learn new things and get along with others. An environment that deprives the child of his basic needs prevents him from becoming all that he can be.

To reach his full growth, every child needs

- Well-balanced, nutritious meals and snacks to restore his energy.
- Both active and quiet activities during his day, with time for exercise and needed rest.
- Protection from harm and a safe environment to grow in.
- Necessary health care and preventive services to insure his future health.

The child's physical growth brings with it his physical identity. He learns about his body by using it. He learns how it looks and works, what it needs, and what the different parts can do for him.

Through his five senses, seeing, hearing, smelling, feeling and tasting, he learns what gives him pleasure and what gives him pain. He is fed when he is hungry. He is held and comforted to make him feel loved and wanted. He is clothed and made comfortable. Through every type of stimulus he receives, the child learns to recognize his physical needs and their associated feelings.

Children may be small in size, but they like to feel "big." A child who wants to do something, or does it well, may say, "Johnny is a big boy." If he is asked to draw a picture of himself, he may draw a person who is physically big.

Parents can help the child by reinforcing the "big" things that he does by himself. A child who is encouraged to think "big" is "big" in his own mind.

Mental Growth

Mental growth is the development of

- The ability to gain and hold knowledge.
- The mental skills necessary to use knowledge: ability to think, plan, remember, imagine, judge, decide, and solve problems.

Intellectual growth is active, manipulative, sensory. It involves *cognition*, mental growth and activity — the act or process of knowing.

Cognition takes root during the early years when the young child's curiosity gives him the urge to reach out in his environment. He wants to touch, taste, smell, ask "why."

Discussion concerning the effects of heredity and environment on the child's intellectual development is an age-old battle. The present view sees both heredity and environment as important in all areas of a child's growth.

Parents can do much to help the child develop his givens in an environment that promotes learning. They can

- Help the child to trust his world and the people in it. He needs to feel secure and safe, before he is ready to explore his world and accept new knowledge.
- Provide ways for him to use his body and learn what it can do: run, jump, climb, cut, paste, dance. He needs to develop his large and small muscles through activities that use them. He must do things that make him think.
- Teach him to reason and generalize. He needs to have time to think, plan, and make decisions that affect him.
- Give him experiences that promote language development. He needs to talk things over; tell how he feels about things; listen to stories, poems, records; and take part in other language-building activities.
- Provide him with all that he needs to develop a healthy body that can help to create a healthy mind.

Emotional Growth

Emotional growth refers to the feelings and desires that the child has and the ways through which he learns to deal with them. How he responds is closely related to how he feels about himself.

Fig. 11-10 Children may be small in size, but they like to feel "big." With his brother's hat on, Johnny *is* a "big" boy.

- A child who has a healthy self-image likes himself and believes he is a worthwhile person. If he does not like himself — or if he believes others do not like him — he may show this in his behavior. He may become aggressive or withdrawn to hide his feelings. He may hit or hurt another child because he himself hurts inside.

- What a child learns about himself comes from those who love him and those he loves. Every child needs to feel wanted and loved. He needs to know that there are people who care what happens to him. He needs to know that his parents enjoy him and like him, just the way he is.

- The child who feels safe, secure, and wanted in his home and expanding community develops a sense of value and self-esteem. He is willing to try new things, because those he loves have confidence in him and in his ability to do things for himself and by himself.

- A child who thinks well of himself is able to accept limits set on his behavior. His trust in his parents helps him to do what they say is good for him. By accepting limits, he learns to cope with things that do not go his way.

- A child needs many opportunities to be with other children to learn how to control himself and get along with others.

Social Growth

Social growth refers to the child's progress in how he acts and reacts during interactions with others in his environment. Although all children pass through the same patterns of growth, life experiences bring happiness to some and leave others unhappy.

Differences in how life treats the child may result in differences in his personality. Some children may be friendly and cooperative. Others may be hostile or timid.

Each child responds in his own way to the people in his life. In turn, he is affected by these same social relationships.

Parents who recognize the importance of a child's experiences in his social group may be able to help the process.

- The child learns how to act in a group, by imitating those he cares about. A child who sees the socially accepted behavior of his parents accepts it as a model for himself. Parents must remember that their child does what he sees them do.

- The child learns to listen by having others listen to him. It is important for parents to talk with — not to — the child. Communication is a two-way street for parents and their child.

- The child learns to be polite when others are polite in their dealings with him. The words he uses and the things he says are a reflection of what he hears and sees in his world.

SUMMARY

All persons who work with children need some guidelines to help them know what to accept and what to reject in what they read and hear about children.

Concepts that are important in the study of child development include growth, maturation, development, and learning. How these words are defined and described depends upon the point of view taken.

Four major viewpoints are sketched to explain the concept of learning: (1) learning occurs because growth simply takes place; (2) learning takes place because people of all ages respond to rewards and punishments; (3) learning takes place because people respond automatically to certain kinds of stimuli;

Section 4 Child Development and Parent Enablers

and (4) learning takes place because the child uses his present mental ability to understand new concepts.

Children grow and develop in ways that follow a similar pattern. As they are alike, so are children unique persons.

People differ in their beliefs concerning what takes place and what it is that develops. Views include nature (heredity, or givens), nurture (environment) and a middle view that is in between.

Areas of child growth and development include physical growth, intellectual growth, emotional growth, and social growth.

SUGGESTED ACTIVITIES

- Arrange to observe a young child. Plan five one-hour visits.

    a. Get several sheets of paper. Fold them into four parts. For each square on a page write the words: physical, intellectual, social, emotional.

    b. Write in the appropriate space behaviors that you can see. Be objective. If you want to include what you **think** about the situation, write your notes on the other side of the sheet.

    c. Continue to observe the child over a period of five weeks. Use a separate sheet of paper for each observation. Be sure to put the date on each sheet.

    d. At the end of the five-week period, examine each growth area very carefully. Look for

    (1) Behaviors that continue to recur.
    (2) Behaviors that decrease or stop altogether.
    (3) Behaviors that show that the child is developing skill in the area.

    e. Make a summary of your observations for each area.

    f. Write a page or two telling about the child's growth and development as you see it, based on your observations.

    g. Share your findings with your class.

    h. Compare the child that you observed with one that a classmate observed.

    (1) In what ways the growth patterns are alike.
    (2) In what ways the growth patterns are different.
    (3) The behaviors that make each child a unique person.

    i. Discuss your experience as one in which you learned by "doing."

- Plan a panel discussion with members of your class. Discuss one of the growth areas: physical, intellectual, emotional, and social.

- Interview several parents. Ask them to share some of the problems that they have in helping their children in one of the growth areas. Carefully avoid questions that are too personal (i.e., "invasion of privacy"). Share your findings with your class.

REVIEW

A. Define each of the following.

    1. Child development   6. Rote learning
    2. Growth   7. Givens
    3. Maturation   8. Nature
    4. Development   9. Nurture
    5. Learning   10. Cognitive map

B. Name and briefly describe the four theories of learning that are presented in this unit.

C. Give three different views that describe development and what it is that develops. Tell how you describe development from your own point of view.

unit 12 what infants learn and parent enablers

OBJECTIVES

After studying this unit, the student should be able to

- Define the terms *infant, personality,* and *enabler.*
- List at least five characteristics of a child during each of the following periods: 0-6 months; 6-12 months.
- State four basic needs of the infant, giving parent enablers that help meet these needs.
- Describe four activities or aids that can stimulate the child's ability to see, listen, feel, and taste.

A child is considered an *infant* from birth until the time he begins to walk, usually around a year or so of age. During the first year of life he grows, learns, and changes faster than he will at any later time. Each infant grows in his very own way and at his very own rate.

Parents have an important role. They set the stage for the way the infant grows and develops. The start a child gets may affect him far into his adult life, often making the difference between success and failure.

This unit presents information that can be passed on to parents in a simple, direct way. What is given must be viewed with full respect for the individual differences that exist between humans at any stage of development.

The discussion divides the period of infancy into two parts. The first looks at the infant from birth to six months; the second part from six months to twelve months.

BIRTH TO SIX MONTHS

From the moment of birth, the newborn infant shows that he is both alike and different from all the other infants in the newborn nursery of the hospital. He can cry, cough, sneeze, and yawn. He can open and shut his eyes. He responds to light and dark. He can suck milk from his mother's breast, but he does it in his own way. He may nurse hard, tugging away with force. In contrast, another infant may be so slow and sleepy his mother must urge him to stay awake long enough to complete his feeding.

Those who work in the nursery can see behaviors that make each newborn infant a unique person with his own personality and temperament. At the sound of a strong, demanding cry coming from a nursery crib, a

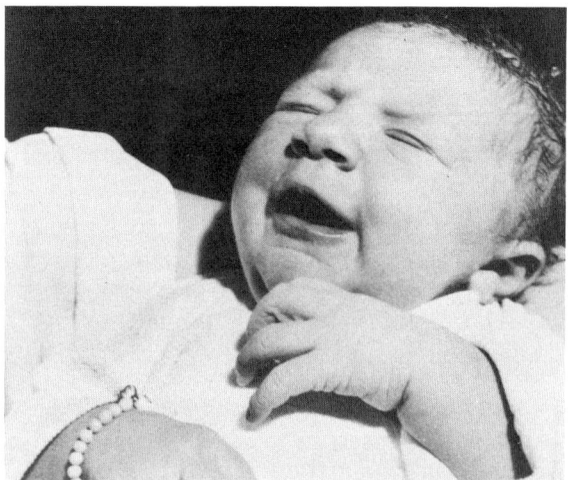

Fig. 12-1 From the moment of birth, there are behaviors that make each newborn infant a unique person with his own personality and temperament.

nurse may exclaim, "There goes the Jones baby. He's hungry again!" Not only does the infant show that he is an individual, but the nurse recognizes him as a person with his own timetable and unique cry.

Characteristics of the Infant

The newborn baby often comes into the world red and wrinkled. He has a soft spot on top of his head that usually closes by the time he is eighteen months old.

His characteristic reactions to his world are much like those of other infants. But he sets his own pattern of behavior. From birth to about three months, he shows certain behaviors.

- May demand a feeding every three or four hours, during the first month. His doctor is the best qualified person to prescribe a feeding plan tailored to the infant's needs.
- Sneezes, yawns, belches, coughs, spits up, cries, hiccups and passes gas. A few swallows of warm water may stop his hiccups.
- Breathes fast, slow, or jerky. May make little sounds in his sleep. (This is no cause for alarm.)
- Sleeps a big part of each day. Needs less sleep as he grows older. Makes the change himself.
- Thrusts arms and legs about when on his back. Can turn his head from side to side.
- Hands are usually fisted. Will grasp an object placed in his hand. At first can hang on to an object and support his own weight if the object is raised.
- Cries when he needs attention: a diaper change, to be fed, is in pain, other needs.
- Responds to human voices. May stop crying when someone speaks to him.
- Cries when he is upset. Can be quieted or distracted when soothed.
- Listens to sounds. May jump when he hears a loud noise.
- Sleeps without being bothered by ordinary household noises. Learns to shut out some noises. No need to have library silence in the house or to have his family tiptoe when near him.
- Smiles by the beginning of the third month.

From about three to six months, the infant makes some dramatic changes. Following his own timetable, he grows and takes on his own *personality* (qualities that make him a unique person with characteristics of his very own).

- Begins to laugh out loud. Likes to hear his voice. Babbles, coos, and gurgles.
- Can focus his eyes and begins to use his hands to reach, touch, or grasp the things that he sees.
- Learns about himself. Discovers his fingers, hands, and later his feet and toes.
- Stares at objects suspended above his crib.
- Pushes up with his arms and raises his head and shoulders when lying on his stomach. Rolls from back to stomach.
- Sits with support. Puts weight on legs when supported around his waist.
- Responds to sounds. May turn his head to seek the location of a sound. Listens to the ticking of a clock. May be pleased by music or voices on radio or television. May be quieted by the sound of voices.
- Likes to have someone talk to him. Makes vocal sounds and smiles back at someone who speaks to him. Likes to be cuddled and fondled.

Section 4 Child Development and Parent Enablers

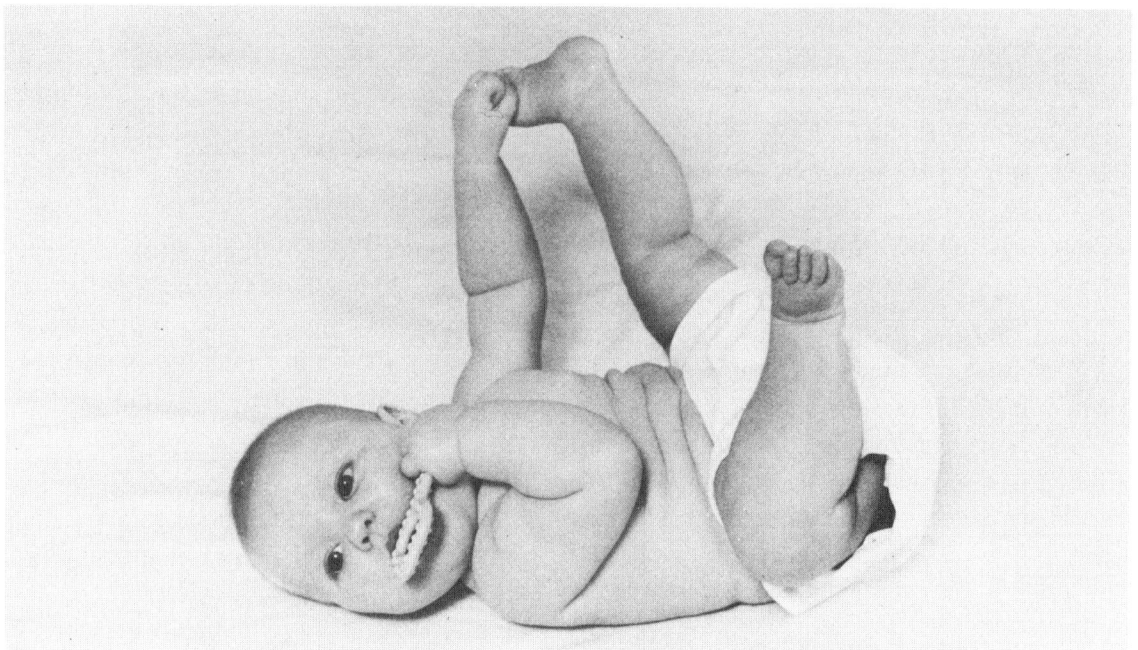

Fig. 12-2 The infant learns about himself. He discovers his fingers and toes and what they can do.

- Becomes excited when he hears his mother's voice or someone else that he knows.
- Shows an interest in toys and objects he can play with, near the end of this period. May fuss if items are removed.

Infant Needs and Parent Enablers

Infants may vary in their rate of development, but every baby grows and learns. Every baby has basic needs that must be met if he is to become a healthy, happy child. And every parent can *enable* (make possible) these needs.

SIX MONTHS TO TWELVE MONTHS

The period of six months to twelve months in an infant's life is marked by great changes in his appearance. Started at birth, his rapid growth continues. He may triple his birth weight by the end of the year.

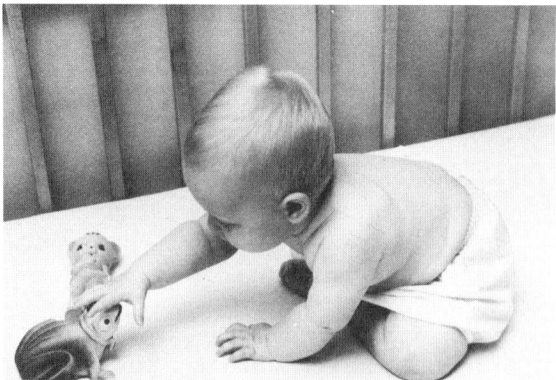

Fig. 12-3 The infant shows an interest in toys and objects he can play with. He reaches for something that he wants.

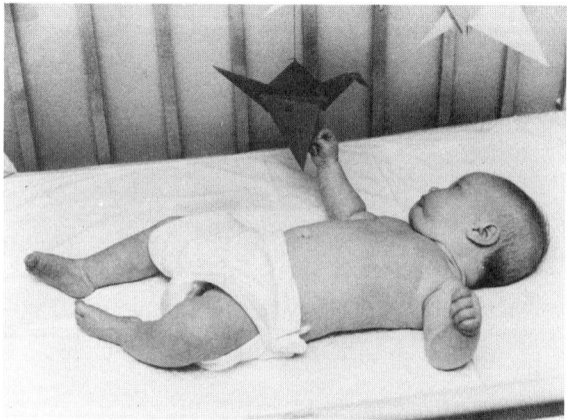

Fig. 12-4 A mobile helps the infant learn to focus his attention on an object.

Unit 12 What Infants Learn and Parent Enablers

A PAPER-FOLDED BIRD WITH FLAPPING WINGS

Directions: Use a square sheet of paper which is of a good quality. Shelving paper, typing paper, and wrapping paper are easily available and inexpensive. When a dotted line is shown, use the line as a guide, creasing the fold very carefully. Checkpoints show how a model should look thus far.

1. Bring A down to B.

2. Fold C over to the right to rest on D.

3. Checkpoint: the model should look like this. Check.

4. Open C slightly.

5. Bring C down to rest on B. Flip the model over to the left so that D is now on the left.

6. Checkpoint: the model should look like this. Check.

7. Repeat step 4: Open D slightly.

8. Bring D down to rest on C.

9. Bring the top layer of G over to the center, folding on the dotted line.

10. Bring to top layer of H over to the center, folding on the dotted line.

11. Checkpoint: the model should look like this. Check.

12. Fold D upward and back, so that G and H meet in the center.

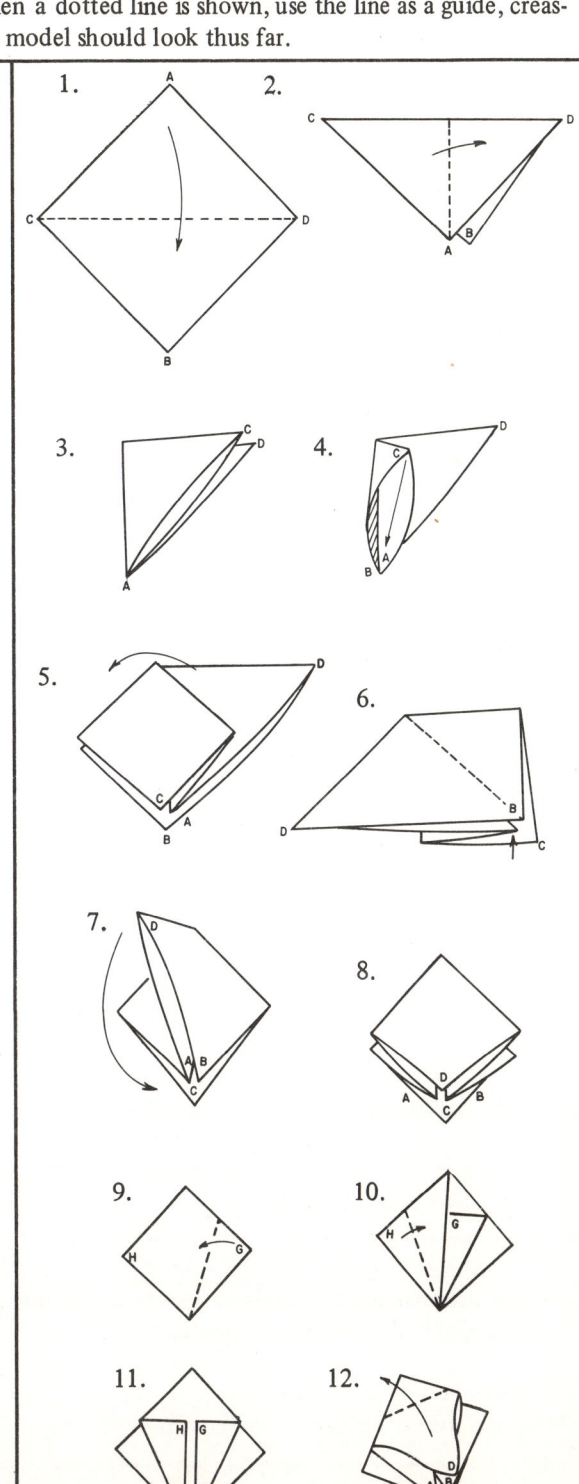

129

Section 4 Child Development and Parent Enablers

A Paper-Folded Bird with Flapping Wings (con't)

13. Checkpoint: the model should look like this. Check. (Note: this is the hardest part of the task. Keep trying.)

14. Flip the model over. Fold on the dotted lines to bring J and K to the center as shown in #15.

15. Repeat step 12: fold C upward and back, so that J and K meet in the center. C should rest on D.

16. Checkpoint: the model should look like this. Check. Fold A up and under to the right, turning it inside out. Do the same for B: fold it up and under to the left, turning it inside out.

17. Fold on the dotted line to bring C down to the right as shown in #18. Fold on the dotted line to bring A down, turning it inside out.

18. Checkpoint: the model should look like this. Check. C and D should touch. A forms the bird's beak; A is turned inside out.

19. Place one hand under the neckline shown at the right, hold tightly. Place the other hand on the tail and pull the tail gently. The bird's wings should flap.

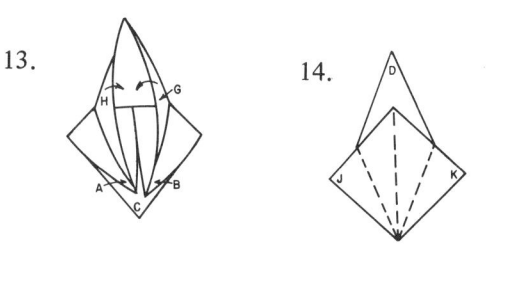

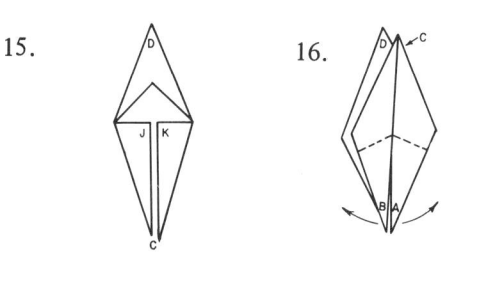

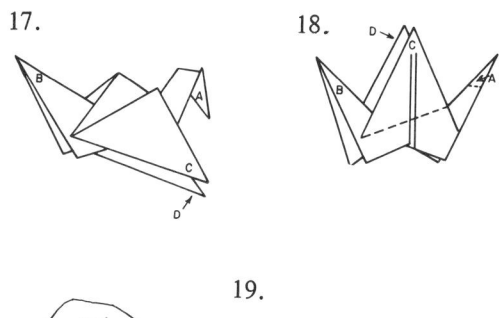

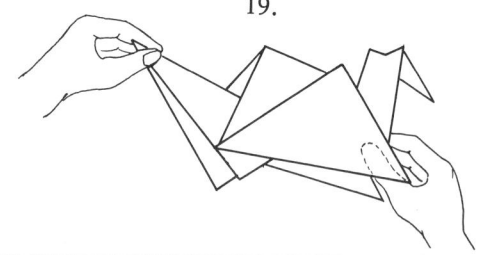

Note: The infant enjoys a paper-folded mobile made of birds on which he can focus his attention. The toddler and preschooler enjoy the bird as a plaything. Older family members enjoy creating the birds for fun and to give them to young children.

For other easy-to-fold models see
Massoglia, Elinor Tripato. *Fun-Time Paper Folding.* Chicago: Childrens Press, 1959.

Fig. 12-5 A paper-folded bird can be made from a square sheet of paper.

Unit 12 What Infants Learn and Parent Enablers

Needs	Parent Enablers
• To feel safe and secure in his world.	• Feed him when he is hungry. • Change him when he is wet or soiled. • Let him set his own pattern for food, rest, and "socializing" with his family. • Set a daily routine that he can depend on. Let him know that he eats after washing his face and hands. He sleeps after a bath. • Show him that he is loved: cuddle, hug, and kiss him, smile at him, sing and talk to him.
• To have protection and a safe environment in which to live and grow.	• Keep his room at a comfortable temperature (about 70° F) day and night. • Limit his visitors during the first few weeks. Discourage visitors from handling him. Increase his contacts with others as he grows older. • Get him out in the fresh air and sunshine. Dress him to fit the weather.
• To feel loved and wanted.	• Hold him when he is being fed, even if he is not being nursed. • Talk to him in a soft, soothing voice when he is upset. • Let all members of the family touch him, pat him, fondle him, and hold him as he grows older. • Let him hear the voices of all family members. • Have all family members do things for him and with him. • Repeat noises that he makes. Talk to him, even though he cannot understand what is said. • Put him where he can see and hear what is going on, while awake.
• To have his physical needs met.	• Provide him with food and vitamins as prescribed by his doctor. • Start a medical record, keeping track of visits to his doctor, problems or allergies that may arise, and any other related facts. • Allow active and quiet periods each day. • Give the young baby freedom to kick and fling his arms, without the restriction of tight bed covering. • Place him on a blanket or mat on the floor for a few minutes each day, to exercise and to feel "free."
• To learn about the world around him.	• Let him listen to the sounds in his world: human voices, clocks, radio, television, thunder, animals, sirens, whistles.

Section 4 Child Development and Parent Enablers

- Suspend a mobile above his crib that he can look at when he becomes aware of objects around him.
- Put an alarm clock where he can hear it tick.
- Place a bright rattle, plastic spoon, or some other small object in his hand. Start when he is very young and watch him as he becomes aware of objects and things that please him.
- Place before him colorful objects that he can see when he is lying on his stomach, raising his head, and pushing up with his arms.
- Play some music and dance with him, holding him so that he can feel rhythmical movements that keep time with the music.
- Make tours of the house with him, to acquaint him with his surroundings.
- Let him have periods in rooms where he can watch a family member at work or play.
- Help him to develop a feeling of being sure about people and things — the idea of "trust" in his world.

Fig. 12-6 Needs and parent enablers.

Increases in height and weight are influenced by factors in the child's environment: income, nutrition, race, sex, and physical health. Heredity also has a major effect on his development.

Some studies indicate that black babies are more advanced in motor development than white babies.[1] The reasons given for this are that genetic factors may influence their growth, or it may be the way that black parents handle their infants.

During this period the child shows a marked increase in energy and activity. Normal development proceeds at a pace set by each child's own timetable for growth, but certain characteristic reactions are seen. The infant

- Rolls over from back to stomach, usually around five to seven months.
- Sits up between six to eight months of age.
- Starts to crawl between seven to nine months.
- Pulls himself up to standing position at about nine to ten months.
- Stands alone and walks anywhere from nine to fifteen months.
- Babbles, squeals, and likes to listen to his own voice.
- Can say "bye-bye" at the end of the first year; responds to "no-no" showing that he understands the command.
- Tries to imitate facial expressions.
- Likes to look at his mirror image and may try to reach out to touch "himself."
- Engages in active, purposeful movements with his body: Tries to get things that

[1] Diane E. Papalia and Sally Wendkos Olds, *A Child's World: Infancy Through Adolescence,* (New York: McGraw-Hill Book Co., 1975), pp. 157-158.

he wants, even when they are beyond his reach. May use one object to obtain another; for example, he may pull a tablecloth toward him to get something on it.

- Experiments with objects in space: Puts objects into containers and takes them out. Crawls around something that is in his way. May crawl across the room to get a toy that he recognizes.

- Recognizes family members: May reach out to them or push them away in protest. Usually withdraws from strangers, but may reach out playfully when offered a toy or object that he wants.

- Plays with a toy or uses it as a social contact by offering it to someone near him: May drop the toy out of his playpen for the person to pick up and hand back to him. Repeats the process like a game that he has invented himself.

- Tests things with his eyes and hands, although he still brings objects to his mouth as he did earlier.

- By the end of the year, he is a determined person who likes to move under his own power: May fuss if picked up while he is crawling where his curiosity leads him.

- Attempts to feed himself: Shows definite likes and dislikes in food, sometimes protests if not permitted to choose what he wants to eat.

- Attracts the attention of his family by repeating actions that make them laugh: Seems pleased with himself and may squeal with delight each time they react to his antics.

Infant Needs and Parent Enablers

There is no tool that can precisely measure the growth and development of any infant. There is no way to draw a line between what he needs at one stage and what parents can do to help him. Each infant must be seen as a human being developing in his own way and at his own speed.

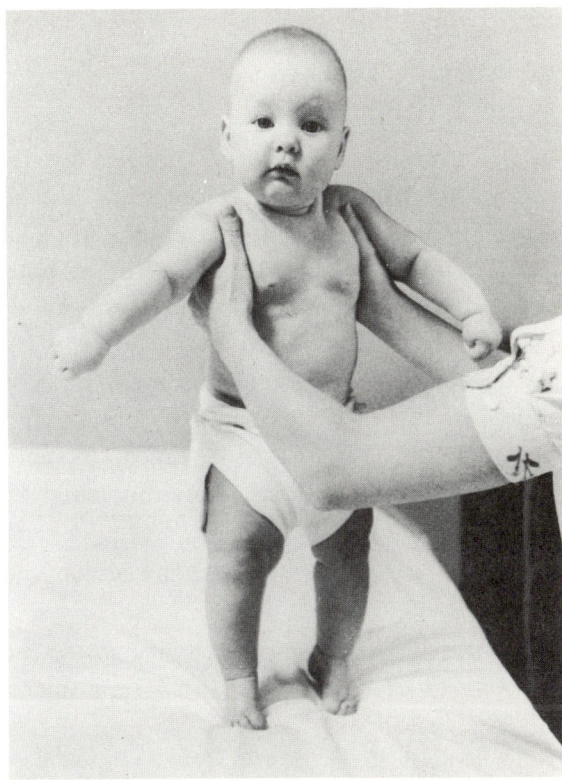

Fig. 12-7 From eighteen to twenty-two weeks, the infant may support his weight when someone holds him in a standing position.

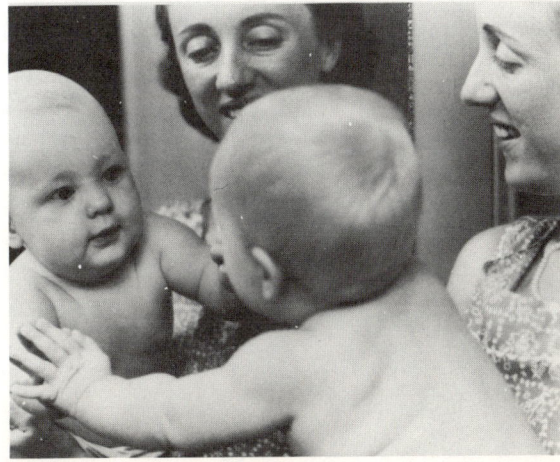

Fig. 12-8 The infant likes to look at his mirror image and may reach out to touch "himself."

Section 4 Child Development and Parent Enablers

Many of the tasks parents perform for the younger infant may be broadened and expanded with him as he continues his first year of growth. Listed are basic needs of the infant, and parent enablers to help him during the second half of his first year of life.

ACTIVITIES AND AIDS TO FOSTER DEVELOPMENT

The following activities and aids are described to help parents explore what can be done to foster the infant's development. The list is closely related to those things with which the infant has sensory or physical contact in his day-to-day encounters.

Selections must be made on the basis of each infant's own timetable of growth and development. Parents can be urged to create home situations that stimulate the child to act or to react to something near him.

Mobiles: dangling toys to hang above the baby.

- Attach a strong piece of twine across the width of the crib. With string, suspend

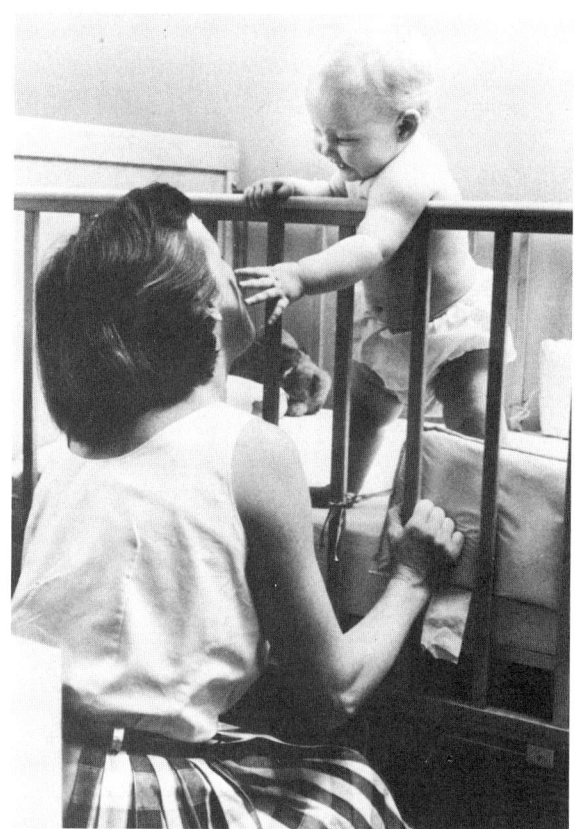

Fig. 12-9 The infant likes to have someone play with him and may reach out to touch his playmate.

Fig. 12-10 From twelve to fifteen months the child may be ready for new developmental tasks. He likes to look at picture books and make his own marks on paper.

134

Needs	Parent Enablers
• To feel safe and secure in his world.	• Love him, hold him, sing and talk to him. • Continue a routine that he can depend on. Make sure he has a time to get to know all family members, especially his father. • Play with him and let him know that he is loved and wanted. • Be patient, consistent, and respond to his needs promptly.
• To have protection and a safe environment in which to live and grow.	• Keep poisonous materials beyond his reach when he is crawling. Protect him from contact with heaters, stoves, electrical cords, and anything else that can hurt him. • Give him toys that can be washed and kept clean. Avoid things with sharp edges or parts that he can remove. • Continue his outdoor play. Let him come in contact with other children, especially those who will talk to him and play games with him.
• To feel loved and wanted.	• Play games with him and describe what he is doing or seeing during daily routines. • Talk to him and use words to label objects, events, and people in his world. • Let him see people who come to visit. Help him increase his ability to accept and trust new faces. • Praise him when he makes sounds or imitates them — or does anything that can be praised. Let the speaker's tone give the infant a feeling of acceptance. • Accept his attempts to feed himself, praising him for his efforts. Promote the development of his self-image, a "can do" attitude. • Let him view his mirror image. Put a mirror where he can see himself while in his playpen (be sure that it is not within reach.)
• To have his physical needs met.	• Increase his food intake as prescribed by his doctor. Give him only one new food at a time. Let him get used to the feel and taste of it. • See that he gets his immunization shots early. By his first birthday, he should have protection from polio, diptheria, measles, smallpox, whooping cough, and lockjaw. His doctor knows what he needs. • Provide many ways for him to get exercise, fresh air, and sunshine. See that he gets sufficient rest time.

Section 4 Child Development and Parent Enablers

• To learn about the world around him.	• Give him many opportunities to crawl and explore his immediate world. • Give him toys that stimulate his curiosity and sharpen his ability to see, reach, listen, grasp, focus his eyes, and respond in some way. • Let him seek sounds that he knows, such as the ticking of a timer placed somewhere in the room. • Take him outdoors to hear the sounds in his world: cars, trucks, airplanes, sirens, barking dogs, and meowing cats. • Place things that he can reach and touch on the floor: stuffed animals, soft towels, plastic bowls, metal pans and similar items. • Give him a chance to experiment with sounds: touch piano keys, ring a bell, shake rattles, squeeze toys. • Let him play in the water at bath time: splash, wet a cloth, float a toy, and become aware of what he can do with water and in it.

Fig. 12-11 Needs and parent enablers.

spoons, ribbon, cloth, plastic rattles, and rubber jar rings from the twine.

- Make bright-colored paper-folded birds. Attach them to string and suspend from the ceiling.

- Hang a prism from the window frame. Place the child's crib so that the prism sends flickering colors near him.

- Tie bright-colored objects to the crib slats on his right and left sides. Place them where he can see them when he turns his head.

- Sew tiny bells to strips of cloth. Suspend them across the crib slightly to the left or right of the infant. Place them where his arm movements can touch the bells, but not so that they can hit him. This is suggested for the very young infant who will not grasp the objects and place them in his mouth.

Music and sounds for listening.

- Sing nursery rhymes to the infant or play records and tape recordings of songs with a strong rhythmic beat.

- Tape-record the soothing voice of a parent. Place the recording where he can hear it. Use it to quiet him, especially when he is fussy and his parent is busy.

- Put an alarm clock on a chair near his crib. Add another clock to vary the sound.

- Wind up a musical toy animal and place it near him.

- Tape-record the sounds that he makes. Play them back to him.

- Play story records for him, even though he cannot understand what is said.

- Play soft, soothing music when it is time for him to sleep. Use music of other moods when he is awake.

- Place him near the radio or television set where he can hear voices. He may learn to recognize the voice of a newscaster as a "friend" who can quiet him when his parent is busy.
- Play games like "pat-a-cake," and "peek-a-boo."
- Make noisemakers by putting beans, pebbles, or bottle tabs in a plastic bottle; glue bottle cap securely. Do the same with small-size coffee cans that have plastic lids. Put noisemakers in the can and glue plastic lid in place.
- Sew tiny bells on the sleeve of a shirt that he wears when he is awake. Place them where he cannot reach them or put them in his mouth.

Toys for comfort and cuddling.

- Make a soft, cuddly toy animal.
- Make a tiny pillow of soft cloth. Stitch brightly colored designs on one or both sides.
- Fasten several colored terry cloth patches on his crib sheet where he can see them and feel them. Try patches of other kinds of material that have a different "feel."

Things to reach for.

- Put small, safe objects in his crib to let him practice reaching for them: plastic spoons, unbreakable cups, small blocks, small aluminum pans.
- Try putting some objects on a chair beside his crib. Have some there when he wakes up in the morning (he may let his family sleep a bit longer).
- Place bits of dry cereal or raisins before him at feeding time. Give him a chance to reach for the objects and taste and handle them until he is satisfied. Praise him when he eats them.
- Put floating objects in his bath water. Hold him while he tries to reach for them. Make sure that he feels secure and safe in the water.

Things to touch and taste.

- Place before him things that he can touch and taste: bits of banana, dry cereal, a quarter of a seedless orange. Vary the size, color, shape, and texture of the food — keeping within the diet plan set by his doctor.
- Let him touch and taste new foods himself. Make sure that his fingers are clean when he reaches for food that is spoon-fed.
- Give him different objects, in a wide variety of shapes, colors, and sizes, that can be thoroughly cleansed. Let him "discover" for himself what has a taste and what is tasteless. Include bits of food so he can find something that is edible.

SUMMARY

A child is considered an infant from birth until the time he begins to walk. During this period, he grows, learns, and changes faster than he will at any later time.

Each newborn infant has behaviors that make him a unique person with his own personality and temperament. Each infant has his own timetable for growth and development.

Infants respond to people, things, and events in their environment. Parents play an important role in helping the infant respond in a way that fosters his positive development.

All infants have basic needs that parents can meet. The infant needs

- To feel safe and secure in his world.
- To have protection and a safe environment to live and grow in.
- To feel loved and wanted.

Section 4 Child Development and Parent Enablers

- To have his physical needs met.
- To learn about the world around him.

The infant grows rapidly and may triple his birth weight by the end of his first year. Increases in height and weight are influenced by factors in the child's environment: income, nutrition, race, sex, and physical health. Heredity also has a major effect on his development.

There are many ways in which parents can enable (make possible) the infant's positive growth. Each child must be seen as a human being developing in his own way and at his own speed. Activities and aids used with infants must be appropriate for the child as an individual.

SUGGESTED ACTIVITIES

- Locate the parent of an infant. Try to interest her in exploring ways that her baby can learn through parent enablers.
    a. Find out the exact age of the infant, in months. If the infant was *premature* (born before full term), subtract that time from the age figured in months.
    b. Select from this unit ten or more enablers that are appropriate for the child in question. Show the list to the infant's mother and ask her to choose five activities that she is willing to try with her baby.
    c. Prepare for the parent any necessary materials needed for the activity. The parent may have some of the things on hand and offer their use. Just remember to be considerate and not place a task-burden on the parent.
    d. Write exactly what the child does or tape-record (with permission) the entire activity. Replay the tape, so that the parents can hear it before you share it with your class. If they have any objection to the outcome, make another recording that they can be comfortable with.
    e. Bring the materials used and the recording to class. Share both with your peer group.
- Compare your findings with those of other members of your class. Determine similarities and differences in the way that the infants responded.
    a. Note which activities appealed to the greatest number of infants. Discuss why this may be.
    b. Note which activities were rejected by the infants. Make a list of reasons why *any* infant would reject these activities. Go down the list to see which reasons might apply to the individual infant.

REVIEW

A. Define each of the following.
   1. Infant
   2. Personality
   3. Enabler

B. List at least five characteristics of an infant during each of the following periods: zero to three months, three to six months, six to twelve months.

C. List five basic needs of the infant as described in the text.

D. Describe one activity or aid that can stimulate the child's ability to do each of the following: see, listen, touch, taste.

unit 13 what toddlers learn and parent enablers

OBJECTIVES

After studying this unit, the student should be able to
- Define and describe the term *toddler*.
- Tell what can be expected of a child when he enters the period in which he is considered to be a toddler.
- Describe at least ten characteristics that toddlers seem to have in common.
- Describe at least one activity or aid that can stimulate toddler growth in each of the following areas: physical, intellectual, social, emotional.

A child is considered to be a toddler from the time he begins to walk until he approaches the age of three. Some babies begin to walk as early as nine or ten months of age, and some do not walk until the age of eighteen months. However, walking is most common at thirteen to fifteen months — the entry period of the present discussion.

ENTRY BEHAVIOR

By the time a child begins to walk, he has more than tripled his birth weight and has learned a great deal. As he enters this period, there are some things about him that can be observed on a "can do" or "cannot do" basis.

- Some children are weaned; others may want to satisfy the sucking need with a bottle or pacifier well into the second year.
- Walking may take place with assistance, or the toddler may be able to get about by himself. He may keep his legs wide apart, bending his knees to steady himself while walking. He may be somewhat knock-kneed or bowlegged. When he wants to get about more quickly, he may revert back to crawling or creeping if he still feels unsteady on his feet.
- Has begun to talk and has a vocabulary of several words that have meaning for him and can be understood by others. He may understand many more words.
- Responds to the moods of people around him. If he sees someone laugh, he laughs; his mood matches what he sees. If someone should cry, the toddler may sob as if his heart is breaking. He knows when someone is pleased or displeased with him and his mood shows it.
- Self-confidence depends largely upon the freedom given to him as an infant. If his parents have been patient and have permitted him to explore his world, he may be willing to face new things. If he has been restricted too much, he may enter his next stage with much dependency on others.
- Has outgrown his playpen and likes to play on the floor. Shouts and squirms with delight when someone joins him in his play activities.
- Mealtime pattern has been set. He is probably down to three meals a day with a morning and an afternoon snack.

THE TODDLER EMERGES

The toddler is like a "bundle of energy" that is constantly in motion. He might also be called the little "runabout," for he likes to run about and explore every nook and corner of his world.

His abilities broaden and expand as he gains control of his muscles. He gets in and out of things. He goes up and down stairs. He climbs over furniture and crawls under tables and chairs.

As the toddler gains control of himself and his surroundings, he may seem to be stubborn or contrary. He is like a dedicated scientist who lets nothing stand in the way of his work.

The toddler's increased activity makes him prone to accidents. Objects that he plays with must be free from sharp edges. Things that can harm him must be kept where he cannot reach them. Some safety rules are listed:

- Medicines and household cleaning preparations should be kept in locked places.
- Pot handles should be turned toward the back of the stove, so that the toddler cannot reach them. Back burners should be used in preference to front ones.
- Gates can be used to limit the child's access to stairways or rooms that have no doors.
- Baby-sitters must be made aware of what things the toddler must avoid, if the objects cannot be removed.
- Emergency telephone numbers should be posted where they can be located quickly in case of an emergency: poison control center, baby's doctor, hospital or community emergency squad. A person taking care of the child during his parents' absence should always know how to contact them.

Teaching the toddler to stop undesirable behavior is a problem that calls for much thought and, often, action. When a parent wants some act to stop, the first response is often to spank. The child may stop what he is doing, but he may also end his natural desire to explore and learn about his world. Thus, a spanking may do more harm than good.

The child's problem may be that he does not understand what is expected of him. When he enters an area where he is not to go, the best action is to pick him up and put him where he should be. A quiet but firm "no" may help him to understand that a limit is being imposed on him.

When he tries to touch a forbidden item, another quiet but firm "no" may stop his action. Removing the object or replacing it with something to distract him may help. Toddlers usually respond well to spoken commands when parents demonstrate what is to be done.

During his efforts to learn about his home and what is in it, the toddler may meet objects and events that frighten him. An overloaded washing machine may give a loud, thumping sound. A television set may suddenly flash a practice emergency alarm. A telephone receiver left off the hook may cause a telephone operator to send out the strange buzz sound that calls attention to the problem. A friendly dog's lapping tongue may cause the child to think that he is about to be eaten by the animal. These and other situations call for reassurance and comforting until the child gets used to things that are new and strange to him.

The toddler's interest in gaining control of himself may serve well when his toilet training begins. Control of his bowel movements can come only

- When he has developed muscular control.
- When he understands what is expected of him.

Section 4 Child Development and Parent Enablers

- When he can feel the urge to empty his bowels.
- When his training is accompanied by patience and praise.
- When he is not punished or criticized for having an occasional "accident."

Most toddlers are ready for toilet training around eighteen to twenty-four months. Individual differences must be considered, however. Bowel control comes first and bladder control later. It may be some time later before the child achieves night control. In all aspects of toilet training, praise when he performs well can increase the chance that he will try again.

GENERAL CHARACTERISTICS OF THE TODDLER

Each toddler seems to share certain characteristics with others in this stage of

Fig. 13-1 A young child goes forth to learn about his world. He can see, touch, taste, smell, hear.

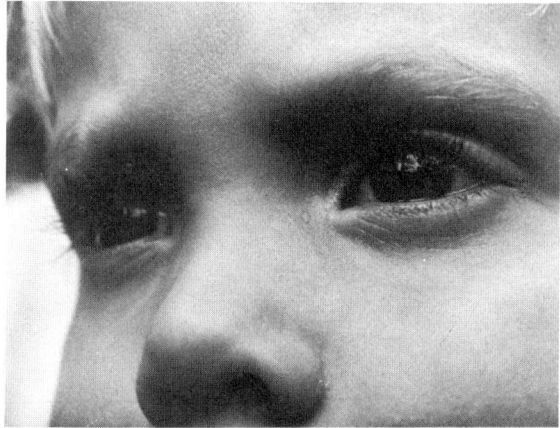

Fig. 13-2 He sees his world through wondering eyes.

Fig. 13-3 He touches the soft fur of his dog. He holds him close and learns about feelings and love.

development. He has an increasing ability to recognize people, objects, and events in his life. He shows an intense interest in the world about him, examining everything that he sees. He feels, touches, tastes, smells — and learns.

Listed are some characteristics that the toddler shares with his peer group.

- Possesses a great deal of energy that keeps him constantly in motion.
- Tries to master motor skills by his efforts to push, pull, drag, lift, or climb anything within his reach.
- Moves into the family set where he may be frustrated when he learns that other persons have needs that may infringe on his freedom.
- Gets into situations that create the need for limits to be imposed on him for his own protection and safety.
- Needs constant supervision.
- Likes to make a production of bathtime, mealtime, and bedtime. Rituals give him a sense of security.

Fig. 13-5 He smells flowers. He learns that a rose has a pleasant scent.

Fig. 13-4 He tastes ice cream. The cold, sweet refreshing taste pleases him.

Fig. 13-6 He tests things in his world to learn more about them. Do dogs like to smell flowers, too?

- Likes to have familiar things remain where he knows they belong. Tends to be puzzled when things are moved. May put moved objects back in their original place.
- Speech begins to serve him in getting what he wants.
- Responds to "no" when adults tell him to stop something. He learns to say "no" when he wants others to obey his command. Becomes angry at frustrations.
- Tries to do things for himself, wants to dress and feed himself.
- Likes push-and-pull toys that he can handle.
- Enjoys things that he can take apart, put together, push, pull, or ride.
- Likes to scribble with crayons, marking anything that he can. Tears, crushes, or marks paper.
- Responds to music and stories. Likes rhymes and stories about himself. His listening span is very short.
- Imitates adults in what they do. May be puzzled when he finds that he is not permitted to do everything that adults may do. May display his anger.
- Parents often expect too much of him, failing to recognize that a child is not a little adult. He cannot be held responsible for his actions.
- Plays among other children, but is unable to play cooperatively with them. Treats other children like objects. Skills of social contact are somewhat primitive.
- Has no concept of time, except the here and now. It is very difficult to make him hurry.
- Responds more to his mother than anyone else. Continues to withdraw from strangers and may seek his mother for reassurance that all is well.

A YOUNG CHILD'S CONTINUING NEED

Even though the toddler seems to be somewhat independent, he is still very much in need of mothering. This means his need for the kind of attention that a mother gives when she "does what comes naturally."

Mothering is described as a natural drive that seems to tell a mother when to feed, comfort, or scold her child. It is what she does when she loves her child and wants to provide the best care possible. The mother's actions come from her heart and may not be seen within the pages of a book. Mothering takes place when the child's mother (or surrogate mother)

- Holds him, loves him, and gives him signs of approval.
- Comforts him when he is hurt and takes measures to ease that hurt.
- Shows an interest in what he does and says.
- Praises him for a job well done and praises him again whenever he repeats the performance.
- Says "thank you" when he does something as a favor, letting him know that he is appreciated.
- Develops his self-image by accepting him as he is.
- Feeds him, clothes him, and lets him know that he is loved and wanted.

TODDLER NEEDS AND PARENT ENABLERS

The progress that the toddler makes depends much on what his parents do to help him. With guidance, he can become a healthy, happy child ready to face his next tasks in living and learning. Without help, he may be unable to understand his world and comply with its demands.

Physical Growth	
Needs	**Parent Enablers**
1. Growth rate is slower than in infancy: • Requires less food in proportion to his body. • Needs all daily requirements, despite poor appetite.	1. Make necessary adjustments: • Provide less food, but a well-balanced diet. • Create meals that are different in color and texture to spark his interest in food. • Let him feed himself, even though he makes a mess. • Set a fixed time for meals and see that he is part of the family group. • Make meal time a pleasant experience.
2. Is always on the go: • Needs conditions for being active. • Needs a safe place for his play.	2. See that nothing handicaps him: • Give him clothes, shoes, and socks that fit. • See that he has outdoor play and exercise. • Provide for adequate rest time between periods of play. • Allow floor space for indoor play in bad weather. • Give him a safe place in which to climb, run, jump, and explore.
3. Hands are becoming more skilled in handling things: • Needs opportunities to build his large and small muscles. • Needs work-play materials that are simple but challenging.	3. Provide work-play materials that require very little coordination at first. Progress to other things as child develops increased skill: • Climbing equipment, big blocks, push-and-pull toys. • Cardboard cartons or wooden boxes (no splinters) in which to climb in and out. • Hollow barrels to crawl through. • Steps and planks for climbing. • Kiddie cars, rocking horses, ride-a-stick animals, and other body-movement toys. • Big blocks for building. • Small blocks for carrying, building, and piling. • Sand, water, clay, and other raw materials. • Large crayons for marking. • Large books, puzzles, and nesting blocks. • Large beads and spools for stringing.
4. Increased muscular controls makes toilet training possible: • Needs patience and understanding.	4. Follow the child's cues: • Start training when he seems to understand what is expected of him.

• Needs to know how to take care of himself: how to go and how to wash hands afterward.	• Be patient and considerate. • Do not criticize him when he has an "accident." • Keep extra clothing on hand in case of "accidents." Let him help change himself. • Have a step-on box or stool that he can use to reach the sink. Let him wash his own hands after using the toilet. Colored soap may be an attraction.

Fig. 13-7 Physical growth: needs and parent enablers.

Intellectual Growth	
Needs	Parent Enablers
1. Intellectual growth is spectacular: • Needs time, space and things to help him grow.	1. Provide an environment that stimulates mental activity: • Give him books with pictures, nursery rhymes, and simple stories. • Read to him or make up stories about him or his life. • Have plants and other growing things for him to observe. • Give him things for make-believe play: cloth scraps, pots and pans, jewelry, baby dolls, purses, shoes, and other items. • Let him work with materials that help him create: clay, crayons, paint, finger paint, music makers.
2. Speech is beginning to serve his purposes well: • Needs to hear good language. • Needs to listen.	2. Provide him with appropriate models for imitation: • Do not use baby talk. • Use words to describe things around him. • Let him listen to stories, poems, radio and television shows for children, records, tapes. • Call attention to sounds that he can hear in his environment: sirens, bells, bird calls, animal sounds, motors, thunder, and the like. • Encourage him to use language to express his feelings and needs.
3. An awareness of physical relationships is being developed: • Needs to see likes and differences.	3. Present many opportunities for developing thinking skills: • Give him toys that fit in a certain fashion: puzzles, wooden inlay puzzles, nesting blocks, pegs to fit in board or box with matching holes.

• Needs to further develop sensory perceptions.	• Give him household items that can be ordered by size: nesting measuring cups, spoons, bowls. • Help him to develop concepts of elements in his world: shapes, sizes, forms, color, number, and time. • Let him identify objects, listen to sound, feel materials in his environment, taste-smell things that are edible, smell other things.

Fig. 13-8 Intellectual growth: needs and parent enablers.

Social Growth	
Needs	Parent Enablers
1. Increased mobility gives the child a greater acquaintance with his world: • Needs to understand things and activities in his environment.	1. Provide many opportunities for contacts with objects and activities in his world: • Let him learn to identify natural sounds: birds, rain, sounds of animals, wind, thunder, human voices, music. • Help him to understand that sounds cannot hurt him. • Let him learn about mechanical sounds in his environment: bells, clocks, sirens, trucks, engines, musical instruments. • Help him to understand that some sounds are warnings that tell him to keep away.
2. Increases awareness of himself as a person with rights and responsibilities: • Needs to know what he is permitted to do and what he must avoid. • Needs to learn to cooperate and relate to other people.	2. Provide him with experiences that develop his self-image: • Let him see himself in a mirror and have him point out his facial features and body parts. • Use his name often so that he knows it is his "very own." • Praise him often for jobs well done. • Be quiet but firm when telling him what he must not do. • Be kind and polite with him as with any other person.
3. Skills of social contact are somewhat primitive: • Needs to be comfortable around people. • Needs to understand his own place in the world.	3. Provide opportunities for him to broaden the range of people that he knows: • Permit him to meet persons who visit his home. Introduce him properly. Encourage him to respond in an appropriate way. • Reassure him when he meets new people and things for the first time.

Section 4 Child Development and Parent Enablers

• Needs to be with children in his own age group.	• Take him on trips in his community to help him develop new concepts. • Create situations for him to be with other children: at home, in the play yard, in a toy-lending library, or in any other place where he can be supervised.

Fig. 13-9 Social growth: needs and parent enablers.

Emotional Growth	
Needs	Parent Enablers
1. Increased desire to manage his own life creates problems for the toddler: • Needs to depend on the familiar before he can reach out to the new. • Needs to learn to cope with his feelings. • Needs constant reassurance that everything is "O.K." • Needs help in understanding the meaning of sharing with others.	1. Provide situations that help him learn to trust in his world and feel able to produce what is expected of him: • Establish routines that become familiar activities that he can expect and understand: bedtime, mealtime, playtime. • Give him a sense of order: he washes his hands before meals; he takes a nap after lunch, he goes outdoors after his nap. • Avoid head-on clashes by removing things that he must not touch. Offer him an attractive substitute when he wants things that he can not have. • Keep directions simple and clear. Make sure that he understands them. If he does not respond, his parent should promptly see that the child follows through on what is to be done. • Give him attention and plenty of love. • Listen to him, hug him, smile at him, and praise him to make him feel good inside. • Keep his meetings with other children short, simple, and supervised. • Use a good formula for keeping his playmates down to a number that he can cope with: one playmate for each year of the child's life.

Fig. 13-10 Emotional growth: needs and parent enablers.

Always allowing for individual differences, there are many ways by which parents can help the child grow and develop: physically, intellectually, socially, emotionally.

PLAY MATERIALS TO FOSTER DEVELOPMENT

Play materials are aids that the child uses during his play activities — activities often called a child's work. Play is the means by which he learns how to learn. In his play the child tests his wings as he copes with his world of time, space, things, people, and animals.

Listed are some play materials that foster the toddler's development. What is selected must match the child's interest and maturity level.

Pull toy

- Materials needed: shoebox, glue, four plastic lids, magic marker, string.
- With the magic marker, draw lines to make the plastic lids look like wheels.
- Place the box on a table. Glue the lids on the box so that each is flush to the bottom of the box. Attach a pull string to the box.
- The box is ready to carry lightweight objects.

Pillow hill

- Materials needed: an old bed sheet and several pillows and chair cushions.
- Place the sheet on the floor. Put the pillows on top.
- Let the child climb up and down the pillows and cushions.
- The child can arrange and rearrange his "hill."

Chair tunnel

- Materials: several straight-backed chairs.
- Turn the chairs over so that their backs touch the floor.
- Let the child crawl under the tunnel created by the closely-packed chair backs.

Cardboard tunnel

- Materials: several large cardboard boxes.

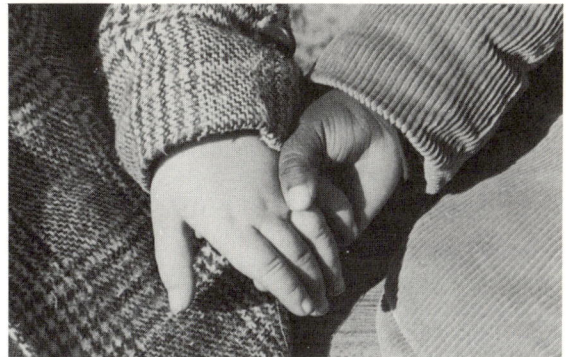

Fig. 13-11 As he leaves this stage, the young child may be ready for "special" friends. Sometimes he likes the comfort of a friend with whom he can watch the wonders of their world.

- Cut out the end of each box. Attach several to make a tunnel. Let the child crawl through it.

Nested cans

- Materials: several cans of different sizes (that can be nested), masking tape.
- Make sure that rims have no sharp edges. Fasten masking tape around the rim of each can to ensure safety.
- Let the child experiment to nest or stack the cans.

Carton blocks

- Materials: several clean half-gallon milk cartons, several quart cartons, masking tape, scissors.
- Cut off tops of two cartons of same size. Push them together and fasten block with masking tape.
- Make blocks of two different sizes.
- Let the child experiment and build.
- Parent can create some simple structures that the child can imitate as a matching game.

Sorting game

- Materials: an egg carton, an assortment of buttons containing some that are alike and some that differ.

- Place buttons on the lid of the open carton.
- Child sorts buttons and places them in the sections of the egg carton.
- Other objects such as bottle caps, rubber bands, paper clips, beans, and the like may be added.
- After the child experiments, his parent can show him other ways that he can imitate in sorting the objects.

Noisemakers

- Materials: a coffee can with matching lid, glue, pebbles, or buttons.
- Put pebbles or button in a can. Glue the lid securely.
- Let the child shake the can. Play music to accompany his rhythmical movements.
- Let him experiment with sound by placing different objects in another can to hear the new sounds that result when the can is shaken.

Art gallery

- Materials: wrapping paper, crayons, glue, old catalogs and magazines.
- Attach the paper to the lower part of a wall in his room or to the bottom part of a door.
- Let him color on the paper or paste on pictures that he chooses from the catalogs and magazines.
- Pictures and decorations may be holiday themes.
- Make him understand that he marks and pastes pictures only in his very own place.

Shopping bag

- Materials: two large paper sacks, masking tape, string.
- Put one sack inside the other. Keeping the double thickness, fold down the top edges of the bags several times (about 1 1/2" to 2" width). Continue until the bags are about one-half their original height.
- Secure the edges with masking tape. Make holes and attach string to make a handle for carrying.
- Let the child color the bag or paste pictures from magazines on it.
- He can use the bag to carry toys and other light objects.

SUMMARY

A child is considered a toddler from the time he begins to walk until he approaches the age of three. Walking is most common from thirteen to fifteen months.

The toddler is constantly in motion and likes to explore everything in his world. He needs a safe environment in which to grow and learn.

His interest in gaining control of himself serves well in toilet training. Most toddlers are ready for toilet training around eighteen to twenty-four months, but children vary. For his own protection the toddler needs certain limits set on his freedom to move about. Things that can hurt him should be put beyond his reach, if possible. A quiet but firm "no" may help him learn to avoid off-limit places and things.

Parents can do much to foster the child's growth and development through play materials and activities.

SUGGESTED ACTIVITIES

- Try to interest the mother of a toddler in exploring ways that her child can learn as suggested in this unit.

  a. Taking into account the age and possible interests of the child, make a list of activities that you can show the parent.

  b. Have the parent select activties that she would be willing to try with her child.

  c. Prepare for the parent any necessary materials needed for the activities.

  d. Write exactly what the child does or tape-record (with permission) the entire activity. Replay the tape, so that the parent can hear it before you share it with your class. If the parent has any objection to the outcome, make another recording that she can be comfortable with.

  e. With her consent, try some of the activities yourself. Follow the directions given in d.

  f. Bring all of the materials to class and share them with your peer group.

  g. Compare your findings with other members of your class. Discuss fully.

REVIEW

A. Define and describe the term *toddler* as used in this unit.

B. List at least five characteristics of the child who enters the period in which he is considered to be a toddler.

C. Identify ten characteristics of the toddler.

D. Tell what happens to a child when mothering takes place.

E. Identify a need that is associated with each statement below that is concerned with the child's growth.

  1. Growth rate is slower than in infancy.
  2. The toddler is always on the go.
  3. The toddler is using speech to serve his purposes.
  4. Increased mobility gives the toddler a greater acquaintance with his world.
  5. The toddler's skills of social contact are somewhat primitive.

F. Describe at least one thing that a parent can do to stimulate the toddler's growth in each of the following areas: physical, intellectual, social, and emotional growth.

unit 14 what preschoolers learn and parent enablers

OBJECTIVES

After studying this unit, the student should be able to

- Define and describe the following terms: preschooler, sense of autonomy, locomotor movements, nonlocomotor movements, manipulative skills, handedness, seriate.
- Tell what can be expected of a child when he enters the period in which he is considered to be a preschooler.
- Describe at least ten characteristics of the preschooler.
- Identify five needs of the preschooler and corresponding parent enablers.

As the child approaches his third birthday, he enters the period often called the *preschool age* — the time that precedes formal schooling. The preschool child — the three, four, and five year old — is one who has a new sense of direction. He has discovered himself as a person in his own right and is ready for many new experiences.

ENTRY BEHAVIOR

The preschooler enters a new phase in his life — new in the sense that he is ready and eager to test the nature and limits of his own individuality. He has plans and ideas and wants to carry them out. He has an "I can do" attitude.

Allowing for the individual differences, a thumbnail sketch can be given of the child who is now entering the preschool age.

- Shows marked development in large muscle coordination, but small muscles are not well developed.
- Eye-hand coordination is still very limited.
- Can accept necessary limits and restraints on his behavior.
- Wants adult approval and is willing to comply with adult demands to get it.
- Can be given a limited amount of freedom to go beyond his immediate home environment.
- Usually takes care of his own toilet needs, but may be so wrapped up in his play that he "forgets" to attend to his needs.
- Can feed and dress himself with little or no help. His skill depends on how much he has been permitted to do for himself as a toddler.
- Imitates adults and others in their language, manners, and habits.
- Shows increased skill in use of language; can make himself understood and express ideas.
- Asks countless questions to satisfy his curiosity.
- Likes to help around the house and may sometimes irritate family members with his "helpfulness."
- Although still very close to his mother, he finds his father more important to him than in the past.

- Endless motion continues, but he is able to deal with longer periods of quiet activity.
- Shows his fatigue by being restless, irritable, or negative.

GENERAL CHARACTERISTICS OF THE PRESCHOOLER

The preschooler is much like a looking glass image of the people around him. What he does and what he feels develop out of what he learns from those who love him and whom he loves best. He looks, he imitates, and he learns.

From his contacts with other people, he learns to trust them and develops feelings about himself. When his needs are met and he is loved and praised for what he does, he learns to like himself. Only when he can trust people in his world can he realize his own sense of self.

The child with a healthy self-image is able to develop a *"sense of autonomy"* — of being able to stand on his own feet. This push toward independence comes in part from his increased maturity level. His parents also play an important role in helping him seek and find autonomy. They permit him to move about and are nearby to give him assurance when he returns to his homebase.

Very often the preschooler may lead adults to think he can perform on a high level at all times. When he comes back for help or reassurance, it is apparent that he still needs to experiment and learn about himself, his abilities, and his limitations.

It is important that the child's parents, and the other persons in his life, help him to build a sense of self and autonomy. Some suggestions are listed.

- Show a friendly, honest interest in him and what he does.
- Accept him as he is.
- Help him to do things for himself without pressuring him.
- Give him the right to make mistakes and to feel secure in learning by trial and error.
- Permit him to make decisions that affect him: what he will wear, what he wants for dessert, what he will play with, what gift he wants to give someone.
- Help him to find out about alternatives — what it is like to have different choices. Let him learn to make a choice and live with it.
- Be understanding when he must face the consequences of his own behavior.

As the preschooler advances during this period, he becomes more dependable and obedient. He has an increased capacity for friendship and is at his best in small groups. His autonomy increases, but he still needs to be able to count on adults for security in facing the unfamiliar and unexpected.

Fig. 14-1 The child with a healthy self-image is able to develop a "sense of autonomy" — of being able to stand on her own feet.

Section 4 Child Development and Parent Enablers

DEVELOPMENTAL STAGES

Any effort to describe a preschooler makes it necessary to face the fact that there is a wide range of differences between children of the same age group. A child may have the physical appearance of a five year old, but may act out his feelings like a three year old. Another child who is three years old may talk with the vocabulary of a child far beyond his years.

All aspects of a child's development — physical, intellectual, social, and emotional — continue to intertwine. They make him the unique person that he is.

A developmental view of the preschooler follows. Each area is presented somewhat in the order of advancing age.

Physical Development

During the early part of this period, the child's development is confined to his *gross* (large) muscle control. He uses his senses and his body to explore and learn about his world. He develops a *body image:*

- Learns about his body parts in relation to each other.
- Finds out what his body parts can do.
- Knows the difference between right and left.
- Can tell directions that relate to his body position: behind, by the side of, before, above, under, in front of, in back of, for example.
- Likes his body and what it can do for him.

Through his body movements, the child gradually masters *locomotion* — the ability to make his body act for him. He develops *locomotor movements* — he can move his body from one place to another. He can

- Crawl
- Walk
- Skip
- Slide
- Climb
- Run
- Hop
- Leap
- Jump
- Gallop

He learns to master *nonlocomotor movements* — he can move his body while it stays in one place. He can

- Push
- Pull
- Bend
- Twist
- Swing
- Turn
- Stretch
- Shake
- Bounce
- Reach

As he gains greater control of his body movements, he develops *manipulative skills* — his body movements relate to an object. He can

- Hit
- Throw
- Catch
- Kick

During the time he gains control of his gross muscles, he also experiments with fine

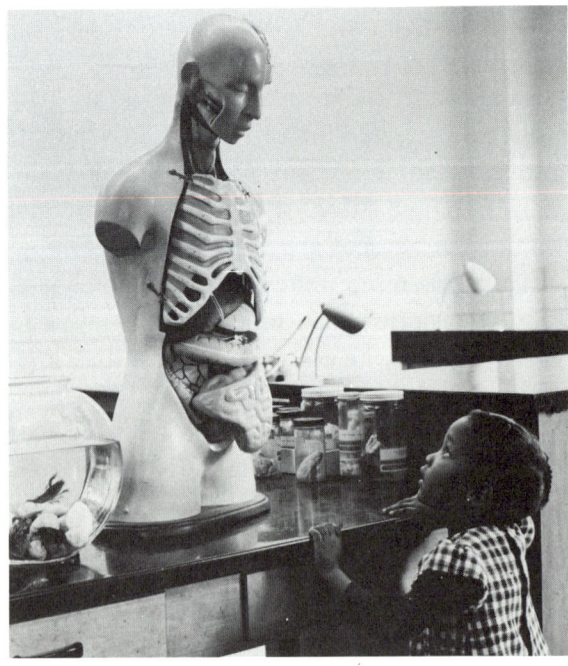

Fig. 14-2 Young children are interested in their bodies. Shown is a young child who is interested in another body — a model of an adult which she sees on a study trip.

muscle activities. His eye-hand coordination shows development. He masters thumb-finger grasp. He establishes *handedness* — uses one hand in preference to the other.

Activities that he enjoys help to develop control and coordination of his hand movements. He learns to

- Button his coat
- Fasten a zipper
- Tie a shoelace
- Draw with crayons, paint, and chalk
- Cut, paste, and tear things
- Sort objects
- Play with peg boards
- Build with blocks
- Mold clay and play dough
- String beads
- Trace with templates
- Create designs with template shapes
- Use a paper punch
- Press a stapler
- Squeeze a nose dropper

Intellectual Development

The preschooler's eagerness to meet new things and new experiences is in full swing. His wide scope of interests leads to increased knowledge. His endless questions help to broaden and expand his language facility. His thinking skills are growing.

It is not necessary or even desirable to push the preschooler into school-type things. But through play materials and games he can develop many new skills.

The following tasks are given as a broad framework to indicate what is possible. Only the maturity level of the child and his interests can make the learning tasks real for him.

Visual perception

- Knows nine colors: red, white, blue, yellow, orange, green, brown, black, purple. Uses color names in his conversation.
- Identifies sizes: large, small, middle sized.
- Recognizes numbers (few or many according to ability) and can count objects to meet his needs.
- Perceives basic shapes or forms: circle, square, heart, triangle, rectangle, star. Uses shape-terms in conversation.

Auditory discrimination

- Listens to sounds and can tell what they are: animals, human voices, natural sounds, and mechanical sounds in his world. May shut out sounds that are annoying or frightening.
- Responds to instructions.
- Imitates sounds that he hears.

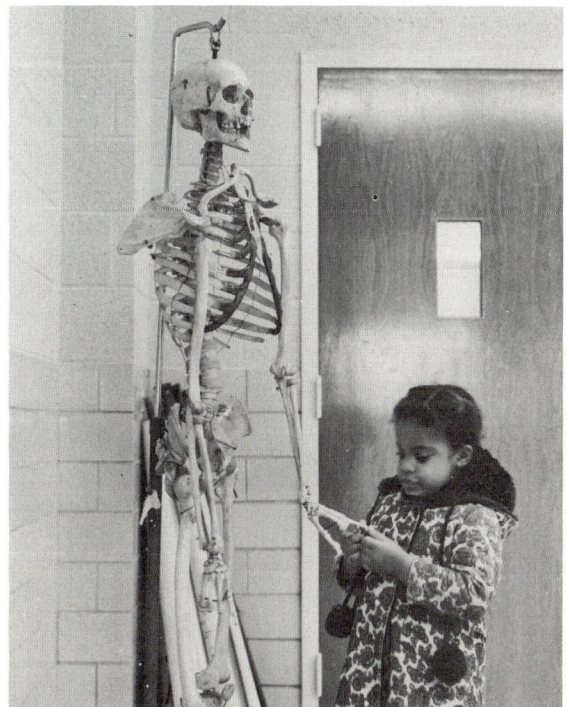

Fig. 14-3 The preschooler can count objects to meet needs: a skeleton has five "bony" fingers — 1-2-3-4-5.

- Can recognize differences in sounds of words.
- Listens to music and tries to carry a tune.
- Can locate the source of a sound (finds a ticking timer that is hidden where he can get it).

Touch sensitivity

- Feels things in his environment: cloth, food, toys, pots and pans, walls, tree trunks, sidewalks, wood, sand, stones, dirt, plants, fur on animals. May handle small living things (insects, frogs, worms).
- Can tell the difference between hot-cold, soft-hard.

Taste-smell recognition

- Smells things at home and away: food, odors, perfume, flowers, smoke. Rejects unpleasant odors.
- Tastes foods. Has likes and dislikes.

Thinking skills

- Learns to *seriate* — order by size (smallest to largest) or some other quality.
- Can *classify* objects — place them into categories (such as all blue balls or all big balls).
- Can *group* (combine) objects.
- Can *regroup* (take groups apart).
- Can show *one-to-one correspondence* (consider two properties of an object at one time).
- Can recognize some *cause-effect relationships* (something takes place because of something else): milk spills if the glass is placed too close to the table edge.
- Can use number concepts (according to ability).

Language development

- Follows directions. Can give simple directions of his own.

Fig. 14-4 Young children are sensitive to loud noises. They may shut out sounds that are annoying or frightening.

Fig. 14-5 Preschoolers explore their home environment. A vine provides an opportunity to see, touch, taste, and smell fruit — and hear the juice burst forth as teeth bear down on it.

- Carries on a conversation.
- Engages in dramatic play.
- Matches tones or sounds that he hears.
- Listens to rhymes and can repeat them.
- Retells stories that he hears.
- Makes up simple stories of his own.
- Helps to make experience charts.
- Likes to hear songs and tries to follow along.
- Enjoys songs with finger plays and body movement.
- Uses his imagination with puppet play.

Personal-Social Development

The child enters the preschool period with very limited social skill. He is primarily interested in himself and what he wants. He has no capacity to share — "I" and "mine" are his rule.

As he meets other children in play, he learns to be more cooperative. Gradually he learns to share and take turns. He likes to be with other children and begins to have special friends, but these change often. He quarrels easily.

The tendency to be a showoff is very strong in the preschooler. He brags about his parents and things they can do. He talks about himself, often communicating with laughter. This expanding sense of self is a part of his growing-up process.

During his interactions with people in his world, the preschooler meets some desirable goals.

- Appreciates the rights of others.
- Expresses sympathy.
- Recognizes differences between people and respects these differences.
- Relates to small groups of children.
- Changes his behavior when group-work demands it.
- Helps in small tasks around the house: sets the table and helps clear it, runs errands, picks up toys.
- Makes good company if people are patient with him.

Emotional Development

The preschooler tends to be jealous and may compete for the affection and approval of the adults in his life. If a new baby comes into the family, he may feel fear and anger toward his parents. He may see the baby as someone who has come to take his place.

Jealousy may be displayed in different ways or it may not be seen at all. The child may show open anger toward the baby or his parents. He may disguise his feelings, instead. The result may be nightmares, "accidents" (wetting his pants), temper outbursts, or other adverse behavior — signs that all is not well.

Several other behaviors related to the child's emotional development are listed.

- Cannot distinguish between truth and untruth and may be upset when accused of "telling lies" — something that he does not understand.
- Thinks faster than he can talk, a problem that may cause him to begin stuttering.

Fig. 14-6 A conversation can be a serious matter even to a very young child.

PRESCHOOLER NEEDS AND PARENT ENABLERS	
1. Large-muscle development	1. Provide play equipment and materials which call for large-muscle use: • Swings, climbing bars, gym sets, rope ladders. • Wagons, scooters, tricycle, wheelbarrow, doll carriage, sled. • Auto tire to roll, hoop, roller skates (learner type, at first). • Plastic punching bag, inflated rubber balls, other things to punch. • Bean bags, peg-and-mallet sets, ten pin game, paddle with ball attached. • Auto innertube for water play.
2. Release of energy	2. Provide adequate space (indoors and outdoors) in which child can run and play: • Designated area for outdoor play. • Indoor area he can call his own.
3. Fine-muscle development	3. Provide materials that promote fine-muscle skills: • Blocks, puzzles, interlocking wooden forms, log-building set, hammer and peg set, counting frame. • Clay and play dough, crayons, finger paints, water colors, blunt scissors, paste, paper, template, paper punch, stapler.
4. Development of perceptual skills	4. Provide materials that help him think: • Alphabet set, printing set, play typewriter, lotto, inlay puzzles. • Games that require sorting, matching, categorizing, seriating. • Clock dial, scale, counting frame, magnet, thermometer, soap bubble set, play telephone. • Books, story records, songs and games in music, view master with slides, filmstrips.
5. Language development	5. Provide opportunities for hearing and using language: • Listening to stories, poems, records, human voices. Meeting people. • Labeling things that he sees, makes, or has in his room. • Discussing things that he shares with others: trips, television shows, shopping trips, holidays, his home.

	• Materials for pretending (role-play): dolls to dress and undress, farm and zoo animal sets, toy cars and trains, airplanes, boats, trucks, puppets, shoes, ties, gloves, vests, hats, kitchen and other home utensils that cannot hurt him, empty food cans and cartons.
6. Social development	6. Provide situations in which he can learn to assume responsibility for his own behavior: • See that he has children with which to play. • Involve him in family projects. • Let him make decisions and live with the outcome. • Give him tasks to perform and let him know what the consequences are for nonperformance. Follow through. • Let him mingle with visitors in the home to learn social behavior.
7. Emotional control	7. Provide guidance in helping him cope with sadness, grief, and other personal problems that may arise: • Help him to accept what he cannot change: hospital stay, death, loss of parent through divorce or separation, prison, surrogate-parent or stepparent, physical handicap (poor vision, loss of hearing, motor or physical problems, allergies that impose limits, disease, skin irritations, etc.). • Use *bibliotherapy* (stories that highlight a character's problem and the way the person copes with it). • Let him play out his fear through role-play.

Fig. 14-7 Preschooler needs and parent enablers.

- May have fears that are real or imagined: the dark, animals, old people, death.
- May have an imaginary playmate who is real as life to him.
- May resist attempts to discipline him, but responds to action that is consistent and considerate.

ACTIVITIES AND AIDS TO FOSTER DEVELOPMENT

Feel Box

- Cut two holes in the side of a hatbox or cardboard carton.
- Place some objects in the box.

- Have the child reach in with both hands and touch something.
- Ask him to describe what he has, using terms such as hard, soft, furry, rough, smooth.
- Let him take out the object and give its name. Provide the name if he does not know it.

Food Fun (a five-sense experience)

- When pie is being prepared for dessert, let the child learn.
- Give him some pie dough to roll out. Let him add a sprinkle of cinnamon and some sugar. Bake the dough. Let him eat it.
- Discuss the experience: the feel of the dough, pressing the rolling pin down on it, smelling the cinnamon (tasting it — uh!), the "sandy" feel of the sugar, the baking smell, the end product taste.
- Let him help make some small pies for the family. When the oven is turned on, write desired temperature on a slip of paper (for older child). Let him set the oven. For the pies, he can roll the dough (parent puts it into pan), spoon the filling into the pie shell (counting as he goes along). He can roll the top crust which parent transfers to pan. Child can prick crust and press down edges with a fork.

Plate Pictures

- When the family is served foods such as spaghetti with sauce, gravy, or chocolate pudding, let the child help clear the table and scrape the plates clean.
- Let him use his index finger to draw pictures on the bottom of some of the plates.
- Afterward let him experiment with warm and cold water in washing his hands with and without soap. Have him decide which method does the best job.

Now Smell This

- Dab several wads of cotton with a different extract for each: chocolate, lemon, orange, cinnamon, vanilla, mint, strawberry (spices may be used instead).
- Place each wad in a well-washed baby food jar.
- Ask the child to smell each jar, telling what the smell makes him think of.

Tasting Fun

- Prepare for snack time a variety of foods that differ in appearance, taste, and texture: a small piece of cheese, celery, orange, tomato, apple, banana, carrot.
- Have him compare the foods in color, texture, and taste.
- Let him tell what he likes best.
- Have him experiment to see what salt or sugar does to the taste of the foods.

What Is This Sound?

- Child turns away from person playing with him.
- Child is asked to identify sounds that a person standing behind him can make:

Fig. 14-8 Experiences with paint help the preschooler develop fine muscles. Freedom to experiment helps the child learn what paint can do.

crush paper, clap hands, shuffle feet, tap with a pencil, whistle, imitate the vocal sound of an animal, display a ticking clock.
- Positions are reversed. The child makes the sounds for his partner to guess.
- If recorded sounds (natural or mechanical) are available from a toy-lending library (or other source), they may be used, too.

SUMMARY

A child is considered a preschooler from the time he approaches his third birthday, until he enters school ready for his formal education. He has an "I can do" attitude. The preschooler seeks a sense of "autonomy" or independence — of being able to stand on his own feet.

The development of body image — what his body can do — is an important part of the child's development. He can use his large muscles with increasing control. He begins to develop skill in small-muscle control. Toward the end of the period he has greater coordination in hand movements. Handedness is established, and he begins to write.

The child's intellectual development makes it possible for him to face the new tasks required of him during his formal schooling. He is eager to learn about his world and asks endless questions.

The preschooler needs many opportunities to develop his muscular control, perceptual skills, language skills, social behaviors, and emotional control. His parents play an important role in helping him to face his tasks with success.

SUGGESTED ACTIVITIES

- Locate the parent of a preschooler, or ask if you can volunteer in a preschool center to work with a child.
    a. Taking into account the child's stage of development, select from this unit some activities for the child.
    b. Prepare workplans for the activities. Show them to the parent (or preschool teacher) for comments and approval to use the plans.
    c. Try the activities with the child. If possible, tape-record your sessions, so that you can share them with your peer group.
    d. Replay the tape and ask yourself the following questions:
        (1) Was the child interested in the activity?
        (2) Did the child do a lot of talking? Did he ask questions, give reasons, tell "why," "how," or "where?"
        (3) If the lesson were to be done again, what changes would you make, if any?
    e. Share your findings with your peer group. Discuss the likes and differences in the interests and abilities of the children who shared your lesson.
    f. Make up some original activities for the child that you worked with. Show them to the parent (or teacher). Use them if approved. Share them with your class.

Section 4 Child Development and Parent Enablers

REVIEW

A. Define each of the following.
   1. Preschooler
   2. "Sense of autonomy"
   3. Gross muscle control
   4. Body image
   5. Locomotor movements
   6. Nonlocomotor movements
   7. Manipulative skills
   8. Handedness
   9. Seriate
   10. Bibliotherapy

B. List at least five suggestions for helping a child to develop a "sense of autonomy."

C. List ten locomotor movements that the preschooler can master before his formal schooling begins.

D. List ten nonlocomotor skills that the preschooler can master before his formal schooling begins.

E. List four manipulative skills that can be developed as the child gains greater control of his body movements.

F. Describe at least ten characteristics of the preschooler as described in this unit.

G. Identify five needs of the preschooler and corresponding parent enablers.

Section 5 Materials for Home-Based Learning

unit 15 firsthand experiences

OBJECTIVES

After studying this unit, the student should be able to

- Describe the terms *firsthand experiences* and *learning episodes.*
- Identify five general questions asked by persons who plan activities for children.
- Tell four ways by which concepts can be built.
- List five home visitor tasks by which parents can be helped to identify, select, and carry out worthwhile firsthand experiences for the young child.
- Identify five concepts and appropriate learning activities for the young child that foster concept development.

The young child may be surrounded by many opportunities for learning. Unless he has someone to help him get started, he may never know how to learn about his world and discover what is in it.

This unit looks at ways by which parents can use resources in the child's world to help him learn through firsthand experiences. The direct contacts which the child has with objects, things, and events that he can see in his everyday life are called firsthand experiences.

GROWTH CHARACTERISTICS AND LEARNING EXPERIENCES

It is not possible to list activities that meet the needs of all children who have similar growth characteristics. Human beings are complex and varied. No child can perfectly fit any list that attempts to describe him and his peer group.

The growth characteristics presented in the preceding section cannot be accepted as valid for all children. Each list stands for a central point from which a child may deviate. No list is to be used as a match-and-pair formula. All learning experiences provided must be in harmony with the growth characteristics of the individual child for whom plans are made.

Figure 15-1 presents questions that are raised by the people who make plans for young children. These are listed with a related question that parents may ask. Responses are presented as home visitor tasks.

DEVELOPING A COGNITIVE MAP THROUGH FIRSTHAND EXPERIENCES

In unit 11 a cognitive map is described as "all the concepts (interrelated ideas and experiences) which a person develops and uses to guide his behavior." Through firsthand experiences in his world, the child can add vast numbers of concepts to his storage bank of information. There are four ways

Section 5 Materials for Home-Based Learning

GENERAL QUESTION	PARENT'S QUESTION	HOME VISITOR TASKS
What growth characteristics do children show at this stage of development?	Where is my child?	Help parents examine the child's growth: physical, intellectual, social, emotional: • How is the target child like his peer group? • How does he differ? • What activities does he choose at play? • How long does he concentrate on a task? • Can he use oral language to express himself?
What kinds of social behavior does a child of this age normally display?	What kinds of behavior does my child display?	Help parents study their child in his home life and in his peer group: • Does he play with other children; are they older, the same age, younger? • Does he display behavior that is appropriate for his stage of development? • Does he consider the rights of others when he is at play? • Is he accepted by his group? • Does he show any of the following traits: friendly, fearful, shy, aggressive, anxious, temper outbursts, negative action? • How does he handle his feelings? • How does he interact at home?
What developmental tasks are set for children who are in this stage of their development?	What tasks and problems does my child face?	Help parents determine the needs of the child: • Note areas in which he is not performing to his ability. • Identify the child's developmental needs which can be met by parents.
What activities and learning experiences can help children meet success with their tasks to enable the next stage of growth?	How can I help my child achieve success with his tasks and problems?	Find activities that can meet the child's stated needs: • Listening activities

		• Number relationships
		• Art and craft work
		• Music enjoyment
		• Dramatic play
		• Physical exercise and play
		• Contacts with the world of physical and natural sciences.
		• Social situations with peer group and other persons.
How can the child's learning experiences be evaluated?	How can I tell if the things that I choose are right for my child?	Help parents to evaluate the child's behavior when he is at work on a task: • Does he ask questions — why, what, when, where, how? • Does he want to tell others about his activities? • Does he talk about or show what he accomplishes? • Does he show signs of being happy in his work? • Does he think of new activities or things to do which grow out of a task?

Fig. 15-1 Questions and responses that help in selecting the learning experiences that best meet the needs of the individual child.

by which parents can help the child to build concepts.

Discriminate Learning

Through *discriminate learning*, the parent points out the differences between things:

- An apple has a shape which is different from that of a pear (but both are fruit).
- A circle is different from a square (but both are shapes).
- A mail carrier's job is different from that of a fire fighter (but both help people in the community).
- A cottage is different from an apartment house (but both are places where people live).

Classification

Through *classification*, objects or ideas are grouped according to the ways that they are alike:

- A rooster and a hen belong to the same family; (a rooster is a male and the hen is a female).
- A pond has water in it just as a lake does (but a pond is smaller than a lake).

Definition

Through *definition*, the parent tells what the word means in terms that already have meaning for the child:

- The mayor is the person who is in charge of things in the city. He works with other people to get jobs done.
- Some pandas are small, reddish brown animals somewhat like a raccoon. Other pandas look like black and white teddy bears.

Context

Through *context*, parents point out the meaning of an unfamiliar word by calling attention to how it is used:

- The princess lived in a beautiful castle that was as big as an apartment house; (*castle* must mean a large building where people live).
- The children gave their father an ottoman, so that he could rest his feet on it; (*ottoman* must mean a footstool).
- The little girl has a bruise that did nothing more than make the skin around the bruise turn a bluish color; (*bruise* must be a "hurt" that does not bleed).

The child's cognitive map grows as he discovers new things that have meaning for him. His cognitive map is formed, changed, and enlarged by every experience the child has. Parents have an important role in helping the child to make his cognitive map all that it can be.

FIRSTHAND EXPERIENCES IN THE CHILD'S WORLD

Firsthand experiences can be used to help the child gain accurate concepts of things in his world:
- People
- Objects
- Qualities
- Events (happenings)
- Processes
- Relationships between things

A list of firsthand experiences is given in figure 15-2, a breakdown of home and family life concepts. Learning episodes are presented for each concept. A *learning episode* is a bit of learning which is complete in itself. It may stand alone, or it may be related to other learning episodes centered around a like theme.

The concept of learning episodes is helpful in demonstrating the need for parent skill in tapping all opportunities as soon as they arise. Home and family life concepts are taught during the course of everyday life. The key to learning is knowing how to make use of the home as a laboratory for learning.

In the list that is presented, no attempt is made to set an age level. Selections can be made only with full respect for each child as an individual — for his maturity level, past experiences, needs, interests, and ability to understand.

The learning activities listed are suggestions to help parents lead the child toward things which he wants to know or needs to know. Parents can be guided in choosing what is appropriate for the target child.

The learning episodes identified with home and family life do not begin to name all of the ways that parents can help children learn. No doubt parents can add many other ideas to those given. A partial list of the many other themes around which parents can create learning episodes is given:

The Farm

- Kinds of farms.
- What can be seen on a farm: fields, pastures, orchards, woods, streams, ponds, buildings, animals.
- How the farmer uses objects and space.
- Farm work and machines that help to do it.

Unit 15 Firsthand Experiences

CONCEPTS	LEARNING ACTIVITIES IN EVERYDAY LIVING
Home and Family Life	
• Father and mother are responsible for their family.	• Count family members. Learn full names. • Find out about the work of parents. Learn that a parent can work in the home, outside the home, or in both places. Visit the place(s) where outside-the-home work takes place. • Make a photo mobile of the family.
• Each family member has duties at home and away.	• Help the child to understand how parents provide the family with food, shelter, clothing. Take child shopping for food. • Talk about the work of other family members. • Talk about the need for family members to practice thrift. • Talk about manners. • Help child to make a chart listing ways he can help at home.
• Everyone needs a home.	• Have the child talk about his home: type of house, number of rooms, colors inside and outside, family members who live in it. • Let child draw pictures of his family to place in a scrapbook. • Collect photographs of family members doing different things. • Have child make a shoebox house. To make the rooms, use pictures from mail-order catalogs. Paste them around the inside of the shoeboxes. Make pipe-cleaner dolls to serve as family members. Dress them with clothing models cut from catalogs. Show the child how to use the dolls in dramatic play. Encourage him to make up his acts.
• People need good food to have strong bodies and keen minds.	• Have child help in buying food: note prices, names, sizes, containers, etc. Let him match words on a grocery list with words on canned goods. Make a play store. • Let child help prepare foods: measure dry and liquid ingredients, set oven temperature, whip cream, count eggs, etc. • Let him bake a cake or cupcakes, using a prepared cake mix. • Call his attention to things that take place: steam, bubbles, freezing food.

167

Section 5 *Materials for Home-Based Learning*

	defrosting food, grinding, chopping, slicing, cutting, mashing, boiling, baking, etc.
	• Help him count cookies, eggs, rolls — by the dozen. Let him weigh things.
• Plants and animals provide people with food.	• Visit a farm. Walk around to see things.
	• Name animals that provide food.
	• Locate pictures, filmstrips and stories about food and how it is grown.
	• Let the child plant a food that he can eat. Plant something in a deep dishpan to grow indoors.
• Relatives are people who have a place in our extended family.	• Identify relatives: grandmother, grandfather, aunts, uncles, etc.
	• Make a family tree. Have the child put photographs on it.
	• Have child make greeting cards to send to relatives on special occasions.
	• Bring together family and relatives to help the child develop a feeling of having roots.
	• Acquaint child with his cultural or ethnic heritage: food, language, special objects or events. Help him develop pride in his heritage.
• Families need other workers who provide services to the home.	• Let child find out what workers do: painters, plumber, electrician, laundry or dry cleaner, carpenter, etc. Visit a home that is being built in the neighborhood. Observe it from start to finish.
	• Find stories and books that can give the child more information about workers.
• People need clothing.	• Help child to understand that the climate and weather affect the choice of clothing.
	• Provide child with samples of clothing material to see and touch: cotton, wool, silk, leather, rubber, linen, furs.
	• Make a picture book of different kinds of clothing that can be worn in the four seasons. Use catalogs or newspaper pictures.
	• Make labels for scrapbook pictures, even though child cannot read them. Use words to explain things and built his vocabulary.
• Families can have fun together. (See unit 21)	• Find group games that the family can play.
	• Make games: a checker set can be made from the side of a cardboard box. Use soft drink bottle caps for checkers.

Unit 15 Firsthand Experiences

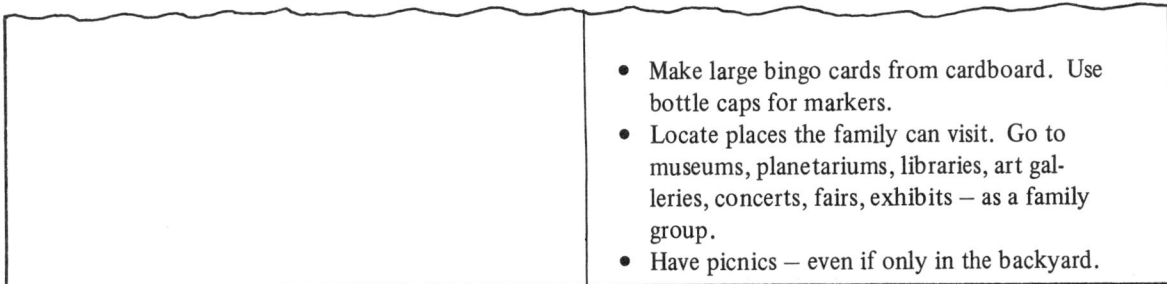

- Make large bingo cards from cardboard. Use bottle caps for markers.
- Locate places the family can visit. Go to museums, planetariums, libraries, art galleries, concerts, fairs, exhibits — as a family group.
- Have picnics — even if only in the backyard.

Fig. 15-2 Young children learn concepts through daily living experiences.

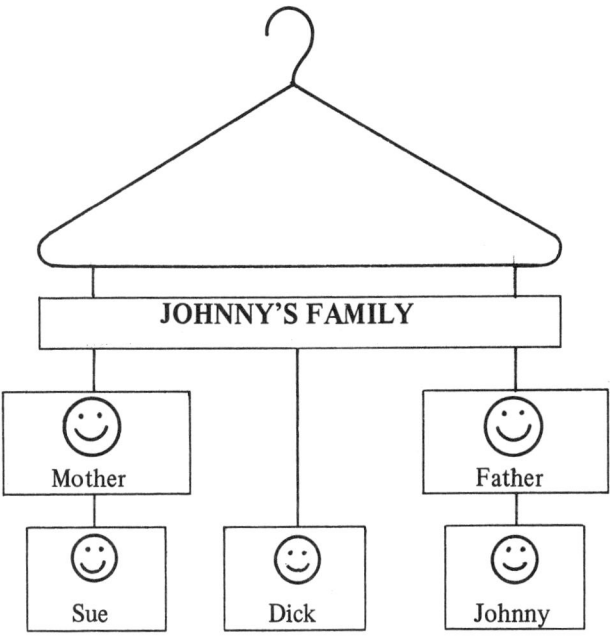

Fig. 15-3 A family mobile can be made to help the young child to see his family as a unit.

☺ THINGS JOHNNY REMEMBERS ☺

1. He keeps away from things under the sink.
2. He does not touch things that can hurt him.
3. He says "thank you" and "excuse me."
4. He speaks in a nice voice.
5. He does not yell at people.
6. He shares and takes turns.
7. He knocks before opening closed doors.
8. He helps his family.
9. He asks permission before he uses something which does not belong to him.
10. He puts away his toys when it is time to do it.
11. He is considerate of others when he uses the bathroom.
12. He makes sure that his dog does not bother neighbors.

Fig. 15-4 Making a chart of things that the child remembers to do is helpful, even if he cannot read it. It gives meaning to printed words and makes him feel good about himself, too.

Section 5 Materials for Home-Based Learning

SOME WAYS A YOUNG CHILD CAN HELP AND LEARN AT HOME

1. Set the table: count forks, knives, chairs, napkins, plates, etc. (Learns to count and classify things.)
2. Get food from the refrigerator at mealtime. (Learns food names firsthand. Follows directions.)
3. Help measure liquid and dry ingredients. (Learns about the relationships between things: 1 cup, 1/2 cup, 1/4 cup.)
4. Put his own clothes away. (Learns to assume responsibility for himself.)
5. Learn to answer the telephone: "The Jones' home, Johnny Jones speaking." Or, "Johnny Jones speaking." (Learns social amenities — good manners.)
6. Dial a telephone number for parents. (Learns a skill that can be tapped in family emergency.)
7. Water plants and take care of family pets. (Learns to assume responsibility that goes beyond his own needs.)
8. Bring in newspaper (Learns to be helpful)
9. Pay the newspaper person (with parent nearby) and examine coins at the same time. (Learns to identify and use coins for goods and services: penny, nickel, dime, quarter, half-dollar. Learns paper-money terms by looking at number words. Learns to classify money.)
10. Help to fold laundry and put it away. (Learns to associate clothes with family members. Learns to perform service in family life. Learns to assume responsibility. Learns to match like things: blue sock with blue sock, etc.)

Fig. 15-5 Some ways to help a child learn.

VOCABULARY LIST: Home and Family Life

air	checker	fork	house
alarm	child	freezer	ingredients
attic	chop	fruit	knife
aunt	clean	fur	language
baby	clothes	furnishing	light
bake	cocoa	furniture	lighting
basement	coffee	gas	linen
bed	comb	game	liquid
blend	concrete	girl	manners
boil	conditioner	glass	matches
boy	cook	gloves	milk
bread	cotton	grandfather	mirror
brick	count	grandpa	mitten
brother	cut	grandmother	mix
brush	daddy	grandma	mother
bubbles	dog	grind	museum
build	doll	group	nylon
butter	dry cleaner	hat	plant
cap	electrician	health	plate
carpenter	electricity	heat	play
carpet	fair	heating	piano
cat	family	help	picnic
ceiling	father	hobby	plumber
cement	fire	home	potato
cereal	food	hot	polite

Unit 15 Firsthand Experiences

Vocabulary List (Con't)			
quilt	shop	stucco	vegetables
radio	silk	table	ventilation
rayon	sink	tea	ventilator
refrigerator	sister	telephone	visitor
recorder	size	television	wash
roof	slice	temperature	water
room	sofa	tools	wear
rug	stairs	toys	weather
safety	steps	towel	whip
scissors	stereo	uncle	wires
screen	spoon	underwear	work
sheets	stove		

Fig. 15-6 Shown is a partial list of words related to the home. When parents explain what words mean, the child can build new concepts on those he already knows.

- Foods from the farm: vegetables, milk, fruits.
- Planting a garden: taking care of it, harvesting.

Pets
- Animals that can be pets.
- Care of pets at home.
- How to keep pets from bothering neighbors.

How People Go Places (Move)
- Buses, cars, taxis, trucks.
- Passenger trains, freight trains, subways.
- Bicycles, motorcycles.
- Boats, ships.
- Airplanes (some persons are trained to use space ships).

Events and Happenings
- Holidays (can be a time for celebrating with friends).
- Birthdays (self, family, relatives, friends).
- Current happenings (discussing things that the child hears on radio, television, or by word of mouth). Explain things that he sees and asks about. Calm his fears.
- Personal experiences.
- Elections (concept of choosing people to be "in-charge" of things in town or country). Say, "Election day is the time people *vote* — choose — other people to be in charge of things that we care about."
- Weather changes (understanding lightning, thunder, rain, snow.) Observing: clothes used in different seasons, storm windows being put up, screens being stored, moth-prevention measures taken, listening to weather forecasts and checking what does happen, keeping a thermometer outdoors and keeping a record of each day's temperature, etc.
- Parades.
- Exhibits, festivals, fairs, circus.
- Space exploration: let them watch related programs. Find answers to their questions. Call attention to magazine and newspaper pictures that show things seen on television. See how much child can recall from television program.

Section 5 *Materials for Home-Based Learning*

MOREHEAD PLANETARIUM PROGRAM GUIDE

WONDER OF THE SKY

Suggested for 3, 4, and 5 year olds

The planetarium narrator will welcome the children in the Sky Theatre to put them at ease in unfamiliar surroundings. The planetarium "teacher" — the Zeiss Projector — will be introduced and an explanation of what it will do will be given. Using the projector and special effects the children will experience the daytime and nighttime sky as seen from their backyard.

CONCEPTS TO BE DEMONSTRATED IN THE PLANETARIUM:

1. The sun moves in the daytime sky giving the earth life.
2. The sun is a star like those you see at night only much closer.
3. At night we can see the moon, stars and planets.
4. American Indians told stories about star patterns in the sky.

STUDY QUESTIONS:

1. What is the sun? (It is a star, a ball of hot gas in the sky.)
2. What does the sun do for us? (It gives us light, warmth, and makes the trees and flowers grow. It also makes it possible for birds and animals and people to live.)
3. What can we see in the nighttime sky from our backyard? (Stars, moon and planets.)
4. What did the American Indians see in the sky among the stars? (Some of the animals he met in the forest such as bears and birds, as well as Indian braves and maidens.)

Fig. 15-7 The parent selects WONDER OF THE SKY, a program designed for children three, four, and five years old. (Source: Morehead Planetarium, University of North Carolina, Chapel Hill, N.C.)

A PARENT-CHILD STUDY TRIP TO A PLANETARIUM

The Situation

- Described is a study trip that a parent takes with a young child. Follow-up learning activities are included.
- Home visitors can use the outline to demonstrate how a study trip can be a meaningful experience to the child.

Preplanning

- Parent finds out about programs which are planned.
- Parent selects WONDER OF THE SKY, a program designed for three, four, and five year olds.
- Parent obtains a guide that gives background information, including cost.
- A reservation is made and confirmed.
- The date and time are recorded on the family calendar. The child is involved. He encircles the date. As days pass, he marks them off on the calendar.
- Parent makes transportation plans.

Unit 15 Firsthand Experiences

Introducing the Idea to the Target Child

- The child naps longer one day, so that he can stay up until dark that night.

- Parent takes child outdoors to look at the nighttime sky.

- Child talks about what he sees. Parent calls attention to group of stars. New words, with consistently brief explanations, are used as parent and child talk:

    Star: heavenly body; something that looks like a faraway point of light, a distant sun; something that is shown as having five points when pictures are drawn or made in another way. (Attention is called to stars seen on the flag, for example. Parent draws on child's previous knowledge to help him understand the present concept.)

    Constellation: stars that have their own (fixed) group.

    Planet: a heavenly body that rotates (turns around like a wheel).

    Satellite: a small planet that revolves (travels in a path) around a larger one.

    Moon: the satellite that revolves around the earth. It shines by reflected (mirrorlike image) light that the sun throws back to it. Parent later uses a mirror and lamp to show "reflected" light.

- Parent makes no effort to "drill" information into the child. Comments and information are in conversationlike tone. Objective is to make child familiar with the words and to associate meaning with them. Parent sets the stage for what child is to see at the planetarium.

- Parent repeats nighttime learning episode once, twice, or more times — as child shows interest.

- Daytime talks define the *sun:* a star; a ball of hot gas in the sky; a star about which the earth and other planets revolve (travel in a path).

- Parent calls attention to the need for eye protection from direct rays of the sunlight.

- Child has opportunities to talk about his experience.

- Parent takes child to the public library. Books about stars are found. Parent and child select books that are appropriate for the child. Parent selects book from which to gain information (or review) necessary to answer questions the child may ask.

- Planetarium is too far away for parent to let child see building before the visit. A photograph of the planetarium is obtained. Child can see where he is to go.

- Child sees photograph of the planetarium teacher (the Zeiss Planetarium Projector) and learns that it is very, very big.

- Child sees photographs of behind-the-scene work at the planetarium. He learns that loud sounds may be heard. Lights may go on and off. He learns that both are manmade. Parent knows that young children are sensitive to loud noises. The child is less apt to fear something that he knows about in advance.

Going to the Planetarium

- Parent gives child money to pay the bus fare. Attention is called to the price of the tickets and the coins used.

- Child is encouraged to talk about what he sees on the way.

- Child pays for planetarium tickets, too.

Section 5 Materials for Home-Based Learning

Fig. 15-8 The child sees a photograph of the planetarium teacher (the Zeiss Planetarium Projector) and learns that it is very, very big.

- Parent and child visit planetarium exhibits before the show.

- Child is able to see the planetarium projector before the lights are dimmed. Parent calls attention to things that were said before the trip. Child is well at ease.

The Program in Action

- A narrator welcomes the young children and tells them about the Sky Theatre and what they will see there. She tells them that they will see the daytime and nighttime sky as if they were in their own backyard.

- When the lights are dimmed, the child shows signs of fear. His parent reaches out and holds his hand. The child is at ease again.

- The young children present show great interest in what is going on. A common frame of reference gives them an opportunity to go beyond "talk." They discuss the things that they see together.

- When the program is over, the target child takes another look at things that interest him.

Fig. 15-9 If a child can see how sound effects are made, he is less likely to be frightened by what he sees and hears.

Follow-up Activities

- Child tells his family about the trip.
- Parent acts as scribe (one who does the writing) for the child. The parent writes what the child dictates. (Both sets of grandparents are to get a letter from him.) He signs the letters with his name (written, if he can, or a "scribble" that

174

Unit 15 Firsthand Experiences

Fig. 15-10 Children look at planetarium exhibits before the show starts.

Fig. 15-11 A narrator welcomes the young children. She tells them about the Sky Theatre and what they will see there.

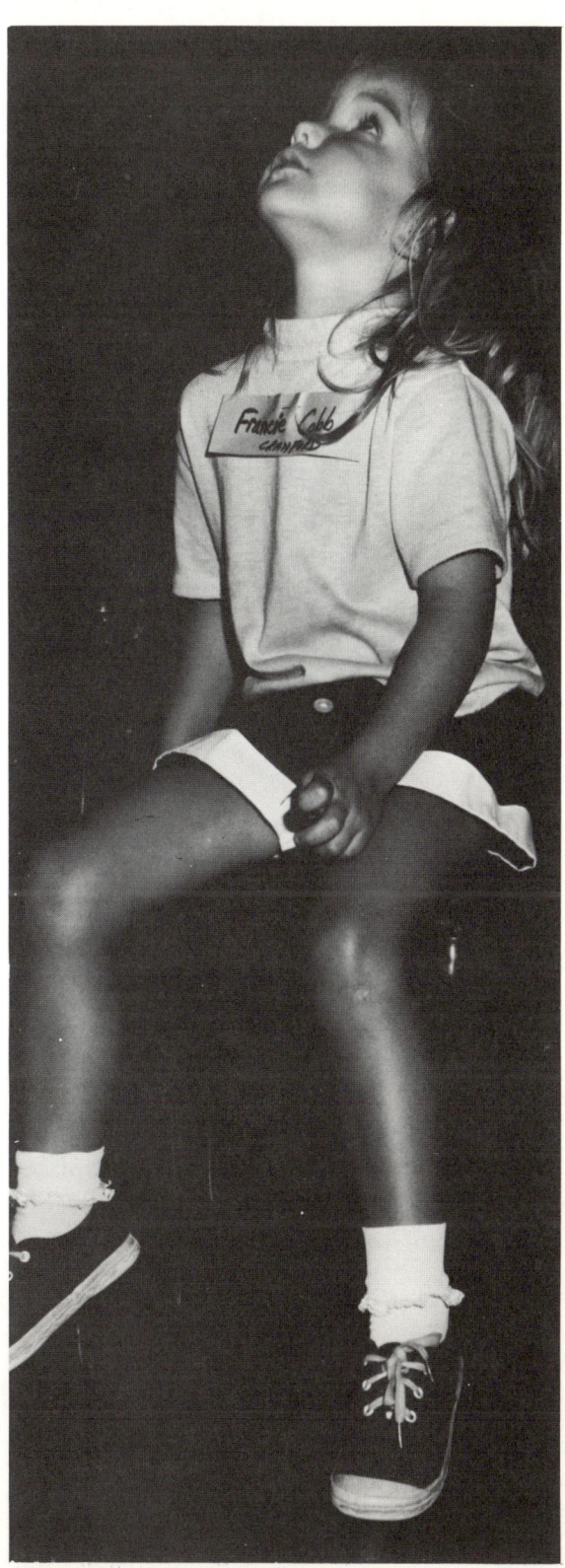

Fig. 15-12 A preschooler shows great interest in the story of the sky.

175

Section 5 *Materials for Home-Based Learning*

Fig. 15-13 A common frame of reference gives a young child an opportunity to go beyond "talk." He can discuss things with a friend who sees what he does.

stands for his name). Letters are taken to the post office where child buys stamps and mails his letters himself.
- He goes outdoors another night to see the stars again. Child uses many words that he heard during his trip.
- Parent helps child to make a five-pointed star (see unit 16). He pastes stars on the windows in his room.
- Parent and child work together to make a shoebox peep show of constellations (see unit 16).

THINGS TO REMEMBER

It is important that parents understand that the ideas listed are not intended to be school-type learning. What is presented must be in keeping with cues that the parent gets from the child. When a child shows a definite interest and asks to hear more, the parent can go on. Any attempt to "push" the child into a learning episode may cause him to balk and can lessen his desire to learn.

Firsthand experiences are things that happen during the course of everyday life. The sun, the moon, and the stars are things that the child can see. *Natural questions* (those that he asks himself) come up all the time. A trip to the planetarium (or another local place) suitable for a learning episode can help to give the child some answers to his questions. The trip may spark other questions that lead him further in his desire to learn about his world and what affects it.

Firsthand experiences include watching other people do things, too. A child who watches a woman using a sewing machine has a firsthand experience. Seeing a crane at work when a building is being built is a firsthand experience. Meeting people from other countries and listening to them speak is a firsthand experience. The list is one that is hard to end.

SUMMARY

Firsthand experiences are direct contacts which the child has with objects, things and events that he can see in his everyday life. All experiences must be in harmony with the growth characteristics of the individual child for whom plans are made.

Five questions are raised by people who make plans for young children: (1) What growth characteristics do children show at this stage of development? (2) What kinds of social behavior does a child of this age normally display? (3) What developmental tasks are set for children who are in this stage of their development? What activities and learning experiences can help children meet success with their tasks to enable their next stage of growth? (5) How can the child's learning experiences be evaluated?

Parents ask five corresponding questions: (1) Where is my child? (2) What kinds of behavior does my child display? (3) What tasks and problems does my child face? (4) How can I help my child achieve success with his tasks and problems? (5) How can I tell if the things that I choose are right for my child?

Concept learning helps a child to develop his cognitive map. Concepts can be learned through discriminate learning, classification, definition, and context.

Firsthand experiences can be used to help the child gain accurate concepts of things in his world: people, objects, qualities, events (happenings), processes, and relationships between things.

A learning episode is a bit of learning which is complete in itself. It may stand alone, or it may be related to other learning episodes centered around a like theme. Parents can provide many learning episodes for the child. Study trips are good ways to provide firsthand experiences that enhance learning.

SUGGESTED ACTIVITIES

- Prepare a list of study trips that can be made in your immediate community.

    a. Locate a parent who is willing to let you plan a study trip for her child and accompany her when the trip is made.

    b. Go over your list with the parent, to find a study trip that is appropriate for the target child.

    c. Try to use no-cost activities, unless the parent makes other selections for which she pays her own expenses (you should expect to pay your own way).

    d. Make your plans. The planetarium trip described in this unit may spark ideas for your trip. Perhaps you may be able to take a trip to a planetarium, too.

    e. Prepare an account of your experience, using the following headings:

    The Situation
    Preplanning
    Vocabulary List
    Introducing the Idea to the Target Child
    Follow-up Activities
    Evaluation

    f. Make the vocabulary list in two parts. A pretrip list is made to prepare the parent for explanations that may be necessary. Words that are related to the study trip are identified and defined. Sometimes the simplest words are the most difficult to explain. Check the words in a dictionary. A list of words that come up during the trip should be kept and added to the first list.

    g. Evaluate (tell how good) the experience, using three headings: what you learned, what parenting skills the parent gained, and what the target-child learned.

    h. Share your experience with your class. Listen to what they did.

i. Duplicate and exchange study trip reports with your peer-group. Place them in your workplan file.

j. Be sure that material obtained from other persons bears the name of the contributor. A person must always be given credit for his work.

REVIEW

A. Define and describe the terms.
   1. Firsthand experiences
   2. Learning episodes
B. State five general questions asked by persons who plan activities for children.
C. Identify and describe briefly four ways by which concepts can be built.
D. List five home visitor tasks by which parents can be helped to identify, select, and carry out worthwhile firsthand experiences for the target child.
E. Identify five concepts and appropriate learning activities that foster concept-development in the young child.

unit 16 objectives and activities

OBJECTIVES

After studying this unit, the student should be able to

- Define and describe the terms *curriculum, organized experiences, self-concept, self-esteem,* and *identity.*
- Identify three sources of objectives and tell how they contribute to the home-based curriculum.
- Select, for each area of concern described in this unit, four related objectives and activities.

This unit deals with the curriculum for a home-based early childhood program. *Curriculum* is defined as all of the organized experiences which a parent provides to help the child learn at home.

Organized experiences are those thought-through opportunities for learning which a parent can

- Plan ahead: intended activities.
- Seize on-the-spot opportunities: unplanned learning episodes which fit a need the parent can recognize.

CURRICULUM FOR HOME-BASED PROGRAMS

Educators can guide parents who wish to explore ways to build a home-based curriculum for their young child. It is crucial to point out that there is no single way by which a child can master a concept or learn a skill. To plan for a given child, it is necessary to

- Identify goals and objectives which are on the child's level of understanding and need.
- Select methods by which goals and objectives can be met.
- Locate learning media which increase the probability that desired change in behavior takes place — that the child gets, holds, and uses what is taught.

Sources of Objectives

Three sources of objectives are identified. The first is the child. What the child can do and what he should be able to do must be identified. The difference between the two is called a *need*. The needs of the child are based on his growth and development in all areas: physical, intellectual, social, emotional. What a child wants to do is also a need and is considered. In like manner, what he does not want to do is another cue to a curriculum which responds to the child's needs. For example, a parent wants a child to take music or dancing lessons. The child balks. Forced involvement may be harmful to the child.

The child's needs must take top priority in plans made for him. The curriculum must lead to his positive growth and development.

The child's group must also be considered a source of objectives. The child's group consists of the people who care about him — what he does and what happens to him. Included in this category are

- His parents: parents have the right to bring up their child according to their

Section 5 Materials for Home-Based Learning

own beliefs and value system. Therefore, what they say should "count."

- His cultural group: People in a society have ideas concerning the way that the young in that group should be raised. Certain things are accepted by use or offered by law.

Parents may see society's objectives as learning to do the "right" things, and living a "good" life. Both affect what goes into the curriculum and the direction it takes.

Specialists are also sources of objectives for young children. Specialists are all persons who put in their bid for what they feel is "best" for the child. Some specialists are concerned with the child's physical wellbeing; others concentrate on his intellectual development. Some specialists deal with subject matter such as language, science, art, music, and the like. Each contributes to goals which are like those set for all schooling. People who work with young children and study their behavior give vital information. It is necessary to put that information in a form which parents find helpful.

AREAS OF CONCERN

Each area of concern which follows is based on a like framework.

- The area is defined and described.
- Major objectives for the area are identified.
- Appropriate learning activities are listed and described briefly.

Area of Concern: Self-Concept

The child's *self-concept* is his view of himself as a person: how he is both alike and different from other people he knows. Self-concept includes all kinds of descriptions, verbal expression or mental images, which form in the child's mind. Self-concept has a direct bearing on what the child (or almost any person) says, does, and thinks.

Self-esteem goes beyond the child's view of himself and includes his own inner feelings about what he sees. He may have a high or low level of regard. A high level gives him a good feeling about himself. He can face his world with a positive outlook and a good chance for success. A low level of regard gives him the feeling that he is not worthy or capable of doing worthwhile things.

What the child sees takes root during his early years. His parents are his first source of information about himself. When Johnny hears about the nice things he does, he gets the idea that what he does counts and so does he. When he hears misleading information — "Don't be such a dum-dum" — he may accept the label and live up (or down) to it.

Identity tells the child about his place in his group. He learns who he is, what he is, and where he fits into the world of people. He gains knowledge of his name, sex role, race, and social class. The regard he gives his identity stems from the impressions he gets from those who are significant in his life.

Parents begin the development of the child's self-concept almost from the moment he is born, when they

- Cuddle him, say nice things to him (even though he cannot understand), and love him.
- Hold him close to give him feelings of comfort and security.

Learning Objectives

- To help the child develop a sound and healthy self-concept.
- To make the child feel he is accepted as he is.
- To let him make choices and decisions by which he can learn self-direction.
- To set realistic goals which he can achieve successfully.

- To give him chances to be independent.

Learning Activities

- Body Image Game: The child learns about specific parts of his body and what they can do. He is asked to
    a. Look in a mirror and point to the body parts of his mirror image.
    b. Touch parts of his body and name each part.
    c. Touch corresponding parts on his mother's body.
    d. Find body parts on a doll or toy animal.
    e. Find body parts in pictures of people and animals.
    f. Show different ways his body can move (see unit 14).

- A Book About Johnny (use child's own name): The child puts together a book about himself. His parent helps him to insert
    a. His name, address, age, height, weight, and telephone number.
    b. His father's name, mother's name, and how they can be reached (if not at home during the day).
    c. What he should do if he gets lost (illustrate with policeman when appropriate).
    d. Photographs of himself (with dates taken to follow his growth).
    e. Photographs of family members and relatives.
    f. Drawings which he makes of himself and his family.
    g. Telephone numbers of friends he can call by himself. (Makes a telephone book with pictures of friends, too.)
    h. His name in printscript for him to copy.

- Johnny (use child's own name): The child makes a form like himself and learns more about his own characteristics. His parent
    a. Places a large sheet of wrapping paper on the floor.
    b. Asks child to lie on paper while parent traces his form.
    c. Guides child in putting in his features.
    d. Helps him to cut out form (or parent does it if he is unable to handle scissors).

Fig. 16-1 An older baby learns what a body part can do.

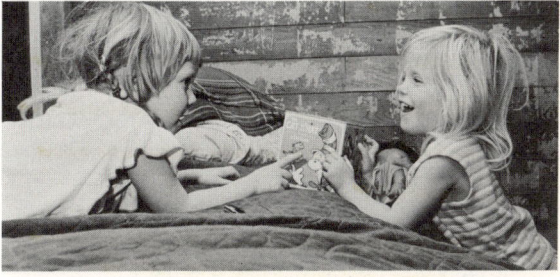

Fig. 16-2 Language development takes place when the child discusses something with a person who shares a like experience.

e. Helps him to finish "Johnny" as he chooses. He can color the rest of the form. He can attach the form to a coat hanger and hang his clothes over it. He can make and fasten with masking tape two like forms; they can be stuffed with crumpled paper or old stockings. He can dress his stuffed "self" and play with it.

- Which Hand Has It?: The parent helps to develop the concept of location by playing a game with the child.

    a. Parent holds object small enough to be covered by fist.

    b. Object is shuffled from one hand to another to give the idea of change of location.

    c. Parent stops and asks child to guess which hand has the object.

    d. If child is able to guess, he then has a turn making the parent guess which hand has the object.

Area of Concern: Language Development

Language development refers to the child's growing ability to learn and use language. It includes both input and output. *Input* refers to ideas which the child gets when he

- Listens for information.
- Follows directions.
- Enjoys and appreciates stories, rhymes, and jingles.
- Listens to television and radio shows.
- Learns through firsthand experiences.
- Hears about the pictures, films, or filmstrips he sees.
- Discusses something with a person who shares a like experience with him.

Output refers to the child's use of language when he

- Talks with friends.
- Makes known what he wants or needs.
- Gives messages and directions.
- Plans and reports on things that concern him.
- Shares ideas with others.
- Tells stories, poems, rhymes, and jingles.

Language development lies at the heart of home-based programs. From infancy, the child needs to build concepts, learn words to describe them, and use words to further his language growth.

Language Objectives

To promote the child's language growth by providing opportunities for him to

- Listen to others.
- Share experiences.
- Acquire a large and meaningful vocabulary.

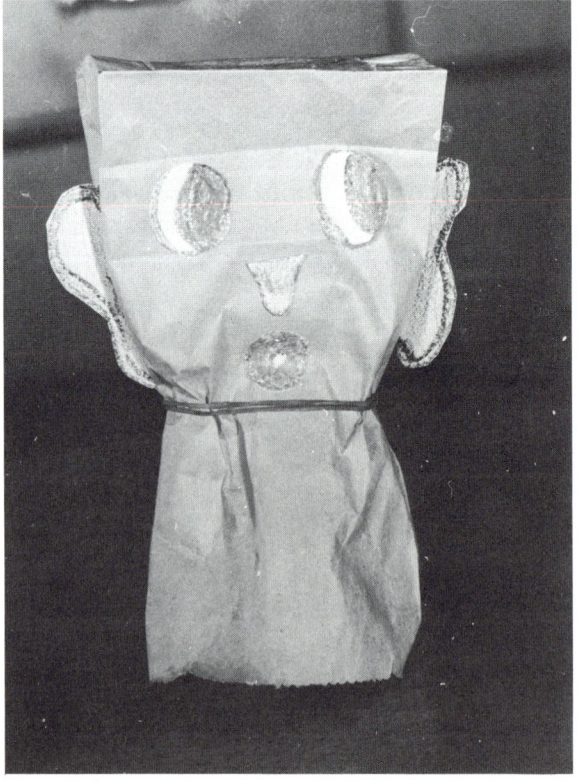

Fig. 16-3 Shown is an easy-to-make paper bag puppet.

- Learn stories, rhymes, jingles, and poems.
- Retell simple stories.
- Overcome "baby talk."
- Follow simple directions.
- Attempt creative language expression: tell stories about his own pictures, use puppets, take part in role-play and creative dramatics.
- Increase his ability to hear and see likes and differences between words (auditory and visual perception).

Learning Activities

- Stories: There are many ways by which stories can promote language growth. The child can

    a. Listen to stories read or told to him.

    b. Look at picture books; tell what he sees; describe what he thinks is happening; tell what people in the pictures might be saying.

    c. Draw and color his own pictures. Make up stories and have his parent write what he says beneath pictures.

    d. Make a scrapbook of magazine pictures which he likes. Dictate story captions for his parent to print for him.

- Puppets: Many easy-to-make puppets can serve the child in his play and add to his language growth. Directions are given for making some simple puppets.

    a. Make a puppet by drawing a face on the palm of a child's hand with colored chalk, a soft lead pencil, or tempera paint. Cut the sleeve of an old shirt, put it on his arm and secure it with rubber bands. Cut off the toe of an old black sock and fringe the edges to make a wig. Slip it over the fingers and trim the front of the wig.

    b. Make a paper bag puppet. Put a small ball of crumpled newspaper in a small paper bag. Paint a face on the bag, and costume it as desired. Put a rubber band around the bag to keep the paper inside. When in use, the child inserts his hand and grasps the newspaper ball.

    c. Cut figures of people from an old mail-order catalog. Staple them to a well-washed "ice-pop" stick.

    d. Make a paper bag mask for a "real-life" puppet. Figure 16-4 shows two young children wearing their own paper bag creations.

- Telephone Use: Toy telephones can be used to help the child develop a useful skill.

    a. Help him make a toy telephone by fastening two empty cans to a long piece of string. See figure 16-5 for directions.

    b. Use a toy model to teach him how to dial. On a card write numbers which he can find and dial. When he gets the idea, let him make a real telephone call to a friend. (It is wise to set

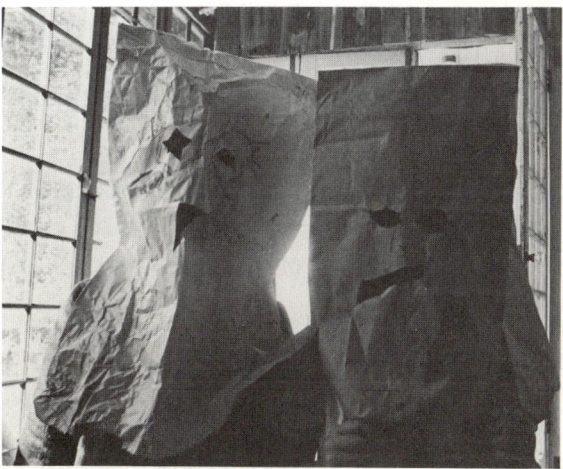

Fig. 16-4 Children make paper-bag masks and become real-life puppets. They feel good about themselves when they make something they can use.

Section 5 Materials for Home-Based Learning

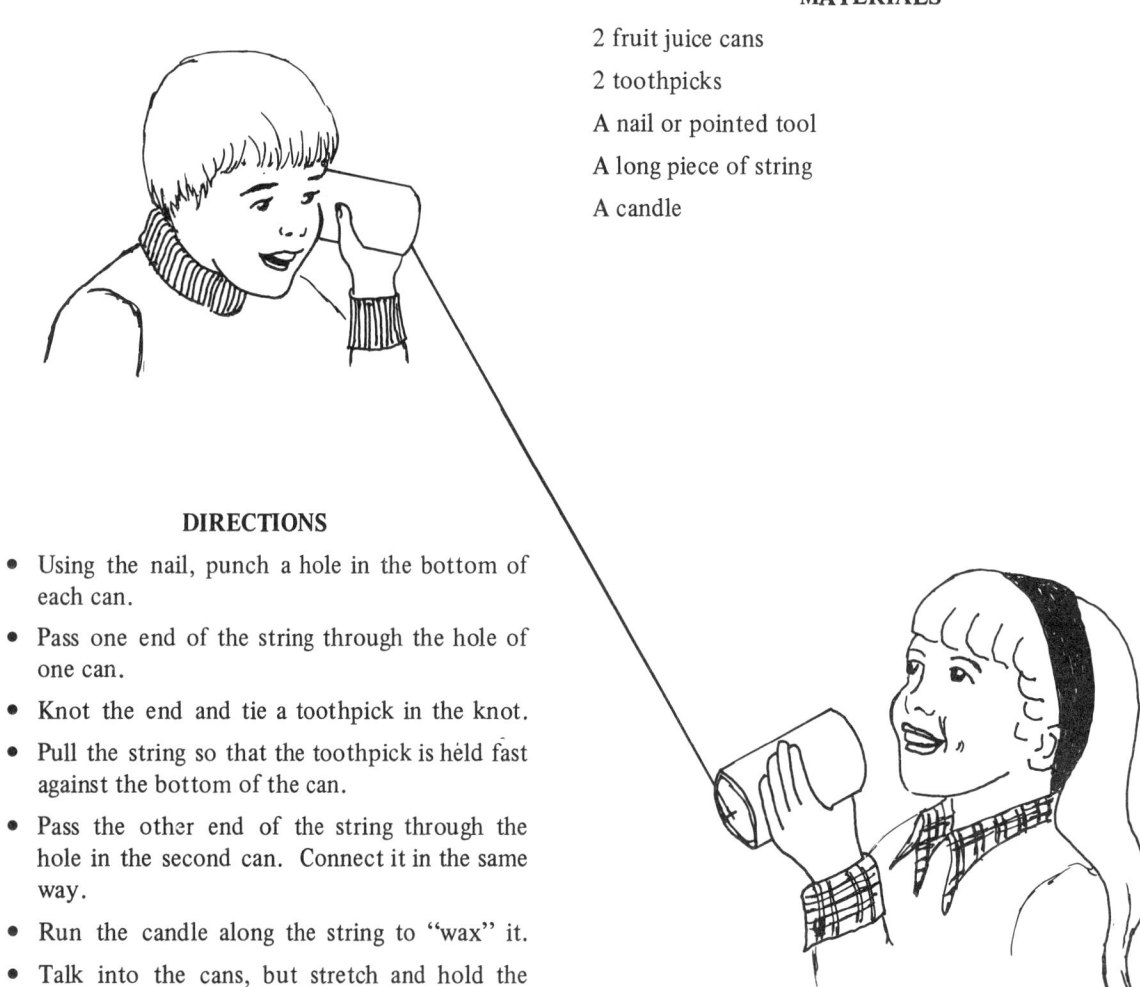

MATERIALS

2 fruit juice cans

2 toothpicks

A nail or pointed tool

A long piece of string

A candle

DIRECTIONS

- Using the nail, punch a hole in the bottom of each can.
- Pass one end of the string through the hole of one can.
- Knot the end and tie a toothpick in the knot.
- Pull the string so that the toothpick is held fast against the bottom of the can.
- Pass the other end of the string through the hole in the second can. Connect it in the same way.
- Run the candle along the string to "wax" it.
- Talk into the cans, but stretch and hold the string tightly.

Fig. 16-5 Directions for making a toy telephone.

limits on the use of the telephone right from the start.)

- Poems, Rhymes, and Jingles: Locate all kinds of rhythmic verse which the child can enjoy. Recite them for and with him.

    a. When he knows a verse, omit a word and let him supply what is missing. Example: Jack and Jill went up the... (hill). Jack and... (Jill) went up the ...(hill).

    b. Use finger plays with nursery rhymes.

    c. Let him dramatize a nursery rhyme. He can be Jack and his parent can be Jill. Play with him to give him the idea of dramatic play. Let him act out other roles which he may enjoy.

    d. Borrow cassette tapes from a toy-lending library. Provide the child with a wide range of poems.

- Typewriters: Letters, the movement of the carriage, and the fact that he can "write" seem to fascinate the child. His interest makes a typewriter an excellent tool for learning.

Unit 16 Objectives and Activities

DIRECTIONS

- Get a cardboard box.
- Glue small bottle caps to the top of the box.
- Place a letter on each bottle cap.
- Check a real typewriter for location of letters before you start.

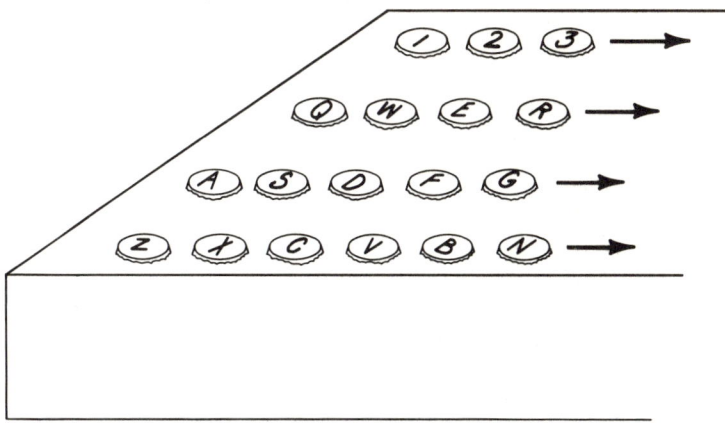

Fig. 16-6 A box with a model keyboard can become a game for learning letters of the alphabet.

a. Help the child make a homemade typewriter from a box. Glue small bottle or tube caps (button size) to a cardboard box as shown in figure 16-6. Use a standard keyboard for placing letters on each key. Play games with the child. Say, "Point to the *g*, find the *c*, and so on."

b. Take him to a toy-lending library where he can practice with the "real thing."

c. Insert a sheet of paper. Show him a card with a word which he knows (dog). Let him find and press each corresponding letter on a typewriter keyboard. Remove the paper. Place the word card above his typed word. Let him check. Give him crayons to illustrate his work.

d. Locate an old typewriter which he can use.

- Fun with letters and words: Letters of the alphabet take on new interest when presented in unusual and colorful ways, figure 16-8.

  a. Make several sets of alphabet letters printed on shapes similar to those shown in figure 16-9. Make a key card (letters written in alphabetical order). Have child place sets in order, using the key card as a guide. Start with one set; proceed to more as child is able.

  b. Newspaper headlines: have him encircle letters. Check them with his key card (or use card to find them).

  c. Encircle words and letters he finds in newspapers, and magazines.

  d. Cut out words that begin like each of the letters of the alphabet. Make an

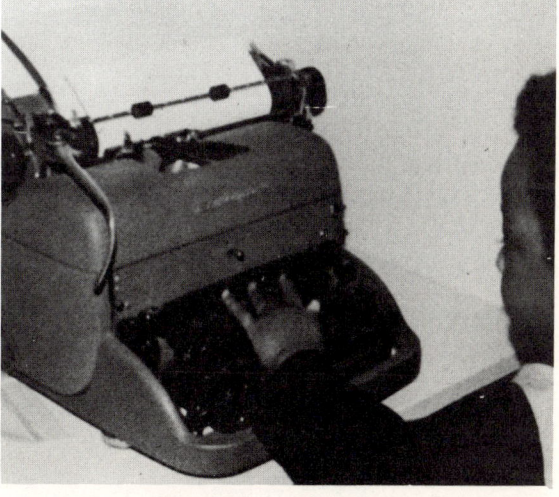

Fig. 16-7 A child uses a real typewriter in a university toy-lending library.

185

Section 5 Materials for Home-Based Learning

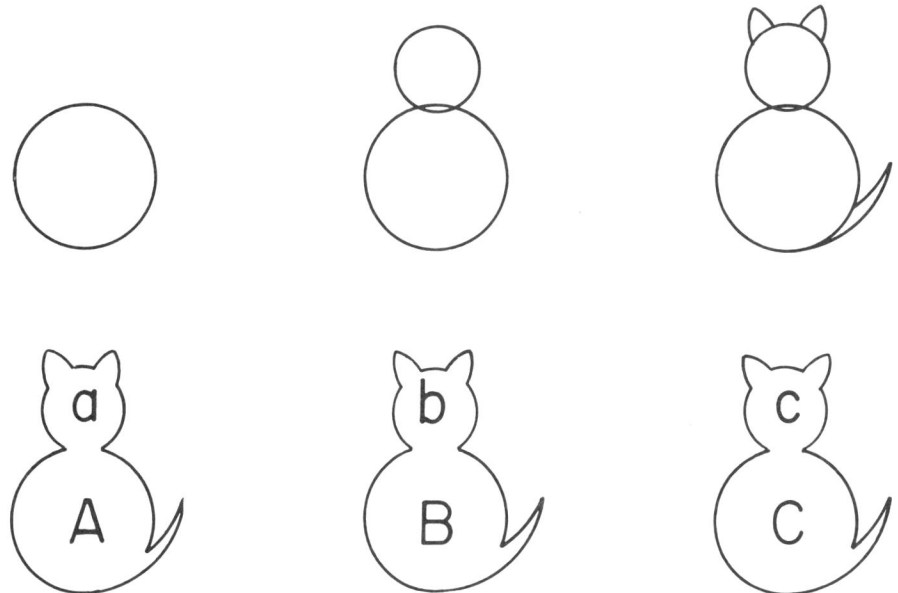

Fig. 16-8 Letters of the alphabet take on new interest when presented in unusual and colorful ways.

Fig. 16-9 Several sets of alphabet letters make a card game.

a b c d e f g h i j k l m n o p q r s t u v w x y z
A B C D E F G H I J K L M N O P Q R S T U V W X Y Z

Fig. 16-10 Shown is a key card containing letters written in alphabetical order.

alphabet book. Paste one letter on each sheet of paper. For each page, add words which begin with the key letter on that page.

e. Play card games with shape-form letters.

f. Cut and mount lists of words (even though he does not know their meanings). Count them. Parent can write totals beneath each column.

g. Let him try to copy letters on shape-forms. He may wish to trace them and make a set of cards for a friend.

h. Encourage him to try to make up his own games with letters and words.

Area of Concern: Science

Science activities help the child to learn about his world and what is in it.

Science Objectives

- To help the child discover his world of things by letting him ask, observe, describe, classify, predict.
- To develop the child's concepts and thinking powers.
- To provide the child with ways by which he can seek and answer some of his own questions.

Learning Activities

- Collect and label pictures: animals, machines, insects, airplanes and spaceships, boats, foods, fabrics, cars, land and water scenes, mountains, trees, flowers, plants.
- Collect specimens of rocks, soil, sand.
- Get some plant cuttings. Put them in water until they take root. Remove them to cans filled with soil. Take care of them. (Two can be prepared. Place one in dark closet, the other on a window sill which gets sunlight. Let child observe results.)
- Go to a planetarium. Observe nighttime sky. (See unit 15)
- Experiment with magnets. Use paper, soil, metal, rocks, pins, wood, to see if they can be held by the magnet. Experiment with many objects.
- Make a pinwheel. Watch the wind make it move.
- Make a weather chart. Observe weather. Listen to weather reports. Place appropriate word on the calendar each day: rain, snow, clouds, fair, cold, warm, sunshine, fog, ice, dew, rainbow, thunder, lightning.
- Let child take care of household pet: dog, cat, fish, turtle, bird. Get library books about pet.
- Make a terrarium.
- Make a toy telephone from two tin cans. (See figure 16-5)
- Increase length of string used. See how far the child can hear a voice when someone speaks into a can. (It may be several hundred feet if string is stretched tightly.)
- Make a seed necklace. Rinse pumpkin seeds in water to clean them. While still moist, make a hole in each. Let child string seeds with nylon thread long enough to make a necklace he can put over his head.

Area of Concern: Mathematics

Children have experiences with numbers very early in life. Through good use of opportunities which arise, parents can set the stage for an understanding of mathematical concepts.

Math Objectives

- To develop an understanding of *set* (group or collection of objects).

- To develop concepts of measurement: big, little, less, more, shorter, taller, heavier, lighter, higher, for example.
- To develop the concept of geometric figures through experiences with shapes: triangle, rectangle, square, cube, cone, cylinder, circle.
- To develop the concept of spatial relationships: near, far, up, down.
- To develop an awareness of money as a universal medium of exchange and learn to recognize U.S. coins and currency.
- To develop an understanding of *numeral* (symbol for a number) relationships: first, second, third, fourth, and so on.

Learning Activities

- Locate and count things in the home which make up a set: dishes, utensils, furniture, gloves, and glasses, for example.
- Compare things with reference to size, weight, and so on.
- Make a stamp scrapbook. (Use cancelled stamps for art collage, too.)
- Counting at home: knives, forks, eggs, etc.
- Measurement: measure child's height and keep record.
- Weight: weigh child and keep record. Call attention to examples; such as weight of food when purchasing, mail (to know required postage).
- Locate channels on television set.
- Volume: help in baking and cooking by measuring ingredients for parent.
- Clocks: note time of favorite television show. Make paper-plate clocks for play.
- Graphs: make a chart to record height at various times during the year.
- Count birthday candles to match each year of child's birth.
- Games (unit 17) to promote number concepts.

Area of Concern: Music

Music is a language understood by people the world over. It can bring much joy to the young child.

Learning Objectives

- To bring music to the child from infancy.
- To stimulate the child's creative expression.
- To help the child feel and produce various rhythms.
- To promote the child's listening skills.
- To help the child explore what his voice can do — sing.

Learning Activities

- Provide ways by which the child can take part in music action and reaction: listen, sing, play, move his body, keep time.
- Use materials in the home to produce sounds:
   a. Rubber bands placed around a box: pluck them.
   b. Glasses filled with different levels of water: tap glass.
   c. Large nails attached to string: hit with another nail.
   d. Pebbles in coffee can, resealed with tape: shake can.
   e. Two old pot lids: clash them like cymbals.
   f. Soda bottle caps, perforated and put on string: shake them.

g. Sandpaper attached to wooden blocks: rub them together.

h. Grains of sand in a plastic box: shake the box.

- Sing to the child, use recordings, or play a musical instrument to accompany songs.
- Play soft background at nap time. Use happy, gay music when child is at play.
- Have family fun singing rounds such as, "Row-Row-Row Your Boat." Sing nursery rhymes with child, too.
- Turn to concert programs on television. Let child see the family look for musical programs for all to hear. Let him choose programs, too.
- Play musical chairs for a family party.
- Tell-a-music story: have child listen to music and tell a story which he "feels" about the music.
- Draw-a-music story: have child listen and then draw a picture of something the music makes him think of.
- Have child listen for music in the air: the wind blowing, trees "swishing" their leaves, birdcalls (He can try to imitate them with parent), water running over stones, a horse galloping, rain pattering on the roof, a windshield wiper moving (He can clap to keep time.)
- Dance team: parent holds child's hands and "dances" with him, using waltz, tango, rock-and-roll, cha-cha-cha, polka, or any other type music available.

Other Areas to Develop

There are many other areas to be developed in home-based learning. Some are listed with comments.

Play. Play is like the looking glass of reality in the child's world. It is the means through which he recreates his world to understand it. He needs many opportunities to

- Dress up and pretend to be somebody else: father, mother, milkman, storekeeper, fire fighter, mail carrier.
- Join his family in leisure time activities.
- Develop his body through the use of equipment.
- Move his body to develop skills: locomotor, nonlocomotor, manipulative.
- Find in play an escape valve for his feelings.
- Express himself in free, aimless, fun-type activity.
- "Do" what he wants to do.

Fig. 16-11 Children need things to do — just for fun and shared play.

Fig. 16-12 A child can get exercise on a swing by using it himself or pushing a friend.

Section 5 Materials for Home-Based Learning

Health. The development of good health habits is an important part of a child's home training. He needs to

- Have regular physical examinations.
- Learn to eat a well-balanced diet and get enough rest.
- Learn to wash hands before eating and after toileting.
- Learn to care for his hair, teeth, and body to keep them clean and in healthy condition.
- Learn how to exercise his body by using equipment himself or helping a friend.

Safety. The safety skills a child learns may save a life – his. Every family should have a well-planned safety program for the entire family. All persons should know

- How to leave the house in case of fire: Fire drills in the home are needed. The child must know what to do.
- How to store cleaning fluids, medicine, and household cleaning preparations and what to do in case of accidental poisoning. Child must learn to keep away from things which can hurt him.
- How to protect young family member from accidents.
    a. Teach child the meaning of safety signs.
    b. Help him to observe traffic lights.
    c. Teach him tricycle (or bicycle) safety rules.
    d. Teach him to swim and observe water safety rules.
    e. Keep family dog from running after cars (child may try to follow the dog).
    f. Teach child to stay away from parked cars.
    g. Make sure that child cannot reach medicine cabinets.
    h. Know where the child is when family car comes or goes.
    i. Help him to know that he must not go with strangers.
    j. Teach him how to get help if his baby-sitter gets sick.
    k. Tell him what to do if parent gets sick suddenly.

Art. Art is woven into all of the activities of a home-based program. Many activities already appear elsewhere in this book. Sensory and creative experiences can come through

- Crayons, chalks, paint, heavy lead pencils, finger paint.
- Clay, play dough, paper.
- Blocks, water, sand.
- Use of all kinds of waste materials.

Note: Activities which appear in this unit are suggestions, only. They are to be selected as

Fig. 16-13 Sensory and creative experiences come through the use of art materials.

190

they fit the child for whom they are intended. The good judgment of the child's parents and the parent educator (home visitor) is assumed.

SUMMARY

A home-based curriculum consists of all of the organized experiences which a parent provides to help the child learn at home. Organized experiences are opportunities for learning which can be planned ahead or used when the opportunity arises.

There is no single way by which a child can master a concept or learn a skill. The method must fit the child.

Three sources of objectives in curriculum planning are the child, the child's group, and specialists. People who work with young children provide information which needs to be presented to parents, in a form they can use.

A child's self-concept is his view of himself as a person. His self-esteem is the way in which he regards himself. His identity tells the child about his place in his group.

Areas to be considered in building a curriculum for home-based early education include: self-concept, language development, science, mathematics, music, play, health, safety, and art.

SUGGESTED ACTIVITIES

- Interview a parent who has a young child ranging in age from 2 years to 5 years.

   a. Ask about learning episodes described in this unit. See how many the child has been exposed to.

   b. Find out if you can work with the child to provide (appropriate) episodes he has not had.

   c. Prepare workplans for learning episodes for which you feel you need help from your instructor. Show your plans. Follow suggestions, if any are made.

   d. Work with the child. See how much parent involvement you can get.

   e. Share your experience with your class.

- Locate other learning episodes listed or described in books, magazines, and newspapers.

   a. Briefly describe each.

   b. Write the correct reference form.

   c. Put them in your workplan files.

- Create original learning episodes which can help the child to meet some of the objectives for each area of concern.

REVIEW

A. Define briefly each of the following.
   1. Curriculum
   2. Organized experiences
   3. Self-concept
   4. Self-esteem
   5. Identity
   6. Need
   7. Numeral

B. State three things which must be done to plan for a given child.

C. State three sources of objectives in building home-based curriculum for young children.

D. Give a basic framework around which a subject matter area may be developed.

E. Write five objectives and five learning activities for each of the following areas described in this unit: self-concept, science, language development, mathematics, and music.

unit 17 creating media for learning

OBJECTIVES

After studying this unit, the student should be able to

- Define and describe instructional objectives for young children.
- Develop learning episodes to help the child match, group and regroup, note similarities and differences, classify, and put objects in a sequence.
- Select appropriate learning activities for the three-to-five-year-old child.

The young child tends to have a strong impulse to handle things and to make something work. He can crush a piece of paper and has a ball to play with. He puts a bag on his head and is an instant spaceman. He takes objects and arranges and rearranges them in ways that please him.

In the process of his play, the child gains not only amusement, but sound educational values, as well. He learns to think through a problem before he starts it. He develops it patiently, step by step. When he finishes his task, he understands how he can use materials to suit his purpose.

The child who finds satisfaction in his tasks is usually one who has a success base on which he can build more success. He learns to do, by doing. He learns to create, by having opportunities to be creative.

This unit explores ways to help the child learn by utilizing his desire to touch, taste, see, smell, and hear. Ideas given are not cookbook recipes to be followed in a 1-2-3 order. They may be viewed more like a snowball which grows larger only after it gets that first push down the hill.

The first part of the discussion deals with learning episodes parents can use to meet specific teaching-learning objectives. The second part is an alphabetized list of creative activities to spark other ways by which the child can learn and have fun.

Attention is called to the fact that because children differ in both interests and experience backgrounds, an episode may not be appropriate for all children. An activity which may be easy for one child may prove more difficult for another in the three to five age group. Parents can recall what was said in earlier units to guide them in making selections.

INSTRUCTIONAL OBJECTIVES

No young child should be put under pressure to reach an objective someone else sets for him. What is done must come at the pace with which the child is at ease and at which he shows interest.

Some people feel that a child can indeed be comfortable when the goal is appropriate and set to give direction to an activity. The view stresses the need for parents and others to know when the child has "arrived" in completing his task.

An instructional objective for a young child is described as one which states (1) what the child is supposed to be able to do after being exposed to the learning episode, (2) the conditions under which he is to do it, and (3) the kind of behavior which is expected and accepted of him in terms of his age, uniqueness as a person, and his past experiences.

Section 5 *Materials for Home-Based Learning*

The activities that follow are designed to promote the thinking skills of the young child. The first five learning episodes are in a workplan format. Parents can gain insight into ways an activity can be used as a learning experience for the child. The other activities are described briefly. They can be helpful in training sessions as exercises for parents to think through. Some parents may be able to see the learning episodes as valuable without a need to examine them further.

Concept: Matching (One-to-One Correspondence)

Skills

- Matching like with like (one-to-one correspondence).
- Seeing similarities and differences.

Objective

- When given a set of alphabet cards, containing uppercase letters written in manuscript, the child should be able to place each card in one set under its mate in the other set.

Materials

- Two sets of cards with uppercase letters in manuscript.

Procedure

- Take five cards (A, B, D, E, K) from one set and place them on the table.
- Give child five like cards from the other set. Have them place his cards under their match in the key set.
- At first avoid letters that are similar (O, Q, X, Y). Continue the game until child uses all letters.

Checks (Questions to ask the Child)

- Which letters did you have trouble with? Which letters were the easiest to do? Which letters look almost the same? Where are they different? How can you remember them?
- In what other ways can we group the letters?
- Would you like to play the game with a friend?

Leads

- Arrange a key set in A-B-C order. Have child match them.
- Write letters on cards of unlike colors or shapes.
- Staple to a card letters written on scraps of silk or wool, for example.

Concept: Sets (The Same or Different)

Skills

- Seeing similarities and differences.
- Comparing sets to separate those which are different.

Objective

- When shown four like letters and one which is different, the child should be able to cover the one which is different.

Materials

- Paper, a magic marker, bottle caps.

Procedure

- Trace a bottle cap to make a row of five shapes. Write in manuscript; A A B A A. Have child observe closely.
- Let child place bottle cap on letter which is different.
- Progress to other groups. Larger groups may be used. Child may be asked to cover more than one matching letter at one time.

Checks (Questions to ask the Child)

- How did you know which letter to cover? What did you look at?
- What else can we do to separate the one which is different (cross it out, erase it, tear it out, cut it out, for example)?
- How can I help you to play this game with a friend? (Write the letters. Show him how to write the letters. Make many more sets of letters to arrange, rather than write them in sets.)

Leads

- Make an alphabet bingo game. Use letters on cards.
- Find likes and differences in words found in newspaper. Child states which letter he seeks. Puts an X on all he finds. Counts. Seeks other sets. Determines largest found.

Concept: Sequencing (Putting Things in Order)

Skills

- Placing things according to some order (size, pairs, etc.)
- Making judgments.

Objective

When given two sets of measuring cups, the child should be able to place them in at least one sequence: largest to smallest, two by two, nested, for example.

Materials

Two sets of measuring cups, paper, and crayon or magic marker.

Procedure

- Place unnested measuring cups before the child. Let him experiment to see what he can do with them.
- Show him some other ways to use the cups: nest them, arrange them by two's, trace the rims to make circle designs (repeating a sequence several times), draw circle people, arrange cups from largest to smallest.

Checks (Questions to ask the Child)

- What do we call the shape of the rim (round, circle)? How many cups do you have? What are two cups of a kind called (pair, set)? Show me the largest cups. Show me the smallest.
- Which arrangement do you like best? Why?
- Can you put in order other things, such as two sets of nested bowls and measuring spoons?

Leads

- Have child "test" sizes by using water to experiment with measuring cups. Use dirt or sand for dry measure.
- Sequence other home items: cans, dishes, shoes, socks.

Concept: Classifying (Putting Things in Their Group)

Skills

- Seeing relationships between objects.
- Forming judgments.
- Developing the ability to categorize.

Objective

When given unsorted objects, the child should be able to use some of them to make at least three different groups of things that have something in common.

Materials

Any number of the following (or similar) objects which the child knows: buttons, zippers, spools of thread, spoons, sewing needles, bottle caps, dry beans, pumpkin seeds, peach pits, combs, brushes, mirrors, toothbrushes, cups, forks, handkerchiefs, socks.

Procedure

- Have child work with items to experiment.
- Help him to classify things: (1) things to help in health care: comb, brush, toothbrush, mirror; (2) things related to clothes: buttons, zippers, thread, sewing needles. Other groups can be used.

Checks (Questions to ask Child)

- How can you tell what things go together?
- How did you make up your mind what to do with the things?
- When we put things in a group, what do we call it (set)?

Leads

- Have child shop with parent and put away purchased goods.
- Let child help in sorting laundry — talk with him about groups.

Concept: Grouping and Regrouping (Put Together-Take Away)

Skills

- Counting objects.
- Taking away a part from a whole; putting together like parts.

Objective

When given a coat hanger with five clothespins fastened to the bottom, the child should be able to put together or take away combinations up to the sum of five.

Materials

Ten snap clothespins attached to a wire coat hanger.

Procedure

- How many clothespins do you see? Count them.
- Push one clothespin away from the others — "take away" one clothespin. How many are left? Count them: 1-2-3-4.
- "Put together" the one clothespin with the four. How many are together? Yes, five are together again.
- Let child experiment with the clothespins. If he is able, keep adding more — one at a time. Let him find new groups.

Checks

- Let's see if you can do these put-together and take-away jobs: put together 3 and 2, 4 and 1, 2 and 2. Take away 1 from 5, 2 from 3, and so on.
- Let's see how many different put-together and take-away jobs you can make up yourself.

Leads

- Put together: count forks, spoons, and knives for setting the table.
- Take away: cookies from box, eggs from carton, for example.

THINGS TO MAKE AND DO

Animals I Know

- Find pictures of animals which the child can recognize. (Perhaps he can find some in magazines.) Mount them on cards. Label them.
- Make a matching set of labels for a game.

Unit 17 Creating Media for Learning

Beach Bag

- Cut a circle (about two yards across) from an old shower curtain. About two inches in from the edge, sew on a strip of wide bias tape. Leave an opening for a drawstring.
- Cut a smaller circle of cardboard (about 12 inches) and place in the bottom of the bag. Pull drawstrings. The bag is ready.

Bell Cutouts

- Take a sheet of paper and fold it in half.
- Draw a bell form as shown (keep paper folded).
- Cut out shape. Open the fold. A bell is there.

Bleach Bottle Santa Claus

- Give the child some tempera paint, a brush, some cottom, and glue. Let him

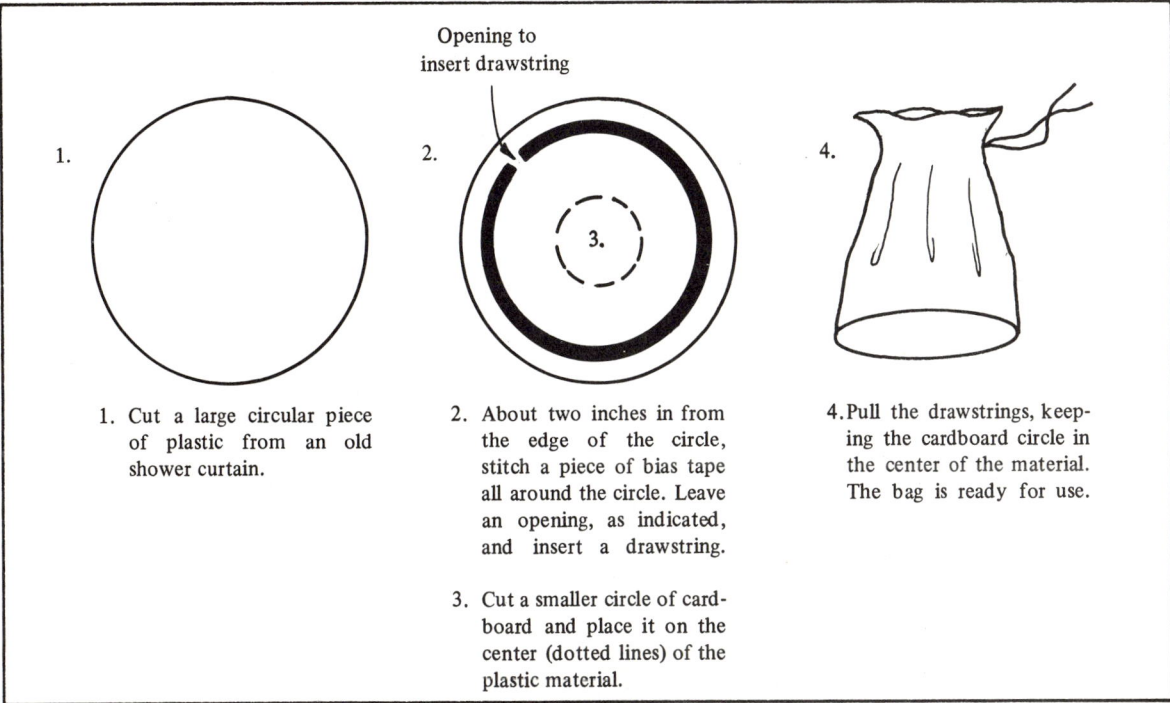

1. Cut a large circular piece of plastic from an old shower curtain.
2. About two inches in from the edge of the circle, stitch a piece of bias tape all around the circle. Leave an opening, as indicated, and insert a drawstring.
3. Cut a smaller circle of cardboard and place it on the center (dotted lines) of the plastic material.
4. Pull the drawstrings, keeping the cardboard circle in the center of the material. The bag is ready for use.

Fig. 17-1 A beach bag can be made from an old shower curtain.

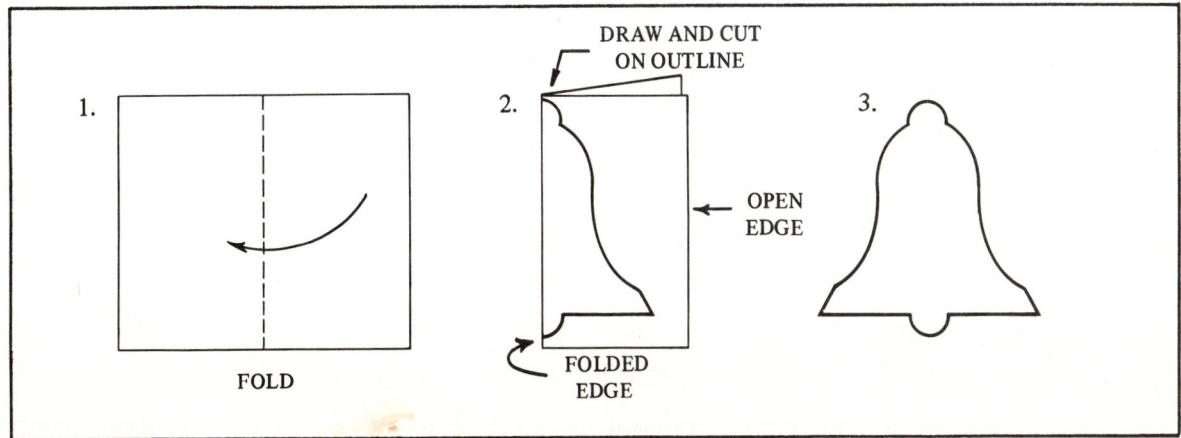

Fig. 17-2 A bell is easy to make and has many uses.

Section 5 Materials for Home-Based Learning

make a Santa Claus. Do not show him the model, but try to spark his own creative ideas.

- See if he can make other things from bleach bottles.

Blue, Blue, What is Blue?

- Provide child with nine sheets of colored paper: red, black, blue, green, orange, purple, yellow, brown, white. Label each sheet with its color name.
- Let child find things in magazines to match colors. Mount.

Bottle Cap Bracelet

- Get about five caps from soft drink bottles. Remove the linings from the caps and set them aside.
- Place some glue in the center of each cap. Carefully press down a string of ribbon long enough to tie into a bow on child's wrist.
- Add some more glue to the lining of each cap and replace the lining to hold the ribbon securely.
- Variation: Use only one cap and put a clock face on top of it by pasting on it a small circular piece of paper with a clock face drawn on it.

Bubble, Bubble, Bubble

- Place some soapy water in a large plastic cup. Add a few drops of glycerin. Let the child blow bubbles with a straw, bubble pipe, or large-tubed piece of macaroni.

Button Faces

- Give the child a box of assorted buttons and a pie tin.

Fig. 17-3 Shown is a model of Santa Claus made from an empty bleach bottle.

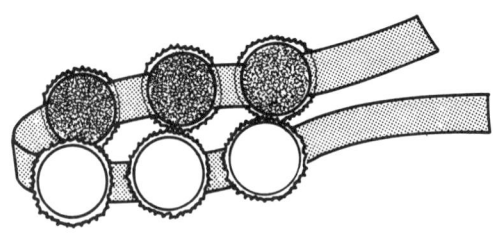

Fig. 17-4 A bottle cap bracelet or wristwatch can delight the young child.

Unit 17 Creating Media for Learning

- Let him make faces with the buttons.
- Variation: A more advanced child can make pictures by mounting buttons on a sheet of paper, plastic covers, or cardboard.

Calendar Game: Clap for the Winner
- Place on the floor an old page from a large wall calendar.
- Have child try to drop a small object (button, bean, penny) on a number.
- Whenever he drops the object on a number, the other player(s) clap(s) for him (while he counts, or they do).

Catalog Caper
- Get two old mail-order catalogs. Let child find photographs of ten things that he likes. Parent locates ten matching things in the second catalog.
- Both sets of pictures are mounted. Child shuffles cards. He lays them out and tries to find a match for each.

Dot Pictures
- Trace pictures from an old coloring book.
- Put dots around the outline shape of each picture.
- Put a clear sheet under each picture and trace only the dots for each (put picture to window). Child connects dots.
- For the child learning his numbers, a dot with a number can be used with some of the outline drawing added.

Fig. 17-5 A touch picture is fun to make.

Section 5 Materials for Home-Based Learning

Feel My Name

- Write child's name in large letters. Help him trace the letters with the rubber tip of a bottle of mucilage.
- Let him shake salt on the mucilage while it is still wet.
- He can "feel" his name.
- Variation: Draw pictures with the rubber tip, shaking salt on the wet mucilage as the picture takes form, figure 17-5.

Food Fun

- Mix the child's favorite pancake batter.
- Preheat slightly greased pan or griddle.
- Spoon small amount of batter on pan to make silver-dollar-size pancakes. Cook like regular pancakes.
- Note: Babies and toddlers can use them as finger food. Older children can prepare them for the younger ones.

Hand and Footprints

- Lay a sheet of wrapping paper on the floor. Trace the child's foot. Make several footprints.
- He can keep a copy to see how much his feet grow. He can mail one to a grandparent or relative. He can make a set of number cards by putting numbers on prints. He can make a foot picture by drawing in features or whatever he can think of.
- Trace his hand. Draw a turkey using his five fingers.

Get-Well Card

- On a sheet of paper, parent writes the greeting:
  Dear Somebody (insert person's name),
    Get well.
      (Child draws a picture)
- Parent signs name of child, or he does it himself.

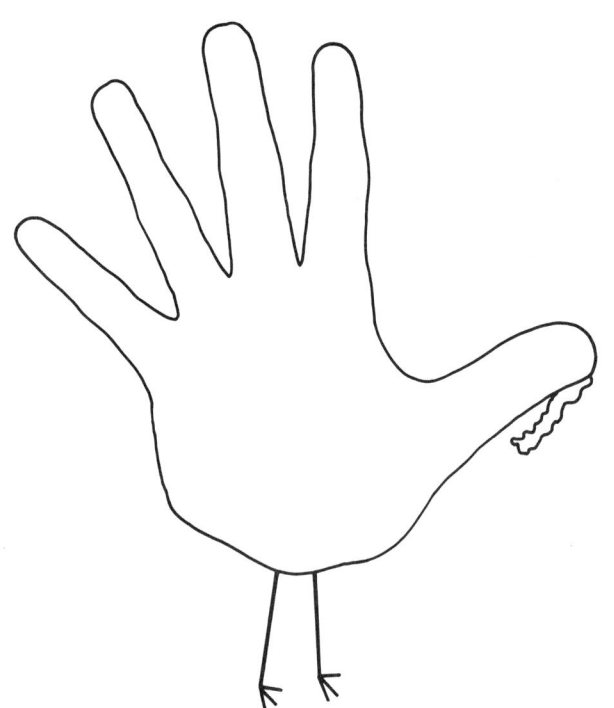 

Fig. 17-6 Hand and footprints make a fun activity.

- Letter is taken to the post office for a stamp and mailing.

Growing Up

- Make a tape measure (five inches wide) from heavy wrapping paper (double thickness). Place numbers showing each inch from one to fifty. Tack to the back of the child's bedroom door.
- Measure the child's height. Mark the place with a snap clothespin bearing the child's name. Move clothespin as the child grows. Whenever child is measured, put the date right where the clothespin is placed.

Paper Lanterns

- Have the child fold a sheet of drawing paper. Give him crayons to color the paper, covering all of it.
- Guide him in cutting from the fold up to a guideline, as shown in figure 17-7.
- Open fold and staple both ends together to make a lantern.
- Add string for a handle and hang lantern in a child's room.

Magic Garden

- Fill dish three-fourths full of salt.
- Dampen the salt with laundry bluing.
- Add a few drops of food coloring.

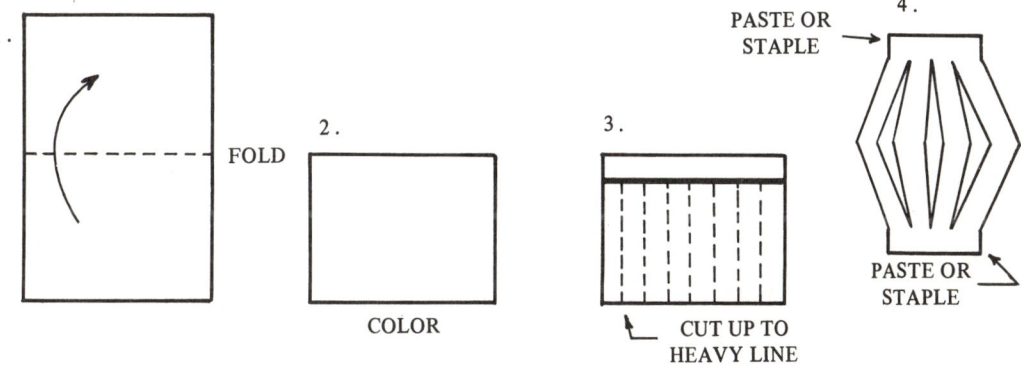

Fig. 17-7 An easy-to-make paper lantern.

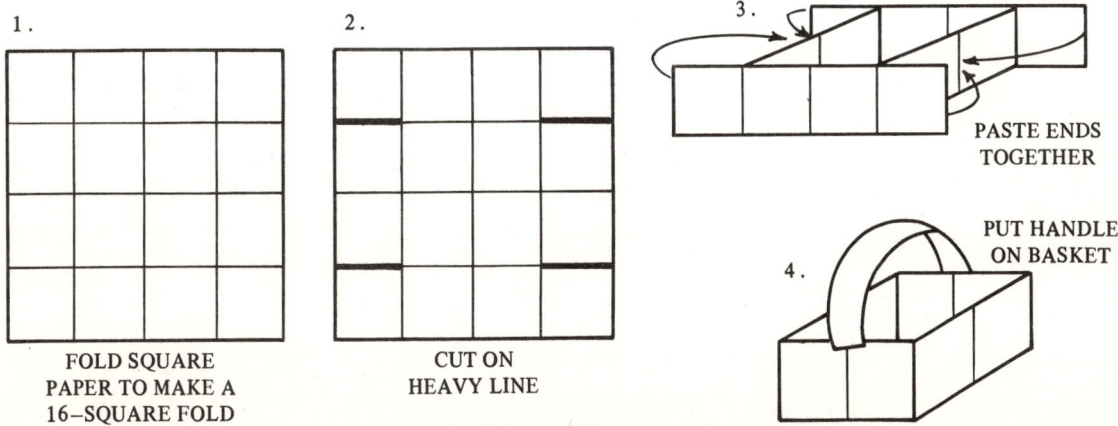

Fig. 17-8 A party basket is a useful object.

Section 5 *Materials for Home-Based Learning*

- Set dish aside where child can observe it.
- About three days later "flowers" will be in full bloom.
- Variation: Repeat the experiment. Instead of food coloring, use a few drops of Merthiolate. Have child observe. The "flowers" in the two gardens are slightly different.

Party Basket

- Get a square sheet of colored paper. Fold as shown in figure 17-8 to make sixteen squares.
- Cut as shown. Paste sides together to make a basket.
- Put handle on basket for a May basket. Use basket as a nut holder for a birthday party.

People, Animals, Things

- Child and parent look at picture books. Object is to find pictures of people, animals, or things.
- Each word (people, animals, things) can be written on a separate sheet of newspaper. Child finds magazine pictures and mounts them under one of the headings.

Fig. 17-9 Pie-plate faces can be a fun job for all the family.

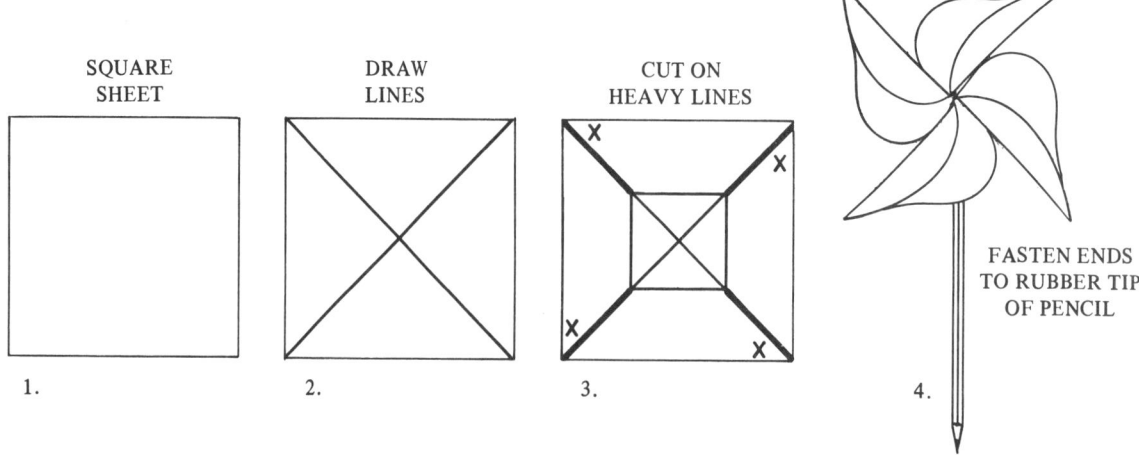

Fig. 17-10 A pinwheel is easy to make and is more than a toy. The child can use it to see the wind at work.

Unit 17 Creating Media for Learning

Pie-Plate Faces

- Give child scraps of paper, paste, and a pie plate. Let him cut features to make a pie-plate face.
- The family join in the fun. Each member makes one.

Pinwheel

- Cut a five inch square of paper. Draw lines so that they cross at exactly the center of the square. On each line, make a dot one-half inch from the center. Cut in from the corners of the square along each of the four lines. Stop at the dots, figure 17-10.
- Bend in to the center the corners marked with an X. Run a pin through the four corners and attach the pin to the rubber tip (eraser) on a pencil.
- The child moves the pinwheel rapidly to make it twirl.

Play Santa Claus

- Child cuts from old catalog things he wants to give to his family as gifts. Family is urged to go along with the fun — as if real things were received.
- Role play and pantomime combine to make this a fun game.

Shirt Art

- Let child draw a picture or design on thin paper such as tracing or onion skin. Use wax crayons.
- Lay design face down on an old white T-shirt.
- Run a hot iron over the back of the paper.
- Let the child fill in designs in color.
- Steam to set colors for him: lay shirt, crayon side down, over a few thicknesses of heavy wrapping paper. Place a wet cloth over the shirt and iron with hot iron until the shirt is dry.
- If desired, the child may draw directly on the front of the T-shirt. Colors may be set as described.

Star Shape

- Get a sheet of paper (typing paper is fine). Follow the drawings in figure 17-11 to make a star form.
- Follow the arrow and fold the paper in half (1).
- Find the middle of the line AC (point D). Follow the arrow and fold on the dotted line to bring B to rest on D (2).

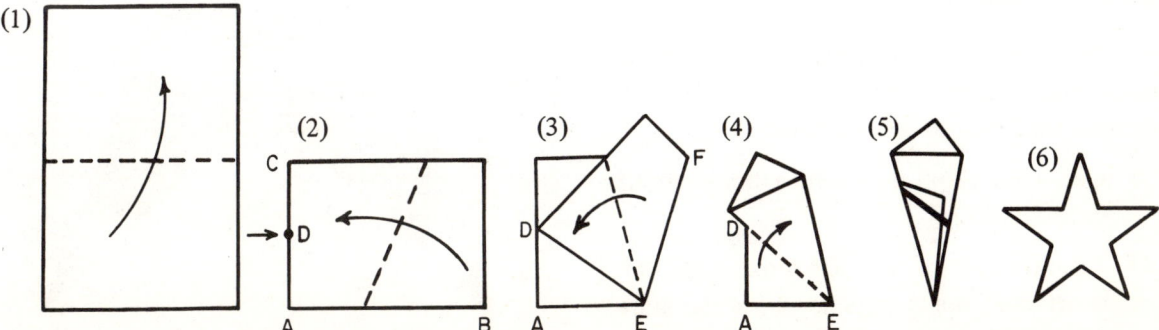

Fig. 17-11 The child's parent can do the folding for the younger child. Other children may be able to follow the parent's step-by-step instruction.

Section 5 Materials for Home-Based Learning

- Fold to bring line EF to rest on line ED (3).
- Follow the arrow and fold point A to the right along line DE.
- Cut on the heavy line shown. (5)
- Unfold. A five-pointed star is there. (6)

Star-Shape Santa Claus

- Use red Christmas wrapping paper to make a large star-shape as just described.
- Talk about the star form. Call attention to the fact that it looks as if it has five body parts: head, two arms, and two legs. Ask how the star can be made to look like "something." Show child the star-shape Santa Claus.
- Provide him with cotton, glue, scraps of paper. See what he can do.
- If he wants to make a star-shape Santa Claus, see if he can add something creative to make it his own. Other things can be made: elves, reindeer, children, people.
- Added use: Paste the star-shape Santa Claus onto a piece of cardboard or heavy drawing paper. Cut out shape. Use as a Christmas tree decoration. Or, make a Santa Claus mobile.

Star-Show Peep-Box

This is a good activity to use with a planetarium study trip. (See unit 15 for a scenario on a visit to a planetarium.)

- Get a shoebox, a pencil, a book about constellations.
- Lift the lid of the shoebox. At one short end, make dots to show the stars in a constellation (Big Dipper). Use the point of a pencil to punch a hole through each dot.
- At the other end of the box, make a round peephole.
- Replace cover.
- Look through the peephole, holding the box up to the light. (window or electric light). The constellation can be seen.

Supermarket Shopper

- Help the child to make a shopping list using labels from cans bought at a grocery store.
- Mount the label as shown in figure 17-14. Use masking tape and a small piece of paper to make a number pocket. Place a strip of paper in the pocket to show how many cans of the item shown are to be bought.
- Have the child make a scrapbook containing staple items the family may need. Each number pocket shows how many items are to be bought at any point in time.

Fig. 17-12 A star shape has many uses. It can become an interesting Santa Claus.

1. On a file card, make a drawing of the Big Dipper. Use a paper punch to make the stars.

2. Place the file card inside one end of a shoebox. Make marks to show where each star should be. With a paper punch, or a pencil point, make holes to show each star.

3. At the other end of the box make a peephole.

4. Put a cover on the box. Hold the box up to the window, or to a light bulb, and look through the peephole. The outline of the Big Dipper can be seen.

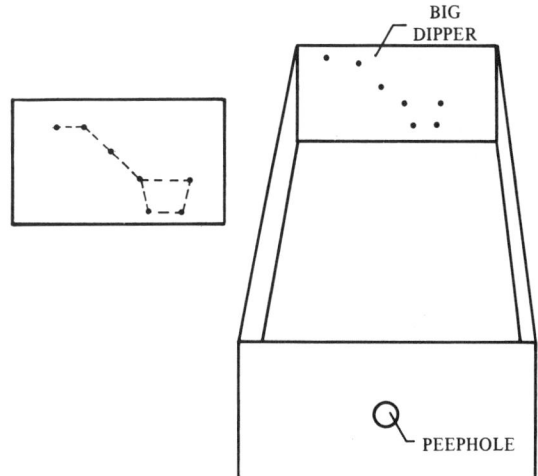

Fig. 17-13 A star-show peep-box can be an activity related to a planetarium visit.

Fig. 17-14 Shown is the supermarket shopper's scrapbook for ordering goods to be bought.

- Child sits in the kiddie-seat of the supermarket cart. He helps parent "find" cans and count them as parent removes them from shelf. Child once again counts cans as they are put away at home.

- The scrapbook keeps the child's hands busy. His task keeps him interested, and the supermarket kiddie-seat cart holds him secure and safe.

What Can You Do There?

- Use mail-order catalogs to locate pictures that show rooms in a house (bedroom, kitchen, living room). Mount the pictures and label them with the room name.

Section 5 Materials for Home-Based Learning

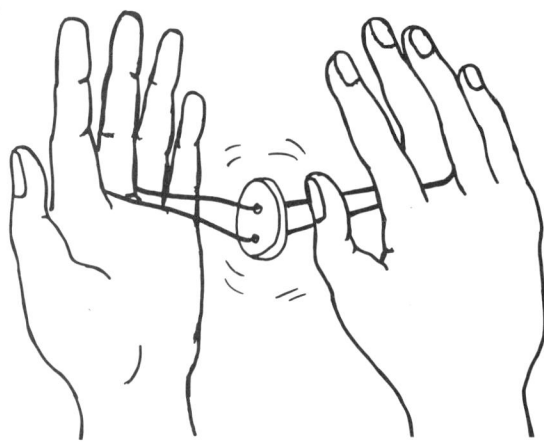

Fig. 17-15 Whirl-the-button can be enjoyed by the whole family. Shown is the button in action.

- Have child tell what he can do in each room. He can also tell what he must not do, "I must not touch things in the medicine chest or under the sink. They can hurt me."

Whirl-the-Button

- Get a large two-hole button and about two yards of strong string. Put one end of the string through each button hole and tie the ends together.
- Place the button in the middle and hold one of the end loops of the string around the middle finger of each hand. Whirl the button around twenty or thirty times until the string is well twisted.
- Move hands apart and then together to make the string wind and unwind. A buzz-saw sound is made.

SUMMARY

The young child has a strong desire to touch, taste, feel, see, and hear things. He likes to make things work.

Parents can use the child's natural impulse to handle things to create learning episodes. Things in the child's everyday life become tools for learning.

The young child needs opportunities to learn in a creative way. He needs a success base on which to build more success.

No young child should be put under pressure to reach an objective someone else sets for him. What is done must come from a pace at which the child is at ease and shows interest. When a goal is appropriate for the young child and set to give direction to his activity, he can indeed learn without feeling any pressure.

An instructional objective for a young child is described as one which states

- What the child is supposed to be able to do after being exposed to the learning episode.
- The conditions under which he is to do it.
- The kind of behavior which is expected and accepted of him in terms of his age, uniqueness as a person, and his past experiences.

Some skills which can be stated in behavioral (instructional) terms include the following concepts:

- Matching: one-to-one correspondence.
- Sets: Finding similarities and differences.
- Sequencing: Putting things in order.
- Classifying: Putting things in their group.
- Grouping and Regrouping: Put-together and take-away activities with objects.

When learning episodes are discussed with parents, attention should be called to an important fact. Because children differ in both interests and experience backgrounds, an episode may be easy for one child but prove more difficult for another. Parents should recall what was said in earlier units to guide them in their selections.

SUGGESTED ACTIVITIES

- Select at least five of the thirty activities described in the "things to make and do" section of this unit. You can work alone, or find a classmate to work with you as a team. For each activity

    a. Identify ways the activity can foster the child's growth: physical, intellectual, social, emotional. Remember that an activity can contribute to one or more growth areas.

    b. Write an instructional objective for each of the five activities selected. Prepare a workplan for each. Get feedback from your instructor. Follow any suggestions offered.

    c. Locate a child for whom the activities are appropriate. Use your workplans with him.

    d. Arrange the five objectives in the order of difficulty seen as the child faces his tasks. Place the easiest first, then the next higher level until all five are listed. Ask yourself these questions:

    (1) Was one task harder than another? If so, why would the task be hard for *any* child (list reasons). Then go down the list to see if any of the reasons apply to the child with whom you worked.
    (2) Which was the easiest task? What made the task easy for the child?
    (3) How can the knowledge gained in this experience help me when I work with other children who are performing the same tasks?

    e. If you worked with someone else, find out how that person made out. Compare the children. Discuss your findings. Report to your instructor and/or your class.

- See how many homemade games and activities you can create to help a child learn the five concepts described in learning episodes presented in this unit. Share and exchange ideas with your class.

REVIEW

A. List skills related to each of the following concepts.

    1. One-to-one correspondence   4. Classifying
    2. Sets   5. Grouping and regrouping
    3. Sequencing

Section 5 Materials for Home-Based Learning

    B.   Identify instructional objectives for young children as described in this unit.

    C.   Discuss fully the following statement drawn from the text: "No young child should be put under pressure to reach an objective someone else sets for him." Give your own views and interpretation of the statement.

Section 6 Modeling Skills

unit 18 identifying the modeling approach

OBJECTIVES

After studying this unit, the student should be able to

- Define the following terms: person model, program model, autotelic discovery approach, responsive model, cognitive curriculum, parent-educator model, object level, index level, symbol level, sign level, orchestration.
- Identify at least five findings that show the effect of parent behavior and attitudes on the child's intellectual development.
- Discuss eight questions that parents and program planners can ask as they explore approaches open to them.
- Describe at least two different model programs.

A *model* is defined as something worthy of imitation. In early childhood education, it may refer to a person or a program. A *person model* is someone the child imitates to shape his own behavior. He may be affected by his peer group. He may model himself after the adults he sees most — his parents. Or, he may imitate other adults in his world. A *program model* is one of the many approaches for teaching children between the ages of three and eight.

THE PARENT MODEL

Parents often choose toy models for their child to play with. They may see in the toy something "good" they hope the child may gain by playing with it.

Sometimes parents urge their child to play with children who show some traits or habits that parents hope may "rub off" on their own child. In their efforts to train the child well, parents may make a careful check of the child's playmates. They may want to know what his friends do at play and how they behave.

Although parents are concerned with toys and friends, they may need to be reminded that they themselves are the child's most important models. Studies have shown the effect of parent behavior and attitudes on the young child's intellectual growth. How well the child does when he starts formal schooling is also related to the behaviors of his parents.

Parents Who Promote Intellectual Growth

Parents who are involved in things that stimulate their own mental activity tend to have children who score well in school work. When parents read, children tend to do the same. When parents listen to music, children often share their interests. Many other parent activities seem to have a similar effect on their children.

Parents who have skills in parenting ("know-how" and "show-how") help to increase the child's cognitive growth and development. These parents serve as a source of information and a model for imitation. Learning tasks, and feedback on how well he does, increase the child's performance.

Parents who talk with their child and challenge him to think and to express his ideas promote positive growth. The child is likely to show more advanced performance than one whose parents do not share his experiences.

Parents who set high standards for their child and help him to achieve them tend to stimulate the child to perform well. Such parents are consistent: good work is praised; poor work is rejected.

Parents Who Promote the Child's Self-Concept

The relationship between a child and his parents is another area of concern. Parents who have a warm, friendly attitude toward their child tend to make him feel safe, secure, and capable of doing things. Parents who think well of themselves tend to produce a child who mirrors their self-confidence and builds his own self-esteem.

Studies indicate that it is not the quantity of time spent with the child that counts, but the quality. One parent may devote much time to a child and still not produce satisfying results. Another parent may give limited time in the form of a warm, close relationship. The high quality parent behavior usually gets the best results.

Parents Who Promote the Child's Independence

The school child who is self-reliant and independent is usually one whose parents let him learn early in life to take care of his own needs. Parents who fall into this group may

- Let the very young child learn early to feed and dress himself.
- Permit the child to gain some experience in making decisions that affect him; what to wear, who to play with, where to play.
- Permit the child to gain some experience in making decisions in the family; choose a menu, select a television show, decide how to give a family party, say where he wants to go for a ride.
- See that the child has a chance to solve many of his own problems: decide what and how he wants to play, work out differences with playmates, choose games and toys he wants to use.
- Set limits by which the child learns to control his own behavior.
- Discipline the child by teaching him that he must face the consequences of his own behavior.
- Let him learn to value his own views by the choices he makes.
- Permit more power and freedom as the child shows he is able to deal with the increase.

THE PROGRAM MODEL

Experts do not agree that there is one best way to teach young children. Different programs are in use in various parts of the United States. Some models lean toward one view of child development, but at the same time borrow from one or more of the others.

What is said and what is done stem from different ways to deal with the same problem: meeting the needs of the young child.

Persons who work with parents need to be aware of workable models in early childhood education. Parents should be involved in exploring options open to their children: what can be done and in how many different ways.

Some parents shop around and then place their child in a particular center, because they like what goes on there. When home-based programs are planned, there seems to be no good reason why those parents cannot have choices, too. Parent educators can provide ideas and activities that appeal to them.

Important Questions to Ask

Parents and program planners can explore what is open to them by asking some important questions:

- Who are the **sponsors** of the model? What do they believe about child growth and development? Do their views tie in with that of the child's parents and family?
- What are the **goals** of the model? Are they appropriate for the target child? Do they compare well with what parents set as goals for their child? Can the same goals or parts be used in the home-based program? What changes, if any, need to be made to accommodate both the child and his parents?
- What are the **tasks of children** in the model? Are they in keeping with the needs, interests, and abilities of the target child? Do the activities reflect ways to meet what parents feel is important for their child?
- What is the **role of parents** in the model? How are they drawn into the program? Will parents in a like-program in the home have equal "say" about goals set for their child?
- What **background and training** is required of those who work in the program? Will parents in the home need special training to carry on the work? Who can provide the training, and how can it be made available to parents?
- What **resources** does the model require? Are they available and adaptable to home-based programs? What costs are involved and how can they be met?
- How is the model **evaluated**? Who says it is "good," and what evidence is given? Are there other groups who use the model? What do they say about it?
- Is the model **adaptable** to a home-based program? If so, how? If not, why not?

MODEL PROGRAMS IN EARLY CHILDHOOD EDUCATION

The following models cover a wide range of views, goals, materials, and methods. They are offered as sources of ideas for building a program for home-based early education. Suggestions are given to set in motion the wheels of thought and action.

No model is posed as being better than another. Decisions concerning their use can be made only in the light of local situations. What is judged "best" is what is "best" for the persons involved: parents, children, and those who help them.

The Responsive Model

The *Responsive Model* was planned for children from low-income homes and different ethnic groups. It can be used with any group, however. This model sets as its goal the development of the child's intellectual abilities and a positive self-image. The model highlights an *autotelic discovery approach* which means that learning activities are self-rewarding.

The autotelic approach lets the child try things out, risk, guess, ask questions and make discoveries without reward or punishment. Autotelic activities include games and materials that help the child (1) develop a skill, (2) learn a concept, and (3) acquire an attitude that can be useful in doing some other task.

Section 6 Modeling Skills

The program is tailored to the individual child who participates. Emphasis is placed on responding to the child's needs, culture and interest. Each child is

- Encouraged to solve problems through discovery: The learning environment is carefully controlled. The child is to make a series of "interconnected discoveries" about his physical, intellectual, and social world.

- Free to explore activities open to him: There is freedom to choose activities within preset limits. If an activity interests him, he can pursue it. If he wishes to switch to something else, he is free to do so. He may even reject the activity at the onset.

- Permitted to work at his own pace and in different ways. Units of instruction, called learning episodes, make use of specific toys, games, or pieces of equipment to meet set objectives. The child searches for solutions to problems in his own way, using as many resources as he can. The teacher guides his discovery of solutions. The child finds out for himself if his choices work.

- Given immediate feedback that tells him whether he is right or wrong: Self-correcting toys are provided in the form of nesting cups, puzzles, and the like.

Learning booths have booth attendants who ask the child if he would like to "play" with something like an electric typewriter. If he says "no," he is not asked again. If he says "yes," the booth attendant lets him explore free play with the typewriter. She may also play a "search and match" game. These activities lead to dictation of stories and finally to the child transcribing his own stories.

- Helped to learn for the joy of learning and is given no external reward or punishment. The reward he gets may be winning a game or completing some task. If he is not able to win, he can stop playing or find another task. The goal is that he undertake a task for its own reward.

The Responsive Model, designed for preschool through third grade, has several parts — one of which is a toy-lending library. Handbooks provide parents with help in the use of the toys. Parents are also trained by a teacher-librarian.

The Bank Street Model

The *Bank Street Model* is designed for children from preschool to third grade. It aims to actively involve the child in his own learning to develop his positive self-image, and to promote his development as a self-directed learner.

A learning environment is provided by which the everyday play activities of the child become a democratic-life situation for learning. Play is seen as the means through which the child interacts with people, objects, and events in his environment. Through his play activities, he is able to develop the ability to satisfy his emotional needs in ways that are acceptable.

Work areas are filled with stimulating materials. They give the child a wide variety of opportunities to learn by motor and sensory experiences. These materials include

- Large and small blocks for building.
- Equipment for sand and water play.
- Housekeeping materials in a special corner.
- Equipment for large motor play.
- Math and Science materials.
- Materials for fine arts and craft work.
- Books, pictures, and other visual media.
- Manipulative materials of all kinds.

The model aims to develop the whole child. It promotes his physical and social well-being by helping his family understand his development and his needs. The model brings the support of community agencies and resources to the child and his family — as they need such support.

The teacher's role is to tailor the program to meet the evolving needs of the child. The child's needs are not seen as preset goals. They are descriptions of the teacher's efforts to study him and learn what he can do and wants to do. She gives him many opportunities to make choices and think for himself.

The materials for learning may be preplanned lessons with direct teaching. Or, the teacher may use an indirect approach by helping the child to develop a skill, concept, or attitude. Study is centered around cooking, caring for pets, and doing chores in the room. Observation and study move to the community where children can solve problems and see relationships in their world of people, objects, and events.

Children may work alone or in groups. There are rules by which the children can organize and manage their activities. They have access to many interest areas which are separated by shelves or dividers. Rooms are seen as workshops where the child may move from one interest area to another with little direction from the teacher.

Parent involvement is encouraged. Parents are able to take part in planning and running the program. They may work as paid or unpaid teacher aides, too. There is an after-school program open to older children in the family.

The Cognitive Curriculum

The *Cognitive Curriculum* is a model designed to teach cognitive or thinking skills for children in preschool through third grade. It is based on the belief that telling and showing do not teach, but that active experience with real objects does.

The program has two major components. One is a classroom program in which the teaching staff focus on the development of skills and concepts. The process of learning is emphasized rather than particular subject matter. The other is a home program which consists of planned visits to the home by classroom teachers or home visitors hired to do the job. Home visitors help parents carry on the child's work on a one-to-one basis with the child at home. Parents are involved as teachers of their own child and help to support the activities of the program.

Teachers in the program need intensive training. They must be able to write detailed daily lesson plans with goals appropriate for their group. They must also be able to prepare individual plans stating specific behaviors desired for each child. A curriculum aide is provided, usually one aide to help each team of two teachers.

Learning opportunities for children are derived from the work of Jean Piaget, the Swiss psychologist. Piaget believes that each step in intellectual growth makes the next step possible.

The Cognitive Curriculum uses Piaget's concepts in the basic framework for the model. Included are four levels of ability:

- *Object level:* the child has experiences with real objects and places. For example, the child sees a telephone, hears it ring, and talks with someone at the other end of the line.

- *Index level:* the child learns to recall an object mentally when he can see only part of it or some part is missing. To the child, the ringing of the telephone stands for the telephone.

- *Symbol level:* the child can use pictures and dramatic play in place of real objects. He draws a picture of a telephone, for example.
- *Sign level:* the child can use words and numerals with meaning. This means that the child represents things through written words and numerals, although this is not stressed for preschoolers.

Four cognitive (intellectual) skills are identified in the program. Some of the related concepts were presented in learning activities described in unit 17. A brief review is given.

- *Classification:* the child learns to see likes and differences among objects. He learns to group them on this basis.
- *Seriation:* the child learns to order objects by size, quality, or quantity (soft to hard, small to large).
- *Spatial relations:* the child develops an understanding of his relation to objects. He acquires body awareness and concepts of position (in-out, near-far).
- *Temporal relations:* the child learns to understand time sequences. Things begin and end. Events can be ordered (first, second, before, last).

The Cognitive Curriculum uses materials found in most traditional preschools. They are used in new and different ways to join a learning experience with an enjoyable activity. All learning activities are labeled work, although there is no sharp line between work and play.

Teaching is done in a step-by-step process. Every activity is designed to meet a set objective. The sequence of tasks is preset. A child learns one concept before moving to a more difficult one.

Interest centers divide the room into four areas: (1) the house and doll area, which is used for role play and body image games; (2) the large motor area, equipped with boards, blocks, and toys for riding; (3) the art area; used for teacher-led activities or for "open" artwork; and (4) a quiet area which contains table-activity materials selected by the teacher to meet set goals. The children may select from puzzles, small cars, trucks, books, beads, and peg boards.

The Cognitive Curriculum involves children in cleanup work. They put away materials and games and tell why they put materials in certain places. In this way, classification and seriation concepts are reinforced.

The Florida Parent-Educator Model

The *Florida Parent-Educator Model* is based on the belief that education must start early and it must start in the home. The program provides a link between what a child learns in a center and what he does at home. A parent-educator (home visitor) assists teachers in a center and works with parents in their homes each week.

There is no preset curriculum or special technique to be used. The program is developmental in the sense that learning tasks are developed that allow the home and school to work together as partners. The curriculum is the product of the parent and the school staff working together to help the child meet his developmental tasks.

The parent-educator is usually a mother from the local community. She works in the center to learn skills she can pass on to parents each week. A teacher supervises the classroom activity of the parent-educator and assists her in planning and carrying out her work in the home.

The parent-educator may perform other tasks that are related to the child's needs. She may act as a liaison between the home and agencies that provide medical, dental, and social services.

The play activities of the child serve as cues to the level of concepts and skills the child attains. The child's play behavior is observed by parents and teachers.

Much language is used with the child's work to help him learn to classify, label, and seriate. As in many other models, activities in the Florida Parent-Educator Model are based on tasks like those important to Piaget.

Tucson Early Education Model (TEEM)

The *Tucson Early Education Model* is based on the belief that full participation in today's society requires certain skills and abilities. The assumption is made that people who lack these skills come from a background which did not build the necessary foundation.

The TEEM model attempts to solve this problem by providing for the early childhood development of four factors, the first of which is language competence. It also provides for the development of an intellectual base made up of skills assumed to be needed for learning; such as classifying, seriating, sequencing, listening and paying attention, making judgments and choices, and the like. There must also be a motivational base with attitudes and behaviors that make it possible to be productive in dealing with persons, objects, and events. Examples are liking school, sticking to a job until it is done, expecting to be successful, and being willing to change. Social arts and skills — the ability to use language in social situations, the ability to cooperate with others, and the ability to read, write and do math — must be developed.

TEEM has no set curriculum or stated set of learning objectives. Each child begins where he is and is guided on his own level and at his own pace. Learning may take place in small group work or in a one-to-one exchange between the child and an adult. Three tasks are identified for the teacher, who must

- Arrange an environment that leads each child to learn.
- See that the children have good models of language and behavior to imitate.
- Reinforce the desired behavior as soon as it occurs.

A *program assistant* receives special training to act as a change agent in the classroom. The change agent

- Carries out program changes when the need arises.
- Introduces new ideas to those who are to use them.
- Helps teachers by demonstrating new ways to reach goals.
- Visits classrooms to see how things are going.

The concept of *orchestration* is used in TEEM. It means that skills and concepts from different subject areas are taught in the same activity.

TEEM was originally designed for Mexican-American children (preschool through grade three). It now includes programs for children of all cultural groups. The involvement of parents helps to bridge the gap between cultures.

AN ECLECTIC MODEL

If parents are involved in building a home-based program for their child, the result may well be called an *eclectic model*. Something seen as eclectic borrows from other sources like itself. When options are open to them, parents may wish to do much "borrowing."

Program planners must be sure that when borrowed parts are combined, they are compatible and result in an appropriate set of learning tasks for the child. They must also suit the viewpoint and needs of the kind of program desired and use the resources available. The borrowed parts must also operate well under local conditions.

A good home-based program is one which has a natural link between the way a child develops and the learning experiences provided. No matter what the base may be, a good program shares certain things in common with all other well-planned programs.

- It makes provision for the child's physical development. It insures a healthy body for a healthy mind.
- It helps the child develop his self-concept, self-esteem, and self-identity. Social development is crucial.
- It helps the child to recognize and respond to a range of feelings in himself and to communicate them to others in acceptable ways.
- It helps the child develop intellectual skills. His experiences help his mind to grow, develop, and make sense of his world.

Fig. 18-1 A good program makes provision for physical activity and development.

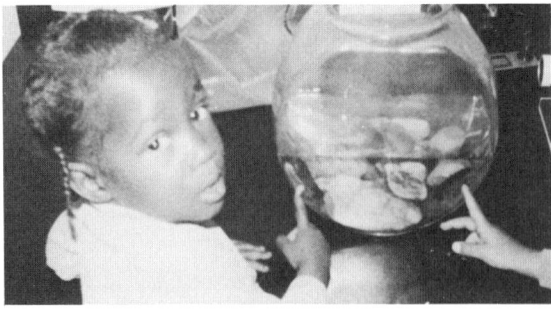

Fig. 18-2 A good program provides the child with experiences that promote language development. Shown is a preschooler using both verbal and nonverbal language.

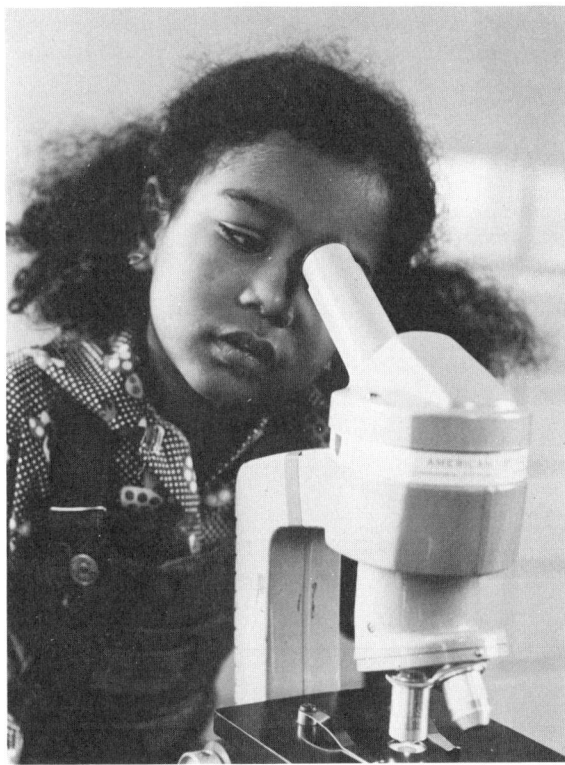

Fig. 18-3 A good program provides children with experiences that hold their interest and stretch their minds.

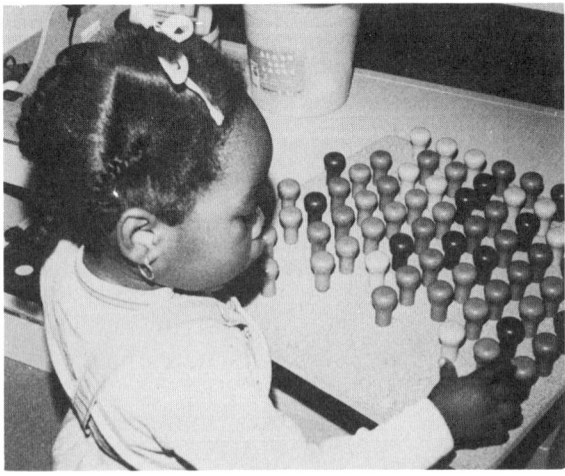

Fig. 18-4 A good program helps the child to develop intellectual skills by classifying, matching, and making judgments.

- It promotes his ability to use language with accuracy and flexibility. It gives him positive feedback.

- It includes relating to other children: working and playing with them and relating to them in many other ways. He learns to respect others: their rights, interests, feelings, and abilities.

- It gives him a chance to form a closer relationship with his parents and family members. He also gains experience with other adults who guide and support him.

- It helps him to relate to a group. His experiences as a part of a group help him to see his own place among others. He learns about group behavior and how he can stay within bounds — without losing his own views and goals.

Planning a home-based program requires careful study and thought. Program models can be studied by reading about them in published reports, books, and articles. If local communities have model programs, perhaps arrangements can be made to visit programs which may be similar or different. Filmstrips are available with accompanying cassette descriptions of some of the programs described in this unit (see list of references).

Designing any program can be difficult. It may be necessary to resolve conflicts of values and beliefs. When people are involved in making plans that affect them personally, they are more apt to accept responsibility for carrying out the plans. This may hold true where parents are concerned.

This unit describes models from which ideas may be gained for home-use. Unit 19 tells how modeling skills can be developed in centers. *Modeling* refers to the "show-how" techniques used by teachers — and by home visitors who work in the home.

Fig. 18-5 A good program helps each child to develop intellectual skills and creative thinking. Shown is a bedroom art gallery and circus made by children in a family.

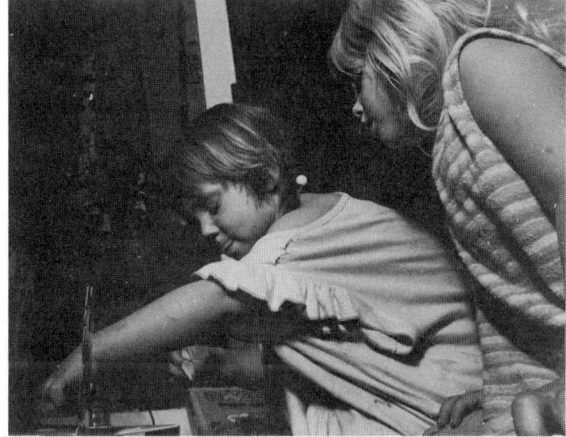

Fig. 18-6 A good program helps children to decide and direct their own learning activities.

Fig. 18-7 A good program helps the child to relate to a group. Shown are children sharing a creative experience.

Section 6 Modeling Skills

SUMMARY

A model may be seen as a person or a program. A person model is someone the child imitates to shape his own behavior. A program model is one of the many approaches for teaching children between the ages of three and eight.

Parents are the child's most important models. There are many studies that show the effect of parent behavior and attitudes on the young child's intellectual growth. Parents who model certain types of behavior tend to have children who imitate them.

Experts do not agree that there is one best way to teach young children. Various programs are used throughout the country.

When programs are planned the following should be considered: sponsors, goals, tasks of children, role of parents, staff training, resources, evaluations, and adaptability. The models described include the Responsive Model, the Bank Street Model, the Cognitive Curriculum, the Florida Parent-Educator Model, and the Tucson Early Education Model (TEEM).

Parents may help to develop an eclectic model — one that borrows from other sources like itself. A good home-based program is one which has a natural link between the way a child develops and the learning experiences provided.

SUGGESTED ACTIVITIES

- Check the yellow pages of your local telephone book under the heading: Schools – Nursery and Kindergarten.

    a. Telephone the directors of two centers. Ask if you may visit to observe and obtain information about approaches to learning used at the center. Try to set a date and a time for your visit.

    b. Follow up your telephone call with a letter to each director in which you (1) thank the director for taking time from her busy schedule to talk with you, (2) make reference to the date and time you plan to be at the center (to make sure that there is no misunderstanding), and (3) include the fact that you are looking forward to your visit, or a similar comment.

    c. Make a list of the questions that follow. Give a copy to the director upon your arrival. Ask if she can give you a few minutes to discuss the questions before you leave. If she does not wish to respond to a question, do not press the issue.

    (1) Who sponsors the program? What is the philosophy on which the program is based?
    (2) What are the goals of the program?
    (3) What are the tasks of children?
    (4) What kind of training is required of the staff?
    (5) What resources are available? Do community agencies and organizations provide services?
    (6) How is the program evaluated?

d. Compare the two centers and the programs they offer.
   (1) See if any of them follow activities along the lines of those described in this unit.
   (2) See how the two centers are alike and how they differ.

e. If the activity is done as a class assignment, the yellow page list of centers can be divided among class members. Perhaps the group may decide to visit in teams of two. The class may wish to make their own plans in carrying out the activity.

CAUTION: Remember that the purpose of your visit is to learn more about programs and how they meet the needs of children. You are not an authority, and must not try to pass judgment on what you may see as "good" or "bad."

REVIEW

A. Define briefly each of the following.
   1. Person model
   2. Program model
   3. Responsive Model
   4. Cognitive Curriculum
   5. Parent-Educator Model
   6. Autotelic discovery approach
   7. Object level
   8. Index level
   9. Symbol level
   10. Sign level
   11. Orchestration

B. Identify and discuss at least five findings that show the effect of parent behavior and attitudes on the child's intellectual growth.

C. Briefly list the questions that parents and program planners can ask as they explore curriculum approaches open to them.

D. Compare two different models described in this unit. Give your own reaction to the program described.

unit 19 working with parents in centers

OBJECTIVES

After studying this unit, the student should be able to

- Describe four tasks seen as important in setting up a program for parent involvement and training.
- Identify four ways by which parents can learn how to become teachers of their own children through center-based training.
- Describe five things parents can learn and do in centers.
- Give an example of how center-based training helps a parent to help her child learn.

The old saying, "Actions speak louder than words," takes on new meaning when it is applied to activities in early childhood centers. Parents can learn how to deal more effectively with their own child by observing and assisting child care workers in the center.

Wishing for parent involvement does not make it happen. Some parents may be afraid to take part for fear they are to be judged. They may need to be reassured before they can feel free to participate.

It is not easy to be a good parent. Early childhood center workers must be aware of the problems that parents face in doing their job. Most parents mean well and want to do what is best for their children. Good parent-teacher relationships are made when each tries to understand how a certain thing looks to the other.

Teachers must face the fact that not all that a parent sees will gain parental approval. Some negative views can be expected. Open discussions concerning what is done, and why, may help to end some of the negative feelings and attitudes a parent may have.

In a center the teacher is a model whose behavior becomes a pattern for the parent to follow. The teachers modeling task is to help parents gain confidence in their own ability to be an effective teacher of their own child and the insight, knowledge, and skills they need to help the child learn, grow, and develop to his capacity level.

A good parent involvement program must be led by teachers who see parents as partners in the teaching-learning process. This unit discusses ways by which a working relationship can be built.

PARENT INVOLVEMENT AND TRAINING

Planning is an important part of any effort to help people learn. To insure an effective program for parents, ways must be found to interest all the people who will be working together.

Teacher Involvement

Teachers must be involved in the early planning of the parent program. People tend to accept plans and ideas they feel are their own. Involving teachers at the onset of the program is one way to get off to a good start. Some ways of involving teachers are listed:

- Examine the program of the center. Take a complete inventory of teacher tasks designed to meet set objectives.

Unit 19 Working with Parents in Centers

Interviewer: _____

Date: _____

Parent Questionnaire[1]

Head Start is a total family program. This means we will seek to provide experiences for parents that will encourage their growth also. These questions give you the opportunity to tell us more about yourself and what you are interested in. We would appreciate your thoughtful answers.

1. What role do you feel you play in your child's life?

2. What would you like Head Start *to be* for your family?

3. How do you feel about standing up for your rights?

4. What things do you like to do?

5. What things are you interested in learning or doing?

6. Do you enjoy being with others in groups?
   ____ School Functions   ____ Scouts   ____ Church Groups
   ____ Room Mother   ____ Neighborhood Groups   ____ Coops
   ____ Other   ____ Community Centers

7. If you had several hours of "free" time for yourself each week, what would you like to do?

8. Head Start encourages parents to take an active role in all parts of the program. Who would you prefer to be involved with? (Please number in the order of your choices.)
   ____ Children   ____ Other Parents   ____ Head Start Workers

9. What types of activities appeal to you?
   ____ Assisting teacher in classroom   ____ Field trips with children
   ____ Helping plan social type events   ____ Preparing foods at home
   ____ Certain office type work   ____ Newsletters
   ____ Phone work   ____ Receptionist
   ____ Hostess at events in your home   ____ Larger group activities
   ____ Serve on the Policy Council   ____ Health Advisory Board
   ____ Center Committee   ____ Acting as leader to small group of parents

10. If you wanted to volunteer, how many hours would you like to spend? (Please circle)

    6 - 4 - 2 - 0

Fig. 19-1 Shown is a parent questionnaire used to draw parents to the center as active participants.
[1](Source: Lane County Head Start, Eugene, Oregon.)

- Identify teacher tasks which can be performed by parents who may serve as regular aides in the center. They may be volunteers or paid workers.

- Identify teacher tasks which can be taught to parents as "learners" in the center. Parents in this group may participate only to learn how to teach their own children.

- Examine the new role of the teacher as an adult educator performing an adult education task — teaching parents how to teach their own children.

Ideas and tasks should be put in printed form. When information is put in writing, it is easier to step back and look at what is there. Tasks can be changed, substituted, or eliminated. The written word also helps avoid conflict or confusion by providing a frame of reference known to all.

Important decisions must be made concerning how parents are to be trained: the method to be used, the person to be in charge of the training program, and ways that the parents are to be involved in their own training. It must be decided what resources and services are available and may be used. A means by which center and home training activities can be linked must be devised. Methods for record keeping (what records are to be kept and in what form) must be planned, as well as a system for evaluating the training program.

Parent Recruitment

A means must be set up by which parents can be recruited. There are many ways by which parents can learn about opportunities open to them at a center: (1) The center can establish a link with agencies and organizations in the community who can tell parents what is available; (2) A child already in a center can take home a letter inviting his parents to take part. A questionnaire can provide information helpful in planning the program; (3) Letters can be sent directly to parents; (4) Telephone calls can be made; (5) Personal visits to homes may attract some parents; (6) Local radio stations may have a time when they are willing to make special announcements of interest to people in the community; and (7) Local newspapers may carry an article telling about the program and inviting parents to come.

Decisions must be made about the tasks and events to be set in motion. Plans should be made for an orientation meeting to give parents important information. Other meetings are included when the program gets underway. Listed are tasks to be accomplished sometime during the training program.

- State the goals of the center. Explain how the goals are to be met.

- Discuss the school philosophy. Tell what the staff believes is important to the young child.

- Discuss the characteristics of the age group at the center. Note ways in which children may differ, even though they are in the same age group.

- Identify and discuss the developmental needs of children in the center age group. Help parents to find out what their child needs.

- Describe learning objectives that tell parents what the child is supposed to be able to do and how he is to do it.

- Show activities that help the child meet his tasks. Have teachers model the behaviors parents are to copy. Discuss with parents what they see.

- Help parents imitate the teacher's model. Give parents help as they need it.

- Let parents evaluate their own experiences. Make each feel that she/he is an important part of the program.

- Be sure to state any limits set on what parents may and may not do. Explain limits set on child behaviors.
- Caution parents to keep in confidence what they see other children do at the center.

HOW PARENTS CAN LEARN IN CENTERS

Parents can learn by the "look and see" method. They look around the center and focus their attention on a teaching-learning activity they can observe. As they watch the teacher work with their child, they can see the child's reaction to what is taught. They learn how materials and activities are used to promote learning. They have a chance to see their child work with other children.

Parents can learn by discussion. They may raise questions concerning what they see in the center. The teacher may explain why a lesson was taught one way and not another. In discussions, parents gain greater insight into learning and how it can be sparked.

Parents can learn by doing some of the teaching themselves. Storytelling and learning episodes modeled by the teacher can be copied by the parent. The teacher supervises the activity.

Parents can learn by sharing their experiences with other parents and learning from them, too. They can discuss common problems and work together to find ways to solve them. Some studies show that a person can find a solution to his own problems better when he is in a group situation.

Parents can learn by carrying on in their homes many of the activities they try out in the center. A home visitor can help the parent, or the parent can work out her tasks alone. She can discuss them later.

WHAT PARENTS CAN LEARN AND DO IN CENTERS

In many centers, formal or informal programs for parents are organized to get their aid in meeting set goals of the school. Some programs are organized much like school courses of study. They teach about child growth and development, parenting skills, and homemaking practices by which the child's home and family life can be improved. Others are informal group meetings where like objectives may be met. What is offered to parents may vary with the goals of the center itself.

Although the tasks of parents may differ there is one thing they share in common. Letting the mother see how the daily program works is like giving her a part in a script about the center. She can follow along with the teacher, receive explanations, and get assistance as her work goes on.

The activities which follow are offered as examples of what goes on in some centers and can be explored in others.

Preparing and Serving Food

Teachers encourage parents to volunteer in preparing and serving food for the center. Parents gain knowledge of the factors which influence nutrition and food practices. They learn important facts about home management and consumer practices; they learn to

- Make sound choices in the food market — choices that are economical and nutritional.
- Plan menus based on child growth and development.
- Select and prepare the kind and amount of food which meets the nutritional needs of the individual child.
- Prepare and store food in a safe and sanitary way.
- Make mealtime an enjoyable experience for the child and help him develop good food habits.
- Expand the child's experiences with food to help him learn about words, textures, colors, smells, measures, and tastes.

Section 6 Modeling Skills

- Involve the child in grownup activities, such as planning meals, marketing (see figure 17-14 for supermarket activity), and preparing and serving food.

Determining Learning Needs

Teachers show parents how a preschool inventory finds some of the learning needs of the child. Parents learn how teachers give preschool "tests" as a way to measure some type of behavior. Teachers discuss the results and provide parents with toys and games designed to promote the desired skills. Some informal learning tests are listed:

- Measuring incoming and outgoing language. The child is asked to point to objects and recall what he was asked to find.
- Checking visual-motor abilities. The child is given toys (blocks, stacking rings, pegs) to see what he can do with them. He is given media such as crayons and paint to see what he can create.
- Testing visual and auditory signals. The child is asked to repeat words or numbers. He may be asked to copy simple designs shown to him, too.
- Testing the child's ability to use expressive language. The child is asked to point to a toy on request (shows ability to receive a message). He may tell about the toy and use descriptive terms in what he says (shows ability to express an idea).

Interacting with the Child

Teachers show parents how to interact with a child on a one-to-one basis. Teachers model storytelling techniques. They also provide models for music activities, artwork, sandbox and water play, games, creative play, and learning episodes. Parents have a chance to work with their own child and with others. Opportunities to work with children other

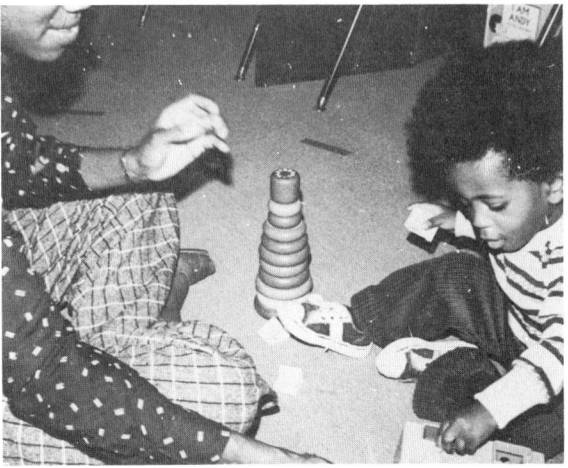
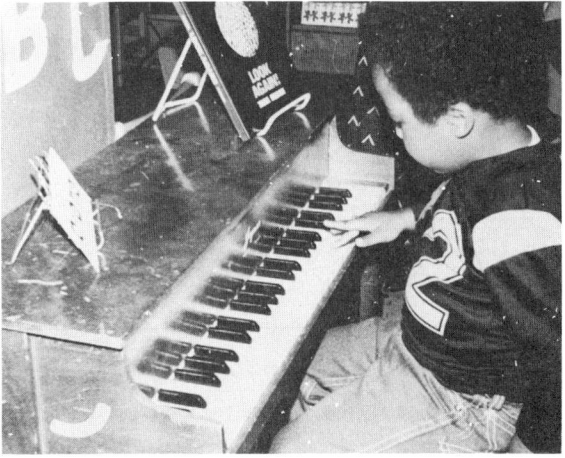

Fig. 19-2 Toys, games, and models provide young children with many learning experiences they can share with adults.

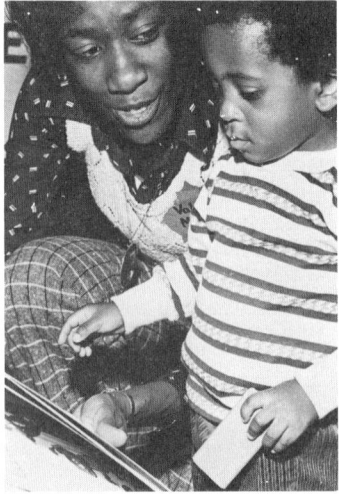

Fig. 19-3 Shown is an effective adult-child interaction taking place.

than their own gives parents a broader view of the meaning of individual differences among children.

Dealing with Child Behaviors

Teachers show parents how to deal with child behaviors in a positive way. Parents learn to look for the "payoff" — the reward that makes a child behave in set ways. Parents learn that rewards can come in different forms: attention, food, approval, or special privileges. They learn ways to weaken undesirable behavior to stop it from occurring. Some ways are listed:

- Find the payoff and stop it right away.
- Try to reason with the child to make him see what is not right about his behavior.
- Give the child a substitute for something he must not touch or do.
- When punishment is necessary it should be done immediately (especially when the child's safety is at stake), but an explanation should be given.

It is important that parents know something about reinforcement and how it works. They need to know that reinforcement must be something the child sees as rewarding. It may be material (tokens, stars, food, candy, toys) or it may be only verbal praise.

Some parents may want their child to develop an internal reward system — the satisfaction the child gets for a task well done. Other parents may wish to give external rewards in the forms mentioned. Teachers should be aware of conflicts that may arise when what a teacher does is not in keeping with what a parent wants to do at home.

What can be stressed is that the behaviors go on when the child gets his payoff. The behaviors tend to stop when the payoff is removed. Parents may be able to see what works best with their child by watching his behaviors in the center.

Meeting to Exchange Ideas

Teachers provide parents with opportunities to meet each other and exchange ideas. Parent meetings at the center bring parents together to share problems and explore solutions. Some parents may find comfort in knowing that others face the same problems they do.

Staff members may take a leadership role in discussions. They may obtain resource materials for parents, or they may invite speakers who can deal with common problems.

Finding Needed Services

Teachers help parents find needed services that exist in the community. Parents learn that there are agencies and organizations who can help them with parenting needs. These include: medical, nutritional, legal, adult education and recreation opportunities, and services in the area of housing and employment — when applicable.

LEARNING AIDS FOR PARENTS

Each program may have learning aids geared to the needs and interests of persons enrolled. In addition to the usual books, films, filmstrips, magazines, and packaged materials for learning, some homemade aids are suggested. These are tailored to the people who take part.

A taped script may be prepared so that parents have access to instant information about the center. One or more cassette tapes can cover the goals, philosophy, and guidelines to let parents see where they fit in.

A set of tapes for each subject matter area touched upon in learning episodes (music, art, math, science, play, social studies) is very helpful. In a very simple and conversationlike way, some objectives are stated

Section 6 Modeling Skills

for each area. Ways that the center tries to meet them are discussed.

A tape about discipline and how parents can use a positive approach to their problems may also be offered. As parents discuss other ideas in meetings, tapes on these topics should be included, too. Parents should be able to borrow tapes for home use.

Newsletters are prepared to let parents know what is going on in the center. One topic of concern is dealt with in each issue to answer and explore questions raised by parents. Parents may be involved in preparing the letter.

Sample lessons in which teachers model the kind of behavior needed to build concepts, develop language skills, and let children solve learning problems may be televised.

A parent at work with her own child may be televised. The parent should see a replay of the tape and make comments about the lesson. The teacher gives positive feedback. Unless the parent gives written permission for the tape to be retained, she should see it being erased. She may be uncomfortable about having a record of what she may see as "mistakes."

A parents' book club may be started. Books may be borrowed by the center from the public library, teachers, other parents, or agencies willing to share them. Books at all reading levels should be included. Topics may be related to sex education, discipline, child rearing, crafts, games for young children, and the like.

A center file of games, stories, learning episodes, mounted pictures, craft ideas — for parents to borrow may be created. The source of all material must be given on the information sheets. The teacher must discourage "pirating" (illegal copy work) by rejecting work copied without the permission of the copyright owner.

A bulletin filled with current news should be kept. Any adult education classes open to parents can be included. Clippings from a local newspaper may be helpful and of interest.

Learning kits geared to what is going on in the center may be developed. Toys, games, and information for parents should be included.

MODELING: AN APPLICATION

The following application of the concept of modeling is a sketch of what can be done over time. The amount of time spent, what is done, and how much is done depends on the local situation. Each task is identified and described. An explanation for parents follows each task.

 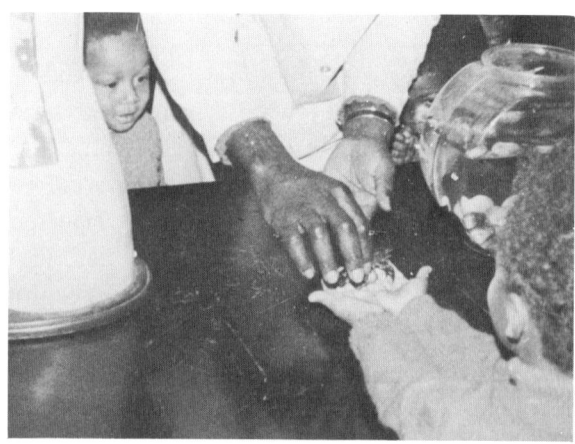

Fig. 19-4 Children are ready to seek new experiences when things hold their interest.

Identify the area of learning: A child learns through his five senses. Plan a lesson that will show how intellectual development expands as the child learns by using his senses.

Describe the characteristics and interests of the child: Call attention to the characteristics of the child who is the same age as the target child. Note that a characteristic is only a frame of reference. It is like trying to predict what a child is like at a certain age. The child

- Enjoys sensory experiences; the "here and now" are his.
- Likes color, sound, movement, and touch stimuli.
- Explores, experiments, and seeks new experiences when things hold his attention.
- Shows a keen and active curiosity in things about him.
- May seek body explorations, not sparked by sex urges and drives, which are of no great concern.
- Asks endless questions and wants answers.
- Shows little interest in remote places or in things of the past, although he may ask about things he sees on television.

Identify developmental tasks for the child: When a child reaches a certain age, there are things that can be expected of him. At different stages, the child likes to do things that other children like him also find interesting. What he learns at one level may help him with tasks at the next higher level. The child of this age needs

- To experiment with many kinds of materials.
- To discriminate in the use of color and sound.
- To handle and learn about many different objects.
- To use simple tools in a safe way.
- To use toys and games designed for learning.
- To go on study trips around his home and in his community.
- To learn new words to express and make clear the experiences he has.
- To expand his range of works to meet his increased need to express his new ideas and understandings.
- To have time to be alone to think about things that concern him without being pressured.

Call attention to ways by which the child can meet his tasks in center activities: The parent should see the many ways by which children in the center use their senses to learn.

- Experiences with color: drawing with crayons, paint, chalk, experimenting in mixing colors, seeing color in nature, choosing things of colors that please them.

Fig. 19-5 A young child needs time to be alone, to think about things that concern him, and to sort things out.

Section 6 Modeling Skills

- Experiences with sound: horns, whistles, machinery, tools, musical instruments, human voices, animal sounds.
- Experiences with touch: balls, blocks, news and different objects of various textures (hard, soft, cold, rough, smooth, sharp), clay, and other items. Call attention to a "feely bag" which can be made at home.
- Experiences with taste: new foods, snacks, tasting parties.

Demonstrate a lesson in which the child has an opportunity to use all of his senses in a learning experience: Play dough is easy to make and can be made at home. Parent should observe what is done.

Teacher: Here is our recipe for making play dough. What do you think we need?

Child: Salt.

Teacher: How can you tell?

Child: That picture looks like a box of salt. And, I see one cup next to it.

Teacher: What do you think that one cup means?

Child: We got [sic] to put one cup of salt in it.

Teacher: Will you measure one cup of salt and pour it in the bowl?

Child: Okay.

Teacher: Can you tell what else we need?

Child: Flour, because I see the flour bag and three cups next to it. Mommy has a bag like that.

Teacher: How nice that we have the same kind of flour. Can you tell how many cups of flour we need?

Child: Three.

Teacher: Will you please measure the flour and put it in the bowl with the salt?

Child: Okay.

Teacher: How much water do we need? Look at the picture of the pitcher and cup. Can you guess how much water we need?

Child: One cup?

Teacher: Right. Now what do you think needs to be done?

Child: We gotta [sic] mix everything up.

Teacher: Right. Now let's see how well you can mix the dough. I'll read the directions while you do the work.

Fig. 19-6 Children learn through their senses in a home-based learning activity.

Unit 19 Working with Parents in Centers

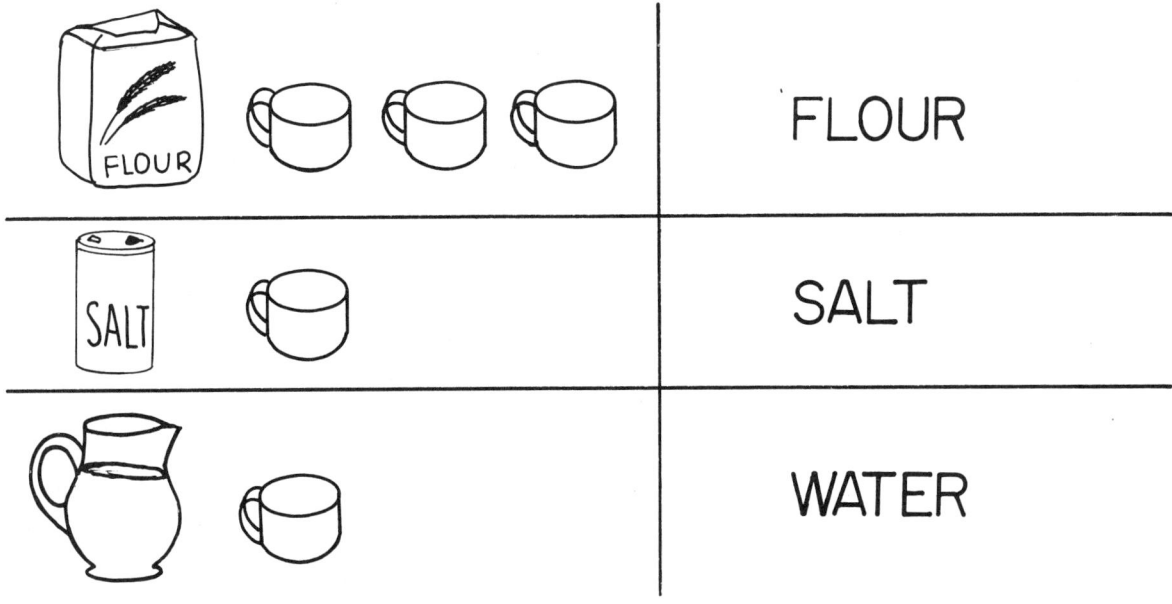

PLAY DOUGH

1. Measure these things.
   - 3 cups of flour
   - 1 cup of salt
2. Mix the flour and salt.
3. Add 1 cup of water, little by little.
4. Mix well until a paste is made.
5. Find out what you can do with the dough.
   - Add some different colors (to make it look good).
   - Add some extract: vanilla or peppermint (to make it smell good).
6. Make something to keep.
   - Roll the dough. Squeeze it. Pat it. Shape it.
   - See what you have.

Fig. 19-7 **Play dough helps the child learn through his senses and is a fun experience.**

The lesson goes on. The child is encouraged to use words to describe how the dough feels. He asks if he can taste it and does. He spits it out. He is given food coloring and some extract, vanilla and peppermint. He finds that the food coloring makes no difference in the taste of the play dough. He tries it after adding flavoring, but spits that out, too. He concludes that "play dough is for play and not for eating."

The child's mother feels the dough and tries to make something with it. The child is delighted with the thought that "a big lady is playing." He imitates the teacher's words when he says to his mother, "Good work! You did a good job."

Identifying desirable outcomes: The teacher calls attention to some desirable outcomes of the activity. She points out that the child is able to

Section 6 Modeling Skills

- Use material safely.
- Learn by the use of his senses.
- Work on a task which does not require too much supervision for his safety.
- Deepen his interests through enriching experiences.
- Develop his creativity.
- Respect the ideas and work of others.
- Show patience and interest in finding his own answers to things that concern him.
- Observe to learn more about things in his world.

Transferring the parent's experience to the back-home situation: One of the first comments parents often make is that they wish they had a place to "keep all those things." Perhaps the best way to respond is to convert the problem to a challenge for all parents: How can we find storage space for the child's things? Some ways shown to be helpful are listed. Parents of children in the center may add other ideas.

- Get several cardboard boxes from a supermarket. Cut each box down to a height which can be slipped under the child's bed. To teach the child to sort and classify things, place a picture on the box showing what goes in it. The box may also be labeled (even though the child cannot read the words) to give meaning to the printed symbols. The child should be helped to pick up before he leaves for another interest. When he develops the pickup habit, he can do the task himself.
- Keep a box of toys for the toddler and preschooler in any room where he may be. When his own things are available, he is less apt to handle other things — especially those he is not to touch. A

HELPING IN A CENTER
• Register children for the program.
• Go on field trips as teacher-aides.
• Make things to sell in the school fund-raising Flea Market.
• Help one or more children with learning tasks.
• Prepare and give parties on birthdays and holidays.
• Work with children in discovery centers for learning.
• Read stories to children.
• Operate machines for the teacher or children: tape-recorder, movie projector, record-player, filmstrip projector, etc.
• Help with art, sewing, or cooking activities.
• Help plan and prepare low-cost meals.
• Paint old furniture to be used in the center.
• Collect wood and waste materials for craft work.
• Develop learning materials for teachers.

Fig. 19-8 Shown are some ways by which parents help others and help themselves, too. **Parent skills come with practice.**

low-cut box can be placed under a sofa or a chair. An attractive long tablecloth can conceal a box kept under a table.

- To provide space for playing games and writing, the parent may be able to obtain lap trays which can be stored where the child plays. He can sit on the floor and use the lap tray like an Oriental chow table.
- The bottom of an inverted cardboard box makes a nice table for play. The top is removed and a space large enough for the child to put his legs through is cut in one side. The box may also be used for toy storage when turned with the top up.
- Other storage places may be a drawer in the kitchen or bedroom, a closet, shop-

ping bags placed on a doorknob, wastebaskets, clothes hampers, and many other items which can be used on a temporary basis.

Games and toys described in other units can be made for the child. With things to do, storage space, and a place to work, the young child can learn to organize his own time.

SUMMARY

Parents can learn how to deal more effectively with their own child by observing and assisting child care workers in a child care center. Teachers can model behavior for parents to copy.

Teachers should be involved early in planning programs for parent involvement. A list of tasks for parents should be made. Teachers assume a new role as adult educators — teaching parents how to teach their children at home.

Ideas and tasks should be put in printed form. A plan for recruiting parents is needed. A plan to be followed in the training program is necessary.

Parents can learn in different ways at the center. They can "look and see" and learn by observation. They can learn by discussion. They can learn by doing some of the work themselves. Parents can also learn from each other by sharing ideas and answers to problems.

In working at the center, parents can learn about child growth and development, parenting skills, home management, consumer practices, and foods and nutrition needs of children. Skills in working with children can also be learned.

SUGGESTED ACTIVITIES

- Contact the director of one of the centers you visited in the past. Ask if you can do the following:

    a. Make a list of ways parents assist in the center.

    b. Observe parents at work on their tasks.

    c. Attend a meeting for parents.

    (1) Make a list of questions parents ask to get information.
    (2) Make a list of things parents say to give information.
    (3) Identify ways in which parents share and help each other to solve their parenting problems.

    d. Interview a parent who helps at the center.

    (1) Ask what the parent likes to do best at the center.
    (2) Ask how the parent thinks more people could become involved in the parent program.
    (3) Ask for any word of advice which the parent may offer for you to take back to your class — made up of persons who plan to work in centers.

    e. Share your findings with your class. Exchange information. Make a complete list of all ways parents help in centers in your community.

    f. Discuss both positive and negative (if any) comments parents make concerning their work. How do you think the information gained can be used to improve adult education when people work with parents?

Section 6 Modeling Skills

REVIEW

A. Describe four tasks that are important in setting up a center-based program for parents.

B. Identify four ways by which parents can learn how to teach their own children.

C. Describe five things parents can learn and do in centers.

D. Give an example of how center-based training helps a parent to teach her own child.

Section 7 Family Development

unit 20 the family unit

OBJECTIVES

After studying this unit, the student should be able to

- Define and describe the term *family*.
- Discuss five contributions the family makes to the growth and development of the child.
- Identify and describe the four stages of the family life cycle as discussed in this unit.
- Discuss at least two ways in which sibling rivalry may be prevented or lessened.
- Identify five concerns which affect family life.

The *family* is a universal unit in society. It consists of persons who are united by marriage, blood, or adoption ties, and share a common home. These persons live together in a face-to-face association in which there are well-defined roles for family members. They interact with each other according to ways acceptable to their social group.

A person can be a part of at least two basic family units. The one into which he is born or adopted and the one which he helps form by marriage.

A family may lack either the father or the mother — may have only a single parent or a parent substitute. A family may sometimes consist only of siblings.

Since the beginning of time there have been families. The universal role of the family includes

- Childbearing: giving birth to children and carrying on the family line.
- Child rearing: helping the child to grow and develop.
- Child socialization: helping the child to learn about his culture, how to be comfortable in it, and how to make his contributions to it.
- Regulation of the child's behavior.
- Economic support.

SIGNIFICANCE OF THE FAMILY UNIT

For years people thought of a good home as one which provided certain things. The home was said to be a "good" home if it provided food and adequate clothing, a well-kept, clean house, and enough money to let the family live according to the accepted scale of living in the community.

Today this view is only part of the picture. The family is seen as the setting in which the child first meets life. His family is the miniature world in which the child takes his first steps in learning about his world and what is in it. It is where he builds habits and skills and learns to meet his problems.

The family may well be the greatest force in the child's life for, or against, his full growth. The family has a key role as the molder of the child's environment to permit full and rich development. Some contributions of the family are described.

The family produces the child and gives him ties with the past, present, and future. All societies must replace themselves if they are to survive. This need to go on is met almost universally in family groups. When the child is born, he stands as a replacement for his family group. The cultural pattern or way of life shared by his group is transmitted to the child by his family. There is no "beginning" to any generation. Each family group has "oldsters" who pass on what they know to the incoming group. The child grows, matures, and the cycle is ready to begin again.

The family cares for the child and trains him. The human child is helpless for a very long period. His family gives him food, shelter, and clothing. They protect him from dangers he is unable to cope with because of his immaturity and lack of experience in life's ways. In his family group, he learns that living in a world of people makes it necessary to have some rules to go by. There must be rules to insure the rights of all members of the group, to enable group members to live together and get along, and to provide people in the group with a method by which they can relate to each other.

The home is the first place where manners are learned through the examples set by parents and other family members. It is important that parents see that behaving in a socially acceptable way means much in the development of the child's self-concept. When other people accept him, he has a feeling of worth. He gets this by doing what his group expects of him. Good models for imitation can feed the growth process.

The family introduces the child to his society. The child learns about his world of people, objects, and events. He learns what people in his society share. He is linked to his larger society and learns how to get the support he needs from the larger system.

The family provides the child with an intimate group. Human beings have a basic need for love, affection, and a feeling of "belonging." The young child must have these needs met if he is to become a social being. Studies show that this closeness is crucial in the early years of the young child's life. Lack of love and attention can leave an emotional scar which can affect him for the rest of his life.

The family helps to regulate the child's behavior. The child learns how others in his family expect him to behave. He himself comes to feel that their way is both right and good for him. His family may use love-oriented techniques to discipline him: praise, isolation, and the withdrawal of love. This approach tends to make him act in certain ways because he finds that the set behavior is self-rewarding. They may use material-oriented techniques, such as rewards in the form of tokens, candy, or the withdrawal of privileges, or they may use physical punishment. The child gets his "payoff" when he does what is expected of him. Both approaches aim to teach the child how to behave in his group. The family provides a set of rules by which members guide their actions. They give some type of feedback when the child does well or when he does not do so well.

The family establishes a basis for the child's value system. The child learns to value what other family members value. When he sees an older sibling help with a family task, the child gets the idea that helping is a part of family life. Each family member learns to live with people by accepting a share of the work in the home. When work is shared, happy family living is possible. Sharing in the home helps to bring about "togetherness" in the family. It is not always a means of being together physically, but it may mean sharing feelings, love, values, and ambitions.

The family helps the child to develop an understanding of male-female roles. Young children have an interest in what their parents do in the world of work. Parents can do much to break away from old-time views concerning boy-girl activities. A boy who learns about foods and food preparation has a lifelong skill. A boy who learns how to bathe a baby develops a useful skill to tap when he is old enough to baby-sit. The knowledge gained may come to his aid in later years, when he has a child of his own. Young girls need to know from early childhood that there are no limits imposed on them. Opportunities to role play the work of adults help children to understand options open to men and women. The attitude each child develops stems in part from the direction his family takes.

The family helps the child develop his self-concept, self-esteem, and identity. The child is the mirror-image of the people about him. He takes his cues from his parents and other family members. Only as they feel that they count can they help the young child to feel that he counts, too.

THE FAMILY LIFE CYCLE

The family takes form when two people marry and establish their home. There are many tasks to be faced by the husband and wife who are seen as a team. The couple set goals for their future. Goals are linked with values both share: what they have, what they

Fig. 20-2 A boy who learns about foods and food preparation has a lifelong skill.

Fig. 20-1 When he sees his older brother help with a task, the young child gets the idea that "helping" is a family affair.

Fig. 20-3 A boy who watches and talks about how to bathe a baby is learning a useful skill.

want, how they will work together to get it. Responsibilities are identified and decisions made concerning the way in which the goals will be met. Housing, furniture, and home equipment are needed. Schedules may need adjustments when both parties work outside the home. New associations in the community may take form as the couple take on citizenship roles as a family unit. New relationships are established with each other and with in-laws, relatives, friends, neighbors, and other social or business groups. Plans for children in the future may be made.

With the knowledge that a baby is on the way, the family must face new concerns. The woman looks toward her new role as mother — adding this to her existing roles as woman and wife. The man must face his new role as father — adding it to his existing roles as man and husband. The anticipated arrival of a baby brings questions that need to be resolved:

- Is the present house large enough to accommodate a child?
- What changes in finances must be made to meet added expenses?
- What views do the prospective parents share with regard to childrearing?
- What steps (if any) should be taken to protect the family in case of loss of income? Accident and health insurance, social security, bank and credit unions, and the like, may be discussed.
- How can the mother-to-be get necessary prenatal care to insure her own good health and that of her unborn child?
- Where can both parents-to-be learn how to give the child the best care possible from the moment of birth? What do they need to know and understand about child growth and development to be successful parents?

Fig. 20-4 Young girls need to know from early childhood that there are no limits imposed on them. Shown is a "young child's play that becomes a young woman's profession."

Parents resolve their problems in their own way. How they do it is related to the type of home they create. A *child-centered* home gives the child whatever he wants. He is the focus of all decisions from sunrise to sunset. Parents think that they do him a favor when they give him his own way. They may go so far as to sacrifice their own hopes and dreams to shower the child with material things in life. An *adult-oriented* home is one in which the parents "boss" the family and make all decisions for them. A child has little or nothing to say about things that concern him. One or both parents tell him what to do and in what way to do it. A *family-centered* home is like a small community where members share in the decision-making process. Each child is free to voice his opinion and is made to feel that what he thinks is important. His family let him discuss his problems and thus make him feel that he is a worthy person who counts. The child is able to develop a positive view of himself and learns that he need not be afraid of what is new and different.

When a family has more than one child, each newcomer makes it necessary for the family to make room for him. Parents must recognize the growth needs of each child and provide for them. Family income must stretch to reach more persons. The life of the family expands when the child enters school. Increased family activities in the community may bring more expenses.

Like the young robin who learns to fly and leaves the nest, so do young adults leave when their time comes. Parents face new changes in their own way of life. Expenses may start to decrease, unless the departing child needs the financial help parents may be

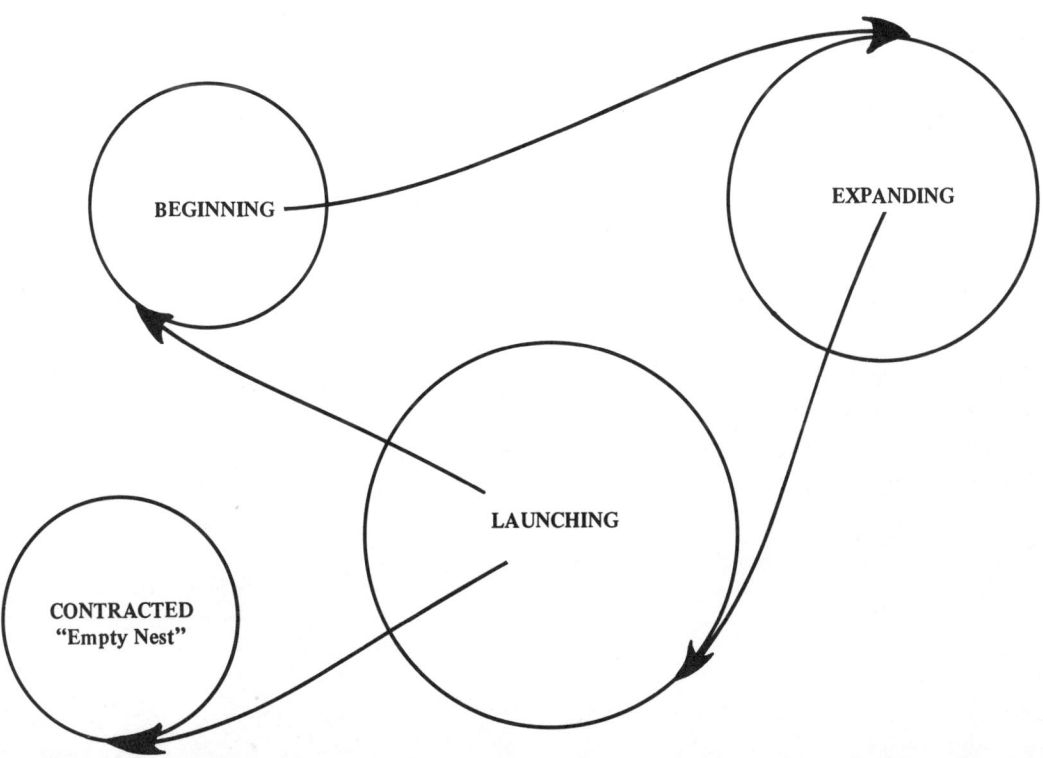

Fig. 20-5 Shown is the family life cycle: beginning, the childless couple; expanding, increase in family size; launching, maximum size at start of stage; contracted, "childless" couple, the "empty nest."

able to give. Housing needs may decrease if married children do not move in with their parents. The family circle widens as young adults marry, have children of their own, and include in-laws as part of the family group. If she has not combined a career as a homemaker with work outside the home, a mother may wish to reenter the work world. New training and new adjustments face her and her husband.

When young adults leave home, the family shrinks and all that remains is an "empty nest." As their offspring face a new life of their own, so can parents find a new world for themselves. They have more time for friends, hobbies, and each other. New interests in church or community affairs may give new ways to find fulfillment in life. Activities with their children and grandchildren may have real meaning and bring them much happiness.

An important task of adult educators is to include in their parent programs all phases of the family life cycle. Young parents need not give up their own lives when they have children to raise. Outside interests can help people to grow and develop as persons as well as parents. Leisure time activities can stand by as a source of productivity when parents face their "empty nest."

Figure 20-5 shows the family life cycle as a continuous process. The family begins and expands; children are launched and on their own; the basic family contracts and the nest is empty. The young adults stand as replacements in their group and the cycle of life and living begins all over again.

SIBLINGS

When a second child is expected, parents must begin early to tell the firstborn he is to have a brother or sister. It can be a good time to take a step forward in the child's sex education. The questions a child asks can be answered at his level of understanding and interest. Simple but honest responses to his questions are the rule.

Preparing for a New Family Member

Letting the young child see infants may spark his desire to know more about babies and what they do and need. He can observe someone taking care of a baby. His attention can be called to the helplessness of the infant. He learns that the new family member may be a playmate sometime, but not at first. Thus he does not build his hopes too high and can accept an infant who must grow before he can "go."

The young child can help his own mother get ready for the new baby. Shopping for things the baby will need can give the young child a new sense of worth. He may be permitted to make some choices: perhaps selecting the color of a blanket or an article of clothing.

Allowing a child to help in finding space and things for the baby tends to improve his self-image. He finds that his parents respect him and what he thinks and likes. He feels that he is a worthy person with good ideas. Praise for his help can add to his sense of well-being.

When children must double-up in a room, there are ways to get help. Figure 20-6 shows

Fig. 20-6 Shown is a way extension agents help to stretch space.

how extension agents helped to stretch space. Drawers can be used for toys, clothes, blankets, and other items.

Avoid Sibling Rivalry

It is unlikely that there is a family with more than one child in which some rivalry does not take place. This need not be if parents take steps to prevent it from happening.

The child who is involved in preparing for the baby may look at the situation in a positive way. The parent's task is to build on that good attitude. From the moment of the second child's birth, parents must avoid making comparisons of any kind between him and his brother or sister. It should be a rule. The rule may be broken at times, but "trying" may keep the score down.

Promoting Cooperation

The home is the first place where social behavior is learned. Through the examples set by parents and other family members, children learn how to get along and to belong.

From the time he is little, each child needs to feel that he is part of the family — to share in work and play. The young child can help set and clear the table and do other easy chores. Tasks are discussed in preceding units.

A young child needs to learn to respect the property and privacy of other family members.

- He needs to know what his limits are in the use of space and things in the home.
- He needs to respect the privacy of his parents and other family members, by knocking when doors are closed.
- He needs to learn to ask before he touches or takes things which do not belong to him.
- He needs to learn to accept the fact that there are times when others have rights to family space. When guests come, a simple statement can help, "We have company, let's take your toys to your room where you can go on playing;" or, "Brother and his friends will be watching the ball game on television tonight. Let's find something that you can do in your room."

Fig. 20-7 Big Brother and all of the "Indians" have fun with their newspaper headdresses.

Fig. 20-8 Siblings learn to cooperate by sharing a common experience. Young children feel they are loved and wanted in the group.

There is no doubt that some conflict will take place between siblings. It is part of growing up and learning how to get along with others. When children have an opportunity to talk over the things that upset them, they can find ways to work them out.

Children need to know what they may do and what is expected of them. Parents must expect of each child only what he is mature enough to give. Each child in the family should grow at his own pace and in his own way.

FORCES WHICH AFFECT THE FAMILY

The world of today is one of rapid and constant change. Forces at work bring on new roles and new ways of life. It is not an easy task for some people to cope with what is happening.

Some resist change because it does not tie in with their own value system. They are satisfied with things as they are. Other people may feel the need for more drastic change along the same lines. Each sees the same thing from a different point of view.

How each family deals with change is an individual matter. It is helpful to identify some of the problem areas and open the door to discussions in parent groups. Parents may find that they themselves can be change agents. Some may wish to make an effort to redirect things that they see as a threat to their family life.

Listed are some concerns that may spark discussion groups:

- Technological changes bring forth raised standards of living which create new problems in the home.
- The increase of women in the outside world of work makes it necessary to resolve new and different family problems.
- More effective methods of population control may limit family size, but take away some of the advantages of having several children in a family.
- The changed status of men and women make it necessary to look at family roles from a new point of view.
- More child caregivers are needed to accommodate families, when both parents work.
- The increased stress on being an individual ("doing your own thing") may affect the way that parents see their parenting tasks.
- Alternate life-styles and one-parent families create new child-rearing problems.
- Things families did for themselves in the past must now be shared with other social agencies.
- Television programs are both a positive and negative source of education for children.
- Agencies outside the home have created a decrease in the power of the family over its members.

SUMMARY

The family is a universal unit in society. The role of the family includes childbearing, child rearing, child socialization, and regulation of the child's behavior and economic support.

The family has a key role as the molder of the child's environment to permit his full and rich development. The family produces the child and gives him ties with the past, present, and future. The family cares for him and trains him. The family teaches the child manners. The family introduces the child to his society. The family provides the child with an intimate group. The family helps to regulate the child's behavior. The family establishes a basis for the child's value system. The family helps the child to develop an understanding of male-female roles. The family helps the child develop his self-concept, self-esteem, and identity.

The family life cycle includes four phases: beginning, expanding, launching, and the contracted phase often called the "empty nest."

Sibling rivalry can be prevented to some degree. To avoid problems, parents should never compare their children. Cooperation is important in teaching children how to get along and to belong in the family.

The world of today is one of rapid and constant change. Forces at work bring about new roles and new ways of life. An opportunity to discuss common concerns may help parents learn how to deal with change.

SUGGESTED ACTIVITIES

- Arrange to have several visitors come to your class (at different times) to talk on topics related to family life. Let them know that you are interested in knowing more about the effect of family life on the young child.

  a. Check your resource file to locate agencies that can share one of their members for an hour or so.

  b. Make your contacts, following some of the suggestions made in other units. Be sure to say that you are unable to pay a fee for their time. Listed are some people you may be able to get and examples of what they may be able to discuss.

  Social worker

  >How families can get aid
  >Kinds of problems social workers deal with
  >Examples of how people are helped
  >Approaches to drugs and alcoholism
  >Child abuse and neglect
  >Problems of poverty-level parents
  >Problems of affluent parents

  Public health nurse

  >How families can get aid and in what way
  >Importance of family health care
  >Problem areas in the care of children
  >Diseases of young children
  >Immunizations: what, when, and why

  Public safety worker

  >How families can get help
  >Importance of home safety inspection
  >How to make a safety checklist
  >What to do in case of safety violations
  >Rodent control in the home
  >Making home a safe place for the young child

Marriage counselor or minister
- How families can get help
- Husband-wife inputs to a happy marriage
- Financial problems and marriage failure
- Importance of good communication in families
- Young children and marriage failure

Recreation worker
- How families can take part
- Recreation as a family bond
- Physical activities and good health
- Body-building activities for home use
- Recreation in the community

Home visitor
- How families can take part
- Home learning activities
- Teaching the young child at home
- Helping parents to help their child

- Ask foreign visitors or people who have visited other countries to talk about their experiences and observations of family life.

- Ask some senior citizen to visit your class to talk about family life in the "good old days."

    a. If they cannot come to your class, ask if you may tape record an interview to share with your class.

    b. Try to find out if they think that the "old days" were really "good."

    c. Compare what they say with what takes place in families today.

- Make a bulletin board display of the past, present, and future life in families. For the "future," try to imagine what family life will be like. Be as creative as you can. (Who knows? You may guess right!)

REVIEW

A. Define and describe the term "family."

B. Discuss at least five ways in which the family helps the young child to grow and develop.

C. Identify and describe the four stages of the family life cycle as described in this unit.

D. For each stage of the family life cycle, make a list of tasks parents must meet. Use textbook material, other books, talk with parents, observe families.

E. Explain the meaning of sibling rivalry and give an example. State what you think can be done to resolve a similar problem.

unit 21 the play way to family development

OBJECTIVES

After studying this unit, the student should be able to

- Describe five ways by which the play way can promote family learning and provide recreation.
- List at least four things a parent can do to get ready for the play way to family development.
- Describe an activity to promote each of the following: nature study, community understanding, need for physical exercise, and the pleasure to be gained by living and learning in a family.

It is the aim of every home-based program to help each child grow physically, intellectually, socially, and emotionally. The desired outcome is a happy, healthy person who lives a rich and full life in his world. The play way can help reach this goal.

FOLLOWING THE PLAY WAY

The *play way* to family development is described as the use of interesting mental, physical, and social activities to promote learning and provide recreation. It is the means through which the family

- Helps each member learn about people and how to get along with them.
- Gives each member a sense of security and achievement in his daily living.
- Accepts each member as a worthy person and helps him to discover and develop his own talents.
- Recognizes that people learn more easily from real life situations which they can understand.
- Provides opportunities for members to learn and be familiar with their background of cultural and national heritage.
- Builds attitudes, skills, and appreciations seen as necessary for living in a democratic society.
- Emphasizes the need for personal responsibility to the community, state, nation, and world.
- Promotes an understanding of the need to use wisely and conserve both human and natural resources in the environment.

To use the play way to family development, planning is necessary. Planning helps to move each child toward constructive learning experiences and away from what interferes with learning. Planning for the play way can be compared to turning on a light switch in a dark room. The things are already there; the light makes it possible to see them.

The world is full of rich opportunities for learning. Much of what can be used is right in the home and community. Sometimes it is necessary to "turn on the light switch" to explore with parents what can be seen and done.

A DIALOGUE WITH PARENTS

Following is a face-to-face dialogue with parents. No effort is made to describe the parents: their personalities, their education, or their experience in life's ways.

What is drawn for use in the at-home situation must be done in the light of local needs. Each parent must be viewed as an "adult learner" who brings to the situation a different set of attitudes and experiences. This must help decide how to approach a parent and what to say.

It is important that parents are part of the planning process. Change agents must remember that in a dialogue two voices are heard.

Talking Things Over with Parents

In the business world there is a time-honored belief that the best combination for success consists of two partners. One brings in the business, and the other handles the goods.

Your must link with your community to become a real partner in the education of your child. Take him out in his world. Assume a leadership role in making that world his laboratory for learning and joyful living.

The first task is to take inventory in your community. Ask yourself these questions: What is out there that can help my child learn about his world? Is there a museum, art gallery, zoo, toy-lending library, picnic area, planetarium, recreation center, or some other place to go?

Find out how you can make use of what is offered. Each community runs things in its own way. Ask your home visitor to help you make a list of places you can visit and keep within your family budget. If a person cannot afford an admission charge, there are ways to get around this.

Making the Selection

The second task is to choose something from your list. Get help in selecting trips and activities that meet the interests and maturity level of your child. The best way to hold a child's interest is to find things that he cares about. Your child may give you some clues to go by.

For example, imagine that your child comes home one day and says, "Johnny Jones went to the zoo with his mother." Your child may really be trying to give you another message. He may be saying, "Johnny Jones went to the zoo with his mother. I'd like to go to the zoo, too."

Seize the ball and run — don't walk! Ask him right away, "Would you like to go to the zoo, too?" The chances are good that he says "yes." Go with him and have a good time, too. If by any chance he says "no," wait awhile and try again; he may change his mind.

Maybe you can invite Johnny over for milk and cookies. While he is with you, say that you are pleased that he went to the zoo. Then let him tell you about it. If your child is like others in his group, Johnny's story can make him ripe and ready for a trip to the zoo.

Ask your home visitor to help you find experiences that are suitable for your child. Perhaps she can help you build a family file of things to see and do.

Getting Ready for Action

The third task is to get all information that you can before you carry out your plan. If you are taking a study trip, see if you can learn about things that are there. Perhaps your home visitor has pamphlets which can help you with this task.

If you are unable to get information before the trip, do not worry about it. You and your child can learn together. If he asks you a question which you cannot answer, tell him the truth. Say, "I don't know; let's find out." Never try to bluff your way out. When he learns the truth, he may feel that you tried to put one over on him. Next time, he may not believe what you say — no matter what it is. He may not even bother to ask you in the first place.

If your plan is to teach your child how to do or make something, try it yourself first. Make sure that you can do what you want him to do.

The Action

The fourth task is to carry out your plans. Do and say things that make your child feel that your are glad to be with him. Let him see that you are enjoying yourself, too.

Give him a chance to talk about his experience. Let him tell you how he feels about it. Listen to what he says. Treat him with respect. Let him know that he is a person who has ideas that count. Let him know that he counts, too.

If your activity is a study trip, give him time to talk about what he sees. He may need time to put his thoughts into words. Respond with words that make him feel good.

You might say, "That's a very good idea. I'm glad you told me about it." Or, "I'm glad you saw that. It is very interesting. I might have missed it, if you had not told me about it. Thanks a lot."

If your activity is to make or do something, praise him often. Then praise him again. Remember to expect him to do, accept what he does, and respect him and his performance.

THINGS TO DO, SEE, AND MAKE

There are many things that families can do together. All family activities can become valuable learning experiences.

Family Hike

One of the most exciting things a family can do together is to take a hike. Not only is it fun, but it is body building as well. A wagon or stroller can be taken for wee ones who may tire easily.

In the spring and summer, the family can look for birds, flowers, and animals. Each person can have a score card. The first person who sees a bird gets one point. If someone sees a bird of another color, he gets a point.

The game goes on, and each person who names something new gets a point. Something is "new" if it is something not yet seen. It is also "new" if it is a different color from something already seen.

Kite Contest

Children or parents can make kites for themselves and those too young to do so. Some kites are simple enough for preschoolers to make with help.

The kite contest can take place in an open field or playground. Caution the family to keep away from overhead wires. Call attention to the direction of the wind. Let children see how the wind helps the kite to go up.

The objective of the contest is to see how long the kite can be kept in the air. Even young children can be successful in this contest.

Balloon Experiment

On a windy day, everyone can have fun with balloons. While young children play with their balloons, older children may fill several balloons with *helium,* a very light non-inflammable gas used to inflate balloons. Attach to each balloon a self-addressed, stamped card with a note along these lines:

"Please fill in the blanks and mail the card. Thank you. Place where the balloon was found _____ (city or town). Day the balloon was found _____. Time it was found _____."

Older children can find out how far the balloons were able to go. They are sparked with the fun side of science. They may wish to go on to learn about wind, weather, and a host of other topics.

Young children in the family watch what goes on. They get the idea that finding out about things is a worthwhile activity.

Family Nature Study

Nature study helps a child to understand things in his world. It can spark his desire to learn more about what he sees and hears. Listed are some ways for family members to learn about the world of nature:

- Find out what grows in the yard. Learn the name of each plant.
- Make a collection of scenic postal cards, shells, pressed flowers, leaves, wood samples, tree bark, kinds of soil, grasses, ferns, feathers, seeds and similar items.
- Keep a flower garden outdoors or in a dishpan indoors.
- Keep a vegetable garden outdoors. Teach young family members to identify each vegetable and give its name.
- Make a terrarium. Let the family go into the woods to find plants for it.
- Make an aquarium. Let young children choose what to put in it.
- Attract birds by means of a bird bath. Learn the names of birds that come. Listen to bird calls. Try to imitate them. Have young children draw pictures of what they see.
- Collect acorns. Make acorn animals. For example, pipe cleaners may be attached to make an insect.
- Make an animal scrapbook for young family members. Let the children help collect pictures for it. Write stories that they dictate for the book.
- Go hunting with a camera. Take pictures of things that are of interest to the family.
- Study water life. Find moss, algae, water plants, turtles, frogs, beetles. Let young children go along. Caution them about safety rules when near water.
- Go fishing. Learn names of fish in the ocean, stream, or lake near home. Again — safety rules for small fry.
- Keep a pet of some sort for the children to take care of. Make a chore chart so that the work is shared by all.
- Study animal tracks. Scouts in the family can make impressions with plaster of Paris.
- Make an impression of a young child's foot. Let him paint his "foot" with water colors. He can keep it in his room, or give it as a gift to someone who can use it as a paper weight.
- Learn to recognize some of the dangerous plants. Make sure that family members know how to recognize plants like poison ivy. Tell them why they must keep away from poisonous plants.
- Put a thermometer on an outdoor window frame. Make and keep a temperature chart. Help family members to make use of the chart. They can learn how to dress according to the temperature.
- Look at cloud shapes. Try to see "pictures" in the clouds. Let children learn about different clouds. Even a young child can learn about rain clouds.
- Model out of clay dough things seen on nature walks.
- Visit a museum, zoo, sea aquarium, planetarium, farm, or public garden.

Swim Contest

The objective of this contest is to make sure that each family member can swim. Each learns to swim where Red Cross lifesavers are on guard. A *Red Cross lifesaver* is a person who takes and passes a special test to qualify for water-safety work.

Young children can learn to swim, and older ones who know how can go on to higher level tasks. Water-safety instruction or diving lessons may have appeal to older children in the family. Parents may wish to take lifesaving as a skill to tap if it is ever needed.

Teach children two safety rules: Never swim alone. Never swim unless a lifeguard is on duty.

State Fair

Many communities have fairs and carnivals which can be fun for the family. Members may wish to exhibit something at the fair.

One or more trips to the state fair can be worthwhile for all. Firsthand views of livestock, plants, craft work, and exhibits — plus the excitement of people hurrying to and fro — can be a peak experience. Some of the excitement may linger years after the event is over and become the fond memories of childhood.

Neighborhood Cheering Squad

If family members or other children in the neighborhood play in ball games, take the family to see a game. Get a group together to cheer for the "home team." This helps to build a spirit of togetherness.

When a big league game is shown on television, let older children invite friends in for coke and popcorn while the game is on. Young children can have other types of activities — to go with their coke and popcorn. The family learns that home is a place for friends and family. They find it is a nice place to be.

Social Services

These are things families can do together to help others:

- Make paper-folded birds to decorate a Christmas tree. (See unit 12 for directions.) Workers in a rest home for the elderly, a hospital, church, or public place may welcome the help.
- Raise plants in tin cans. Cover them with gay paper. Give them to friends and neighbors on holidays, birthdays, or other special times. A plant is a nice greeting for a new neighbor.

Fig. 21-1 A family making paper chains for a Christmas tree.

Fig. 21-2 Some children in a family sent valentines to their neighbors. This is how they gave a clue to their identity.

- Make a joke book for a veterans' hospital.
- Make a scrapbook of animal pictures for a nursery school.
- Help a community group fix toys to give to needy children at Christmas time.
- Make a valentine for all the neighbors on the block. Hang them on doorknobs. Give them a clue to your identity. Figure 21-2 shows how one family "signed" their valentines.
- Make puppets and give a show for family, friends, or neighbors. Invite mothers, fathers, and children.
- Ask the Junior Red Cross or American Field Service to help find a "pen pal family" from another country. Have your family members learn about the customs of the pen pal family. Exchange friendly letters. Tell them about things that your family does.
- Have your family help with a community cleanup job or scrap-saving task. Make it a project for the whole family; do not leave out the little ones.
- If your family has things from another country, share them with other people. Take your children to see things that other families share.

Stories and Books

Parents can set a special time for stories each day — a time to read to young children and show them the pictures. Storytime can be more than a listening experience. It is a time for children to be with those they care about.

Sometimes there are people in a community who have a special way to tell stories. Perhaps one lives in your community and is willing to share this ability.

A play library can be made in the basement or attic. Boxes are nailed together to make a frame. Wrapping paper is used as walls. Newspaper can serve as well.

A cub scout den mother may have cubs working on storytelling awards. Invite them to visit, so the children can tell their stories and earn their award.

Parents should find out when the local library has its storytelling time. They should take the children as often as possible.

Fig. 21-3 Shown is a child sharing things she collected when her family lived in Japan.

Fig. 21-4 Storytime is more than a listening experience. It is a time for children to be with those they care about.

Family Picnic

Families should have a picnic even if it must be in the backyard. The children can plan the menu. If a park is nearby, perhaps hot dogs or hamburgers can be cooked on a grill provided in the park. If not, pack a lunch and set off for a good time.

There are many homemade games to play. Children have fun and learn creative ways to make up new games. The following games are taken from a family file of games which the children liked. Some of the games are their own ideas.

Keep Your Beans Dry: Fill a large tub of water. Float a small pie pan on the water. Give players ten beans each. One at a time, the beans are tossed. Each player tries to place his beans in the pie pan. Score is kept as appropriate for the age group.

Muffin Tin Toss: Place a muffin tin on the table. Give each player ten bottle caps. Child tries to throw his bottle caps into the muffin tin. Score is kept as appropriate for the age group.

High Skydive: Place an empty vegetable can on the ground. Give each child ten toothpicks (or used match sticks). He drops each, one-at-a-time, and tries to "high skydive" right into the can. Score is kept as appropriate for the age group.

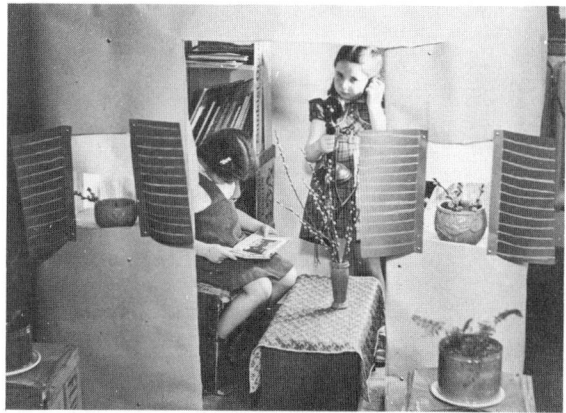

Fig. 21-6 These young children made their own play library.

Fig. 21-5 Shown is a volunteer worker telling a story with a Japanese storytelling kit.

Fig. 21-7 "Keep Your Beans Dry" is a good picnic game for all family members.

Section 7 Family Development

Box the Card: Place three cardboard boxes on the ground. Child gets an old deck of cards. He tries to toss each card into one of the boxes. Score is one point for each card that lands in a box. The person with the highest score is the winner.

Clothespin Bowling: On a picnic table, set up snap clothespins like tenpins in a bowling alley. A marble, golf ball, or tennis ball is the "bowling" ball. The older the child, the smaller the ball should be. The game can be played like bowling. Young children, especially those who hear about bowling activities in their home, find the game a "grown-up" thing to do.

Airport: Make paper-folded airplanes. Help the young family members, or make their planes for them. Place a large cardboard box on the ground. Children stand around the box. Each player flies his plane and tries to land it on the box. Keep score as desired.

Airplane Race: Children fly their paper-folded planes in a field. The person whose plane goes the farthest is the winner. All family members can play this one.

Tie Me Quickly: One or more players can take part. The task is for a player to unwind a ball of twine around himself (he is timed). When several people are playing, the ball of twine is passed around the group, and each person says, "Tie me quickly." The game is ended when there is no more twine to unwind. The winner is the person or persons who finish the task first.

Wash Day: String a clothesline between two trees. Tie a handkerchief in the middle to divide the line into two sides. Each of the players gets ten clothespins. The winner is the first person who pins all of his pins on his side of the line. The game can be played as a relay. This game can be played indoors by using two chairs for the clothesline.

Fun in the Family Car

People who travel have an opportunity to let family members make up games to play in the car. Here are some games which can be played right around town when the family is going someplace.

Red Car Mine: Each child selects a color. He gets one point every time a car of his color goes by. He calls out, "Red (or his color) car mine." Prepare file cards before the trip starts. Give one to each child. He can make his own tally marks to keep his score. For safety reasons, use crayons instead of pencils for scores.

Gas Stations: Each child selects a gas station. When a gas station appears on his side of the car, the player gets a point. The person with the highest score wins the game.

License Numbers: Each child selects a number. When he sees his number on a license plate, he gets one point. This is a good number game for preschoolers.

License Colors: Players select a color other than that of their own state. A point is scored each time that color is seen on a

Fig. 21-8 A preschooler follows the twine around the group in "Tie-Me-Quickly." He is cheering for his sister's team.

Unit 21 The Play Way to Family Development

license plate. Older children may play this game as a game of "states."

Daisy, Goldenrod, Clover: Players select flowers which are apt to be seen along the way. Every time the flower is seen, the respective player gets a point. This can be done with trees, too.

Puppets: Make paper bag puppets before the trip starts. The children make up plays as they drive along.

Music Makers: The children are encouraged to sing songs that they know. Rounds are lots of fun. Each person starts a new line until everyone is singing a different part of the song. Twinkle, Twinkle, Little Star and Are You Sleeping, Brother John? are songs young family members may know. If not, they can learn.

Pay for the Gas: When the family stops for gas, young children may watch the numbers on the tank. When it is time to pay, one of the children is helped to make the payment. His attention is called to the coins or bills used. Older children can do their own figuring to check the "accuracy" of the register.

Holiday Specials

Do something special to observe holidays. One need not be of Irish origin to enjoy the fun of St. Patrick's Day. An Irish stew and a lime salad may add a festive touch to the day. Hamburger stew is a good substitute for Irish stew, figure 21-10.

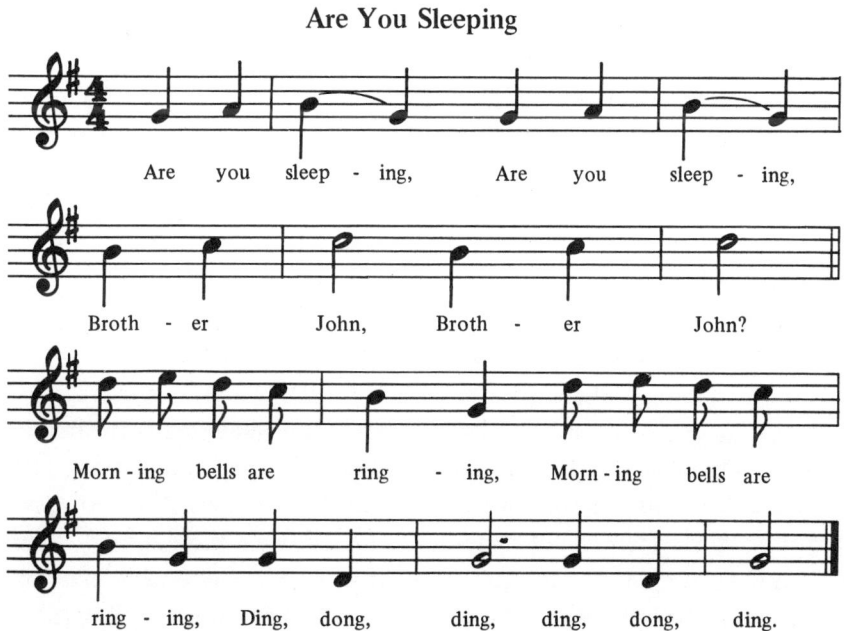

Fig. 21-9 Young children are delighted when the family sings a song they know.

> **HAMBURGER STEW**
>
> 3 medium potatoes, pared and diced
> 2 medium carrots, diced
> 1 1/2 pounds ground beef
> 2 small onions chopped
> 2 cups milk
> 2 teaspoons salt
> 1/2 teaspoon Accent (monosodium glutamate)
> 1/2 teaspoon pepper
> 1 tomato cut in small pieces
>
> Combine ingredients and bake in a covered 3 quart casserole at 325° Fahrenheit about 1 1/2 hours. Remove cover during the last half hour of cooking. Makes 4-5 servings. *Note:* This is an easy recipe for a young child to prepare. Parent or older child in family can clean and cut vegetables. The young child can take it from there.

Fig. 21-10 Young children like to do things that grownups do in the family. Hamburger strew is a meal-in-one which a small child can prepare. It is a good substitute for Irish Stew on St. Patrick's Day.

On Halloween the family can have their pumpkin and eat it too. Pulp taken from parts cut to make the features can be cooked and eaten. Pumpkin seeds can be prepared for eating by washing them thoroughly and placing them in a thin layer in a shallow pan. No seasoning is added. The pan is put in a 350° oven for fifteen to twenty minutes. The seeds are stirred frequently. If desired, seasoning (salt and butter or parmesan cheese) may be added before serving. The seeds are served hot.

Young children enjoy Easter fun activities. Eggs can be colored as a family task. Easter baskets can be made from small paper bags. Figure 21-11 shows an easter rabbit basket which can be made by a very young family member.

The children can make valentines to decorate the home on St. Valentine's Day. It is easy to learn to cut a paper heart with a pair of scissors. Figure 21-12 shows how to fold the paper and where to cut.

The list of things to do on holidays can be one that the family makes. Newspapers, magazines, library books, and homemaking-type television shows are a good source of ideas. Part of the learning experience is that of finding out what can be done. The important point to remember is that what takes place must be the play way, an enjoyable experience for all.

SUMMARY

The play way to family development means using interesting mental, physical, and social activities to promote learning and provide recreation. Planning with families is an important part of the process.

Parents must link with the community to be a real partner in the education of their children. The community is a laboratory for learning.

Parents should explore all ways through which children can learn. It is important that parents enjoy what is done, too.

Unit 21 *The Play Way to Family Development*

Cut

Front

Rear

Cotton Tail

Directions: Keep bag closed. Draw outline as shown. Cut on dotted lines. Staple the rabbit's ears as shown. Turn him around. Put a wad of cotton for his tail.

Fig. 21-11 Easter baskets can be made from small paper bags.

Fig. 21-12 A heart is easy to make. Fold a piece of paper. Cut on the dotted lines.

Section 7 Family Development

SUGGESTED ACTIVITIES

- Find a family with whom you can try some of the activities described in this unit.

    a. Have parents select what they would like to try with their children.

    b. Involve the children in making the plans, if possible.

    c. Let your class know how the activities turned out. Compare notes with classmates to see which things were most popular.

- Make a calendar of activities to do each month of the year.

    a. Interview parents you know to find out what their children enjoy. Add these inputs to your calendar.

    b. Check with teachers to learn more about the interests of young children. Add to your list any new activities the teachers may suggest.

    c. Go to the library and get some books about parties. Add to your list ideas gained from the texts. (Be sure to credit the sources.)

- See if your instructor can make arrangements for you to have a game party in your class. Plan to use some of the games described in this unit. Try to make up some games of your own. Invite a family to join you.

- Try some of the nature study ideas yourself. Go with a classmate. Make a list of things that you think a child would do or say if he were with you. Report your activities to your class. Let them decide if you have described things a child might really do and say.

REVIEW

A. Describe briefly five ways by which the play way can promote family learning and provide recreation.

B. List four things a parent can do to get ready for the play way to family development.

C. Select from text material an activity to promote each of the following: nature study, social work, exercise, and family-sharing.

Section 8 Record-Keeping and Evaluation

unit 22 developing a record system

OBJECTIVES

After studying this unit, the student should be able to

- Explain the importance of records in a home-based early childhood program.
- List five questions which must be asked and answered by program planners.
- Identify and describe records which may be needed for the following: administrative records, family records, target-child records, and home visitor records.
- Tell how a parent can begin a growth and progress file which can be kept up by the child as he grows older.

Obtaining information and keeping records is a major task for the home visitor and other staff members. Good records hold a crucial place in all educational programs. In home-based programs they provide

- The information needed to know children and their families and to base plans upon their needs.
- A point of departure in comparing a person's first performance with what he does as he moves forward in the program.
- A means for studying each program and using data to see how the program meets set objectives.
- Data to help improve the program by showing what does and does not work well under certain conditions.
- Sound, reliable facts that justify a continuation of the program.
- Information for other persons who may wish to start a similar program.

IMPORTANT QUESTIONS ABOUT RECORDS

1. Why are records important to the program?
2. What information is needed?
3. How can worthwhile records be developed for the program?
4. How can administrators be sure that the staff uses records wisely and well?
5. What security measures are to be set to safeguard confidential information?

Fig. 22-1 Program planners are faced with several questions that must be asked and answered.

PLANNING FOR RECORD KEEPING

The planning of a record system should involve as many persons within the program as have any reason to make use of the data. This means that all members of the staff have an opportunity to speak and plan. A good guide to follow is that many minds have many ideas. Ideas are the seeds of progress.

From the very beginning, accurate up-to-date records must be kept for the home-based program. Planners are faced with several problems to be resolved. They must understand why records are important in the program. The purpose for which the records are kept helps to determine what kind of record keeping is necessary. Planners must determine what information is needed; only when there is a real purpose should information be gathered. Worthwhile records must be developed for the program. They must be usable and in a form that has meaning for those who are to use them.

Administrators must be sure that the staff uses records wisely and well. Those who obtain information need training to do the job. Those who interpret the information must be qualified to do so. Those who use the information need guidance with their tasks. Security measures must be set to safeguard confidential information. Information must be kept confidential, yet made available for use. The local staff must have knowledge and skills that qualify them to plan for the best use of their product.

SUGGESTED PROCEDURES FOR DEVELOPING RECORDS

Following the "many minds have many ideas" approach, the staff does *vertical planning*. This means that all staff persons (both up and down the line) carry out some of the following tasks:

- A survey of existing forms is made. These may be national, state, or local forms used in similar programs.
- The staff examines forms. A discussion takes place. Local needs are identified.
- A written summary is made of staff suggestions. Discussion follows. Changes or additions are made.
- The staff decides what should be put in their records and why.

- Trial forms are prepared, taking into consideration space, instructions for recording data, and ease in doing it.
- Storage space is found, considering size of folders, space needed, and content of the record (confidential or not).
- Improvements are made as new needs come to light when records are used.

ESSENTIAL RECORDS

No attempt is made in this unit to specify what records are to be kept. Since a record system is planned ideally to meet the needs of the users, a listing does not serve as the goal for all programs.

The best use of such a listing takes place when planners use it as a checklist. If a record is needed, it can be adapted to local situations. Items to be included on the record are selected when they can be used well by the staff.

Administrative Records

Every program needs a clear line of authority that states what tasks go with which jobs. It must be clear who is to make administrative decisions and record the information which must be filed. Included are policy, budget, staff hiring, summary reports, and other items.

With each task comes the need to get the information, record it, and use it as necessary. Examples of such records follow:

- Personnel: application, interview, employment record.
- Budget: staff salaries and program funds.
- Inventories: facilities (when appropriate), equipment, and supplies.
- Reports to appropriate persons: summary statements, program progress,

evaluation, funds and their use, sponsor-required information, personnel evaluations.

- Insurance protection: forms for requesting adjustments when private cars are used for business purposes (example: home visitor's insurance rates may go up), possible suits against the program because of home visitor's line-of-duty activities and Workmen's Compensation insurance.

Family Records

Since home-based education is concerned with all family members, data is needed about them. A basic record is prepared for each family served. The file must be brought up to date regularly.

Basic information obtained for family records includes much of the following:

- Registration forms:

    Interview and screening

    Date of entry into program

    Termination with reason (if family is dropped or leaves).

- Family information:

    Father's name, occupation, education, health

    Mother's name, home or job status, education, health

    Children in the family: sex, name, birth dates

    Ethnic identity (for program planning purposes)

    Language(s) spoken in the home (dominant one)

    Religion (if needed for specific purpose)

    Family strengths

    Family problems

    Other persons living with family: name, sex, age

- Parent participation:

    How they are involved in program

    Services provided family members

    Skills parents can share with staff and other families

Target Child Records

The *cumulative record* is the most widely used means of recording the individual growth and development of a child. Data which reflect the positive direction of the child's growth are kept.

While note may be made of negative behavior, it is important that the record show it as part of a pattern and not an accident. Behavior that takes place only once or twice may be misleading if it is placed in a cumulative file.

- Physical condition and maturity (health card):

    Height and weight

    Inoculation and immunizations

    History of childhood diseases

    Vision and hearing tests (with follow-up record)

    Dental and medical checkups (date of last check)

    Physical disabilities, if any

    Strengths in the child's development

    Problem areas or physical needs which can be seen

    Any other information which might affect the child's ability to learn

- Intellectual growth:

    Inventory of child's concepts of people, objects, and events in his world.

    Attention span and willingness to follow directions

    Level of language development; ability to give and get messages.

    Visual-motor ability

Section 8 Record Keeping and Evaluation

```
                    CHECKLIST OF LARGE MOTOR SKILLS
    Child's name _____ Date _____

    Directions: Place a plus sign (+) if the child can do it. Place a minus sign (-) if he cannot
    do it.

    1. Locomotor Movements

        ____ Runs forward.                  ____ Slides
        ____ Runs backward.                 ____ Rides tricycle
        ____ Hops on one foot.              ____ Walks on stairs with alternating feet
        ____ Hops (jumps) on both feet.     ____ Climbs up and down (jungle gym).
        ____ Skips with one foot.           ____ Gallops
        ____ Skips with both feet.

    2. Nonlocomotor Movements

        ____ Bends down.                    ____ Pushes and pulls.
        ____ Stretches upward.              ____ Twists and turns body.

    3. Manipulative Skills

        ____ Throws ball.                   ____ Catches ball.
        ____ Rolls ball.                    ____ Bounces ball.
```

Fig. 22-2 A checklist is helpful in testing the child's large motor skills.

Development of abilities concerned with identification of objects, seriating, sequencing, classification, memory, and spatial relationships

Formal and informal tests the child may take; name, score, interpretation, use of results, follow up

- Social-emotional development

Evidence of child's ability to cope with his world

Evidence of willingness to cooperate and relate to other people.

Evidence of attitude toward rules and set limits

Identification of behaviors that show acceptance by his peer group (as seen in anecdotal records)

Anecdotal records (descriptions of observed behaviors)

Emotional behavior and relationships with others

Display of attitudes or special interests

Language development

Behavior at work and play

Home Visitor Records

Record keeping by the home visitor may vary much from one program to another. Certain records and reports can be found in general use. Some of these follow, but no effort is made to list them in any particular sequence.

- Registration of family: home visit screening form.

- Child interview sheet: checklist of behaviors to assess the child's intellectual skills, language development, socioemotional growth, and physical well-being.

- Observation report: description of child's behavior during screening interview.

- Home visitor report:

    Objectives and activities.

```
                                    Interviewer  _____
                                    Date         _____

                              SCREENERS OBSERVATION

Observation of Child      _____
_____
_____

Child's Behavior at Interview    _____
_____
_____

Parents comments regarding child   _____
_____
_____

Parents attitude toward child     _____
_____
_____

Stimulus in Home     _____
_____
_____

Other observed or discussed problems   _____
_____
_____

ie. discipline: _____
Marital Status:   Mother & Father ____   Mother only ____   Father only ____   Divorced ____
                                                                               Separated ____
                                                                               Widowed ____

Housing information:   Live in house ____      Apt ____    Housing Development ____
                       Mobile Home ____        Other _____
Neighborhood information:   Crowded ____    Playgrounds ____    Sparsely populated ____
                            Other _____
```

Fig. 22-3 The screener's observation is a part of the child's cumulative record.

Materials needed.
Follow up of last visit.
Progress made.
New problems identified and referrals.
Evaluation of visit.
Plans for next visit.

- Time and expense report:

Extra time put in at night or on weekends.
Parking fees and highway tolls.
Mileage expense claim, direct gas purchases.

- Agency referral forms: referring families to local services needed and available.

Section 1 Family and Personal Medical History
          Family History
          Personal Medical History
Section 2 Schools Attended
          Nursery-Kindergarten
          Public or Private Schools
Section 3 Mathematics
Section 4 Language Development
          Listening
          Speaking
          Reading
          Writing
Section 5 Social Studies
          Early Childhood Experiences
          School Experiences
Section 6 Science
Section 7 Creative Expression
          Fine Arts
          Arts and Crafts
          Other: music, dance, physical expression
Section 8 Tests
          Readiness (standard or homemade)
          School-Type (standard and teacher-made)

Fig. 22-4 Sections included in Growth and Progress File.

- Family services record: help given to members and in what way, follow-up of services and outcome.
- Diary of work tasks.
- Anecdotal records kept of child.
- Home visitor's self-evaluation report: evidence of growth as a helper of others and as a self-directed learner.

A Team Approach

When the first visit is made, or when an interview takes place, home visitors often work as a team. Both observe and make mental note of what takes place. With the exception of names, birth dates, and the like, nothing is written until after the team leaves the home. Sometimes people feel uncomfortable when someone is writing down what they say.

Working as a team helps the home visitors to get what they need from the interview without creating this problem.

Home visitor reports should be completed as soon after a visit as possible. When reports are put off, information tends to become less clear. A daily diary or cassette tape recording of informal activities can be helpful in meeting the need for a quick report.

Information gained is fed to the staff for preview. Social workers, health coordinators, and speech specialist gain insight into the kinds of services that may be needed.

Follow-up checks pinpoint problems. The home visitor keeps in touch to insure the continuation of what is needed.

RECORD KEEPING BY PARENTS

If parents are to be effective teachers of their own children, they need to know how to keep track of each child's progress. This includes growth in all areas of the child's development.

The *Growth and Progress File* (G & P File for short) can be adapted to meet the goal for record keeping.[1] A G & P File is a bound cumulative record which parents themselves keep. It includes several sections as shown in figure 22-4.

Getting Started

The G & P File for home use can be a homemade loose-leaf notebook. Materials needed include: two large notebook rings, cardboard cut to size for two covers, subject matter dividers, and paper.

The title of each section is written on dividers. Entries can be made as described in this unit. Parents may find other ways that suit them better. The author of the *G & P File* gives this advice to parents.

[1] Elinor T. Massoglia, *Growth and Progress File,* (Washington, D.C.: American Service Publishing Company, 1956).

FAMILY HISTORY

Name	Relationship	Illness (or) Abilities

Fig. 22-5 A family medical history is an important part of the child's G and P File.

"You begin your recording with the birth of your child. Even the fact that he was premature may give the kindergarten teacher further insight into the social development of a child in contrast to that of his classmates."

"Premature birth may enable a child to enter school a whole year before full term would have permitted. This immaturity may need careful guidance during the first three years. He is not as old as his contemporaries and, therefore, should not be pressed to 'keep up' with them if he seems unready."[2]

Making Entries

The first section is concerned with family and personal medical history. Family history may include both positive and negative traits seen in the family line:

- Allergies and organic defects in either parent or other family member.
- Diseases found in the family line: diabetes, heart trouble, sickle-cell anemia, and the like.
- Life span of grandparents and others.
- Outstanding traits or abilities: intellectual, physical, and creative.

Personal medical history begins with the child's birth. Figure 22-6 shows a birth entry. If this child has signs of learning problems as he grows, two facts may be of interest to those who want to help him: (1) he was premature, and (2) his head was grasped with forceps during delivery. Premature birth may suggest that he is a bit behind when compared with his peer group. Forceps may suggest an injury during birth. Only persons qualified can get further information and interpret the full data. The parent's entry shows one source of data that may be important.

Another entry shows the kind of information which may be kept. Shot records may be kept on a health card designed for that purpose.

[2] Elinor T. Massoglia, "You Can Help Your Child Get Better Grades in School," *U.S. Lady Magazine* (Sept.-Oct. 1956):55.

Section 8 Record Keeping and Evaluation

PERSONAL MEDICAL HISTORY

Date	Age	Subject	Details
1/30/75		Birth	Difficult birth. Almost two mos. premature. Forceps used in delivery. Child weighed 3 lbs. 10 oz. Remained in hospital for 5 weeks.
9/15/75	9 mo.	Strep throat	Difficulty in breathing. High temperature. Showed signs of being sensitive to penicillin. Was able to tolerate it. Doctor says to mention this the next time baby is sick.

Fig. 22-6 The child's personal medical history contains information which can have meaning in his future.

When the home visitor finds that the child has developed a certain skill, she can help the parent place the facts in the G & P File book. Information can be put under subheadings such as: date, age at the time, area (math, science, etc.) and achievement.

Samples of the child's work (drawing, writing numbers, worksheets) can be kept in a pocket folder. Each work should bear the date and age of the child at the time. He can learn to compare new entries with old ones and chart his own progress.

Not only does the G & P File provide information to others, it gives the child a chance to look at himself. He can see how he is improving and showing signs of growth. Even a very young child can tell when a drawing shows signs of growth.

When the child is older, he may be pleased with his file. He may feel that his parents really care about him and what he does. He may smile at some of his "baby" things, but he will know how much his family tries to help him move ahead. He may even try harder himself.

When a child reaches the third grade (or perhaps sooner), he can make a folder to hold samples of his work. He can assume responsibility for his own file.

Fig. 22-7 Older children sometimes assume responsibility for their own G & P File Books.

SUMMARY

Good records are important in a home-based early childhood program. Records provide information, a basis for comparison, evidence that objectives are met, data to help improve the program, and facts that justify a continuation of the program.

Planning a record system should involve all members of the staff. Accurate up-to-date records must be kept.

Vertical planning is a good way to get ideas. All members are involved in preparing forms to be used by the local program.

Essential records include administrative records, family records, target child records, and those of the home visitor.

SUGGESTED ACTIVITIES

- Locate and bring to class as many different blank records and forms as you can obtain.
    a. Check your local school system, health department, churches, early childhood centers, and any others available.
    b. Examine the records. See how they tie in with the purposes the makers intended. Tie them in with the objectives of respective organizations.
    c. See how many of them would apply to home-based educational programs.
- Make a checklist for a child's intellectual development.
- Make a checklist for a child's socioemotional development.
- Make a checklist for a child's physical development. Be sure to check other units when making your lists.

REVIEW

A. Explain why records are important in a home-based program.

B. List five questions which must be asked and answered by program planners.

C. Identify and describe the following records: administrative, family, target child, and home visitor.

D. Tell how you would begin a growth and progress file if you were the parent of a newborn baby. You need not follow the form in this unit, unless you want to. Perhaps you can come up with some ideas of your own.

unit 23 evaluation

OBJECTIVES

After studying this unit, the student should be able to

- Define the following terms: evaluation, measurement, pretest, delayed effects, posttest, formative evaluation, summative evaluation.
- Explain why it is necessary to evaluate a program.
- Describe the steps in evaluating a program.
- List the information needed to see if objectives are met in the four components of home-based programs.

Evaluation is the process of assessing the degree to which set objectives are met. Sometimes the focus of an evaluation is on the learner and, at other times, on the program itself. The brief definition stated covers either situation.

An important part of evaluation is *measurement,* an observable description of behavior, objects, or events. Measurement can be expressed in numbers. It is a response to the question, "How much?"

Evaluation is much broader than measurement. It goes beyond the "how much" question and includes value judgments concerning the things described. Evaluation does something with the measurement and responds to the question, "How good is the thing described?"

For example, a preschooler has a set of alphabet cards. He says the name of each letter on the cards and gets a score (measurement) of twenty-six. A judgment (evaluation) is made that says his score is very good.

WHY EVALUATE A PROGRAM

Evaluation done on any program is usually as a basis for decision making to decide either the survival of the program or its future direction. There are other reasons why evaluation takes place.

Evaluation provides an on-the-way check of progress that is being made toward set objectives. If the objectives are well-written, it should be possible at any point in the program to take stock of how well things are going. Evaluation may point out the need to change something in midstream. For example, one area may need more time than was planned, more emphasis may be needed on a particular skill, a certain resource may need to be reexamined, an activity may need some changes, or home visitor training may need to be expanded.

Evaluation provides information for helping those who are to learn. Children and parents enter the program with their own attitudes, interests, and abilities. The evaluation helps the staff meet individual needs.

The learner himself has an opportunity to see how well he is doing. He can learn to set an appropriate standard for himself and to judge his own behavior in relation to the model set for him. He learns to use resources outside himself to make judgments about his work. He also develops a sense of self-evaluation which is realistic and healthy.

Evaluation provides an opportunity to take a look at beliefs set for the total program.

Every program has certain beliefs on which it is based. During the course of events, strengths or weaknesses in the program may come to the surface. For example, home visitors may feel that they need more training than the few allowed. They may find that there are areas of training which need more work before visits are made. Evaluation helps to change or close gaps.

Other beliefs may be related to the children and how they learn. The outcome of an activity may show that a particular belief may need to be changed. Someone may feel that the young child learns to read best in a formal step-by-step way, for example. A child who uses an electric typewriter and learns to read in an informal way gives evidence to the contrary. The step-by-step lessons may continue, but another option is open. Evaluation helps to point to the option and support it.

Evaluation provides a good way to assess some of the objectives which are not easily defined. The staff must not lose sight of the fact that there are goals which are often difficult to measure. It is easy to fall back on measuring things that can be produced and expressed in numbers. For example, emphasis may be placed on the number of children who score high on a readiness test, rather than on examining the basic objectives of the program. It may be important to show evidence that children are developing the ability to examine and interpret facts or that their attitudes are changing. It may be equally important to discover and expose the fact that these broad objectives are not being met.

Evaluation forms a basis for public relations. There may be a need to defend a program. It may range from defense of the budget to a conflict with a parent who questions some activity.

Whether the program must be justified to one or to many, facts are necessary. A sound basis for explanation and justification is found in appropriate and well-stated objectives, carefully measured results, and sound interpretation of the evidence to show how objectives are being met.

Evaluation serves as a morale booster since it allows both staff and participants to develop an awareness of both purpose and achievement. It is easier to accept a need for improvement when people can see and appreciate what has already been accomplished. For example, a parent who can see the positive gains a child makes through toys and games may continue their use. The parent who can see the value of being involved in teaching her own child may stay involved.

WHY EVALUATION MAY BE OVERLOOKED

Evaluation can do much for a program, but it is often overlooked. Why is this? There are no easy answers. Some of the following comments may help to look at the problem.

Evaluation is a complex process. Good evaluation is not easy to do. Perhaps this is why paper and pencil tests are used so often. Finding another way to evaluate something in meaningful terms is hard to do.

Evaluation takes time. Sometimes evaluation is seen as just one more record to keep. The problem may be that the staff does not understand evaluation as a part of the program itself. Evaluation needs to be viewed as a continuous process and not a one-time thing.

Evaluation is turned over to "experts." When an important evaluation must be done, it is sometimes easier to turn the job over to outside "experts." Experts have a real contribution to make. But they serve best when they are brought in to assist as the need arises, instead of entering to tell the staff what to do or not to do.

Unless the local staff defines needs, understands the needs, and plans for improvements, changes will not be understood or supported by those who live with them. This is not easy to do.

STEPS IN EVALUATION

To evaluate a program is to collect evidence regarding its effectiveness. A question is raised, "What is the impact of the program?" In other words, "What is its capacity to cause changes in those who are exposed to it?"

Evaluation seeks an answer to the question by following a series of steps. A brief description of each step is given.

Identify the goals of the program. The goals of the program are the desired learning outcomes. In home-based programs there are goals related to the target child and his growth and development, his parents and their parenting skills, and other family members and needs they may have. There are also goals related to the home visitor and her effectiveness and to the program itself and how well it meets the needs of people exposed to it.

Define the objectives in behavioral terms. It is necessary to specify the behavior that is accepted as evidence that learning takes place. Well-written instructional objectives should say three things: (1) what it is that a learner should be able to do when he masters the objective, (2) the conditions under which he can do it, and (3) the extent to which he can do it.

Choose or make tools for measuring (or describing) the desired behavior. Decisions are made concerning the way in which the behavior is to be measured. It can be done by observations, checklists, tests, interviews, and other tools that come up with the desired information.

Measurements are taken before the *treatment* (learning experiences) to find out where the learner is at the start. This is called *pretest.* The results of the test are converted to a score or level.

Carry out the treatment. The learner is exposed to the program. He works toward set objectives.

Apply the tools of measurement after the treatment. The measurement made at the end of the treatment is called a *posttest.* The results of the posttest are examined to find the degree to which learning objectives are met.

Interpret the results. What do the results mean? The difference between the pretest and posttest is found. When the posttest is higher than the pretest, the difference is called a *gain.* The gain is what is assumed the student has learned. If there is no difference between the two tests, it is assumed that the student has not met the learning objectives.

APPROACHES TO EVALUATION

Two forms of evaluation are used for judging home-based programs — formative and summative.

A formative evaluation is built right into the program. It helps to "form" the program as it is being developed. Formative evaluation is a narrative description of the program. It may study the following:

- Staff training needs.
- Family needs and how they are met.
- Program goals which are developed and met.
- Kinds of services provided for families.
- How the program is organized and administered.
- How effective the setup is.

In formative evaluation things seen as "good" go on. Things seen as "ineffective" are changed. The main concern is to find problems and deal with them right away.

SUMMATIVE EVALUATION PLAN				
Objective	*Sample*	*Instrument*	*Analysis*	*Date*
(Each objective is stated)	(Source from which data are to be collected.)	(Tool or method by which data are collected.)	(How data is to be examined and interpreted.)	(When objective is to be completed.)

Fig. 23-1 A plan for a summative evaluation is shown. Each objective is met according to the same plan.

Objective: To increase the number of families served each month until all families in the target group are being visited at least once a week.

INTERIM REPORT

Reports from home visitors (based on records kept by each) reveal:

MONTH	HOME VISITOR	NUMBER OF FAMILIES SERVED DURING PERIOD
January	_____	_____
February	_____	_____
March	_____	_____
April	_____	_____
May	_____	_____
June	_____	_____
	TOTAL	_____

COMMENT: (A comment would be made to state whether or not goal was met. Other statements might be included.)

Fig. 23-2 Shown is an item which might be included in a summative report.

Formative evaluation procedures in the home-based program may include

- Home visitor reports made on a day-to-day basis. Each home visitor may have one or more weekly conferences with her supervisor.
- Weekly staff meetings to discuss the program's progress.
- Pinpointing problems and finding ways to resolve them.
- Preparing reports and sending them to persons concerned.
- Interim reports to give an on-the-way look at facts and figures. These are examined to chart the progress up to a certain point in time. They are only temporary steps. Final reports are usually submitted later.

A *summative evaluation* sums up everything for a final report. It includes before-after measurements (pretest-posttest). It describes in detail

- The goals of the program.
- Who took part.
- How many took part.
- What the content was.
- How successful the program was for those in it.

Summative evaluation takes place only after a program is completed or has reached a steady state of operations. It is concerned with program outcomes, so that decisions can be made to continue it, reject it, or change it.

An example of a plan for a summative type evaluation is shown in figure 23-1. The needed information is listed. In parentheses, a description of the information is given.

Another example is that of an item which might appear in a summative report. Figure 23-2 shows an objective and the manner in which the information is given. There is a place for a comment at the bottom of the form.

EVALUATING THE HOME-BASED PROGRAM

The objectives of each component in the home-based program are changed to questions to be raised. Some ways to collect data are given. Only the local program can make judgments and answer the "how good" question of their program.

Education Component

The aim of the education component is to help the child by helping his parents. Questions are raised and answered concerning parenting skills.

- Does the parent show the ability to make use of educational opportunities that arise in the course of everyday life?
- Does the parent utilize the resources and services in the community to help the child grow physically, intellectually, socially, and emotionally?
- Can the parent select, plan, and carry out worthwhile learning activities for the target child?
- Does the parent gain useful information and skills through workshops, sewing and woodcraft centers, toy-lending libraries, or other learning situations?
- Can the parent work independently to find appropriate solutions to child rearing problems as they arise?

Questions are raised to see if the child's needs are met in all areas of his growth and development.

Intellectual growth. Has the child developed in his ability to acquire, store, arrange, and rearrange information concerning his world? Does he show curiosity about his world of people, objects, and events? Does he try to learn through self-discovery? Can he use numbers to solve his own problems? Does he try to create things?

Emotional growth. Is the child aware of his feelings? Does he know how to handle them? Does he show consideration for others? Does he accept responsibility to the extent that can be expected at his stage of development? Does he share with others? Does he practice the self-control expected of children in his age group? Does he listen as well as talk?

Physical growth. Does the child have a healthy body? Does he practice good eating habits? Can he recognize his need for rest and get it? Does he get physical exercise? Does he take safety precautions? Does he use good personal hygiene and know why it is necessary?

Fig. 23-3 Does the child try to learn through self-discovery?

Unit 23 Evaluation

Name _____ Date _____

CONCEPT OF SELF (Encircle one)

The child is able to	Never					Always
• Tell his first and last names.	0	1	2	3	4	5
• Tell his address.	0	1	2	3	4	5
• Tell his telephone number.	0	1	2	3	4	5
• Tell father's and mother's names.	0	1	2	3	4	5
• Tell his birthdate.	0	1	2	3	4	5
• Tell how old he is.	0	1	2	3	4	5
• Name his favorite toys.	0	1	2	3	4	5
• Name his favorite foods.	0	1	2	3	4	5
• Name something he dislikes.	0	1	2	3	4	5
• Name something he likes.	0	1	2	3	4	5
• Recognize his feelings: sad.	0	1	2	3	4	5
• Recognize his feelings: happy.	0	1	2	3	4	5
• Recognize his feelings: angry.	0	1	2	3	4	5
• Cope with his feelings.	0	1	2	3	4	5
• Tell what he would do in an emergency when he is home alone.	0	1	2	3	4	5
• Tell what he would do if he were lost in a department store.	0	1	2	3	4	5
• Tell what he would do if he went for a walk and got lost.	0	1	2	3	4	5

Fig. 23-4 A checklist is helpful in rating the child on self-identity. Many other items can be added as the local staff sees fit.

Fig. 23-5 Does the child recognize feelings and know how to deal with them?

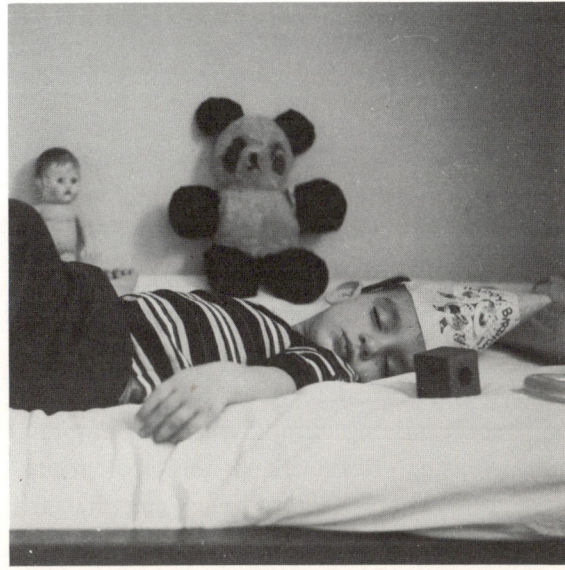

Fig. 23-6 Does the child recognize his need for rest and get it?

Language growth. Does he use language to suit his needs? Is his language development adequate for his growth stage? Can he receive and transmit ideas, feelings, and information? Can he listen to stories with attention? Does he try to make up his own stories?

Health Component

The aim of the health component is a healthy mind in a healthy body for the child and his family. Questions to be asked and answered are suggested.

- Is the child receiving the full range of health services to cover nutrition, dental health, physical and mental health, and safety education?
- Does the child have his health record up-to-date with respect to immunization, fluoride treatment, and other preventive measures to insure good health?
- Are measures taken, as needed, to help all family members improve their present health? Are measures taken to help them keep in good health?
- Do parents know what services are available for health care and how to get it? Do parents see that family members get the services needed?

Social Services

The aim of the social services component is to help all parents resolve the problems that they face at home, at work, and in their community. Questions to be posed are listed.

- Does the parent know about social services that provide help with problems: psychological services, drug counseling, job training, employment counseling, housing, financial aid, and recreational programs? Is there evidence that the parent uses services when needed?
- Does the family take part in community affairs?
- Are family members involved in community projects in which they can both give and gain benefits?
- Are family needs being met in this component?

Sources of Data

The collection of data is very important. Some ways to get information about the child are listed.

- Make a brief sketch of the child's early developmental history. Note whether he was slow or rapid in weaning, walking, talking, teething. See if there is a pattern of growth that is his very own.
- Prepare a health history: immunizations, illnesses, accidents, any handicaps. Include nutrition and rest habits.
- Talk with parents and other family members to learn about the child's social-emotional habits. Observe child. Listen to what he says. Ask him about himself.
- Keep samples of the child's work. Include drawings, stories dictated, a rough sketch or two of the type of block building he does, arts and crafts work.

Fig. 23-7 Can the child receive and transmit ideas, feelings, and information?

Unit 23 Evaluation

Denver Developmental Screening Test, W.K. Frankenburg and J.B. Dodds. Denver, Colorado: Ladoca Project and Publishing Foundations, Inc., 1970 (Revised Ed.)

1. **Purpose**

   To establish the developmental level a child has achieved. Test was originally intended to be a screening device to help detect children with early signs of deficiencies in the areas tested. It is not intended for program evaluation, but many groups use it to provide data concerning the child's developmental level.

2. **Age Level**

   Children aged two weeks to six years.

3. **Content**

   Consists of 105 tasks, of which a child is tested on about 20. Areas include

   - Gross motor and fine motor adaptive (child uses hands, shows ability to solve nonverbal problems).
   - Language (incoming and outgoing messages).
   - Personal-social (self-care and the ability to relate to others).

4. **Scores**

   The child's performance is compared with a scale which indicates the age at which 25, 50, 75, and 90 percent of the children tested can do each task. The test requires that some items be rated by a person who knows the child well. The person giving the test must be familiar with it. Some small props are needed in giving the test.

Fig. 23-8 Described is a helpful inventory test.

8-Block Sort Task (Hess and Shipman, 1968)

1. **Purpose**

   To examine the "teaching" style of the mother when she is working with her child.

2. **Content**

   Mother is provided with a set of blocks. She is shown how they are to be sorted (according to their size and markings). When she understands the procedure, she is asked to teach her child to sort the blocks in the same way.

   The mother-child interaction is tape-recorded. Things considered in the replay of the tape include

   - How the mother explains things to her child.
   - How the child responds to his mother.
   - How the mother gives her child feedback (praise, correction, or other response).
   - Comments and questions asked by the child are examined.

3. **Evaluation**

   The "teaching" style of the parent is indicated by the things she does and says, and how the child reacts to her.

Fig. 23-9 A test which a parent can help to evaluate has much to offer.

- Give formal tests under clinical conditions. These tests must be given and analyzed by an expert. A test is described in figure 23-8.

Section 8 Record Keeping and Evaluation

- Study the child's behavior records and his day-to-day reactions to things in his world.
- Give pretests and posttests to check the gains he makes from the activities of his program.

Information about parents is more difficult to obtain. It is not easy to give a test to a parent. It may not even be wise to do so. This is a matter to decide locally.

Listed are some ways to obtain data about the impact of the program on parents.

- Check the pretest-posttest scores of children to see gains made during the program.
- Interview the parents to see how they feel about what they have learned. See how they feel about the progress of their child.
- Ask parents to fill in a questionnaire that asks the parents to score their own skills and attitudes.
- Observe the parent at work with the child.
- Note how many study trips the parent and child took on their own.
- Give tests that measure parent skills and attitudes. Figure 23-9 describes a test for parents.
- Look at the home environment to see if needed changes are visible.

Evaluating the Home Visitor's Progress

The success of a home-based program rests very heavily upon the home visitor's ability to do her tasks well. She must possess traits and attitudes which move others in the direction of change. Figure 23-10 shows a checklist which can be helpful to those who wish to make a local list.

The tasks of the home visitor are evaluated in three categories: sponsoring-agency, home-visit, and community–related tasks. There are questions to be answered in all categories.

Sponsoring agency tasks. Does the home visitor take part in training sessions? Does she participate in other training as required? Does she seek assistance as needed to improve services to children and their families? Does she submit required records and reports on time? Does she confer at specified times with those to whom she is responsible?

Home visit tasks. Does she develop a plan tailored to the individual needs of each family for whom she is responsible? Does she spend the required time with each family? Does she carry out the day-to-day activities of each family plan? Does she keep the necessary records such as information and referral forms? Is she on call as required by sponsors?

Community-related tasks. Does she know what resources and services are available in the community? Does she understand how to coordinate, integrate, and utilize resources on an "as-needed" basis? Does she prepare and deliver family referrals as required? Does she follow up on all referrals? Does she make parents aware of adult education opportunities in the community?

Job Performance

The home visitor's job performance is what she actually does on-the-job. An evaluation of her job performance is a closer look at the behaviors that she demonstrates.

Listed are things she should be able to do. These items can be used as a basic framework around which a local list of desired competencies can be built.

- Guide parents in understanding and accepting the child as he is.

HOME VISITOR SELF-CHECKLIST

Directions: Read carefully the definition of each trait. Think of your own behaviors on-the-job. Then place a circle around the number which indicates the degree to which you feel you possess the trait.

Definition of Trait	Low				High
1. *Leadership:* ability to act as a change agent to stimulate, guide, direct, and keep parents progressing toward a specific goal.	1	2	3	4	5
2. *Enthusiasm:* the outward expression that shows a strong desire to carry out a task with an eagerness for the activity.	1	2	3	4	5
3. *Resourcefulness:* the capacity for finding worthwhile tasks for parents and their children; the ability to meet sudden or unusual needs successfully.	1	2	3	4	5
4. *Good judgment:* the ability to weigh all options and come up with some desirable end or course of action.	1	2	3	4	5
5. *Cooperation:* the ability to work well with staff members and parents.	1	2	3	4	5
6. *Self-confidence:* faith in one's own ability to carry out tasks to a successful end.	1	2	3	4	5
7. *Adaptability:* the ability to adjust easily to new and different situations.	1	2	3	4	5
8. *Self-control:* the ability to control one's emotions or reactions, especially when under a time of sudden stress or conflict.	1	2	3	4	5
9. *Initiative:* ability to start new things or another course of action.	1	2	3	4	5
10. *Considerateness:* the ability to have empathy for parents with problems; the ability to understand, appreciate, and share the problems or difficulties of others.	1	2	3	4	5
11. *Sense of humor:* the ability to see the funny aspect of a situation; the ability to keep up good spirits.	1	2	3	4	5

Fig. 23-10 Self-evaluation is an important part of the ongoing process of evaluation.

- Show how things and activities in the home can be learning experiences for the child.
- Introduce and demonstrate how to use toys and games for learning at home.
- Help the parent to make toys and games.
- Help parents plan and serve nutritious meals.
- Demonstrate physical activities which are both body building and fun.

- Show parents how resources in the community can be used as rich study trips for the child.
- Guide the parent in developing competence as a parent-teacher.

Program Evaluation

The program itself is evaluated by drawing data from the evaluation of the four components. Judgments are made and based on certain facts. They may include

- Number of children and families reached.
- Improvement and/or increase of services offered to children and their families.
- Identification of any new ways to deliver services or in the administration or staffing of the program.
- The outcome for children: physical, intellectual, social, and emotional growth and development.
- Evidence that the program has stimulated others to seek a like-source of services to children and their parents.

A Team Approach to Evaluation

Evaluation is a team task. Therefore, it is necessary for all members at all levels to have a basic understanding of evaluation. This unit attempts to help the home visitor meet that need.

The home visitor plays a vital role in evaluation. The data which she gathers is used to make decisions concerning the program and those in it. Accurate data is crucial. Sometimes it may be necessary to provide some subjective views, but they must be identified as such.

Finally, in evaluation there is always the risk that evaluators are looking at the wrong things. It is also possible that there may be some *delayed effects* of the program. These are outcomes that do not show up until some other point in time. Evaluation as a continuous process may help to examine delayed effects.

SUMMARY

Evaluation is defined as the process of assessing the degree to which set objectives are met. Measurement is an observable description of behavior, objects or events which can be expressed in numbers. Measurements ask, "How much?" Evaluation asks, "How good?"

Evaluation may be done as a basis for decision making. It may provide an on-the-way check of progress being made toward set objectives. Evaluation provides information about people and beliefs and forms a basis for good public relations. Evaluation can be a morale booster.

Evaluation may sometimes be overlooked because it is a complex process. It takes time and sometimes it is turned over to outside experts.

Steps in evaluation include the following:

- Identify the goals of the program.
- Define the objectives in behavioral terms.
- Choose or make tools for measuring (or describing) the desired behavior.
- Carry out the treatment.
- Apply tools of measurement after the treatment.
- Interpret the results.

Two forms of evaluation are used in evaluating home-based programs: formative and summative. A formative evaluation helps to form the program as it is being developed. A summative evaluation sums up everything for a final report.

To evaluate a home-based program it is necessary to convert each objective to a question. Data is collected to answer the question. Judgments are made to decide whether or not objectives are met in the four components.

Evaluation is a team task. Each member needs an understanding of the process.

SUGGESTED ACTIVITIES

- Ask your instructor to make arrangements for you to visit the testing center of a college or university nearby. Try to do some of the following activities.
    a. Examine tests designed to measure certain skills in young children.
    b. Observe a test being given (a two-way mirror is sometimes used for student observations).
    c. If possible, borrow a test (an old one may be shared) which you can give in class to a peer.
        (1) Read the directions carefully. Study them.
        (2) Follow the direction in giving the test. (Read them orally to be exact).
        (3) Have your instructor help the class to find out what the results mean.
- Ask your instructor to role-play with you in a testing situation. When you make your responses on the test; "speak" your answers, too, so that the class knows what you are doing. Evaluate the test with your instructor.
- Go back to some of the early units in this text. As a class (or as an individual) do some of these things.
    a. Make a checklist of things an infant should be able to do.
    b. Make a list of things a toddler should be able to do.
    c. Make a list of things a preschooler should be able to do.
- Ask a young child to draw a picture of both a man and woman. Bring your pictures to class. Compare the pictures.
    a. See if the class can guess the age of each child-artist.
    b. See if there is a difference between the pictures made by children who are the same age.
    c. See if the pictures reveal anything about the child (judging from the size of his drawings, colors used, subjects drawn).

REVIEW

A. Briefly define each of the following.
   1. Evaluation
   2. Measurement
   3. Pretest
   4. Delayed effects
   5. Formative evaluation
   6. Summative evaluation
   7. Posttest

Section 8 Record Keeping and Evaluation

B. Explain why it is necessary to evaluate a program. Try to include some ideas of your own.

C. Describe briefly the steps in evaluation, as discussed in this unit.

D. Tell what information is needed to see if objectives are met in the four components of home-based programs.

Appendix

APPENDIX A TEXTBOOK REFERENCES

Bergevin, Paul. *A Philosophy for Adult Education,* New York: Seabury Press, 1967.

Brim, Orville, G., Jr. *Education for Child-Rearing.* New York: The Free Press, 1965.

Duvall, Evelyn Millis. *Family Development.* Fourth Edition. New York: J.B. Lippincott Company, 1971.

Erikson, Erik H. *Childhood and Society.* New York: W.W. Norton, 1963.

Giesy, Rosemary, ed. *A Guide for Home Visitors.* Nashville, Tennessee: Demonstration and Research Center for Early Education, George Peabody College, 1970.

Gulick, Luther and Urwick, L., eds. *Papers on the Science of Administration.* New York: Institute of Public Administration, 1937.

Havighurst, Robert J. *Developmental Tasks and Education.* Third Edition. New York: David McKay, Inc., 1974.

Hess, Robert J. and Croft, Doreen J. *Teachers of Young Children.* Boston: Houghton-Mifflin Company, 1972.

Knowles, Malcolm. *The Modern Practice of Adult Education.* New York: Association Press, 1970.

Lippitt, Ronald, et al. *The Dynamics of Planned Change.* New York: Harcourt, Brace and World, Inc., 1958.

Loomis, Charles P. *Social Systems.* Princeton, New Jersey: D. Van Nostrand Company, Inc., 1960.

Maslow, Abraham H. *Motivation and Personality.* New York: Harper, 1954.

Massoglia, Elinor T. "You Can Help Your Child Get Better Grades in School." *U.S. Lady Magazine,* Sept.-Oct. 1956.

Massoglia, Elinor Tripato. *Growth and Progress File.* Washington, D.C.: American Service Publishing Company, 1956.

Massoglia, Elinor Tripato. *Fun-Time Paper Folding.* Chicago: Children's Press, 1959.

Murphy, Lois B. and Leeper, Ethel M. *Caring for Children* (Numbers One Through Nine). Washington, D.C.: United States Department of Health, Education, and Welfare, 1973.

North, A. Frederick, Jr., M.D. *Day Care: Health Services: A Guide for Project Directors and Health Personnel.* DHEW Pub. No. (OCD) 73-12. Washington, D.C.: United States Government Printing Office, 1972.

Papalia, Diane E. and Olds, Sally Wendkos. A Child's World: *Infancy Through Adolescence.* New York: McGraw-Hill Book Company, 1975.

Programs and Community Resources for Day Care. Durham, N.C.: Day Care Task Force, Community Planning Services, August 1973.

Ross Laboratories. *The Phenomena of Early Development.* Columbus, Ohio, May 1974.

Seefeldt, Carol, and Dittmann, Laura L., eds. *Family Day Care.* DHEW Pub. No. (OHD) 73-1054. Washington, D.C.: United States Government Printing Office, 1973.

U.S. Department of Health, Education, and Welfare, Office of Child Development. *A Guide for Planning and Operating Home-Based Child Development Programs.* DHEW Pub.

Appendix A

No. (OHD) 75-80. Washington, D.C.: United States Government Printing Office, June 1942.

———— *Infant Care.* DHEW Pub. No. (OCD) 73-15. Washington, D.C.: United States Government Printing Office, April 3, 1975.

———— *Report of a Joint Conference: Home Start/Child and Family Resources Program.* DHEW Pub. No. (OHD) 74-1072. Washington, D.C.: United States Government Printing Office, June 1974.

U.S. Department of Health, Education and Welfare, Education Division: U.S. Office of Education. *Report of the National Conference on Parent/Early Childhood Education.* Denver, Colorado: United States Government Printing Office, 1975.

U.S. Department of Health, Education and Welfare, Office of Child Development. *The Home Start Demonstration Program: An Overview.* DHEW Pub. No. (OHD) 74-1069. Washington, D.C.: United States Government Printing Office, 1973.

———— *Your Child From 1-6.* DHEW Pub. No. (OHD) 73-26. Washington, D.C.: United States Government Printing Office, 1973.

APPENDIX B SELECTED BIBLIOGRAPHY

Reading is a personal experience. Therefore, a wide selection of textbooks is offered to meet the needs of learners who may differ in background experience, interest, and ability.

Locating appropriate books from which to gain information is a part of the learning experience. Students are urged to create their own reading lists.

A special effort should be made to share new information. It is not necessary for everyone in a group to read the same material. Sharing helps to make the most of time and effort.

The book list provided may be examined by individual students, or by study groups. Texts listed under "References" are not repeated here and should be included in the search for ideas and information. Other reading material located by the class can be added to the basic list that follows.

SECTION 1: GOALS AND OBJECTIVES

Beal, George M. et al. *Social Action and Interaction.* Ames, Iowa: Iowa State University Press, 1966.

Bereiter, Carl and Engelmann, Siegfried. *Teaching Disadvantaged Children in the Preschool.* Englewood Cliffs, New Jersey: Prentice-Hall, Inc., 1966.

Evans, E. Belle, et al. *How to Plan, Develop and Operate A Day Care Center.* Boston: Beacon Press, 1971.

Hildebrand, Verna. *Introduction to Early Childhood Education.* New York: The Macmillan Company, 1971.

Hymes, James L., Jr. *Teaching the Child Under Six.* Columbus, Ohio: Charles E. Merrill Publishing Company, 1968.

Landreth, Catherine. *Preschool Learning and Teaching.* New York: Harper and Row Publishers, 1972.

Law, Norma, et al. *Basic Propositions for Early Childhood Education.* Washington, D.C.: Association for Childhood Education International, 1965.

Martin, Beatrice D. *Teaching Young Children.* Albany, New York: Delmar Publishers, 1975.

Montessori in Perspective. Washington D.C.: National Association for Education of Young Children, 1966.

Watson, Goodwin, ed. *Concepts for Social Change.* Washington, D.C.: National Training Laboratories, NEA, 1967.

SECTION 2: ORIENTATION TO HOME VISITING

Beadle, Muriel. *A Child's Mind.* Garden City, New York: Anchor Books (Doubleday and Company, Inc.), 1970.

Bereiter, Carl. *Must We Educate?* Englewood Cliffs, New Jersey: Prentice-Hall, Inc., 1973.

Click, Phyllis. *Administration of Schools for Young Children.* Albany, New York: Delmar Publishers, 1975.

De Regniers, Beatrice, et al., eds. *Poems Children Will Sit Still For.* New York: Scholastic Book Services, 1969.

Durkin, Dolores. *Teaching Young Children to Read.* Boston: Allyn and Bacon, Inc., 1972.

Appendix B

Goldstein, Joseph, et al. *Beyond The Best Interests of The Child.* New York: The Free Press, 1973.

Griffiths, Daniel E. *Administrative Theory.* New York: Appleton-Century-Crofts, Inc., 1959.

Halpin, Andrew W. *Administrative Theory In Education.* Chicago: University of Chicago Press, 1958.

Jenkins, Gladys Gardner and Shacter, Helen S. *These Are Your Children.* Fourth Edition. Glenview, Illinois: Scott, Foresman and Company, 1975.

Larrick, Nancy. *A Teacher's Guide to Children's Books.* Columbus, Ohio: Charles E. Merrill Publishing Company, 1960.

Parker, Ronald and Dittman, Laura L., ed. *Staff Training.* Day Care Bulletin No. 5. DHEW Pub. No. (OCD) 73-23. Washington, D.C.: United States Printing Office, 1971.

The American National Red Cross. *Standard First Aid and Personal Safety.* Garden City, New York: Doubleday and Company, Inc., 1973.

VanderVen, Karen D. *Home and Community Influences on Young Children.* Albany, New York: Delmar Publishers, 1977.

Yamamoto, Kaoru (ed.) *The Child and His Image.* Boston: Houghton Mifflin Company, 1972.

SECTION 3: PARENTS ARE ADULT LEARNERS

Baker, William E., et al. "The Creative Environment Workshop," *Young Children* 26(4) March 1971.

Beckhard, Richard. *How to Plan Workshops and Conferences.* New York: Association Press, 1956.

Boone, Edgar J., et al. *Administration of Adult Education.* Washington, D.C.: Adult Education Association of the USA, 1965.

Dreikurs, Rudolf, M.D. *The Challenge of Parenthood.* New York: Hawthorn Books, Inc., 1958.

Hallenbeck, Wilbur C., et al. *Community and Adult Education.* Washington, D.C.: Adult Education Association of the USA, 1962.

How to Use Role Playing and Other Tools for Learning. Leadership Pamphlet # 6. Washington, D.C.: Adult Education Association of the USA, 1955.

Ingalls, John D. *A Trainers Guide to Andragogy.* Revised Edition. (SRS) 73-05301. Washington, D.C.: Social and Rehabilitation Service, U.S. Department of Health, Education, and Welfare, 1973.

Kidd, J.R. *How Adults Learn.* New York: Association Press, 1975.

Lorge, Irving, et al. *Adult Learning.* Washington, D.C.: Adult Education Association of the USA, 1965.

Lorge, Irving, et al. *Psychology of Adults.* Washington, D.C.: Adult Education Association of the USA, 1963.

McMahon, Ernest E. *Needs – of People and Their Communities – and The Adult Educator.* Washington, D.C.: Adult Education Association of the USA, 1970.

Miller, Harry L. et al. *Processes of Adult Education.* Washington, D.C.: Adult Education Association of the USA, 1965.

Miller, Harry L. *Teaching and Learning in Adult Education.* New York: The Macmillan Company, 1964.

Pickarts, Evelyn and Fargo, Jean. *Parent Education: Toward Parental Competence.* New York: Appleton-Century-Crofts, 1971.

Treasury of Techniques for Teaching Adults. Washington, D.C.: National Education Association, 1964.

Verner, Coolie. *Adult Education.* Washington, D.C.: The Center for Applied Research in Education, Inc., 1964.

_____ *A Conceptual Scheme for the Identification and Classification of Processes.* Washington, D.C.: Adult Education Association of the USA, 1962.

SECTION 4: CHILD DEVELOPMENT AND PARENT ENABLERS

Baker, K.R. *Understanding and Guiding Young Children.* Englewood Cliffs, New Jersey: Prentice-Hall, 1967.

Bloom, Benjamin S. *Stability and Change in Human Characteristics.* New York: John Wiley and Sons, 1964.

Bohannan, Paul. *Love, Sex and Being Human.* Garden City, New York: Doubleday and Company, Inc., 1970.

Brazelton, T. Berry. *Infants and Mothers: Differences in Development.* New York: Delacore Press, 1969.

Briggs, Dorothy. *Your Child's Self-Esteem: The Key to His Life.* New York: Doubleday, 1970.

Caldwell, Bettye M. and Ricciuti, H., eds. *Review of Child Development Research.* Vol. 3. Chicago: University of Chicago Press, 1973.

Cohen, Dorothy H. *The Learning Child.* New York: Pantheon Books, 1972.

Ginott, Haim. *Between Parent and Child.* New York: The Macmillan Company, 1965.

Gordon, Ira. *Baby Learning Through Baby Play.* New York: St. Martin's Press, 1970.

Hartley, Ruth E., et al. *Understanding Children's Play.* New York: Columbia University Press, 1952.

Jones, Molly Mason. *Guiding Your Child From Two to Five.* New York: Harcourt, Brace and World, Inc., 1967.

LeMasters, E.E. *Parents in Modern America.* Revised Edition. Homewood, Illinois: The Dorsey Press, 1975.

Maier, Henry W. *Three Theories of Child Development.* New York: Harper and Row, 1969.

Ross Laboratories. Booklets on Child Care. Columbus, Ohio.
  Becoming A Parent. September 1974.
  Caring for Your Baby. February 1973.
  Your Baby Becomes A Toddler. June 1974.
  Developing Toilet Habits. May 1973.
  When Your Child Is Contrary. May 1973.
  Your Child's Appetite. December 1974.
  How Your Child Learns About Sex. September 1974.
  Your Child Goes to the Hospital. January 1969.

Appendix B

Your Child and Sleep Problems. February 1972.
Your Child's Fears. May 1974.
Your Child's Progress In School. June 1971.
Your Children and Discipline. November 1974.
You and Your Adolescent. June 1971.
When Your Child Is Unruly. April 1973.

Yarrow, Marian, et al. *Child-Rearing: An Inquiry into Research and Methods.* San Francisco: Jossey-Bass, 1968.

SECTION 5: MATERIALS FOR HOME-BASED LEARNING

Barry, James C. and Treadway, Charles F. *Kindergarten Resource Book.* Nashville, Tennessee: Broadman Press, 1965.

Bits and Pieces: Imaginative Uses for Children's Learning. Bulletin # 20A. Washington, D.C.: Association for Childhood Education International, 1967.

Clarke, Louise. *Can't Read, Can't Write, Can't Talk Too Good Either.* Baltimore, Maryland: Penguin Books, Inc., 1974.

Ellis, Mary Jackson. *Finger Playtime.* Minneapolis: T.S. Denison and Company, Inc., 1962.

_____ *The Kindergarten Log.* Minneapolis: T.S. Denison and Company, Inc., Vol. I, 1955; Vol. II, 1960.

Furth, Hans G. *Piaget for Teachers.* Englewood-Cliffs, New Jersey: Prentice-Hall, 1970.

Hainstock, Elizabeth. *Teaching Montessori in the Home: The Pre-School Years.* New York: Random House, 1971.

Hanna, Lavone A. et al. *Dynamic Elementary Social Studies.* Unit Teaching. Third Edition. New York: Holt, Rinehart and Winston, Inc., 1973.

Hoffman, James and Hoffman, Joan. *Prekindergarten Discoveries.* Minneapolis: T.S. Denison and Company, Inc., 1966.

Landeck, Beatrice. *Songs to Grow On.* New York: William Morrow, 1959.

Leeper, Sarah Hammond, et al. *Good Schools for Young Children.* Third Edition. New York: The Macmillan Company, Inc., 1975.

Lowenfeld, Viktor. *Your Child and His Art.* New York: The Macmillan Company, Inc., 1957.

Machado, Jeanne. *Early Childhood Experiences in Language Arts.* Albany, New York: Delmar Publishers, 1975.

Mager, Robert F. *Preparing Instructional Objectives.* Palo Alto, Calif.: Fearon Publishers, Inc., 1962.

Mayesky, Mary et al. *Creative Activities for Young Children.* Albany, New York: Delmar Publishers, 1975.

Torrance, E. Paul. *Guiding Creative Talent.* Englewood Cliffs, New Jersey: Prentice-Hall, Inc., 1962.

U.S. Department of Health, Education, and Welfare. *Project Headstart: Equipment and Supplies.* (OCD) 0-367-631. Washington, D.C.: United States Government Printing Office, 1969.

Wylie, Joanne, ed. *A Creative Guide for Preschool Teachers.* Racine, Wisconsin: Western Publishing Company, 1972.

SECTION 6: MODELING SKILLS

Andrews, Matthew. *The Parent's Guide to Drugs.* Garden City, New York: Doubleday and Company, Inc., 1972.

Auerbach, Arline B. and Roche, Sandra. *Creating a Preschool Center: Parent Development in an Integrated Neighborhood Project.* New York: John Wiley and Sons, 1971.

Becker, Wesley. *Parents Are Teachers: A Child Management Program.* Champaign, Illinois: Research Press Company, 1971.

Behavioral Analysis Sponsors. *A Token Manual for Behavior Analysis Classrooms.* Lawrence, Kansas: University of Kansas Department of Human Development, 1970.

Cohen, Donald J. and Brandegee, Ada S. *Serving Preschool Children.* DHEW Pub. No. (OHD) 74-1057. Washington, D.C.: United States Government Printing Office, 1974.

Craig, S.K. *Bibliography for Use in Head Start Training and Career Development.* Head Start Career Developments, Vol. 1, No. 4. Washington, D.C.: National Institute for New Careers, 1970. (Available from Information Clearinghouse.)

Goodman, Early O., Jr. "Modeling: A Method of Parent Education." *The Family Coordinator,* January 1975.

Gordon, Thomas, Dr. *P.E.T.: Parent Effectiveness Training.* New York: Peter H. Weyden, Inc., 1970.

Hymes, James L., Jr. *Behavior and Misbehavior.* Englewood Cliffs, New Jersey: Prentice-Hall, Inc., 1955.

Kritchevsky, Sybil, et al. *Planning Environments for Young Children: Physical Space.* Washington, D.C.: National Association for Education of Young Children, 1969.

McNanama, John J. *An Effective Program for Teacher-Aide Training.* West Nyack, New York: Parker Publishing Company, 1972.

Nimnicht, Glen, et al. *The New Nursery School.* New York: General Learning Corporation, 1969.

Palmer, M.W., ed. *Day Care Aides: A Guide for In-Service Training.* Teacher Training Edition. New York: National Federation of Settlements and Neighborhood Centers, 1968.

Todd, Vivian Edmiston and Hunter, Georgennie H. *The Aide in Early Childhood Education.* New York: The Macmillan Company, 1973.

Training for Child Care Staff. New York: Child Welfare League of America, Inc., 1963.

SECTION 7: FAMILY DEVELOPMENT

Arbuthnot, Mary Hill. *Children's Reading in the Home.* Glenview, Illinois: Scott Foresman Company, 1969.

Cherry, Clare. *Creative Movement for the Developing Child.* Palo Alto, Calif.: Fearon Publishers, Inc., 1968.

Dodson, Fitzhugh, Dr. *How to Parent.* New York: Signet, 1970.

Hallett, Kathryn. *A Guide for Single Parents.* Millbrae, Calif.: Celestial Arts, 1974.

Hardge, Beulah and Gray, Susan W. *Helping Families Learn: A Home-Based Program.* Nashville, Tennessee: Demonstration and Research Center for Early Education, George Peabody College, 1974.

Hopman, Anne B., ed. *Helping Children Learn Science.* Washington, D.C.: National Science Teachers Association, 1966.

Appendix B

McCary, James Leslie. *A Complete Sex Education for Parents, Teenagers, and Young Adults.* New York: D. Van Nostrand Reinhold Company, 1973.

Otto, Herbert A. *The Family in Search of A Future.* New York: Appleton-Century-Crofts, 1970.

Play — Children's Business: A Guide to Selection of Toys and Games. Bulletin # 74. Washington, D.C.: Association for Childhood Education, International, 1969.

Public Health Service, Department of Health, Education, and Welfare. *TV and Growing Up: Impact of Televised Violence.* (Report to the Surgeon General's Scientific and Advisory Committee on TV and Social Behavior) Washington, D.C.: United States Government Printing Office, 1972.

Pugmire, M.C. Weller. *Experiences in Music for Young Children.* Albany, New York: Delmar Publishers, 1976.

Schulz, David A. and Rodgers, Stanley F. *Marriage, The Family and Personal Fulfillment.* Englewood Cliffs, New Jersey: Prentice-Hall, Inc., 1975.

Smith, Robert. *Discovering Music Together: Early Education.* Chicago: Follett Educational Corporation, 1969. (Note: coordinated records are available with text.)

SECTION 8: RECORD KEEPING AND EVALUATION

Ahmann, J. Stanley and Glock, Marvin D. *Evaluating Pupil Growth: Principles of Tests and Measurement.* Third Edition. Boston: Allyn and Bacon, Inc., 1967.

Bronfenbrennor, Urie. *A Report on Longitudinal Evaluations of Preschool Programs, Volume II: Is Early Intervention Effective?* Office of Child Development, DHEW Pub. No. (OHD) 74-25. Washington, D.C. United States Government Printing Office, 1973.

Cohen, Dorothy H. and Stern, Virginia. *Observing and Recording the Behavior of Young Children.* New York: Teachers College Press, Columbia University, 1958.

Gordon, Ira J. *Early Child Stimulation Through Parent Education: A Final Report to the Children's Bureau.* U.S. Department of Health, Education, and Welfare. Institute for Development of Human Resources, College of Education, University of Florida, June 1969.

Herman, Jerry J. *Developing an Effective School Staff Evaluation Program.* West Nyack, New York: Parker Publishing Company, 1973.

Krathwohl, David R. et al. *Taxonomy of Educational Objectives.* New York: David McKay Company, Inc., 1956.

Schaefer, Earl S. "Parents as Educators: Evidence from Cross-Sectional, Longitudinal and Intervention Research." *Young Children,* April 1972. National Association for the Education of Young Children, Washington, D.C.

Stanley, Julian C., ed. *Compensatory Education for Children Ages Two to Eight: Recent Studies of Educational Intervention.* Baltimore: The Johns Hopkins University Press, 1973.

Thorndike, Robert L. and Hagen, Elizabeth. *Measurement and Evaluation in Psychology and Education.* Third Edition. New York: John Wiley and Sons, Inc., 1969.

Wilkerson, David. *Parents on Trial: Why Kids Go Wrong — Or Right.* New York: Hawthorn Books, Inc., 1967.

APPENDIX C DEPARTMENT OF HEALTH, EDUCATION, AND WELFARE

To insure "a national commitment to providing all American children an opportunity for healthful and stimulating development during the first five years of life,"[1] several important events took place.

- The Office of Child Development was established within the Office of the Secretary, U.S. Department of Health, Education, and Welfare on July 1, 1969.
- Head Start (a program launched in 1965 by the Office of Economic Opportunity) was delegated to OCD.
- The Children's Bureau established in 1912, a responsibility of the Social and Rehabilitation Service of HEW, was transferred to OCD in September 1969.
- The Office of Child Development became a part of the new Office of Human Development on April 1, 1973.

Within the Office of Human Development, OCD is concerned with the positive growth and development of the nation's children. The target includes "all children from conception through early adolescence."

Some major efforts of OCD are listed.

- Dealing with child abuse and neglect through a nationwide effort aimed at the prevention and correction of problems of child abuse and neglect.
- Promoting education for parenthood as a part of the secondary school curriculum.
- Improving the quality of services to children requiring foster care.
- Furthering the adoption of minority children and hard-to-place children through improved standards for adoption.
- Developing guidelines for State and local licensing regulations for day care services.
- Expanding the existing communication system to provide more people with information on child rearing and development.
- Exploring the Child Development Associate (Program) as a new kind of professional in the child care field: a person whose qualifications are based on performance, rather than on courses or credits.
- Conducting research to develop more effective ways to deal with child-rearing problems, and to determine the effectiveness of programs that now exist.
- Modeling new and effective ways to deal with child-rearing through centers designed for parent-child-teacher interactions.
- Working with other agencies to identify needs, recommend action, or strengthen and reinforce existing efforts.
- Supporting legislation to meet goals set for improving services to all children.

Volunteers are an important part of all programs designed to help children. Persons who wish to help can find suggestions in this book. Section 1 contains the names of many agencies and organizations that encourage volunteer workers. The local Community Action Agency, Board of Education, or Mayor's office may be able to locate specific programs in need of help.

---

[1] U.S. Department of Health, Education, and Welfare. *Office of Child Development.* DHEW Pub. No. (OHD) 75-6. Washington, D.C.: United States Government Printing Office, 1975.

Appendix C

Information related to OCD activities is available through State and Regional HEW offices. They are listed with the office address and areas covered by each region.

Region	Address	Areas Covered
I.	Department of Health, Education and Welfare: OHD, OCD John Fitzgerald Kennedy Federal Building Government Center Boston, Massachusetts 02203	Connecticut Maine Massachusetts New Hampshire Rhode Island Vermont
II.	Department of Health, Education, and Welfare: OHD, OCD Federal Building 26 Federal Plaza New York, New York 10007	New Jersey New York Puerto Rico Virgin Islands
III.	Department of Health, Education, and Welfare: OHD, OCD Post Office Box 12900 Philadelphia, Pennsylvania 19108	Delaware Maryland District of Columbia Pennsylvania Virginia West Virginia
IV.	Department of Health, Education, and Welfare: OHD, OCD Peachtree-Seventh Building 50 Seventh Street, N.E. Atlanta, Georgia 30323	Alabama Florida Georgia Kentucky Mississippi North Carolina South Carolina Tennessee
V.	Department of Health, Education, and Welfare: OHD, OCD Room 712 New Post Office Building 433 West Van Buren Street Chicago, Illinois 60607	Illinois Indiana Michigan Minnesota Ohio Wisconsin
VI.	Department of Health, Education, and Welfare: OHD, OCD 1114 Commerce Street Dallas, Texas 75202	Arkansas Louisiana New Mexico Oklahoma Texas

Appendix C

VII.	Department of Health, Education, and Welfare: OHD, OCD 601 East 12th Street Kansas City, Missouri 64106	Iowa Kansas Missouri Nebraska
VIII.	Department of Health, Education, and Welfare: OHD, OCD 9017 Federal Office Building 19th and Stout Streets Denver, Colorado 80202	Colorado Montana North Dakota South Dakota Utah Wyoming
IX.	Department of Health, Education, and Welfare: OHD, OCD Federal Office Building 50 Fulton Street San Francisco, California 94102	Arizona California Hawaii Nevada American Samoa Guam Trust Territory of the Pacific Islands
X.	Department of Health, Education, and Welfare: OHD, OCD Arcade Building 1321 Second Avenue Seattle, Washington 98101	Alaska Idaho Oregon Washington

APPENDIX D HOME START TRAINING CENTERS

Home Start Training Centers[1] are listed without the names of persons in charge, because assignments sometimes change. Communications may be addressed to the director, using the appropriate address listed.

Regional clusters are indicated. The Wichita, Kansas, center is funded by Region VII.

Home Start Training Center West Central West Virginia Community Action Association, Inc. 804 Ann Street, P.O. Box 227 Parkersburg, West Virginia 26101	I, II, III
Home Start Training Center Clinch-Powell Educational Cooperative Harrogate, Tennessee 37752	IV (except Mississippi)
Portage Project 412 East Slifer Portage, Wisconsin 53901	V, IMPD (east and midwest)
Head Start/Home-Based Training ARVAC, INC. (Arkansas River Valley Area Council) P.O. Box 248 Dardanelle, Arkansas 72834	IV (Mississippi only), VI
Home Start Training Center Kansas Children's Service League 1365 N. Custer Wichita, Kansas 67203	VII
Home Start Training Center 67 South Main Street Millville, Utah 84326	VIII, X
Coordinator Home Start Training Center 3225 Mill Street Reno, Nevada 89502	IX, IMPD (west)

---

[1] U.S. Department of Health, Education, and Welfare, Office of Human Development. July 14, 1975.

APPENDIX E SELECTED AGENCIES AND ORGANIZATIONS CONCERNED WITH THE EDUCATION OF YOUNG CHILDREN

The names and addresses of agencies and organizations are presented. Students are encouraged to seek further information through library resources. For each group, they should

- Find out when and why the group was organized.
- Identify and describe goals and activities.
- Examine publications.

One member of the class may wish to obtain information by writing directly to one or more of the agencies and organizations listed. The list may be divided, so that all groups are contacted.

Many organizations send brochures to students. Be sure to mention student status.

American Association for Elementary-Kindergarten-Nursery Educators, 1201 16th Street, N.W. Washington, D.C. 20036.

American Home Economics Association, 2110 Massachusetts Ave., N.W. Washington, D.C. 20036.

Association for Childhood Education International, 3615 Wisconsin Avenue, N.W., Washington, D.C. 20016.

Black Child Development Institute, 1028 Connecticut Avenue, N.W. Suite 514, Washington, D.C. 20036.

Child Study Association of America, 9 East 89th Street, New York, New York 10010.

Child Welfare League of America, 44 East 23rd Street, New York, New York 10010.

Council for Exceptional Children, 1411 Jefferson Davis Highway, Arlington, Va. 22202.

Day Care and Child Development Council of America, Inc., 1401 "K" Street, N.W., Washington, D.C. 20005.

National Association for the Education of Young Children, 1834 Connecticut Avenue, N.W., Washington, D.C. 20009.

National Congress of Parents and Teachers, 700 North Rush Street, Chicago, Illinois 60611.

National Council on Family Relations, 1219 University Avenue Southeast, Minneapolis, Minn. 55414.

Parent Cooperative Preschool International, P.O. Box 40123, Indianapolis, Indiana 46240.

Society for Research in Child Development, University of Chicago, 5801 Ellis Avenue, Chicago, Illinois 60637.

U.S. Department of Health, Education, and Welfare. (Obtain information and publications list from Regional offices listed in Appendix B.)

In the pursuit of information concerning the organizations and agencies listed, the following texts may be helpful:

Glassman, Lynne. *Directory of Resources on Early Childhood Education.* Arlington, Va.: Council for Exceptional Children Information Center, pp. 13-17.

Gale Research Company. Encyclopedia of Associations, Vol. 1, National Organizations of the United States, Edition 7. Detroit, Michigan.

ANSWERS TO REVIEW QUESTIONS

SECTION 1 ANSWERS TO REVIEW QUESTIONS

Unit 1

A. Definitions are in student's own words.

   1. A *need* is described as any gap that exists between what is and what ought to be.
   2. *Intellectual growth* is the development of thinking processes that help the learner acquire, store, arrange, and rearrange information concerning his world.
   3. *Emotional growth* is being sensitized to one's feelings and knowing how to handle them: learning to feel "good" about oneself.
   4. *Social growth* is getting along with others — showing consideration, accepting responsibility, sharing, practicing self-control, and listening as well as talking.
   5. *Physical growth* is developing a healthy body through good eating habits, rest, physical exercise, safety precautions, and personal hygiene.
   6. *Language growth* is using communication skills as a two-way process — receiving and transmitting ideas, feelings, and information.
   7. *Learning* is a change in behavior. It occurs as the individual interacts with his environment, fills a need, and is thereby able to cope with his environment.

B. Any five of the six statements listed can be used as correct answers.

   1. Positive correlation between parent skills and child success.
   2. Phenomenal sale of books on parenting.
   3. Involvement of parents in Head Start.
   4. Parents seek information from family service agencies.
   5. Success of early home-based programs.
   6. Home Start Demonstration Programs (HEW) have implications for all parents.

   Other data that can be supported are acceptable.

C.
   1. Child's total development from birth to school years.
   2. Early detection of health and educational handicaps.
   3. Home environment and learning opportunities in it.
   4. Competence of parents as teachers of their children.
   5. Influence of families in total process of child development.

D. In the students own words: Ideas gained from chapter, gleaned from supplementary readings, or discussed during interviews with early childhood educators.

E. Any five of the six statements listed can be used as correct answers.

   1. Learning should be problem centered.
   2. Learning should be experience centered.
   3. Experiences should be meaningful to the learner.
   4. Experiences must be geared to the learner's mental, physical, and social maturity.
   5. The learner must have feedback about progress he is making toward his goals.
   6. The security of the learner must be protected.

   Other appropriate responses are acceptable.

Unit 2

A.
   1. *Situation:* location in which a program is placed; the circumstances, conditions or state of affairs the location gives to the program.
   2. *Program components:* people, places, and things that make possible home-based programs; education, health, social services, and parent involvement.

3. *Education:* the process of lifelong learning that begins at birth and ends with death; it can be informal: unplanned, unstructured, or without any recognizable or stated goals.
4. *Random experiential learning:* something that just happens during the everyday course of a person's life; it is a learning experience.
5. *Formal education:* learning that is planned and directed toward identified goals and objectives; guided by someone qualified to do the job; sponsored by those who offer the opportunity on a credit or noncredit basis; organized as a voluntary or compulsory experience; and usually given recognition upon completion of the course or program.

B. 1. *informal*   6. *informal*
    2. *formal*   7. *formal*
    3. *informal*   8. *informal*
    4. *formal*   9. *formal*
    5. *formal*   10. *formal*

C. 1. To help the child by helping his parents.
    2. In student's own words: Information drawn from unit or which is appropriate.
    3. Any goal listed under health component or researched.
    4. To help all parents resolve the problems that they face at home, at work, and in their community.

Unit 3

A. 1. b. A plan deliberately made to change the way something is done.
    2. a. It is a simple process that can be described briefly.
    3. b. The principal said, "I think that you should be able to find about fifty preschoolers among the families in our school district."
    4. c. They should ask for ideas and discuss them after everyone has had an opportunity to contribute.
    5. c. The authority figure's (figures') official approval.

B. 1. a. Give out balloons naming an organizational meeting date.
        b. Send a truck around town with a billboard attached telling about program highlights or naming a meeting date. "Canned" music may be attached to truck.
        c. Show on TV selected scenes from a "family fun" session in a home.
        d. Have radio and TV interviews to let program participants themselves spread the word.
        e. Involve high school students in the program as part of preparent education courses in high school.
        f. Make "happy face" program button to distribute in local shopping center.
    2. In student's own words.   3. In student's own words.

SECTION 2 ANSWERS TO REVIEW QUESTIONS

Unit 4

A. Definitions are in student's own words (from text material).

    1. A home visitor is a person who goes to an assigned home to help parents become efficient teachers of their young child.
    2. Job description tells the general duties that are to be performed by the home visitor.
    3. Job performance tells what the home visitor actually does on the job to carry out specified objectives.
    4. A change agent is a person who is trained to identify, plan, and bring about needed change.
    5. Home visit tasks are the jobs that the home visitor must perform in meeting the needs of the child and his parents.

B. 1. Sponsoring agency tasks
    2. Home visit tasks
    3. Community-related tasks

Answers to Review Questions

C. In student's own words (from text material).
D. 1. Tasks to be performed
   2. Enabling skills to perform the tasks
   3. Educational requirements necessary to develop the enabling skills
   4. Experience needed to develop competence in performing the tasks
E. 1. b. Can do something special.
   2. c. Vary.
   3. c. Adult-oriented activities.
   4. b. Sizing up each situation for an informal give-and-take.
   5. d. Personality and past experiences of the home visitor.

Unit 5 ANSWERS TO REVIEW QUESTIONS

A. 1. e.   2. f.   3. d.   4. g.   5. a.   6. b.   7. c.
B. Responses are in student's own words.
   1. To provide a framework for decisions concerning direction of work, goals, and strategies.
   2. Name of activity, goals, background information, suggested learning activities, materials and resources, procedures, checks or evaluation techniques, leads (what next?), references, notes.
   3. Subtopics can be drawn from figure 5-8 or any other related sources.
   4. As approved by instructor.

Unit 6 ANSWERS TO REVIEW QUESTIONS

A. Definitions are in student's own words.
   1. A sponsor is the organization that employs the home visitor and to whom she is responsible.
   2. An organization is a human system that has an arranged way for people in the system to behave — in their thinking, feeling, and acting in the system. They can be identified with the system. They interact with each other. They carry out their tasks.
   3. The administrative process involves making decisions for the organization and seeing that goals are achieved.
   4. The line of authority tells who is responsible to whom in the organization.
B. Planning, organizing, staffing, directing, coordinating, reporting, and budgeting.
C. Preservice training takes place before the worker starts a job. In-service training takes place while the worker is doing the job.
D. Workers can improve their skills. Improved worker-skills help to improve the quality of work in the program. A person who studies and learns new skills may be able to go ahead to another job with more responsibility.
E. A response drawn from ideas gained in studying this unit.

Unit 7 ANSWERS TO REVIEW QUESTIONS

A. Definitions are in student's own words.
   1. A delivery system is a combination of parts
      - that are interrelated.
      - that contribute to a specific operation.
      - that produce information that "feeds back" to other parts of the system.
      - that produce continuous interaction between parts and thereby help to maintain the system.
   2. Inputs are what goes into a system.
   3. Outputs are observable behaviors that come out of a system.
   4. Feedback is knowledge of results that go back to the objectives of the system.

Answers to Review Questions

5. Evaluation means looking at something to see how good it is.
6. A mobile classroom is a specially designed classroom van, or remodeled bus, that travels to different areas for the purpose of holding demonstration classes for children and their parents.
7. A toy-lending library is a place where parents can learn how to use educational toys, games, and other materials — borrowing for home use what they learn how to use in the library.
8. Observation-participation means that the parent watches the home visitor teach a skill, then she practices the skill herself.
9. Dependence-independence means that parents work from a position of dependence on the home visitor toward independence in teaching their child themselves.
10. Before-assessment determines what the parent can already do before training begins.

B. 1. Any five of the below, or other appropriate ways are acceptable.

   Home visitors
   Mobile units
   Toy-lending libraries
   Parent cooperatives
   Pediatricians
   Community learning centers
   Child development centers

2. Family relationships and roles
   Family cultural and ethnic living patterns
   Family in relation to the community
   Family hopes and aspirations

3. Parents enter the program.
   General assessment is made.
   Rationale for desirable change is established.
   Objectives are set.
   Before-assessment is made.
   Observation and participation takes place.
   Parent works from state of dependence to independence.
   After-assessment is made.
   Evaluation takes place.
   Parent is recycled if more practice is needed.
   Parent exits if competent and confident in using skill.
   Parent reenters system to gain more skill.
   Cycle continues again.

4. In students own words based upon the content of this unit, or other appropriate sources.

5. In student's own words.

SECTION 3

Unit 8 ANSWERS TO REVIEW QUESTIONS

A. 1. All of the child rearing tasks performed by parents themselves, and needed services they obtain for their children.
2. A mature person who studies because he wants to learn.
3. The art and science of helping adults learn.
4. The science of teaching children.
5. Something that has no purpose beyond the activity itself.
6. A task which comes up at a certain point in a person's life and which he must master to achieve success with later tasks.
7. The result of developmental tasks careted by three conditions, as described by Havighurst.

293

Answers to Review Questions

      8. Something that occurs over and over again.
      9. That which occurs when something interferes with a person's development.
     10. A feeling that everything is all right.

B.   In student's own words (drawn from text material).

C.   In student's own words (drawn from text material).

Unit 9 ANSWERS TO REVIEW QUESTIONS

A.   Definitions in student's own words (from text material).

B.   1. Determining parent needs.
     2. Organizing situations for parent learning activities.
     3. Presenting appropriate opportunities for learning to the right person, in the right way and at the right time.
     4. Evaluating the learning experience.
     5. Reinforcing new parent behaviors.

C.   Any eight of the following ten are acceptable.

    1. Interview   6. Seminar
    2. Buzz groups   7. Simulation
    3. Brainstorming.   8. Role-playing
    4. Demonstration   9. Skits
    5. Discussion   10. Workshops

D.   In student's own words (from text material and personal preference given in a logical way).

E.   Any fifteen of the twenty-six learning media listed in the unit.

Unit 10 ANSWERS TO REVIEW QUESTIONS

A.   Definitions in student's own words (from text material).

B.   Specifically listed in introductory paragraphs.

C   1. In student's own words.
     2. Any or all of the following.
        a. The entire group comes together.
        b. Announcements and introductions can be made.
        c. Workshop procedures are described.
        d. Important information is given about the central theme or workshop purpose.
        e. Resource people or the staff can get the ball rolling.
        f. Questions can be answered to make sure that every one understands what is to take place.
     3. Individual responses according to student's experiences.
     4. Individual responses according to student's choice.

SECTION 4

Unit 11 ANSWERS TO REVIEW QUESTIONS

A.   Definitions in student's own words (from text material and other reading from which student may wish to cite).

B.   1. Development theory: learning occurs because growth takes place.
     2. Reinforcement theory: people of all ages respond to rewards and punishment.
     3. Association theory: people — and animals — respond automatically to certain kinds of stimuli.
     4. Cognitive theory: the individual uses his present mental ability and knowledge in learning new concepts.

C.   In student's own words (from textbook material and personal preference).

Answers to Review Questions

Unit 12 ANSWERS TO REVIEW QUESTIONS

A. 1. Infant: child from birth until the time that he begins to walk.
    2. Personality: qualities that make a person unique with characteristics of his own.
    3. Enabler: what a parent does that meets the child's needs.

B. Responses are specifically listed in text material.

C. 1. To feel safe and secure in his world.
    2. To have protection and a safe environment to live and grow in.
    3. To feel loved and wanted.
    4. To have his physical needs met.
    5. To learn about the world around him.

D. In student's own words (from text material or other self-selected source).

Unit 13 ANSWERS TO REVIEW QUESTIONS

A. Toddler: the period that extends from the time a child begins to walk until he approaches the age of three. Walking is most common from thirteen to fifteen months.

B. Responses are specifically listed in text material.

C. In student's own words (from text material or other self-selected sources).

D. (In student's own words)
    - He is loved, held, and given signs of approval.
    - He is praised, comforted, and shown that he is appreciated.
    - He is accepted as he is.
    - He is fed, clothed, and shown that he is loved and wanted.

E. In student's own words. Some responses are given.

F. In student's own words (from text material or other self-selected sources).

Unit 14 ANSWERS TO REVIEW QUESTIONS

A. 1. Child from the time he walks until formal schooling begins.
    2. Being able to stand on one's own feet
    3. Good coordination of large muscles
    4. What the child thinks about his body and what it can do for him
    5. The ability to move one's body from place to place
    6. The ability to move one's body while it stays in one place
    7. Body movements that relate to an object
    8. Use of one hand in preference to the other
    9. Order by size (smallest to largest) or some other quality
    10. Use of stories that highlight a character's problems and the way the person copes with them

B. Any five of the seven listed are acceptable as correct answers.

    1. Show an interest in him and what he does.
    2. Accept him as he is.
    3. Help him to do things without being pressured.
    4. Let him learn by trial and error.
    5. Permit him to make some of the decisions that affect him.
    6. Help him to find out about alternatives (choices).
    7. Be understanding when he must face consequences of his own actions.

C. Crawl, walk, climb, run, hop, skip, slide, leap, jump, gallop.

D. Push, pull, bend, twist, swing, turn, stretch, shake, bounce, reach.

Answers to Review Questions

E. Hit, throw, catch, kick.
F. Response in student's own words (from text material).
G. Response in student's own words (from text material).

SECTION 5

Unit 15 ANSWERS TO REVIEW QUESTIONS

A. 1. Firsthand experiences are direct contacts which the child has with objects, things, and events that he can see in his everyday life.
   2. Learning episode means a bit of learning which is complete in itself. It may stand alone, or it may be related to other learning episodes centered around a like-theme.

B. 1. What growth characteristics do children show at this stage of development? (2) What kinds of social behavior does a child of this age normally display? (3) What developmental tasks are set for children who are in this stage of their development? (4) What activities and learning experiences can help children meet success with their tasks to enable the next stage of growth? (5) How can the child's learning experiences be evaluated?

C. 1. discriminate learning: parent points out the differences between things.
   2. classification: objects or ideas are grouped according to the ways that they are alike.
   3. definition: parent tells what the word means in terms that already have meaning for the child.
   4. context: parents point out the meaning of an unfamiliar word by calling attention to how it is used.

D. In student's own words (from text material).

E. In student's own words (from text material).

Unit 16 ANSWERS TO REVIEW QUESTIONS

A. 1. All of the organized experiences which a parent provides to help the child learn at home.
   2. Those thought-through opportunities for learning which a parent can plan ahead or seize on-the-spot.
   3. The child's view of himself as a person.
   4. The regard the child has of himself as a person
   5. Knowledge the child has about who he is, what he is, and where he fits into the world of people.
   6. The difference between what a child can do and what he should be able to do.
   7. Symbol for a number.

B. 1. Identify goals and objectives based on child's level of understanding and need.
   2. Select methods by which goals and objectives can be met.
   3. Locate learning media which increase the probability that desired change in behavior takes place.

C. The child, the child's group, and specialists.

D. 1. The area is defined and described.
   2. Major objectives for the area are identified.
   3. Appropriate learning activities are listed and described briefly.

E. In student's own words (selected from text material).

Unit 17 ANSWERS TO REVIEW QUESTIONS

A. One or more skills as indicated.

   1. Matching like-with-like; seeing differences and similarities.
   2. Seeing similarities and differences, comparing, making judgments, grouping (any of these).
   3. Placing things according to some order (size, etc.); making judgments.
   4. Seeing relationships between things; putting things in their group; forming judgments; developing the ability to categorize.

Answers to Review Questions

   5. Put together-take away; learning to count objects; taking away a part from a whole, putting together like parts.
B. Specifically stated in text material.
C. Responses will vary according to student's own viewpoint.

SECTION 6

Unit 18 ANSWERS TO REVIEW QUESTIONS

A. In student's own words.
   1. Someone the child imitates to shape his own behavior.
   2. One of the many approaches for teaching children between the ages of three and eight.
   3. A program which highlights activities which are self-rewarding and help the child develop a skill, learn a concept, or/and acquire an attitude that can be useful in doing some other task.
   4. A model designed to teach cognitive or thinking skills for children in preschool through third grade.
   5. A model based on the belief that education must start early and in the home. Parent educators work with parents in the home.
   6. Learning activities are self-rewarding and need no external reward or punishment.
   7. Concrete experience with real things and places.
   8. Child can recall an object mentally when he can see only part of it or some part is missing.
   9. Child can use pictures and dramatic play in place of real objects.
   10. The child uses words and numerals with meaning.
   11. Skills and concepts from different subjects are taught in the same activity.
B. In student's own words (from text material).
C. 1. Who are the sponsors of the program?
   2. What are the goals?
   3. What are the tasks of children?
   4. What is the role of parents?
   5. What background and training is required of those who work in the program?
   6. What resources does the model require?
   7. How is the model evaluated?
   8. How can the model be adapted to home-based programs?
D. In student's own words (response selected from text material and the student's personal preference).

Unit 19 ANSWERS TO REVIEW QUESTIONS

A. 1. Involve teachers in the early planning of the program: list teacher tasks; list teacher-tasks parents can do; list things parents can be taught to do in the center and at home; examine the adult education role of the early childhood teacher.
   2. Put ideas and tasks in writing: how parents are to be helped, who is in charge, how parents are to be involved in their own training, resources and services to be used, linking home and school, record keeping, evaluation of the entire program.
   3. Set up a means by which parents can be recruited.
   4. Decide the tasks and events to be set in motion. Providing parents with information: goals, school philosophy, characteristics of children in center age-group, developmental needs of children, learning objectives set for group, modeling for teachers, parent imitation and practice, evaluation.
   Caution: Parents must know limits set for children. They must remember to respect and keep in confidence what they see at the center.
B. They can look and see. They can learn by discussion. They can learn by doing. They can learn when they share their experiences with other parents and learn from them, too. They can learn by practicing their new skills at home.
C. In student's own words (from text material or their observations in centers).

Answers to Review Questions

D. In student's own words (from text material, observations in centers, interviews with parents or readings done in other texts.)

SECTION 7

Unit 20

A. In student's own words (from text material or other related sources).
B. In student's own words (from text material or other related sources).
C. In student's own words:
   1. Beginning: the couple is married; adjustments are made in the new life; plans are made for the future; the couple is childless.
   2. Expanding: childbirth and child rearing take place; the family grows larger.
   3. Launching: children start to leave home and are on their own, the family starts to get smaller.
   4. Contracted (the "empty-nest"): young adults in the family are on their own; the couple is once again "childless."
D. In student's own words (logical responses are acceptable).
E. In student's own words (individual responses according to the student's own views).

Unit 21

A. In student's own words (from text material).
   1. Promotes good relationships between family members.
   2. Develops sense of security and achievement.
   3. Accepts members as worthy and helps develop talents.
   4. Makes learning easier through real life situations.
   5. Builds a base for living in a democratic society.
   6. Emphasizes national and international responsibility.
   7. Promotes wise use of human and natural resources.
B. In student's own words (from text material).
C. In student's own words (suggestions are specifically stated in text material. Any other ideas are acceptable, if they are relevant.)

SECTION 8

Unit 22

A. In student's own words (from text material).
B. Specifically stated in text.
C. 1. Administrative records are those kept by persons responsible for operating the program.
   2. Family records contain needed data about the family.
   3. Target child records list facts and figures which chart the child's growth and development in all areas.
   4. Home visitor records contain child and family data, time and expense reports, agency referrals, plans and results, diary of work tasks, anecdotal records of the child, self-evaluation of the home visitor's work.
D. In student's own words (individual response drawn from student's own ideas or items in this unit).

Unit 23

A. 1. *Evaluation* is the process of assessing the degree to which objectives are met.
   2. *Measurement* is an observable description of behavior, objects, or events which can be expressed in numbers.
   3. *Pretest* is a means of measurement before treatment.

Answers to Review Questions

   4. *Delayed effects* are program outcomes that do not show up until some other point in time.
   5. *Formative evaluation* helps to form a program as it is being developed.
   6. *Summative evaluation* sums up everything for a final report.
   7. *Posttest* is a means of measurement after treatment.
B. In student's own words (drawn from text material and own ideas).
C. 1. Identify the goals of the program.
   2. Define the objectives in behavioral terms.
   3. Choose or make tools for measuring (or describing) the behaviors.
   4. Carry out the treatment.
   5. Apply the tools of measurement.
   6. Interpret the results.
D. In student's own words (drawn from text material).

ACKNOWLEDGMENTS

The author believes that many people are concerned with helping parents to become effective teachers of their own children and, therefore, are willing to provide information and assistance. The following, listed at random, lend support to this belief by their contributions for which the author expresses gratitude.

- Lane County Head Start, Eugene, Oregon: Marcia Hansen, Director, who granted permission to photograph center-related activities and shared material used in figures 19-1 and 22-3. Christine Puetz and Louise Lopez, Head Start teachers, who shared their field experiences. Parents and children who appear in textbook photographs.

- Miriam G. Ricks, Director of the Early Childhood Library Specialist Program, North Carolina Central University at Durham, who shared materials and permitted the author to photograph activities in the resource center.

- Beverly Evans, Head Teacher, North Carolina Central University Nursery-Kindergarten who provided opportunities for the author's students to share workplans with NCCU preschoolers and obtained parental permission for children to be photographed.

- Beverly Bozeman, Director, Colonial Preschool and Kindergarten (Chapel Hill, N.C.) who gave permission to photograph children and obtained parental consent for the use of the pictures.

- William L. Mills, PhD, Associate Professor of Biology at North Carolina Central University who took time to provide preschoolers with an exciting experience in a biology lab, and enabled photographs which appear in the text.

- Janice Christensen, Home Economics Editor, North Carolina State University at Raleigh, who provided photographs from the University Department of Visual Aids, and the agricultural extension agents who appear in some of the pictures.

- James E. Jeffries, Director of Creative Services, Ross Laboratories (Columbus, Ohio) who provided photographs for unit 12.

- Johnnie Jones, III, Extension Agent, Durham County (N.C.) Extension Service, who presented the workshop on terrarium building for the benefit of the author and her students.

- Anthony F. Jenzano, Director of the Morehead Planetarium (University of North Carolina at Chapel Hill), who provided all of the planetarium photographs which appear in the text and permitted the reprint of a program guide.

- Robert J. Senior, M.D., FAAP (partner, Drs. Senior, Shaeffer, Conley, and Christian) who shared professional materials and permitted a brochure to appear as figure 7-3.

- Rosalie Saul, Director, Project S.T.E.P. (Seniors Tutor for Educational Progress), Redding Schools, Redding, Connecticut, who made possible the use of the project photograph appearing as figure 8-4.

- Community Planning Services of Durham, N.C., who permitted an abstract of their material to be used as figure 2-1.

- Alvadee Adams, former editor of *U.S. Lady,* who gave permission to reprint abstracts from the author's writings published by *U.S. Lady.*

Acknowledgments

- David Zeltzer who gave assistance that went beyond photographic work.

The author expresses her gratitude to her students, past and present, who have contributed either directly or indirectly. Their reactions to concepts presented help to orient the text toward the world of the learner.

A special word of thanks is due those who graciously took time to read the manuscript: Dr. Edgar J. Boone, past-President of the Adult Education Association of the United States and Head of the Department of Adult and Community College Education, North Carolina State University at Raleigh, and Dr. Mary Hardin, Child Development Specialist, North Carolina Central University at Durham.

The author recognizes that some of the adult education concepts discussed in this text are gleaned from her recent doctoral studies. She expresses her appreciation to the Department of Adult and Community College Education, North Carolina State University at Raleigh and to those with whom she worked.

She is in debt also to her children who see as fond memories of their own childhood many of the ideas and activities described. The cooperation of other children and parents who gave permission to use photographs of their children is appreciated.

Finally, and most important, the author acknowledges the assistance provided by her husband, who photographed many of the learning activities provided for their own six children, made the final flow-chart drawings, read the manuscript every word of the way, gave and continues to give encouragement, love, and support in all endeavors.

PHOTOGRAPH CREDITS

David Zeltzer: figures 1-4, 1-5, 4-1, 4-2, 4-3, 4-4, 4-5, 4-6, 4-7, 4-8, 4-9, 4-10, 4-11, 4-12, 4-13, 4-15, 4-16, 4-17, 4-18, 4-19, 7-2, 7-4, 7-6, 7-7, 7-8, 7-9, 7-11, 11-2, 14-5, 14-6, 14-8, 16-2, 16-4, 16-13, 18-6, 18-7, 21-4, 23-3, 23-5.

Martin F. Massoglia: figures 1-3, 1-9, 3-4, 5-1, 11-1, 11-3, 11-5, 11-7, 11-8, 11-9, 11-10, 16-1, 18-5, 19-6, 20-3, 20-4, 20-7, 20-8, 21-3, 23-6.

Department of Visual Aids, North Carolina State University at Raleigh: figures 5-2, 6-5, 7-10, 8-1, 8-2, 8-3, 8-5, 13-1, 13-2, 13-3, 13-4, 13-5, 13-6, 14-1, 20-2, 20-6, 23-7.

Alvin D. Lester: figures 2-6, 2-7, 2-8, 5-3, 5-6, 10-5, 10-6, 11-6, 13-11, 14-2, 14-3, 14-4, 16-11, 16-12, 18-3, 19-3, 19-5, 20-1.

Elinor T. Massoglia: figures 16-3, 16-7, 17-3, 17-5, 17-9, 17-12, 18-1, 18-2, 18-4, 19-2, 19-4, 21-6.

U.S. Army Photos: figures 1-7, 21-1, 21-5, 21-7, 21-8, 22-7.

Ross Laboratories, Columbus, Ohio for photographs from *The Phenomena of Early Development:* figures 12-1, 12-2, 12-3, 12-4, 12-7, 12-8, 12-9, 12-10.

Morehead Planetarium, University of North Carolina at Chapel Hill:
Morehead Planetarium staff photographs: figures 15-8, 15-11, 15-12, 15-13.
University of North Carolina Photo Lab: figure 15-10.
R.R. Russell, Jr.: figure 15-9.

Larry Lee: figures 9-8, 9-9, 9-10.

Acknowledgments

Project S.T.E.P. (Seniors Tutor for Educational Progress), Redding Schools, Redding, Connecticut: figure 8-4.

DELMAR STAFF

Director of Publications — Alan N. Knofla
Consultant — Jeanne Machado
Source Editor — Elinor Gunnerson
Copy Editor — Angela LaGatta
Director of Manufacturing and Production — Frederick Sharer
Illustrators — Tanya Harrell, Tony Canabush, George Dowse
Production Specialists — Patti Manuli, Margaret Mutka, Debbie Monty, Sharon Lynch Jean LeMorta, Betty Michelfelder, Lee St. Onge

Materials used in the text have been classroom tested by Dr. Massoglia with her students at North Carolina Central University.

INDEX

A

Accomplishment, stage of, 86
Acting, as communication, 60
Administration, records of, 256-257
Administrators, 56
Agricultural Extension. *See* Cooperative Extension Service
Andragogy, 81
Approval, parental, 220
Art, in home-based programs, 190-191
Assessment. *See also* Evaluation
 of home-based program, 73
Association theory of learning, 116-117
Auditory discrimination, of preschool child, 155-156
Authority, line of, 57
Authority figure, 26
Autonomy
 sense of, 153
 stage of, 86
Autotelic discovery approach, in responsive model program, 211

B

Baby and Child (Spock), 2
Bank Street model program
 materials for, 212-213
 parental involvement in, 213
Basic-4 food plan, 91
 parent skills and, 92
Behavior
 influence of child's needs on, 118
 observable, 67-68
 undesirable, means of stopping, 225
Behavioral change, 91
Behavioral objectives, preconceived, 5
Between Parent and Child (Ginott), 2
Bibliotherapy, 159
Body image, 154
Brainstorming, 25, 96
Budgeting
 considerations in, 62
 definition, 61-62
Business department, role in child-development programs, 15
Busywork, 82
Buzz group, 95-96

C

Career development, for home visitor, 32
Chamber of Commerce, 9
Change
 effect on family, 240
 preparation for, 41
Change agent, 41
 role of, 36
Child, first, special considerations, 236
Child-adult interactions, 224-225

Child care centers
 programs for parents
  dealing with child behaviors, 225
  determining learning needs, 224
  exchanging ideas, 225
  finding needed services, 225
  interacting with child, 224-225
  preparing and serving food, 223-224
 role in parent training, 220
 tasks to be accomplished by, 222-223
Child development
 activities for, 128-137
  comforting and cuddling, 137
  listening, 136-137
  mobiles, 128-130, 134-136
  reaching, 137
  touching and tasting, 137
 areas of, 118
 definition of, 115
 emotional growth, 122-123
 factors affecting, 118-119, 121
 genetic factors in, 132
 mental growth, 122
 physical growth, 121-122
 sequence in, 118
 social growth, 123
Child development centers, 71
Child rearing, definition, 233
Child socialization, definition, 233
Childbearing, definition, 233
Childhood, early
 definition, 3
 educational concerns of, 4
Classes in the Kitchen, 14
Classification, 165, 195-196, 214
Cognitive curriculum model
 ability levels in, 213-214
 cognitive skills in, 214
 components of, 213
Cognitive map, 121, 163
Cognitive theory of learning, 117
College
 role in home-based education programs, 13-15
 weekend, 14
Communication
 flowchart for, 59
 major processes in, 58, 60-61
 role of director, 61
 staff for, 61
 steps in, 58
Communication lines, for home visitor, 43
Community
 elements of, 23
 identification of, 23
 problems in, 22

303

Index

Community (continued)
　questions about, 23
　resource file, 77
　resources, use of, 75
Community Planning Services, 9
Competence, parents' level of, 1
Concepts
　examples of, 165-166
　related to child development, 163-165
Confidentiality, of home visitor, 43
Context, 166
Cooperation, of young children in family, 239
Cooperative Extension Service, 16
　programs of, 76
Coordinator
　and resource persons, 106
　of workshop, 105
Coorespondence, one-to-one, 156
Critical periods, and home visitor, 86-87
Cultural baggage, modifying, 42
Culture
　components of, 42
　definition of, 41
Curriculum
　areas of concern, 180-191
　　art, 190-191
　　health, 190
　　language development, 182-187
　　mathematics, 187-188
　　music, 188-189
　　play, 189
　　safety, 190
　　self-concept, 180-182
　definition of, 179
　for home-based programs, 179-180

D

DARCEE. *See* Demonstration and Research Center for Early Education
Definition, in learning, 165-166
Delivery system
　feedback loop in, 67
　options
　　child development centers, 71
　　community learning centers, 70-71
　　home visit, 68
　　mobile units, 68-69
　　parent cooperatives, 69
　　pediatrician-sponsored groups, 69-70
　　toy-lending libraries, 69
　primary agent of, 68
　results of, 67
Demonstration activity, 96-97
Demonstration and Research Center for Early Education (DARCEE), 36
Dependence-independence roles, 36
Development
　definition of, 116

　different views of, 119-121
　nature view of, 119
　nurture view of, 120
　of preschool child, 154-161
　　activities and aids for, 159-161
　stages of, 86-89
Developmental tasks, of young children, 227
Developmental theory of learning, 116
Dewey, John, 3
Diet
　for newborns, 4
　for young children, 4
Director, responsibilities of, 58
Discussion, as teaching technique, 97
Dyad, in buzz group, 95-96

E

Early childhood. *See* Childhood, early
Early childhood education program models
　Bank Street, 212-213
　cognitive curriculum, 213-214
　eclectic, 215-217
　Florida parent-educator, 214-215
　responsive, 211-212
　Tucson early education, 215
Easter, activities for, 252-253
Eclectic model, components of, 216-217
Economics department, and child-development programs, 15
Education
　as component of home education programs, 13-16
　　aim of, 13
　　competencies of, 13
　　Cooperative Extension Service, 16
　　Department of Education, 16
　　libraries, 15-16
　　universities and colleges, 13-15
　definition, 12
　early childhood concerns of, 3-4
　formal, 13
　home-based, 3
　importance of parents in, 4
　informal, 12
Education, department of, and child-development programs, 14, 16
Education Research Information Center (ERIC), 28
Emotional development, of preschool child, 157-158
Empty nest, 237-238
Enabler, parent as, 128, 131-132, 135-136
ERIC. *See* Education Research Information Center
Erickson, Erik K., 86
Evaluation
　as basis for public relations, 265
　definition, 264
　of delayed effects, 274
　drawbacks of, 265-266
　of home-based program, 74, 268-272, 274

304

of home visitor's progress, 272-274
  kinds of,
    formative, 266-267
    summative, 267-268
  as means of assessing objectives, 265
  as means of examining beliefs of program, 264-265
  as morale booster, 265
  as progress check, 264
  reasons for use of, 264
  of social action programs, 27
  as source of information, 264
  steps in, 266
  team approach to, 274
Experience sharing, as learning activity, 223
Experiences, organized, definition of, 179

F

Family
  adult-oriented, 237
  anticipation of new child, 236
  changes as children leave, 237-238
  child-centered, 237
  contributions to child, 234-235
    cares for and trains child, 234
    develops self-concept, self-esteem, and identity, 235
    develops sexual concepts, 235
    establishes value system, 234-235
    gives child ties, 234
    gives good example, 234
    introduces child to society, 234
    provides intimate group for child, 234
    regulates child's behavior, 234
  cultural and ethnic patterns of, 73
  definition of, 233
  discovering needs of, 71-72
  discussion topics for, 240
  forces affecting, 240
  future plans, 73
  goals of, 235-236
  leadership role in, 71
  life cycle of, 235-238
  meeting needs of, 72, 73-74
  one-parent, 233
  records of, 257
  relationship to community, 73
  relationships, 71
  role of, 233
  significance of, 233-235
  value system of, 41
Family development
  play way to, 243
  tasks in, 244-245
Family development, learning activities for, 245-252
  airplane race, 250
  airport, 250
  balloon experiment, 245-246
  Box the Card, 250
  clothespin bowling, 250
  Daisy, Goldenrod, Clover, 251
  fun in family car, 250
  gas station, 250
  High Skydive, 249
  hike, 245
  holiday specials, 251-252
  Keep Your Beans Dry, 249
  kite contest, 245
  license colors, 250-251
  license numbers, 250
  Muffin Tin Toss, 249
  music makers, 251
  nature hikes, 246
  neighborhood cheering squad, 247
  pay for gas, 251
  picnic, 249
  puppets, 251
  Red Car Mine, 250
  social services, 247-248
  state fair, 247
  stories and books, 248
  swim contest, 247
  Tie Me Quickly, 250
  wash day, 250
Feedback, 6, 14. *See also* Reinforcement
  in child's behavior, 234
  in communication system, 59
  in delivery systems, 67-68
  in responsive model program, 212
Firsthand experiences
  classification of, 165
  context, 166
  definition of, 165-166
  discriminate learning in, 165
  examples of, 166-169
  follow-up activities, 174-176
  study trip to planetarium, 172-174
Florida parent-educator model, 214-215
Food, preparing and serving, 223-224
Forum techniques, 98-99
4-H Clubs, 16

G

Gain, in evaluation, 266
Ginott, Haim, 2
Givens, set of, 119
Grouping, 196
Growth
  characteristics of, 163
  definition of, 115
  intellectual, 3
  language, 3
Growth, child
  emotional, 3, 122-123
  mental, 122

Index

Growth, child (continued)
    physical, 3, 121-122
    social, 3, 123
Growth, toddlers
    emotional, 148
    intellectual, 146-147
    physical, 145-146
    social, 147-148
Growth and Progress File, 260

H

Halloween, activities for, 252
Hamburger stew, 252
Handedness, 155
Head Start programs, 2
Health, in home-based programs, 190
Health care
    agencies, 18
    aim of, 16
    community sources of funds and services for, 17
    goals of, 16-18
Heritage, cultural, teaching about, 5, 15
HEW. *See* U.S. Department of Health, Education and Welfare
Home
    adult-centered, 237
    child-centered, 237
    family-centered, 237
    as learning environment, 1
Home-based programs
    aim of, 243
    components of
        education, 13-16
        health, 16-18
        parent involvement, 19
        resources, 9-12
        social services, 18-19
    educational competencies of, 13
    evaluation of, 268-274
        data sources, 270-272
        delayed effects, 274
        education component, 268
        emotional growth, 268
        health component, 270
        intellectual growth, 268
        language growth, 270
        physical growth, 268-269
        social services, 270
    location of, 9
    situation of, 9
Home Economics department, and child-development programs, 14
Home Start program, 2-3, 9
    goal of, 2
    growth areas of, 3
Home Start Training Centers (HSTC)
    goal of, 27
    utilizing resources of, 27-28
Home visitor
    as adult learner, 87
    aim of, 42
    areas served by, 43
    basic questions for, 42
    career development for, 32
    as catalyst, 38
    as change agent, 36
    critical periods and, 86-87
    definition of, 31
    evaluation of
        agency tasks, 272
        checklist for, 273
        community-related tasks, 272
        home visit tasks, 272
        job performance, 272-274
        program, 274
    expected competencies of, 37
    goal of, 31
    involvement in parental learning, 223
    job description of, 63-64
        agency tasks, 32-33
        community-related tasks, 34
        home visit tasks, 33
    job performance of, 34-36
    as parent educator, 90
    personal characteristics of, 37-38
    persons involved with, 43
    preservice training of, 37
    problems of, 36-37
    processes employed by, 42-43
    purpose of, 42
    qualifications, 32
    record keeping, 258-260
        team approach to, 260
    requirements for success, 64
    resources of, 43
    tasks of, 75-78, 164-165
        educational, 75
        health, 76
        in home-based programs, 78
        social service, 77
    training of, 37
    use of library, 35-36
    workplan example, 52-54
HSTC. *See* Home Start Training Centers

I

Identity
    of child, 180
    development of, 235
    stage of, 86
Identity crisis, definition, 86
Imitation, 120
Incoming impression, as part of communication system, 60

Independence, promoted by parent, 210
Index level, 213
Individual differences, 43-44, 193
Individual study
   for parents, 93
   sample activity, 94
Infant
   birth to six months, 126-132
      characteristics of, 127-128
      needs and parent enablers, 128, 131-132
   definition of, 126
   six to twleve months, 132-136
      characteristics of, 132-133
      needs and parent enablers, 133, 135-136
Initiative, stage of, 86
Input, in language development, 182
In-service training, 57
Instructional objectives, 193-194
Integrity, stage of, 87
Intellectual growth, promoted by parent, 209-210
Interaction, as part of communication system, 60
Interest centers, 214
Intervention, definition of, 41
Interview, 95
Intimacy, stage of, 86

J

Jealousy, in preschool child, 157

K

Knowles, Malcolm, 81
KOR. *See* Results, knowledge of

L

Language
   expressive, 224
   incoming-outgoing, 224
Language development
   definition of, 182
   input, 182
   learning activities for, 183-187
      alphabet cards, 186
      alphabetical order, 186
      poems, rhymes, and jingles, 185
      puppets, 183
      stories, 183
      telephone use, 183-184
      typewriters, 184-185
      using words and letters, 185-187
   objectives of, 182-183
   output, 182
   of preschool child, 156-157
Leadership role, of parents, 81
Learner
   adult, 81, 85-87
      career of, 86
      critical periods of, 86-87
      developmental tasks of, 85
      family situation of, 86
      home visitor as, 87
      marital status of, 85
      values of, 85
   definition of, 81
Learning
   climate for, 5-6
   definition of, 4, 116
   environment for, 117
   experience centered, 6
   feedback in, 6
   principles of, 6
   problem centered, 6
   random experiential, 12
   rote, 117
   theories of
      association, 116-117
      cognitive, 117
      developmental, 116
      reinforcement, 116
Learning, adult
   creating situations for, 90
   principles of
      ability to learn, 83-84
      experience, 81-82
      impatience, 82
      independence, 82-83
      maturity, 83
      motivation, 82
      sensitivity, 83
   role of senior citizens, 84-85
Learning activities. *See also* Language development; Self-concept, development of; Family development, learning activities for; Child care centers, programs for parents
   classifying, 195-196
   grouping and regrouping, 196
   identifying favorable outcomes of, 229-230
   making play dough, 228-230
   matching, 194
   in mathematics, 188
   in music, 188-189
   providing storage space for, 230-231
   in science, 187
   sequencing, 195
   sets, 194-195
   things to make and do, 196-206
      animals, 196
      beach bag, 197
      bell cutouts, 197
      bleach bottle Santa Clause, 197-198
      blue, blue, 198
      bottle cap bracelet, 198
      bubble, bubble, 198
      button faces, 198-199
      calendar game, 199
      catalog caper, 199

Index

Learning activities (continued)
   things to make and do (continued)
      dot pictures, 199
      feel my name, 200
      food fun, 200
      get-well card, 200-201
      growing up, 201
      hand and footprints, 200
      magic garden, 201-202
      paper lantern, 201
      party basket, 202
      people, animals and things, 202
      pie-plate faces, 203
      play Santa Clause, 203
      shirt art, 203
      star shape, 203-204
      star-shaped Santa, 204
      star-show peep box, 204
      supermarket shopper, 204-205
      what can you do there, 205-206
      whirl-the-button, 206
Learning centers, community, 70-71
Learning episode
   examples of, 166-171
   results of, 69
Learning experiences
   classification, 165
   context, 166
   definition, 165-166
   discriminate learning, 165
   guide to selecting, 164-165
   helping at home, 170
   related to growth characteristics, 163
   vocabulary list, 170-171
Learning needs, involving parent in determining, 224
Lecture, 98
Library
   as resource of home visitor, 35-36
   toy-lending, 69
License to act, 26
Locomotion, 154
Locomotor movements, 154
Look-and-see method, of parent learning, 223

M

Male-female roles, understanding of, 230-235
Materials Curriculum Center, 15-16
Mathematics
   for home-based programs, 187-189
      activities for, 188
      objectives of, 187-188
Maturation, definition of, 115-116
Measurement
   definition, 264
   use of, in evaluation, 266
Media
   for learning, 101-102
   mass, 101
Medicine, preventive, 69
Mobile, of family, 169
Mobile units
   for delivery of services, 68-69
   TV correlation with, 69
Mobiles, 128-130, 134-136
Model
   definition of, 209
   home and family, 234
Model, parent. *See* Parent model
Model, program. *See* Program model
Modeling
   tasks in, 227-231
      areas of learning, 227
      child's characteristics and interests, 227
      child's developmental tasks, 227
      means of accomplishing child's tasks, 227-228
      transferring experience to home, 230-231
      use of senses in learning experience, 228
Moderator
   group, 93
   of panel, 98
Mothering, activities of, 144
Mothering concept, 120
Mothers, expectant, care for, 4
Motivation, of adult learner, 82
Motor skills, checklist of, 258
Muscle control, gross, of preschool child, 154
Music
   for home-based programs, 187-189
      activities, 188-189
      objectives of, 188

N

Needs
   definition, 1, 179
   felt, 2
   of infants, 128, 131-133
Newsletter, as learning aid for parents, 226
Nonlocomotor movements, 154

O

Object level, 213
Objectives, instructional, 266
OCD. *See* U.S. Office of Child Development
One-to-one correspondence, workplan for activities in, 194
Orchestration, 215
Organization
   administrative process of, 56
   definition of, 56
   POSDCORB, 57-62
Organizer, child as, 117
Output, 67
   in language development, 182
Outgoing expression, as part of communication system, 60

P

Panel techniques, 98
Parent cooperatives, 69
Parent education
 as cyclic process, 93
 developing parenting skills, 92
 devices of, 91
 instructional methods, 93-100
 method of, 90
 techniques in, 90
 topics for, 100
Parent-educator, 90-91, 98-99, 214
 considerations of, 90-91
 definition of, 90
 skills for large-group activities, 99
 skills for small-group activities, 98
Parent enablers, for preschool child, 158-159
Parent involvement program
 learning aids for parents in, 225-226
 means of contacting parents, 222
 providing storage for learning toys, 230-231
 questionnaire for, 221
 recruitment for, 222-223
 requirements of, 220
 tasks to be accomplished in, 222-223
 teacher participation in, 220-222
Parent model
 promoting independence, 210
 promoting intellectual growth, 209-210
 promoting self-concept, 210
Parent recruitment
 for child education programs, 222-223
 means of initiating, 222
Parent-teacher
 problem solving, 5
 role of, 5-6
Parenting
 description of, 80
 stage of, 86
 as team effort, 80-81
Parents
 as adult learner, 244
 as child development specialists, 2-3
 competence level of, 1
 education skills of, 74-75
 as enablers, 2, 128, 131-133
  for toddlers, 144-148
 gathering information about, 25
 health skills of, 75-76
 involvement in child care centers, 223-225
 involvement in early education, 77
 involvement in home-based programs, 19
 leadership role of, 81
 learning activities of, 223-226
 learning aids for, 225-226
 natural, 1
 preparental education for, 4, 90
 as program builders, 5
 skill development of, 19
 skills for home-based programs, 77-78
 social service skills of, 77
 surrogate, 1
 training programs for, 72-74, 222-223
 without partners, 52
Pedagogy, 81
Pediatrician-sponsored groups role in home-based programs, 69-70
 sample program, 70
Perceiving, as part of communication system, 60
Personality, definition, 127
Physical examination, 76
Piaget, Jean, and ability levels, 213-214
Piggybacking, 25
Pirating, 226
Planetarium, parent-child study trip to, 172-176
Planning
 decisions involved in, 41
 definition of, 41
 in learning process, 220
 long-view, 43-44
 participants in, 57
Play, in home-based programs, 189
Play activities, 148-149
Play dough
 lesson for using, 228-230
 recipe for, 229
Play materials, 149-150
POSDCORB
 budgeting, 61-62
 coordinating, 58
 directing, 58
 organizing, 56
 planning, 56
 reporting, 58-61
 staffing, 57-58
Posttest, 266
Practice, 14
Prenatal growth, 118
Prenatal period, factors affecting, 118-119
Preschool age, 152
Preschool child
 autonomy of, 153
 behavior of, 152-153
 characteristics of, 153
 coordination of, 152
 definition of, 152
 emotional development of, 157-159
 intellectual development of, 155-157
 personal-social development of, 157
 physical development of, 154-155
 toilet needs of, 152
Preservice training, 57
Pretest, 266

Index

Privacy, invasion of, 62
Program assistant, 215
Program model
   childrens' tasks in, 211
   definition, 209
   in early childhood education, 211-217
   evaluation of, 211
   goals of, 211
   parents' role in, 211
   resources of, 211
   sponsors of, 211
Programs, definition of, 3
Project STEP. *See* Seniors Tutor for Educational Progress
Psychology, definition of, 14
Psychology department, role in child-development programs, 14

Q

Questions, natural, 176

R

Record keeping
   family medical history, 261-262
   Growth and Progress File, 260
   for home-based program, 256
   by parents, 260-263
   planning for, 255-256
   team approach to, 260
Records
   administrative, 256-257
   anecdotal, 258
   checklists, 258
   confidentiality of, 256
   cumulative, 257, 259
   developing, vertical planning for, 256
   essential, 256
   family, 257
   home visitor, 258-259
   information provided by, 255
   interpretation of, 256
   questions about, 255
   target child, 257-258
Referrals, 33
Reinforcement
   in behavior training, 225, 234
   positive, 6
   theory of learning, 116
Relationships
   cause-effect, 156
   one-to-one, 5
Resource persons, for workshops, 106
Resources
   community, 11, 34, 75
      agencies, 18
      cautions about, 19
      funds and services, 17
   educational, 11, 100-101
      established institutions, 100
      informal institutions, 100
      mass media, 101
      social organizations, 100
      voluntary organizations, 100
   file, 77
   filing, 9-10, 12
   human, 23
   library, 35-36
   locating, 9
   man-made, 23
   natural, 23
   utilized by home visitor, 43
   workplan file
      construction of, 44-47
      preparing workplans, 47-52
      workplans in action, 52-54
Responsive model program
   autotelic discovery approach in, 211
   components of, 212
Results, knowledge of (KOR), 67-68
Role-playing, 97-98, 120, 235
   in development of male-female concepts, 235
Rote learning, 117

S

Safety, in home-based programs, 190
Safety checklist, 76
St. Patrick's Day, activities for, 251-252
St. Valentine's Day, activities for, 252-253
Science
   for home-based programs, 187-189
      activities for, 187
      objectives of, 187
Self-concept, promoted by parent, 210
Self-concept, development of, 6, 234, 235
   learning activities for
      Body Image Game, 181
      Book About (Johnny), 181
      (Johnny), 181-182
      Which Hand Has It, 182
Self-concept, of child
   definition, 180
   learning activities, 181-182
   learning objectives for, 180
   role of parents in, 180
Self-confidence, of toddler, 140
Self-esteem, 180, 235
   development of, 235
Self-identity, checklist on, 269
Self-image, development of, 144-148, 211
Seminar, 97
Senior citizens, in home-based programs, 84
Seniors Tutor for Educational Progress, 84
Senses, use of, 227-228
Sequencing, 195
Seriation, 214

Sets, 194-195
Sex education, and siblings, 238
Siblings
    avoiding rivalry between, 239
    preparing for, 238-239
    promoting cooperation between, 239-240
Sign level, 214
Signals, visual and auditory, 224
Simulation, 97
Situation, definition of, 9
Skill learning, steps in, 105
Skills
    cognitive, 214
    educational, needed by parents, 74-75
    for home-based programs, 78
    manipulative, 154
    motor-perceptual, 5
    parental development of, 19, 71
    of preschool child, 155-157
    social action as, 23-27
Skit, 98
Social action
    as citizens' skill, 27
    as citizens' tool, 22
    concept of, 22-25
        community identification, 23
        formulation of objectives, 25
        problem determination, 23-25
    essentials of
        communication, 26
        evaluation, 26
        executing objectives, 26
        obtaining approval, 26
        organization of resources, 26
        selection of plan, 25-26
    Home Start Training Centers (HSTC), 27
    national network of resources, 27
    seasonal fluctuation in needs, 25
    utilizing HSTC resources, 27-28
Social action problems
    components of, 24-25
    determining existence of, 23-24
    information sources, 24
    objective approach, 23
    "piggybacking," 25
    subjective approach, 23
Social action programs
    materials for, 28
    role of librarians, 28
Social goals, of preschool child, 157
Social services
    aim of, 18
    components of, 77
    goals of, 18-19
Socialization, process of, 41, 233
Sociology, concerns of, 14

Sociology department, role in child-development programs, 14-15
Spatial relations, 214
Specialists, role in child-development, 180
Spock, Benjamin, 2
Sponsor, 56
Staff
    identification of, 62-64
    job description sample, 63-64
    planning with, 64
    types of, 62
Staff development, 57-58
Staffing
    components of, 57
    staff development, 57-58
Storytelling, as learning activity, 223
Symbol level, 214
Symposium, 99

T

Target child, 31, 41, 257-258
    cultural background of, 41
    records of, 257-258
Task identification, 37
Taste-smell recognition, of preschool child, 156
Teacher
    as child educator, 222
    involvement in parent program planning, 220-222
    as means of finding community resources, 225
    modeling task of, 220, 224
Teacher-learner interaction, 4
Teacher tasks, 220-222
Teaching
    definition of, 4
    demonstration-type, 5
    parents engaged in, 4-5
TEEM. *See* Tucson early education model
Temporal relations, 214
Theory, 14
Thinking abilities, of preschool child, 156
Toddler
    behavior of, 140-141
    bowel control, 141-142
    characteristics of, 142-144
    definition of, 140
    increased activity of, 141
    needs of
        emotional growth, 148
        intellectual growth, 146-147
        physical growth, 145-146
        social growth, 147-148
    safety rules for, 141
Toilet training, 141-142
Tolerance level, low, 83
Touch sensitivity, of preschool child, 156
Treatment, 266
Triad, in buzz group, 95-96
Troubleshooter, 61

Index

Trust, developing, 86
Tucson early education model (TEEM), 215

U

U.S. Department of Agriculture, 16
U.S. Department of Health, Education and Welfare (HEW), 9
    national resource network of, 27
    regional clusters of, 27
U.S. Office of Child Development (OCD), 2
University, role in home-based education programs, 13-15

V

Value system
    establishment of, 234-235
    of family, 41
    home visitor's impact on, 41
Vertical planning, in developing records, 256
Visual-motor abilities, 224
Visual perception, of preschool child, 155

W

Walking, onset of, 140
Workplan
    components of, 50
    example of, in action, 52-54
    outline of, 49
    preparation of, 47
    sample of, 51-52
    topics for, 48-49
Workplan file
    construction of, 44-45
    organization of, 47
    subtopics in, 47
    topics in, 46
Workshops, 98
    after-action report, 113
    characteristics of, 104-105
    checklist for, 111
    committees of, 107, 110
    coordinator, tasks of, 105-106
    objectives of, 109-110
    outline for, 108-109, 110-113
    parental activities in, 108
    planning tasks for, 106-108
    resource persons for, 106
    staff, 106